The Whole Dog Journal

Handbook of Dog and Puppy Care and Training

The Whole Dog Journal

Handbook of Dog and Puppy Care and Training

Nancy Kerns, editor of *The Whole Dog Journal*

with contributions by Pat Miller, CJ Puotinen, and Dr. Randy Kidd

THE LYONS PRESS

Guilford, Connecticut

An imprint of The Globe Pequot Press

To buy books in quantity for corporate use
or incentives, call **(800) 962–0973**
or e-mail **premiums@GlobePequot.com**.

The content of this book has been distilled from articles published in The *Whole Dog Journal.* In many cases, details have been omitted or condensed to concentrate on the results and recommendations. A more in-depth treatment on most of these topics can be found in the original articles published in the magazine.

The Lyons Press is an imprint of The Globe Pequot Press

Designed by Sheryl P. Kober

Library of Congress Cataloging-in-Publication Data
Kerns, Nancy.
   The Whole dog journal handbook of dog and puppy care and training / by Nancy Kerns ;
with information by Pat Miller, C. J. Puotinen, and Randy Kidd.
      p. cm.
   Includes index.
   ISBN 978-1-59228-189-3
1. Dogs. 2. Puppies. 3. Dogs--Training. 4. Puppies--Training. I. Whole dog journal. II. Title.
SF427.K386 2007
636.7—dc22

2007034175

10 9 8 7 6 5 4 3 2 1
Printed in the United States of America

Contents

Introduction vii

1. Puppy Care Basics 1
   Pre-Puppy Preparation 1 • Minding Your Pees and Cues 5 • Oops! She Did
   It Again! 11 • Bite-Me-Not 15 • The Case for Kindergarten 19 • The Social
   Scene 24 • Living with Humans 101 29 • Adoption Advice 34

2. Behavior and Training 39
   Upper-Level Management 39 • A Classical Conditioning Primer 43
   • Practiced Calm 46 • Just Rewards 51 • The Crossover Challenge 57 • Size
   Matters 58 • Super-sized 63 • Remedial Housetraining for Adult Dogs 68
   • Crate Training Made Easy 71 • Greetings and Salutations 76 • Sit
   Happens—The Magic of Clicker Training 80 • Come to Me, Run to Me 84
   • Walk This Way 89 • Oh, Baby! 95 • The Value of Training the Kids 99 • Off
   Limits 105

3. Difficult Dogs 109
   Living with a Difficult Dog 109 • Demolition Dogs 114 • Canine Social
   Misfits 117 • Obsessive-Compulsive Dogs 122 • Relieving Anxiety 126
   • Hyper Hounds 131 • Predatory Dogs 138 • The Incessant Barker 142
   • The "Gift" of Growling 148 • Once Bitten 151 • Rage without Reason 156
   • Reform School 160

4. Nutrition 163
   How to Choose a Food 163 • The Right Stuff 168 • Can? Do! 171 • When
   Foods Go Bad 174 • Variety Is the Spice of Life . . . 179 • Getting a Raw Deal
   182 • It's All in How You Make It 188 • Upgrading to Pasture-Fed 194

5. Dog Safety and Management 199
   Portrait of a Healthy Home 199 • Preventing Great Escapes 211 • Collar, Tag
   and 'Chip 216 • All in a Day's Care 219 • Picking Playmates 222

6. Dog Health: Veterinary Matters, Including Holistic Dog Care
   and Alternative Health Care 231
   Looking for Dr. Right 231 • Pleased to See You! 236 • A Stitch in Time 241
   • Hot Shots: To Vaccinate or Not to Vaccinate 246 • Heartworm: Don't Take
   It Lightly 251 • Keeping Those Pearly Whites Clean 255 • What Promotes
   Bloat? 259 • The Price of Prescriptions 264 • Dangers of Antibiotic Misuse 268
   • Use Corticosteroids with Caution 273

7. Complementary Care: Holistic Care, Acupuncture, Chiropractic,
Herbal Remedies, Aromatherapy, Homeopathy, Massage, and More.....................277
   The Holistic Paradigm 277 • Ancient Art, Modern Science 279 • Animal
   "Crackers" 282 • Smell This, You'll Feel Better 285 • Canines in a Mist 290 •
   Flower Power 292 • Herbal Wisdom 295 • Homeopathy: Tiny Doses, Huge
   Effects 303 • Lay Your Hands on Dogs 308 • Walking in Water 311

8. Cancer...313
   Canine Cancer Crisis 313 • Conventional Cancer Care 319 • Don't Despair;
   Just Care 326 • What Are the Alternatives? 328 • Is Cancer Prevention
   Possible? 338

9. Having Fun with Your Dog..345
   Tricks for Clicks 345 • Agility Ability 350 • Furiously Fast Fun 355 • Take a
   Hike! 357 • Doggie Camp 362 • Going Camping with Canines 363 • Fun and
   Games 367 • Sit, Stay, Cha, Cha, Cha: Musical Freestyle 374

Acknowledgments..377

Index 379

Contents

Introduction

The *Whole Dog Journal* commenced publication in early 1998—timing that proved to be auspicious. In 1998, "clicker training" and other non-force training methods were new enough to be unfamiliar to most dog owners, but their use and popularity were rapidly growing. More and more veterinary practitioners were seeing fantastic results from using complementary or alternative healthcare modalities on their patients, and professional education and training courses were emerging. Echoing a 1990s boom in health foods and biologically appropriate diets for humans, the pet food industry was just beginning to generate diets that were made with top-quality ingredients, as opposed to the sole use of cheap by-products left over from the human food-processing industry.

These three topics—dog-friendly training, holistic healthcare, and nutrition—have been the *WDJ*'s focus from its first issue. Our goal has been to provide well-researched information and practical advice for dog owners, to empower our readers to put what they've read into practice with their dogs immediately. In the past decade, the magazine has ridden the increasing surge of interest in these areas and, I hope, helped build and maintain the wave's energy.

I had the good fortune to be the *WDJ*'s founding editor, so I've been able to guide the development of the magazine from its inception, as well as benefit from the experience and knowledge of its expert contributors. I've used all of the training techniques and most of the healthcare modalities promoted in the *WDJ*'s

pages, and my dogs have been conspicuously better behaved and healthier than when I (before I knew better!) used only old-fashioned, force-based training and conventional veterinary medicine.

The thousands of letters I have received from our readers over the years also attest to the effectiveness of the progressive practices described in the *WDJ*. Training progresses quickly, and because neither force nor fear comes into play, the bond between dogs and owners stays strong and trusting. This sort of training feels good to both parties. It's also gratifying when, trying our recommendation for a new food or supplement, someone sees her dog's perennially itchy skin clear up and dull coat suddenly develop a shine. When someone has spent thousands of dollars on her dog's conventional medical treatments (many of which cause side effects that are almost as worrisome as the conditions they were prescribed to treat) and an inexpensive herbal remedy solves the dog's problem *without* side effects—well, let's just call it a conversion moment.

Today it's considered smart and not "off-the-wall" to take your canine companion to a veterinary chiropractor or acupuncturist for regular treatments, feed him a home-prepared, biologically appropriate diet of raw foods, and conduct most of his training sessions with a handful of treats and a clicker, but no leash. These practices are safe and effective, but there's more to it than that. This sort of enlightened care actually builds and maintains the dog's physical, mental, and emotional health and vitality. In fact, many owners see such an improvement in their dog's attitude and bearing that they start improving their own diets and seek out alternative and complementary medical practitioners to add to their own healthcare team!

This book contains highlights from a decade of the *Whole Dog Journal*. It's my hope that readers familiar with the magazine will appreciate the collection and concentration of some of the *WDJ*'s best work, and that dog owners who have never heard of any of this will be inspired to give all these new dog-care and dog-training practices a try. I'm confident you'll like the results.

The *Whole Dog Journal* editor Nancy Kerns and a canine friend.

P. S. For readers of this book who are interested in learning more about The *Whole Dog Journal*, visit www.whole-dog-journal.com or call 1-800-424-7887.

CHAPTER 1

Puppy Care Basics

Pre-Puppy Preparation
Stop! Don't bring home that adorable pup until you are properly prepared.

Most people spend months preparing for the arrival of a new baby. They're just as likely, however, to bring a baby dog home on a whim, without any preparation at all. Small wonder they find themselves playing catch-up for weeks, months, years, or even end up "getting rid of" the dog as they struggle to recover from the mistakes made in the pup's formative months.

For example, the lack of a crate, puppy pen, or baby gates from day one makes housetraining "mistakes" inevitable. This can set back later housetraining efforts by weeks or even months, as the puppy is triggered to eliminate in spots where he smells remnants of his past "accidents."

The wise puppy-owner-to-be puts much thought into pre-puppy preparation. This falls into three categories:
- Supplies and equipment
- Service providers
- House rules and routines

It allows you to sleep peacefully at night and enjoy dinner and a movie without worrying about what the pup is destroying.

"You're NOT taking me home today?" Don't let that adorable little face make you do something rash; you should have everything in place before he comes home. A lack of a crate and baby gates, for example, may set back your housetraining efforts for weeks.

Supplies and equipment

There's lots of puppy stuff you'll need to make your puppy comfortable, happy, and successful as he learns to adapt to your alien environment.
- **Crate.** A crate is an indispensable behavior management tool; it facilitates housetraining and prevents puppy misbehavior by keeping your dog safely confined when you're not there to supervise.
- **Puppy pen/exercise pen.** This is another extremely useful management tool, but it expands the "den" concept of a crate to a slightly larger area, giving a pup more room to stretch her legs, yet still keeping her in a safe, confined area. Many people include a "restroom" facility, by using a tarp underneath the pen and newspapers on top of that at one end.
- **Tether.** This is a short (about four feet in length) plastic-coated cable with sturdy snaps at both ends. Tethers are intended to temporarily restrain

a dog for relatively short periods of time in your presence, as an aid in a puppy supervision and housetraining program, and as a time-out to settle unruly behavior. They should not be used as punishment, or to restrain a dog for long periods in your absence.

- **Collar, ID tag, leash, and harness.**
- **Seat belt.** Use a car restraint that fastens to your car's seat belts and your dog's harness (never a collar) to keep her safe, and safely away from the driver.
- **Clicker.** Properly used as a reward marker, a clicker significantly enhances your communication with your furry friend and speeds up the training process. (Learn more about clickers in chapter 2.)
- **Treats.** A clicker, of course, is nothing without an accompanying reward. We use treats as the primary reward to pair with the clicker because most dogs can be motivated by food, and because they can quickly eat a small tidbit and get back to the training fun.
- **Long line.** A lightweight, strong, extra-long leash (10 to 50 feet), the long line is an ideal tool to help your dog learn to come reliably when called regardless of where you are or what other exciting things are happening.

Find a good holistic veterinarian. These practitioners tend to have a more conservative approach to vaccinations than conventional veterinarians—important if you want to prevent the mid- to late-life health problems that some experts believe are related to a lifetime of over-vaccination.

- **Kong toys.** If we could buy only one toy for our dog, it would be a Kong, a chew-resistant (not chew-proof) rubber, beehive-shaped toy with a hollow center. A Kong can be used "plain" as a toy, but makes an irresistible treat for any dog when stuffed with kibble or treats that are held in place with something healthy and edible like peanut butter, cream cheese, or yogurt.
- **Balls, interactive toys, fetch toys.**
- **Grooming tools.** Choose combs and brushes appropriate for your dog's type of coat (ask a groomer or vet), shampoo and conditioner, scissors, nail clippers, cotton balls, and toothbrushes. Start using these tools on your puppy early, pairing the experience with tasty treats so she forms a positive association with the task.
- **House cleaning tools, including enzymatic odor removers.**

Service providers

It's never too soon to start researching the corps of professionals who will help you raise your puppy right. That list will include her veterinarian (or veterinarians, including an emergency hospital, holistic vet, and "regular" vet), training instructor, and perhaps a groomer, pet sitter or walker, doggie daycare provider, and boarding kennel. Grab your phone book, make a separate list for each category, and check them out.

Start with a telephone call. If providers can't be bothered to be pleasant on the phone, chances are they won't be nice in person either. Cross them off.

If they pass the phone attitude test, inquire whether you can visit, ask a few questions, and watch them at work. Then visit. Do they handle canine and human clients gently, and with respect? Are the dogs enjoying themselves, or do they at least appear comfortable? Are the facilities clean, without offensive odor? If the answers to these questions are yes, they stay on the list. If not, cross them off. Make notes next to each of the finalists on your list to remind you whom you liked best and why.

Finally, ask for references. Call the references and ask if they've been satisfied with the provider, if they seem reliable and consistently dog-friendly. Then pick your favorite animal care professionals, and let them know you'd like to become a client when your pup arrives. After you've made your final decisions, make a list of names, addresses, and phone numbers to post on your refrigerator along with the phone numbers and locations of your local animal shelters—in case your precious pup should ever get lost.

House rules and routines

Rules and routines are especially important if there's more than one human in the house, to encourage consistency, an important element of successful puppy-raising. When your pup joins your family, she'll experiment with different behaviors to try to figure out how the world works, and how to make good stuff happen—a dog's main mission in life. The more consistent everyone is, the quicker she'll figure it all out.

Your rules and routines will reflect your dog-raising and -training philosophies. To develop a relationship with your dog based on mutual trust, respect, and cooperation, implement nonviolent management and training techniques, and avoid methods that require harsh verbal correction and physical punishment. The better you are at keeping your pup out of trouble and reinforcing desirable behaviors, the less you'll be upset with her and the sooner she'll develop good habits.

Here are some issues for your family to discuss and agree on:

- **Where will your puppy sleep?** We suggest in a crate in someone's bedroom until the pup's at least a year old and fully housetrained and house trustworthy; then her own bed or someone's bed (or wherever else she wants) is okay.
- **Will she be allowed on the furniture?** We're okay with dogs on the furniture within reason—not the kitchen table, of course—as long as it's not creating any aggression or other behavior problems. We like our dogs to ask permission first if we're on the sofa and they want to join us.
- **Where will she be during the day?** The best answer is with you, if you have the luxury of working at home or taking her to the office with you, under direct supervision or leashed and crated, with potty breaks every hour on the hour, at first. If you're not home, she should be indoors, crated—if you can arrange for adequate potty breaks—or in an exercise pen.
- **What games will she be allowed to play?** There are games, and then there are games! Good games like "Tug" and "Fetch" reinforce desirable behaviors. Inappropriate games like "Body-Slam the Human" and "Jump Up and Bite Skin and Clothing" reinforce undesirable behaviors. Be sure everyone in the family is on board with teaching appropriate games, and playing by the rules.

  If family members insist on an inappropriate game like "Jump Up" (biting is never to be encouraged), get them to agree to teach polite behavior first, then teach "Jump Up" on a very specific cue—and allow it only on cue.
- **Who will feed her, when, and what?** Your pup should be able to depend on regular and high-quality meals from a clean bowl in a quiet place. If you choose to make it a child's responsibility, you must supervise to be sure the dog is fed properly. Don't allow anyone to pester her while eating. Rather, have family members walk by and drop extra-special treats in her bowl while she eats, to help prevent resource guarding.
- **Who will train her, how, and for what?** We urge you to train using positive reinforcement methods, starting with housetraining all the way through the most advanced training you choose to pursue. You can have a "primary" trainer, and then encourage the whole family to participate in training activities;

they'll all be living with the pup, and they can all learn to communicate consistently and effectively in a language she understands.

Make a vocabulary list of terms your dog learns and post it on the refrigerator, so everyone uses the same behavior cues. Add to the list as she learns new behaviors. Remember that your dog is never too young (or old) to learn. Check out basic and advanced good-manners training, agility, rally obedience, tricks, flyball, scent detection, musical freestyle . . . the possibilities are endless.

- **How will you correct her for making mistakes?** Positive does not mean permissive. If your pup is well supervised she shouldn't have the opportunity to make many mistakes, but they will happen. When they do, calmly interrupt the pup's behavior with a cheerful "Oops!" and redirect her to something more appropriate. Make a mental note to ramp up your management or training to prevent the situation from happening again.

Puppies develop lifelong habits during the first several months of their lives. Extra management effort early on can save you years of headaches later. If you don't give your pup the opportunity to learn that chewing sofa cushions is fun and feels good on sore gums, she'll earn house freedom much sooner than a confirmed cushion shredder. When you see her heading for cushions or the coffee table leg, offer her a stuffed Kong instead, or engage her in a game of tug.

If she's driving you crazy, grabbing your pants legs, and biting your hands, say "Oops! Time out!" and put her in her exercise pen for a bit. This will give you both a chance to calm down without resorting to corporal punishment. When she realizes that biting makes the fun stop, she'll learn to control her urge to grab.

Sound like a lot to think about? It should! Accepting responsibility for the life of another living creature requires serious thought and commitment. The way you care for your pup will determine whether she spends the rest of her life sharing companionship and love with you or, like too many dogs, gets passed from home to home in search of one where she will be better understood and appreciated. She deserves a lifelong loving home. They all do.

Minding Your Pees and Cues
Training your dog to eliminate on command is easy and rewarding.

The term "housebreaking" grates on our sensibilities like fingernails on a blackboard. What is it that we are supposed to break? This term is deeply rooted in the force-based philosophy of dog training, and immediately gives new dog and puppy owners the wrong mind-set about the process of teaching their dog to urinate and defecate in appropriate places. Breaking implies punishing the pup for pottying in the wrong spot. Training focuses on helping the puppy do it right.

Three-step formula for training behavior

Housetraining is simple. You don't give your puppy the opportunity to make mistakes. You do give him plenty of opportunities to do it right. Simple, however, does not necessarily mean easy. It means making a commitment to manage your pup's behavior 24 hours a day, until he is old enough to be trusted with his house freedom for increasingly long periods of time.

Here is a basic three-step formula for training or changing a behavior. By applying each of these steps you can get your dog to do just about anything that he is physically and mentally capable of, including housetraining.

Step 1: Visualize the behavior you want.
Create a mental image of what you want your puppy to do and what that looks like—in this case, to consistently and reliably go the bathroom outside in his designated toilet spot. You need to be able to imagine how this looks in order to be able to train your pup to do it. If you only envision your puppy making mistakes in the house, you won't have the creativity you need to help him do it right.

Make sure that you don't inadvertently punish the puppy for eliminating outside. If he is whisked back into the house right after he eliminates, he will learn to hold it longer so as to prolong his play and exploration time outdoors.

Step 2: Prevent him from being rewarded for doing the behavior you don't want.
A reward doesn't have to come from you in order to be reinforcing to your dog. It is very rewarding to a puppy with a full bowel or bladder to relieve the pressure in his abdomen. If you give him the opportunity to go to the bathroom in the house, that will feel good to him, and he will keep doing it when he has the opportunity. It will eventually become a habit, and then his preference will be to eliminate in the house. Step 2 requires you to manage your pup's behavior so he doesn't have the opportunity to be self-rewarded by going to the bathroom in the house.

Step 3: Help him do it right and consistently reward him for the behavior you do want.
This is the step that often gets skipped. You need to go outside with your puppy and reward him when he performs. If you toss him out in the backyard and

don't go with him, you won't know if he went to the bathroom or not. Coming back in for a cookie may be more rewarding to him than relieving his bladder, so he waits by the back door, comes in, eats his cookie, and then pees on the rug.

You'll notice that none of the steps involve punishing the puppy for going to the bathroom in the house. Old-fashioned suggestions like rubbing his nose in his mess or smacking him with a rolled-up newspaper are inappropriate and abusive. They teach your pup to be fearful of relieving himself in your presence, and are very effective at teaching him to pee behind the bed in the guest room where you can't see and punish him. Besides, it is much easier to teach your puppy to go to the bathroom in one right place than it is to punish him for going to the bathroom in an almost infinite number of wrong places.

If you do "catch him in the act," simply utter a loud but cheerful "Oops!" and whisk him outside to the proper place. Remember to treat the "oops" spot thoroughly with an enzyme-based cleaner designed to remove all traces of animal waste, such as Nature's Miracle.

Finally, if you really feel you must make use of that rolled up newspaper, smack yourself in the head three times while repeating, "I will supervise the puppy more closely, I will supervise the puppy more closely, I will supervise the puppy more closely!"

To undertake the eight-week housetraining program described below, you will need a properly sized crate; a collar and leash; treats; poop bags; and time and patience. A puppy pen, tether, and fenced yard are also useful. If you are starting with an older pup or an adult dog, you may be able to accelerate the timeline, since an older dog is physically able to "hold it" for longer periods than a young pup. If, however, at any point in the program your furry friend starts backsliding, you have progressed too quickly. Back up to the previous week's lesson.

Effective eight-week housetraining program

Week One: Acclimate your puppy to his crate on his first day in your home, off and on all day.

While you do this, take him outside on his leash to his designated potty spot every hour on the hour. When he obliges you with a pile or a puddle, tell him "Yes!" in a happy tone of voice (or *click!* your clicker), and feed him a piece of cookie.

Dogs who have positive crate experiences when they are young almost always voluntarily hang out in their crates whenever they have the opportunity to do so—even when, like this dog, they have outgrown their puppy crates.

Pick up his water after 7:00 P.M. to prevent him from tanking up before bed (later if it is very hot), then crate him when you go to sleep.

Most young puppies crate-train easily. The crate should be in your bedroom so your baby dog is not isolated and lonely, and so you can hear him when he wakes up and tells you he has to go out. Do not put him in his crate on the far side of the house. He will feel abandoned and lonely and cry his little heart out, but worse than that, you won't hear him when he has to go—he will be forced to soil his crate.

A successful housetraining program is dependent on your dog's natural instincts to keep his den clean. If you force your puppy to soil his crate you break down that inhibition and make it infinitely harder to get him to extend the "clean den" concept to your entire house.

When he cries in the middle of the night, you must get up (quickly), put him on his leash, and take him out to his potty spot. Stand and wait. When he starts to go, say "Go potty!" or "Do it!" or "Hurry up!" or whatever verbal cue you ultimately want to use to ask him to go to the bathroom. If you consistently speak this phrase whenever your pup starts to urinate or defecate, you will eventually be able to elicit his urination or defecation, assuming, that is, that he has something to offer you at the moment. Being able to put his bathroom behavior on cue is an added bonus of this method of housetraining, and a very handy one when you're late for a date, or it's pouring rain or freezing cold outside!

As soon as your pup has eliminated, tell him "Yes!" in a happy tone of voice and feed him a bit of cookie, praise him, tell him what a wonderful puppy he is, then take him in and put him back in his crate. No food, no play, and no bed-cuddling. If you do anything more than perfunctory potty performance in the middle of the night, he will quickly learn to wake you up and cry for your attention.

First thing in the morning, take him out on leash and repeat the ritual. If you consistently go out with him, on leash, you will teach him to use the designated spot for his bathroom. If you just open the door and push him out, he may well decide that two feet from the back door is far enough, especially if it's cold or wet out. For the first week or so, if his bladder is too full to make it safely out the door, you can carry him out, but by the end of the second week he should be able to walk to the door under his own power.

Now you can feed your puppy and give him his water bowl, but be sure to keep him right under your nose. If you have to use the bathroom, he goes with you. If you want to sit down to eat breakfast, he's on his leash under your chair, or tethered by his pillow.

Ten to fifteen minutes after he is done eating, take him out again, repeat your cue when he does his thing, and say "Yes!", treat, and praise when he is done. Also take him out immediately upon the completion of any exuberant play sessions, and whenever he wakes up from a nap.

For the rest of the day, take him out every hour on the hour for his potty ritual, as well as 10 to 15 minutes after every meal. The remainder of the time he must be under your direct supervision, or on a leash or tether, in his pen or in his crate, every second of the day. Judicious use of closed doors and baby gates can keep him corralled in the room with you, but you still need to watch him. If your puppy starts walking in circles or otherwise looking restless, toss in an extra bathroom break.

"But wait!" you cry. "I work all day, I can't take him out every hour on the hour."

Ah, yes, that is why housetraining is simple but not always easy. "Home alone" pups are more likely to end up stuck out in the backyard, where they get left for convenience's sake as the housetraining program drops lower and lower on the priority list. If you haven't yet acquired your pup and you aren't going to be a stay-at-home Mom or Dad, seriously reconsider

This crate is far too small for this puppy, even for the shortest period of time. If a puppy or dog cannot comfortably stand up and turn around in the crate, he is likely to (righteously) protest his confinement. This sort of negative experience could even turn him off crates forever. NEVER force your puppy into a crate that is too small.

Don't leave any puppy in a crate all day. They cannot "hold it" that long, and will be forced to soil the crate. Once a puppy's inborn instinct to keep his "den" clean is broken, it is hard to repair.

the possibility of adopting an older dog who is already housetrained and who may be in desperate need of a home.

If you already have your pup, you will either need to find a skilled and willing puppy daycare provider, or set up a safe, puppy-proofed environment with wall-to-wall newspapers or pee pads, and recognize that your housetraining program will probably proceed more slowly. You cannot crate him for the 8 to 10 hours a day that you are gone—you are likely to destroy his den-soiling inhibitions, cause him to hate and fear his crate, and possibly trigger the onset of separation anxiety.

When you are home, be extra diligent about your housetraining protocol, and as your pup starts to show a preference for one corner of his papered area you can start slowly diminishing the size of the covered space. You will eventually have to add the step of teaching him not to go on papers at all, which is one of the reasons many trainers don't recommend paper training—

you are, in essence, teaching him that it is okay to go to the bathroom in the house, and then later telling him that it is not okay.

Week Two: Continue crating your puppy at night.

Some pups are sleeping through the night by Week Two. Others need nighttime breaks for a few more weeks. During the day, continue to take him out immediately upon waking, 10 to 15 minutes after each meal, and after play and naps.

You can now begin teaching him to associate "getting excited" behavior with going out to potty. This will eventually translate into him getting excited to let you know he has to go out. If you want him to do some other specific behavior to tell you he has to go, such as taking a bow, or ringing a bell, start having him do that behavior before you take him out.

By now, you should be able to tell when your puppy is just about to squat in his designated place. Say your "Go pee!" cue just a second or two before he starts, so that your verbal cue begins to precede, rather than follow, the behavior.

Stretch his bathroom excursions to 90 minutes apart, and start keeping a daily log—writing down the time, whether he did anything outside, and if so, what

For housetraining success, provide your puppy (or new dog) with frequent opportunities to relieve himself in an appropriate place. Don't leave him in the crate longer than he can "hold it."

Housetraining Troubleshooting Tips and Reminders

1. If your housetraining program-in-progress relapses, back up a week or two in the process and keep working from there. If that doesn't resolve the problem promptly (within a day), a trip to the vet is in order to determine if there is a medical problem, such as a urinary tract infection, that is making it impossible for your puppy to hold it. The longer you wait, the more ground you have to make up.

2. If your pup has diarrhea, not only is it impossible for him to comply with housetraining, he may also be seriously ill. Puppies can dehydrate to a life-threatening degree very quickly. Contact your veterinarian immediately.

3. If your paper-trained pup refuses to go on anything other than paper, take a sheet of newspaper or pee pad outside and have him go on that. Each subsequent trip, reduce the size of the fresh sheet of paper or pad until it is gone.

4. If your dog's inhibitions against soiling his den have already been damaged, you may need to remove his bedding from his crate—it is possible that this is now his preferred substrate. Try the bare crate floor or a coated metal grate instead, and set your alarm to wake you up at night as often as necessary to enable you to consistently take him out before he soils his crate.

5. Neutering your male dog between the ages of eight weeks and six months will minimize the development of assertive territorial leg-lifting. Already existing territorial leg-lifting can be discouraged as part of a complete housetraining program with the use of "Doggie Wraps," a belly band made for this purpose.

6. If at any time your reliably housetrained dog begins having accidents in the house, have him examined by your veterinarian in case there is a physical cause.

7. Remember that drugs such as Prednisone can cause increased water intake, which causes increased urination. If it is not a medical problem, evaluate possible stress factors and return to a basic housetraining program.

8. Vigorous exercise can also cause excessive water intake and subsequent urination, as can a medical condition known as polydipsia/polyuria, which simply means drinking and urinating too much.

9. When your dog has learned to eliminate on cue, start asking him to poop and pee on various surfaces, including grass, gravel, cement, and dirt. Dogs can easily develop a substrate preference—grass, for example—and may refuse to go to the bathroom on anything but their preferred surface. If you are ever in a location where there is no grass, you and your dog could be in trouble.

10. If your situation is such that your pup must constantly be asked to wait to go for longer periods than is reasonable, consider litter box training. Lots of people do this, especially those with small dogs and those who live in high-rise apartments. This also resolves the substrate-preference problem.

---

he did. Make note of any housetraining mistakes, and when and where they occurred. While an occasional "Oops!" may be inevitable (we are only human, after all), if you are having more than one or two accidents a week you are not supervising closely enough or not taking him out enough. The log will help you understand your puppy's bathroom patterns over the next few weeks, and tell you when you can trust him for longer periods.

Week Three: Crate your puppy at night.

During the day, try stretching his bathroom intervals to two hours, still remembering to take him out after all meals, play sessions, and naps.

Continue to keep your log, to make sure your pup's housetraining program is on track. This is especially helpful for communication purposes if two or more family members are sharing puppy-walking duties.

Also continue to elicit the desired bathroom signal

Until your puppy is several months old and consistently eliminating outdoors, you must keep her either in a crate, on a leash, or under your direct supervision.

Weeks Five through Eight: Keep crating your puppy at night.

Gradually increase the time between bathroom breaks to a maximum of four hours, plus meals, play, and naptime. You still need to go out with him most of the time, but you can occasionally send him out to his bathroom spot in his fenced yard all on his own, watching through the door or window to be sure he goes to his spot and gets the job done. By this time, accidents in the house should be virtually nonexistent. As long as the program is progressing well, you can begin phasing out your daily log. As your pup continues to mature over the next eight months, he will eventually be able to be alone left for up to eight hours at a time, perhaps slightly longer.

At that point, you can break out the champagne and celebrate—you and your puppy have come of age!

behavior before you take him out, and to use your bathroom cue outdoors, prior to the actual onset of elimination. Over the next few weeks, the verbal cue will begin to actually elicit the behavior, so that you can bring his attention to the business at hand when he is distracted, when you are in a hurry, or when you are in a new place where he isn't sure he is supposed to pee.

By the end of this week, your puppy should be leading you on his leash to the bathroom spot. Look for this behavior as an indication that he is making the connection to the spot that you want him to use.

Week Four: Crate your puppy at night.

Assuming all is going well, stretch daytime intervals to three hours, plus meal, play, and nap trips. Go with him to his fenced-yard bathroom spot off-leash, to confirm that he is going there on his own, without you having to lead him. Continue to keep your daily log, and reinforce your "outside" and "bathroom" cues.

Dogs have their preferences, but it's useful if your dog can eliminate on cue wherever it is most convenient for you.

Oops! She Did It Again!

Submissive urination is annoying, but you can learn how not to cause it.

In the canine world, when one dog wants to show deference to another more dominant dog, he may urinate as a sign of submission. The more threatened he feels, the more likely he is to urinate. This is an involuntary reaction, an instinctive behavior that all dogs are born "knowing" how and when to exhibit.

In a pack of dogs, this programmed behavior is a valuable survival mechanism. Puppies are extremely vulnerable to the wrath of adult dogs in the pack, and built-in submissive responses signal normal adult dogs to automatically shut off the aggression, thus keeping puppies from being hurt. These programmed responses (submission from puppies, turning off adults' aggression) support survival of the pack. As puppies mature, they eventually become more skilled at detecting and avoiding aggression sooner, and no longer need the submissive urination to protect them (except in dire situations, where under a fierce attack this involuntary response may again be triggered).

That's because, unlike normal elimination, which the dog has some control over, submissive urination can quickly become a classically conditioned behavior; the presence of a particular stimulus automatically triggers the response.

Think of Pavlov's dogs, who drooled at the sound of a bell that had been associated with the arrival of food. Pavlov's dogs didn't decide to salivate when they heard the bell—it just happened. A submissive dog doesn't decide to pee when approached—it just happens.

It might take only one episode of punishment for peeing to condition the dog to automatically pee when she sees or hears stimuli that she associates with the punishment. Sadly, the harder the owner punishes, the more the puppy pees in order to acknowledge the owner's superiority and deflect his wrath. The more the puppy pees, the harder the owner punishes.

And "punishment" in this case doesn't only refer to cruel and unusual treatments such as hog-tying the dog

Speaking different languages

Unfortunately for humans, as we raise young puppies and dogs, actions that seem perfectly natural and innocuous to us, such as bending over a puppy or patting him on the head, can be very threatening gestures in the DogSpeak dictionary, and inadvertently trigger the involuntary bladder-release response. It is a relatively common behavior in puppies, and more prevalent in some breeds than others.

If properly handled, puppies usually grow out of the behavior as they mature. However, if an owner misperceives the behavior as a housetraining challenge and punishes the puppy, the problem worsens.

Many dogs who experience submissive urination are sensitive individuals, highly attuned to subtle changes in your voice and behavior. If you tense up, they are likely to unconsciously respond by peeing. In a pack of dogs, submissive puppies involuntarily exhibit this behavior—the ultimate in appeasement gestures.

outside. One loud squawk of alarm from a surprised person may frighten an extremely sensitive individual enough to classically condition her to pee every time she hears a shout, whether it's a happy shout of "Good dog!" or even just, "Honey, I'm home!"

This is clearly an interspecies communication problem that begs the intervention of a translator before it does permanent damage to the relationship between dog and human. Humans don't like dogs who pee in the house, and dogs become fearful and mistrusting of humans who are always yelling at—or worse, hitting —them despite their best efforts to appease.

Train your friends not to lean over your dog, unless they don't mind wet shoes . . .

Get out the cork

The most effective way to modify a dog's submissive urination is to stop doing the things that make him pee. This means avoiding all of the behaviors that are considered threatening to dogs and are likely to trigger the involuntary response.

This may be more difficult than it sounds, as many of the behaviors that are threatening to dogs are instinctive greeting behaviors for humans, such as making direct eye contact, approaching in a straight line (head-on), bending over the dog, patting him on top of the head, and speaking in a loud or deep voice.

Visitors, as well as all family members, must be counseled and frequently reminded to approach and interact with Spot in a non-threatening way until the dog matures and gains enough confidence that he no longer releases his bladder so easily.

It is critically important to avoid getting angry with your dog when an accident or some other misbehavior occurs. Dogs are masters at reading body language, and even a slight stiffening of your body or change in the tone of your voice can release a stream from a very sensitive dog. It is easier to stay calm if you can remember that Spot has no control over his submissive urination—when the stimulus is presented, the response occurs involuntarily. He can't help it.

If you take full advantage of all available behavior management tools it will prevent most incidents from occurring, and will greatly reduce the environmental damage done when an incident does occur, making it easier for you to stay calm in the face of Spot's occasional flood.

How exciting!

Excitement urination is a little different, but a very close cousin to submissive urination. It occurs when a puppy gets so excited that he "wets his pants." Again, this is an involuntary response that the dog cannot control, and nothing is gained by punishing him.

Calm human behavior—body language and voice— are also important with the excitement urinator. Greetings are best accomplished by ignoring the dog until he settles of his own accord, then acknowledging him very calmly and quietly. Give him opportunities to empty his bladder outside on a regular basis, and implement a "Practiced Calm" (see page 46) program so he learns to control his own behavior, eliminating the trigger for the inappropriate urination.

If you have a submissive or excitement urinator, you can be very optimistic. Most dogs can overcome these problems relatively easily with appropriate management and modification techniques.

Make Certain You Treat the Correct Problem

Before you attempt to address your dog's urination problem, you need to clearly identify it to be sure you apply the right solution to your training situation. Here are some of the various house-soiling challenges you might encounter:

Basic housetraining problems:

- *Dog may urinate or defecate in the house, or both.*
- *"Accident" may occur in the owner's presence or outside the owner's presence.*
- *Is likely to follow some pattern—e.g., after eating, waking up from a nap, or after a play session.*
- *Dog may tend to eliminate near the door—an indication that he was trying to go out.*
- *If dog has been punished for inappropriate elimination, he may regularly go to an out-of-the-way "safe" room to toilet, in order to avoid punishment.*
- *Puddles of urine will tend to be large, stools ample and solid.*

Hunker down and allow a shy dog to approach *you*. Keeping your voice quiet, your eye contact indirect, and your movements slow and calm will give the dog confidence and avoid triggering a spill.

Physical or medical problems:

- *Frequent, small amounts of urine, even in crate or bed, is an indication of a urinary tract infection.*
- *Soft stools in small or large amounts or diarrhea is an indication of a gastrointestinal problem.*

Submissive urination:

- *Most likely to occur when dog is being greeted, approached, or reprimanded, either physically or verbally.*
- *Occurs in the presence of humans (or another dog or other intimidating stimulus).*
- *Dog is likely to display one or more other signs of submission, such as ducking head, laying ears back, grinning, tucking tail and/or fast, low, tail-wagging, avoiding eye contact, rolling on back.*
- *May release small or large amount of urine, usually no feces.*

Excitement urination:

- *Most likely to occur when dog is being greeted or otherwise in high state of excitement.*
- *Occurs in the presence of humans or other exciting stimulus.*
- *Dog displays other signs of excitement, such as wiggling, jumping up, ears up, high tail wag, barking.*
- *May release small or large amount of urine, usually no feces.*

If Spot's problem appears to be simple housetraining, then return to square one of a basic housetraining program. If the signs point to a medical problem, a prompt trip to your veterinarian is in order. If you are clearly faced with a submissive or excitement urination challenge, however, then it's time to implement behavior modification for Spot and you.

Prevention vs. Rehabilitation

As with virtually all dog behavior problems, prevention is a far better approach than rehabilitation. If you have the luxury of working within your puppy's critical learning window, you are light years ahead of the game. The more your pup's breed characteristics and individual personality predispose him to dog aggression, the more critical it is that he be socialized during the learning period. The following steps can maximize his opportunities for socialization while minimizing his exposure to disease:

Do intervene if another puppy starts to bully yours.

• DO keep him current on his vaccination schedule. (Some people vaccinate their dogs far more aggressively than others).

• DO invite friends over with their healthy puppies and gentle adult dogs to play with your puppy.

• DO enroll your puppy as soon as possible in a well-run puppy class where classmates are allowed to play together. Again, people vary in their willingness to vaccinate their dogs. Most trainers require proof of vaccinations for all participants. People who use fewer than the usual number of puppy vaccinations may have difficulty finding a trainer who understands and accepts this approach.

The goal: Well-adjusted, social dogs who can romp and play and enjoy the company of other dogs, and resolve minor differences without bloodshed.

• DO talk to the trainer and watch the class first. Puppy play should be closely monitored to avoid bullying of small or timid puppies by bigger, older ones. The facility should be clean indoors and out, and training techniques involving the use of choke chains, prong collars, or physical force should not be permitted.

• DO intervene if another puppy starts to bully yours. A pup can learn to be defensively aggressive if he is frightened by the intensity of another pup's play.

• DO intervene if your puppy starts to bully another. A gentle interruption of the behavior every time it occurs combined with brief time-outs if necessary, offset by praise and treat rewards when he is playing well with others, can keep him on the right track. A time-out is what behaviorists call "negative punishment." The puppy's behavior (being too rough or aggressive) makes a good thing (playing with other puppies) go away. If you are consistent he will learn that he has to be nice if he wants to keep playing.

• DON'T intervene if two pups are engaged in mutually agreeable rough play. Rough play is perfectly acceptable if both pups are enjoying it. Do keep an eye on the participants to make sure they are both having fun, and gently intervene if the tone of play starts to change.

• DON'T take your puppy to dog parks or public areas where lots of dogs congregate. He faces a much greater risk of exposure to disease in those environments.

• DON'T allow your puppy to sniff piles of feces from unknown dogs when you take him for walks around the block.

• DON'T allow your pup to interact with any dogs or puppies who don't appear healthy, and don't allow the owners of sick dogs or puppies to play with yours.

If you follow these simple guidelines, your chances of having a well socialized dog are high, and your disease risk is very low. Remember: Far more dogs face tragic ends to their lives due to poor socialization than to illnesses encountered in well-monitored puppy play groups.

Bite-Me-Not
One of the most important things a puppy needs to learn: bite inhibition.

Bite inhibition is the ability of a dog to control the force of his bite. Without it, even a playful grab at your sleeve when you are wrestling with your dog or a quick snap of shocked self-defense (when you accidentally step on his tail, for example) can result in a serious or painful puncture. In contrast, a dog in those same circumstances who has well-developed bite inhibition can grab your wrist and even gently shake it, or bite at the ankle of the foot that is planted on his tail, without leaving a mark or causing you more than a moment's minor discomfort.

Canine behaviorists theorize that dogs have evolved to develop bite inhibition for good reason. In canine society, dogs normally use escalation of force effectively to get their messages across without inflicting grievous injury upon each other. This is important from a survival standpoint; if pack members consistently punctured each others' skins over trivial issues, they'd risk their own injury and debilitation, even death, as well as that of the pack mates they depend upon for mutual protection, food gathering, and survival. Even when encountering canines from an "alien" pack, the less actual physical engagement, the better the chances of survival for all concerned.

Fortunately for humans, this bite inhibition often transfers to us, as members of our canines' social groups.

How to get it

Bite inhibition is clearly a desirable thing. So how do you get it? Or more correctly, how does your dog get it? It's not something you'll find on the shelf of your local pet supply store!

Bite inhibition has both genetic and environmental components. That is, a dog can inherit the potential to

There is a good reason to put up with those needle-like teeth. Puppies learn lifelong "bite inhibition" from consistent consequences for too-hard and just-right chewing and mouthing. If it is forbidden altogether, they may never develop a "soft" mouth.

use gentle bite pressure from parents who are also genetically programmed to mouth softly, and he can also learn to bite softly. Of course, the more strongly a desirable behavior trait is encoded in the genes, the easier it is to nurture appropriate behaviors. If your pup lacks good genes for bite inhibition, he'll need lots of environmental influence—the sooner, the better.

Genetics of bite inhibition is one of the very important reasons to meet a pup's parents, if possible, when you purchase from a breeder. While sometimes one or both parents simply aren't available for legitimate reasons, if the breeder declines because either of the parents aren't friendly, have bitten in the past, or cautions you to be careful when interacting with them, you may not want to risk purchasing a puppy from those lines. Make it a point to specifically ask if either parent has ever bitten, and if so, the severity of the bite, and how the breeder would characterize both dogs' levels of bite inhibition. If she's not willing to discuss the topic, doesn't understand the question, or seems not to be forthcoming with information, make your puppy-purchase decision accordingly.

If you're adopting from a shelter, Mom and Dad aren't likely to be around. When you can't meet parents, your personal observations during puppy selection—always important anyway—become even more critical. Most puppies will engage in some degree of mouthing—it's how they explore their world. However, if you play with a number of puppies, you'll discover that some mouth your hands gently, others will repeatedly bite hard enough with their wickedly sharp baby teeth to cause pain, and still others will even draw blood.

Those who consistently mouth gently have a healthy degree of innate bite inhibition and/or have learned their lessons well from Momdog and siblings who let them know when they bit too hard. Those who cause pain or draw blood need more lessons. There's a good chance they can still turn into great dogs—and it will take more input on your part to teach them to be gentle with their teeth. The older a pup is, the more effort it will take to install bite inhibition, and the greater the likelihood that you'll be less successful.

One of the reasons it's such a tragedy to remove a pup from his litter too soon is that he'll miss those all-important bite-inhibition lessons from Momdog and sibs. This is also one of the big drawbacks of adopting a singleton—a pup with no littermates. We strongly recommend you wait to take your new pup home until he's at least seven weeks old, preferably eight, regardless of how eager the breeder is to give him up. Your own bite inhibition lessons can never be as effective with your pup as those from his own kin. No matter how hard we try, we just can't speak dog as well as dogs can.

Don't punish!

In past times, and unfortunately sometimes still today, dog owners were counseled to use aversives to try to teach bite inhibition. If a puppy gnawed on your hands, some trainers suggested holding his muzzle closed as punishment, "cuffing" him under the chin with an open palm, or worse, shoving a fist down the pup's throat. In a word . . . "Don't!"

Not only are these methods abusive and have the potential to teach your pup to fear your hands, they can also trigger aggressive responses from assertive or fearfully defensive pups. If they do succeed in putting a stop to the mouthing, you may have taught the pup that his only options are to "Not Bite" or to "Bite Really Hard" rather than the third important option, "If You Must Bite, Bite Gently."

Remember, all dogs bite, given the right (wrong) set of circumstances. With enough provocation, even the most tolerant and gentle of dogs might be induced to put her mouth on human skin. With good bite inhibition, provocation is likely to result in a polite, "Please don't do that" mouth-on-skin warning. Without it, the

Dogs rarely bite without warning, so be alert to the warning signs, such as a flashing "whale eye," which signifies "You're bugging me!"

provoked dog is likely to cause serious damage when he puts his teeth on someone.

The older a dog is when you start trying to teach bite inhibition, the greater the likelihood that, while you may succeed in teaching the dog to consciously use his mouth more gently, he will still fall back into hard biting during times of stress and arousal.

If you have a pup with naturally good bite inhibition, consider yourself blessed, and take steps to preserve this valuable natural resource. If not, start immediately to cultivate bite inhibition.

If you do try the "Yipe!" once or twice and it works, great. If it doesn't, don't keep doing it! Use a calm "Ouch!" or another more composed marker.

Things to do

Play fetch games with your pup to direct his mouth toward appropriate toys to take some of the "wild puppy" edge off his bite. Be sure to give him plenty of exercise daily. A tired pup is a well-behaved pup. Consult your vet for guidance on how much exercise is appropriate for your pup.

Work with his bite inhibition while he's in an exercise pen or on a tether so you can calmly escape his shark teeth. Begin petting him and playing gently. As long as he's not causing pain, even if he's putting his mouth on you with some pressure, continue playing.

If he bites and hurts you, calmly say "Ouch!" and walk away from him. Step outside the reach of the tether, or exit the pen so he can't follow you and continue to bite. The "Ouch!" isn't intended to stop the biting; it only marks the behavior—tells him what he did that made you leave. This is negative punishment: his biting behavior makes a good thing—you—go away.

Wait 20 to 30 seconds to give him time to calm down, then go back to him and calmly resume playing. If he's barking and aroused, wait to return until he settles. As long as he bites softly, continue playing. Any time his bite hurts, say "Ouch!" and leave.

If several repetitions don't seem to reduce hard biting, give him longer time-outs to give him more time to settle.

Over time, as he learns to control his hardest biting, you can raise the bar—use the same methods to gradually shape a softer and softer mouth. When he's no longer biting hard enough to hurt, use your "Ouch" technique for moderately hard bites, then medium ones, then finally, as he outgrows the puppy stage at five to six months, for any bites to skin at all.

If you must handle him when he's being "bitey"—to groom, trim his nails, attach his leash—keep his teeth busy nibbling at treats you hold in one hand while you work with the other, or have a helper feed treats so you have both hands free to groom, trim, or leash.

This method of marking the inappropriate behavior and walking away from the pup imitates, to some degree, the behavior of Momdog and littermates when a pup bites too hard. If needle-sharp teeth clamp too hard on Momdog's tender teats, she may stand up and exit the den. Pups learn to nurse gently to keep the milk bar open. Similarly, when pups play together, if one is too rough his playmate may "Yipe!" and decline to continue the game. Pup learns to inhibit his bite to keep the fun happening.

Some trainers teach owners to give a high-pitched "Yipe!" or "Ouch!" to mimic a littermate's protestations. While this can work with some pups, others find it more arousing—perhaps because we don't really know what we're saying when we try to speak Dog.

Our advice is to skip trying to imitate a puppy "Yipe!" and just use a calm "Ouch!" as a marker. If you do try the "Yipe!" once or twice and it works, great. If it doesn't, don't keep doing it! Simply replace it with a more composed marker.

More tips

Pups with poor bite inhibition can exhibit exceedingly frustrating behaviors. It's easy to lose patience when those needle-sharp puppy canines sink into your skin. Remember that these "sharky" little guys usually love reactions; you're playing into their paws when you lose your temper with them.

Use management solutions such as crates and baby gates so your pup doesn't have access to you when you're dressed up. Have treats and toys handy so you can toss them away from you and divert him when he's approaching with mayhem on his mind. Do lots of work on the tether so you can repeatedly send the message that hard bites make the good stuff go away.

Young children should play with a shark-pup only under direct supervision, and only when the puppy is in a mellow mood. Most pups develop predictable cycles—if you know he's calmest early to mid-afternoon, that's when he can play with the kids. Controlled games only—no running around the backyard squealing while puppy tries to latch onto chubby, tender toddler legs!

If you're doing positive training, with treats—and of course we hope you are—a hard-mouthed puppy can bring you to tears and leave your fingers bleeding as he clamps down on treats. It's reassuring to know it gets easier when they lose their sharp baby teeth at five to six months, but meanwhile you're tempted to stop training, or at least stop using treats! Try these temporary solutions:

- Keep your treat hidden in your closed fist until you feel your pup's mouth soften. Then open your hand and feed the treat from the palm of your hand like you would feed a horse. This teaches the pup he gets the treat when his mouth is soft, and prevents finger-shredding because he's taking it from your palm.
- Use metal finger splints. Available over-the-counter at pharmacies, these handy gadgets protect your fingers and teach him to be soft because most dogs don't like to bite on metal.
- Feed treats from a metal spoon. This keeps your fingers out of his mouth and teaches him to be gentle; again, few dogs like to bite metal.
- Toss treats on the floor instead of hand-feeding. This is a temporary solution, as there are many times in training when it's far preferable to feed from the hand than the floor. On occasion though, it can save your fingers—and your sanity.

It may take a while to see the positive results of your gradual bite-inhibition lessons, but it's worth it.

The Case for Kindergarten
The benefits of puppy training and socializing classes outweigh the risks.

Early socialization and training, especially for breeds that can be aloof and difficult if they don't receive a lot of socialization at a young age, is critically important for the family dog. That's why all puppies benefit from kindergarten classes.

Well-run, positive puppy kindergarten classes can definitely help get people and their puppies off to a good start in terms of basic manners. Trainers agree that the socializing also helps the puppies learn to relate to other dogs in a healthy, appropriate manner.

However, asked to advise puppy owners on the subject of puppy training and socialization classes, many veterinarians warn owners away, describing a frightening scenario in which viruses, bacteria, fungi, and parasites lurk in the air and on the ground wherever puppies breathe or walk. They say that other dogs and puppies, potential carriers of infection, are best avoided until young puppies are "fully protected" by vaccinations or their own maturing immune systems. Most veterinarians believe it is safe to let four-month-old puppies explore the outside world, but some recommend waiting until pups are six or seven months old.

The problem is that a conservative approach may (or may not, as we'll discuss) safeguard puppies from exposure to agents of infection, but it leaves them completely susceptible to the far less easily treated effects of social isolation. Puppies learn important behavioral skills from each other, their mothers, extended families, and any other canine visitors. These lessons, say behaviorists, can't be learned from humans, however motivated or well-intentioned. They can only be learned from other dogs. Early training and play in group classes enhances dog-to-dog communication at the same time that it helps young puppies adapt to new people, new sights and smells, other animals, and the experience of travel.

So what's a responsible canine caretaker to do? Do you really have to choose between sending your puppy to school to contract a horrible disease and keeping him quarantined so that he ends up being euthanized due to a dangerous personality disorder?

Not really. Although there are some risks associated with each approach, educating yourself about the risks will help you take a moderate path, keeping a lookout for signs of trouble, and helping you guide the development of your pup into a physically and socially healthy pooch.

Understanding immunity

It's no wonder that so many people are misinformed about the risks of disease; few have an accurate understanding of the dog's immune system or the reason for a series of puppy shots.

When challenged by an agent of disease (an antigen), a healthy dog's immune system responds by producing disease fighters called antibodies, which are

To Choose the Right Puppy Kindergarten, Do Your Homework *First*

Owners who decide to take young puppies to school can make informed decisions if they ask the right questions. Check with other dog owners, breeders, groomers, veterinarians, dog clubs, shelters, and pet supply stores; look in the phone book, go online, and watch for ads in newspapers and magazines. Keep an open mind: the perfect program for another person's puppy may not be ideal for yours, and vice versa. Then, go look at each school, and ask the following questions of each school you find:

What is the facility like? Is it safe, clean, and comfortable? Is it sufficiently cool in summer and warm in winter? Does the floor surface provide traction? Is there a convenient potty area and trash cans? Are cleanup supplies provided? How large is the training room?

"Space is an issue," says Tracy Atkins. "If the area is too large, the puppies won't interact. If it's too small, the crowding gets stressful and fights can occur. And it should be puppy-proofed!" That means no exposed electrical cords that pups can chew, or furniture that rambunctious puppies can knock over onto themselves.

Does the school screen its students? Some puppies may not belong in puppy kindergarten. Good trainers screen their applicants with care, considering each new puppy's size, age, breed, background, and personality. "Large breed puppies that are five and a half months old or older when they first come to class are a potential problem for smaller, younger puppies," says Atkins. "Unless they received considerable socialization at home, they lack the social skills for puppy kindergarten and should be placed in a class with older puppies."

Does the school make its policies clear? How much do classes cost? What is the schedule? What about cancellations, makeup classes, and refunds? What are your obligations as a client? Detailed phone interviews, orientation classes, clearly defined policies, and printed guidelines help avoid misunderstandings.

What is the school's vaccination policy? Some schools require proof of two sets of vaccines prior to the first class. Most schools accept whatever vaccination schedule a veterinarian recommends, and a

Group classes are an ideal place for pups to learn to concentrate on their handlers' requests—no matter what other distractions are all around them.

Kids may end up spending more time with the puppy than anyone else in the family. Puppy classes give kids what may be their best opportunity to learn how to manage their sometimes overwhelming friends.

few allow unvaccinated puppies. "We don't require proof of vaccination at A Place for Paws," says Dani Edgerton. "We ask owners to state that their pups' health is being cared for as their veterinarians recommend. We've trained 225 puppies in the last three years without any puppy diseases."

How large is the class? Size varies according to location (larger classes are more common in urban areas) and the availability of staff. The larger the class and the more family members who come, the more assistants an instructor needs. Most kindergarten classes have between 4 and 15 puppies.

Are the trainers experienced? The ability to recognize and anticipate breed-specific behavior is important in classes that welcome all puppies of every description. "Some breeds require extra effort at socialization," says Melissa Bussey at Training Tracks Canine Learning Station in Ohio. "For example, Shar-Peis tend to be more reactive and aggressive than most other breeds in my classes, and many German Shepherd Dogs have come with at least a bit of fear aggression toward other dogs." The more a trainer knows about your puppy's breed, especially if it is unusual or challenging, the better.

Even if a puppy never gains this much obedience from his class, he'll gain experience and increased confidence.

Are families invited? "I like my puppies' new owners to take their children to classes so they can learn, too," says Bichon Frise breeder Sandy Leon in Michigan. "The more consistent everyone's behavior is at home, the better life is for the puppy."

What happens in class? How are the puppies trained? Look for schools that emphasize positive reinforcement, praise, appropriate rewards, and meaningful lessons. "My classes are not simply play groups," says Mary Rioux-Forker. "We train the pups to sit, lie down, stay, go to a rug and hang out, walk on a lead, leave things alone, come, be restrained, do a stupid pet trick, ignore distractions (practice impulse control), and do various behavioral exercises to stabilize temperament and get the relationship right between owner and puppy. At the end of class each week, we teach the pups how to act appropriately as they approach other dogs, and we work on gentle, cooperative, appropriate play with guidance from the owners."

Melissa Bussey emphasizes socialization and problem-prevention exercises. Puppies learn that meeting new people, giving up food or toys when asked, getting off furniture when asked, and standing still while being handled all mean great things for dogs. "The earlier a puppy learns that humans hold the key to all the good stuff,"

Don't enroll in the program that's most convenient to your home or schedule without researching it first. Make arrangements to watch a class, meet the instructor, and ask questions before signing up.

she says, "the better. Dogs quickly learn that pleasing their humans makes good things happen, which makes them willing and eager students. This type of training also makes visits to the vet or groomer much easier."

"It is critical that early puppy training not be punitive," says Gail Fisher, "but it takes more than positive reinforcement to make a class effective. Puppy socialization classes that are all play and no training are, in my opinion, counterproductive. They teach puppies to be out of control in a group class, and they reinforce noisy behavior. We can always tell when a dog (of any age) has spent time in such a play class. Those dogs are far more difficult than dogs that had no training whatsoever."

Finally, don't enroll in the program that's most convenient to your home or schedule without researching it first. Pressed for time, many people sign up for the first class they find, planning to cancel if the instructor's training style is incompatible with their own training philosophies. This strategy has landed many people in the uncomfortable position of having to protest or walk out of a class when the instructor did something to their puppies that they didn't like.

Group classes also give pups a chance to observe and get comfortable with strangers, people who have different voices and mannerisms than their owners.

specific to whatever antigen is encountered by the animal. Infant puppies receive temporary protection from disease via the placenta (in utero) and from antibodies in their mothers' colostrum or "first milk." Later, the mother's milk also contributes antibodies.

Each mother provides different antibodies depending on her history of vaccination and other exposures to disease antigens. If the mother has a well-functioning immune system, and a thorough history of vaccination and/or exposure to disease, she will likely contribute a powerful dose of protective antibodies. If, on the other hand, her own store of antibodies is impoverished, due to a dysfunctional immune system, a lack of vaccinations, and/or a lack of exposure to disease antigens, her antibody contributions to her puppies may well be insufficient.

The protection that each puppy receives from his mother (sometimes called "passive immunity") usually lasts for several weeks and gradually fades; also gradually, his own immune system matures and begins manufacturing its own antibodies when confronted by disease antigens. Usually, this immune system matura-

tion occurs at around 14 to 16 weeks. But the exact rate at which the maternal immunity fades is highly variable from individual to individual. This is important to understand, because as long as the mother's powerful antibodies are at work in the puppy's system, his own immune system will not produce its own antibodies in response to exposure to disease antigens.

In most puppies, the maternal immunity fades at some point between 6 and 16 weeks. Vaccines that are administered while the maternal immunity is still strong will be effectively erased from the puppies' systems by the maternal antibodies. That's why it's generally recommended that puppies be given a series of vaccinations separated by a couple of weeks—to make sure that they're not left unprotected for too long between the fade of the maternal immunity and the development of their own vaccine-triggered antibody protection.

The uncertain timing of the maternal immunity fade is also why veterinarians often recommend that puppies stay relatively quarantined until they are 16 weeks old or even older.

Say a puppy receives a typical course of vaccinations at 8, 12, and 16 weeks. Conceivably, his maternal immunity could still be strong enough at 8 weeks (or even 8 and 12 weeks) to nullify those vaccinations, yet fade before his next vaccinations at 12 or 16 weeks. That could leave him vulnerable to disease—without protective antibodies—for a period of a couple of weeks.

Of course, that's not necessarily the end of the world. Exposure to a disease antigen can make an unprotected puppy sick, but it will also stimulate his immune system to produce antibodies to fight that and future exposures to the disease antigen. However, the older he is, the more mature his own immune system will be, and the better it will accomplish that task. That's why the potential "gap" in the puppy's protection is more dangerous when he's 8 weeks old than when he's 12 weeks old.

Making the decision for your puppy: The risk continuum

Way out on the conservative end of the "fear of disease" scale are the people who feel that any increased risk of infection is not worth the benefits of the socialization; these are the "keep pups home until they are six months old" people. At the other extreme of this scale are the people who are comfortable with the possibility that their puppies could become ill, and who allow their puppies to socialize anywhere, anytime. Some of these people use conventional vaccination protocols; some, you may be surprised to learn, use no vaccines at all.

Then there is the "fear of social disorders" scale, which also has its extremists. On one end are those who feel that all puppies must be socialized, no matter what. These people feel that the risk of dealing with illness, or even the death of a puppy, is preferable to raising a social misfit. On the other extreme of this scale are the people who either don't know or don't care about socialization.

It can be difficult to find a balanced place on this four-ended teeter-totter, especially when you weigh one scale of risks and benefits against the risks and benefits of the other scale. But, people do!

New Hampshire trainer Gail Fisher says, "The risk of contracting a communicable disease is minute compared to the nearly 100 percent guarantee that an unsocialized dog will never reach its genetic potential. Since non-genetically based, distrustful, suspicious, nervous, fearful behavior is totally preventable, why would anyone recommend otherwise? Generally speaking, puppies can recover from contagious illness. Shyness lasts for life."

Massachusetts trainer Gerilyn Bielakiewicz agrees. "The best argument I've heard for early training and socialization," she says, "comes from veterinarian and behaviorist Dr. Ian Dunbar, of Sirius Puppy Training in California. He says that it does no good for vets to tell people not to socialize their puppies before they are fully vaccinated if those same puppies end up dead because they can't get along with other dogs or people. Lack of socialization kills more dogs than any disease."

The Social Scene

Dogs who are confident and comfortable in public are made, not born.

The best socialization programs begin while pups are still with their dams. A good breeder begins handling her pups gently and early, just as their eyes begin to open, giving them a positive association with human touch. As they get a little older (five to six weeks) they should start meeting more humans—all shapes, colors, ages, and sizes—who feed them treats and pet them gently. The breeder will need to supervise these interactions closely, as rough handling at this stage can have the opposite effect, teaching the pups that humans aren't safe to be around.

The mother dog's attitude is important at this stage, too. If she is aggressive toward humans, or even just stressed about her pups being handled, the pups can register her attitude and learn this inappropriate behavior. If Mom is calm and relaxed around humans, pups are more likely to be, too.

By the time a pup is weaned at seven to eight weeks, he should already have a positive worldview programmed into his little puppy brain. When you select your pup from a litter, whether you're at a breeder's home or a shelter—or picking one from a box of free puppies on a street corner—choose wisely. Resist the temptation to rescue the pup who hides in the corner. Select, instead, the pup who is outgoing without being overbearing—the one who seems to have a cheerful, "Life is good!" attitude.

Okay, you've adopted a friendly pup with a sound temperament. Good for you! That doesn't mean your job is done, however. You must continue your pup's socialization lessons assiduously until he is 16 weeks old, and then maintain his positive association to the world throughout his life. If you take an eight-week-old well-socialized pup and stick him in your backyard with no outside exposure, the odds are good that you will end up with a problem.

Don't fall for that shy, withdrawn puppy (especially an older pup) unless you are committed to her social rehabilitation.

An outdoor cafe can be an excellent place to find people to help you socialize your puppy. Look for a variety of people—old, young, big, small, etc.—and give the volunteers a few delicious tidbits to feed to the pup.

100 Exposures in 100 Days

Giving your pup 100 positive experiences in his first 100 days with you is not as daunting as it may sound. The most important thing to keep in mind is to control the circumstances so that the experience remains positive for your puppy. When introducing your pup to children, for example, put your body between your pup and any overeager, rambunctious kids until you have a chance to tell the kids how they must behave if they want to meet the puppy. Don't let a baby clamp his hand onto any part of the puppy's anatomy, or hand the puppy to anyone who is in danger of dropping her.

It's also best to bring an ample supply of extra-tasty treats anywhere you take the pup. When someone sees your puppy and starts making the inevitable "Oh what a cute puppy!" approach, hand the person a couple of treats and ask if he would feed them to the pup as he pets her. Or bring along your puppy's favorite stuffed toy, and give it to the person so he can offer it to your puppy. Keep an eye on your puppy's response; she should be happy, confident, and obviously pleased to see any and every new person approaching. If she appears frightened or overwhelmed, think about how you can make the interactions more rewarding for her.

Seek out people who look different: people with hats or canes, on bikes or skateboards, in uniforms and formal wear.

You'll find many opportunities in your own neighborhood to start your list of 100. You'll also want to get into the habit of taking your pup with you to as many safe places as possible, to enhance his socialization and to start him on his path to being your well-behaved companion, welcome wherever you go.

We suggest you keep an actual written list of your pup's socialization exposures, with a goal of a minimum of one new exposure per day until you've reached the 100 mark. If you put a little effort into it, we're betting you'll get there well before your 100 days are up—more likely in half that time! Here are some suggestions to start you off:

(1) Your mail carrier. Snag him on his daily rounds and ask him to feed your pup a tidbit or two. Start an early positive association with this daily visitor to your home.

(2) Your UPS or FedEx person. Add a little extra power to the positive association with uniformed visitors to avoid trouble later.

(3) Your neighbors. Actually, this can count toward many of the exposures on your list if you live in a diverse neighborhood. If your neighborhood is homogeneous, try a park or the bench in front of your local library. Look for tall men, (4) short men, (5) tall women, (6) short women, (7) skinny men and (8) skinny women, (9) portly men and (10) portly women, (11) babes-in-arms or babies in backpacks or slings, (12) babies in strollers, (13) women pushing babies in strollers, (14) toddlers, (15) older children, (16) tweens and (17) teens, (18) men with beards, (19) people with hats, (20) people with backpacks, (21) people with umbrellas, (22) people in wheelchairs, (23) people using walkers and crutches, (24) kids on bikes, (25) kids on scooters, (26) kids on skateboards, (27) kids playing basketball . . .

. . . and all of the above in various ethnic groups.

Then add locations to your list, including your (28) bank, (29) vet's office, (30) pet supply store, (31) copy center, (32) hardware store, (33) puppy kindergarten class, (34) outdoor cafe, or (35) any place of business that doesn't have a "No Dogs" sign on the door.

Okay, you're one-third of the way there. You get the idea, and get to think up the rest. Be creative, and remember to control each interaction to keep it positive for your pup.

A dog who was well-socialized should exhibit confidence and poise in any setting, interacting comfortably with people wearing any manner of dress.

The health dilemma

Puppy owners are often counseled by their veterinarians to keep their baby dogs cloistered safely at home until they are fully immunized at age four to six months. Looking at the situation purely from a physical health perspective, this makes good sense. You certainly don't want to risk exposing your pup to nasty distemper or parvo bugs.

From a mental health perspective, however, it's horrible advice. You only have two to three more months to give your pup an unshakable faith in the goodness of the world. You cannot afford to wait until those shots are done. During this period, you want to give your pup at least 100 new positive exposures and experiences, to "vaccinate" him against the possibility that he will feel compelled to bite someone. It's not a guarantee against biting, but it's by far your best chance of ending up with an adult dog who is friendly and safe.

Fear periods

At one time in the last several decades, much ado was made about a pup's "critical fear periods." Behaviorists attempted to pinpoint those periods

Puppy Care Basics

Rescuing the Shrinking Violet

Cautions and common sense aside, it's human nature to want to rescue the doggie in distress—the pup who shrinks away from human contact and looks at the world with fear in her eyes. If you are the rescuer type, you have my respect and admiration. Many poorly socialized pups are rescued and go on to live happy and normal lives because their rescuers recognized the daunting task they faced, and made a solid commitment to do the work.

Here are some tips for you if you know that your heart will someday be captured by the challenge of an unsocialized pup:

- *Get her as young as you can. The benefits of staying with her litter until eight weeks of age are outweighed by the benefits of getting started with socialization.*
- *Or, give her the best of both worlds: take the entire litter, or at least several of the pups, and start them all on the road to a happier life. Then be sure to find capable, knowledgeable adopters for her siblings when they turn eight weeks—adopters who will continue with remedial socialization.*

- *Avoid the temptation to keep more than one pup. They are likely to bond to each other more closely than to you, which makes your socialization challenge many times more difficult. Even well-socialized littermates or same-age pals that are raised together can become highly stressed while separated from their buddies.*
- *Have a solid understanding of counter-conditioning and desensitization, and make a strong commitment to practice this with her every single day.*
- *Read* The Cautious Canine *by Patricia McConnell, and* Dogs Are From Neptune *by Jean Donaldson, two books that clearly explain how to work with poorly socialized dogs using counter-conditioning and desensitization.*
- *Be prepared to assertively protect your pup from unwanted advances by well-meaning strangers who want to pet your puppy. You must not let people pet or harass her until she is well-socialized enough to tolerate petting and harassment.*
- *Know that love is not enough. Many well-meaning rescuers think that giving a psychologically neglected pup a home filled with love will be enough to "fix" the problem. Don't fool yourself. Love is an important part of the equation, but it will take a lot of work as well.*
- *Be prepared for heartache. Some poorly socialized pups—most likely those who are genetically sound—do respond well to remedial socialization and grow into reasonably well-socialized adult dogs. Others don't.*

If you don't succeed in enhancing your pup's social skills, are you prepared to live with a fearful dog who may be at high risk for biting you, your visitors, children, and goodness knows who else? Or to make the difficult decision to euthanize, so she doesn't have to live a life of fear and stress?

Your dog may never be this comfortable with children, but she should understand the rudiments of living and playing with humans, and how to accept contact (perhaps not this much!) from family, friends, and relative strangers.

of time in puppyhood during which a "bad experience" would scar a pup's psyche for life. More recently, we have come to realize that, although pups do seem to go through periods during which they are more fearful than others, that time can vary from one pup to the next. Rather than wrapping your pup in cotton wool for a designated period, it makes more sense to watch him closely and ensure that he has mostly good experiences, especially if he seems to be going through a cautious stage.

Even if something does frighten him, it's not the end of the world—you can set up a counter-conditioning and desensitization (CC&D) program (see page 127) to restore a positive association with that particular stimulus, and your pup should recover nicely.

Lifetime socialization

Now your pup is 16 weeks old. You've reached the end of that magic socialization window, your "100 exposures" list is all checked off, and your pup loves the world. Are you done? Hardly.

Like your training efforts, which continue on into adulthood and throughout your dog's entire life, you are never done with socialization. You've laid a very solid foundation; that's something to be proud of.

Much of that will be lost, however, if you toss your four-month-old pup into the backyard and cease all exposure. He still needs to meet and greet people, go places with you, and continue to share your world and your experiences, if you want him to continue to be the happy, friendly puppy he is today. And, of course, that's what you want!

Living with Humans 101
Ten things every dog should know (for your happiness, and his survival).

There are certain basic behaviors that all dogs need to know if they are going to survive in human society. Generally, the only ones who are likely to live happily ever after in their original homes are those dogs who are regarded as "good" by their owners.

The definition of a "good dog" depends on the defining party. If you could ask a dog, he may say something like, "Oh that Jake! He's a darned good dog! He can knock over any garbage can or jump on any counter for food, he trees cats with ease, he can chase most cars until they stop, and he can hear strangers coming from miles away and bark until they are gone! What a great dog!"

But if you asked a human to describe a "good dog," chances are they would not mention any of the life skills that a real dog's dog might display, such as an ability to scavenge for food or hunt and kill small animals. Rather, most people tend to regard good dogs as those who have learned to trade (or at least modify) many of their natural canine behaviors in favor of those that are acceptable to the human members of their families.

While some (or all!) of the Top 10 Things we describe below might seem overly elementary to an experienced and responsible dog owner, many dogs in training classes—and animal shelters—lack several or many of the following skills. Certainly, a committed canine caretaker should be willing to manage or overlook her dog's shortcomings; we are not perfect, nor should we expect our dogs to be. However, the less you have to manage or overlook, the more pleasant life will be for the both of you in the long run.

Put a check mark next to each of the 10 life skills that your dog has already successfully mastered. If you can check all 10, congratulations! You and your canine pal are well on your way to a lifetime of happiness

Your dog must be taught the rules of proper play: how and when to share, and how his teeth can and cannot be used. Start when he's young!

and good times together. If you have to skip some, you might want to get to work and help your dog become an even better companion for you.

1. **How To Live and Play Well with Humans**

   This may seem like a pretty broad topic. It is, in fact, the root of many of the ones that follow. Specifically, however, this means that your dog needs to accept that many human rules simply make no sense from a canine perspective. For example, humans have this incredibly bizarre habit of leaving food around uneaten. Really good food! Large chunks of prey animal—right out in plain view, on the kitchen counter, on the coffee table ... what creature in his right mind would not eat high-value food when the opportunity presents itself?

   Yet humans do just that, and expect their dogs to do the same. Although this exceptional example of canine self-control is often taken for granted, the dog who leaves the roast beef sandwich unmolested on the coffee table when his human takes a potty break in the middle of the Rose Bowl Parade deserves to be held in high esteem by his human caretaker.

   Other examples of bizarre human rules include a taboo on drinking water from the freshest water source in the house (a thing humans call a toilet), and an expectation that their dogs not perceive an open door as an open invitation to dash through.

Our dogs also must adapt to what probably seems to them to be very odd human play behavior. Dogs play with tooth and claw—jumping up, biting, body-slamming—while most humans want their canine playmates to keep their teeth to themselves, and to refrain from jumping up and body-slamming, even in play, unless expressly invited.

Dogs are capable of learning these eccentric human rules, and they learn best when their humans understand that it is a dog's nature to eat available food, drink fresh water, go through openings at will, and roughhouse in play. In each of these cases, proper management—not allowing the dog to be rewarded by the natural but undesirable behavior—and consistent reinforcement for alternative, preferable behaviors can get the job done.

2. **How to Accept Intimate Contact from Family, Friends, and Relative Strangers**

Throughout your dog's life, you will expect him to happily accept being touched and handled by all sorts of people: family, friends, strangers on the street, children in the schoolyard, veterinarians, groomers, and more. Dogs, however, do not come already programmed to love attention and touch. While some seem more naturally inclined to like human contact than others, all dogs must be socialized—ideally from a very early age—and taught to accept, even enjoy intimate touch. Even something as apparently innocuous as a pat on the head is foreign to a dog's natural instincts and nonverbal communication style.

The best puppy raisers begin an intensive socialization program starting when pups are four weeks old (or even younger), by exposing them to gentle handling and touch from an increasing number and variety of humans as the days and weeks pass. Handling ears, touching paws, and

examining teeth and private parts should all be accompanied by rewards—treats, toys, praise—so the pup comes to believe that humans and human touch make very good things happen. This concept should be instilled in his little dog brain well before he reaches the advanced age of four months.

Dogs who are stressed by human contact are far more likely to bite, and bite seriously, at some point in their lives. If your dog missed that all-important socialization period between four weeks and four months, you will need to work hard to make up for lost time. At this late stage, you can probably improve his willingness to accept contact, but he's not likely to be as social as he could have been. A strong commitment to a program of counter-conditioning and desensitization is in order, and you may need the assistance of a behavior and training professional to maximize your success.

3. **How to Share**

In the dog world, possession is generally nine-tenths of ownership, and even a small, lower-ranking pack member can often successfully fend off other dogs' threats to her food and other valuable objects. Dogs will share with each other—when they choose to. You probably expect your canine family members to share happily and willingly, each and every time you decide that what's hers is yours. Resource guarding is, in fact, a relatively common behavior with dogs, ranging from mild tension when folks are playing in the dog's food bowl, to serious aggression with potential to maim.

You can start early in a puppy's life to ensure against food guarding by teaching her that your approach is not a threat to her possessions, but actually brings more good stuff. When she's eating, approach her bowl and drop several high-value treats, one at a time, into her bowl. When she has something she shouldn't, trade her for something better, instead of chasing her around in anger, scaring her and putting her on the defensive. If she consistently gets something wonderful when you approach, and rarely loses the good thing she has, she will not resort to resource guarding—she won't need to!

If your dog is already a resource guarder, seek the help of a qualified positive professional to help you work with it. This is a dangerous behavior, and one that should be addressed by someone who is confident and capable.

4. **When and Where to Go Potty (and Where and When Not to)**

Dogs do come genetically programmed not to soil their own dens, so this is one human rule that makes pretty good sense to them. They may wonder why we insist on living in such large dens when small ones are so much cozier, but once they realize that the whole house is a den, housetraining usually comes along with relative ease.

The trick is to manage the dog's behavior through crates, pens, tethers, leashes, and direct supervision, so he doesn't have the opportunity to get in the habit of using any part of your house/ den as his bathroom. Meanwhile, take him outside frequently and consistently enough so that he gets in the habit of relieving himself outdoors.

Remember, it's a much simpler training challenge to teach him to go in one right spot than it is to teach him not to go in an almost infinite number of wrong spots.

5. **How to Be Alone**

To a wild dog, "alone" is synonymous with "danger." A puppy, especially, is at high risk for being eaten if he is left without the protection of the pack. Although they are thousands of years from their wild ancestors, many of our domestic dogs still experience a residual anxiety when they are left alone. In extreme cases, dogs can develop a condition known as separation anxiety—the equivalent of a panic attack when left alone—and can cause great damage to their environments and injury to themselves. While crates can be used with some destructive dogs to safely contain them while unat-

tended, crating is rarely a solution for unfortunate dogs with separation anxiety, as close confinement can send them into a panic frenzy.

To prevent separation anxiety, accustom your new puppy or dog to being left alone gradually during the first few days he is with you, perhaps crated or tethered while you move around the room, occasionally returning to him when he is calm and quiet. Calm departures and returns will also help him learn to be matter-of-fact about your comings and goings.

When this procedure causes him no discernible stress, begin stepping out of the room—for just a few seconds at a time, then longer and longer as he shows that he can handle it. Avoid returning to him when he is fussing—if he learns that fussing makes you return, you will teach him to fuss harder and harder, until he develops a full-blown anxiety attack when you are out of sight.

If your dog has signs of mild separation anxiety, the above program can also work, although it may take longer than a few days. If your dog has a serious anxiety condition, you will probably need the assistance of a professional, and perhaps anxiety-relieving drugs, to see improvement.

By nature, dogs are pack animals and may feel vulnerable and anxious when solitary—no matter how cozy their physical environment. They have to be taught to be comfortable spending time alone.

6. When, Where, and How to Use Teeth

There are lots of uses for a dog's teeth, and all of them are acceptable, if properly directed. Dogs eat the meals you give them with their teeth; obviously, that's okay. The best way to keep dogs from eating what they shouldn't is to manage their behavior to prevent access and reward for counter-surfing, and to train a positive "Leave it" exercise.

Dogs also chew with their teeth. This, too, is normal behavior, and it behooves you to provide your pup with plenty of appropriate chew objects (a stuffed Kong being our favorite) while he is developing his chewing preferences. Once he zeroes in on suitable chew objects and matures past the experimental puppy stage, your own personal possessions should be reasonably safe. For this reason, keep all new dogs crated when you can't supervise them until they are at least a year old, gradually giving them increased house freedom as long as they show you they can handle it.

Dogs play with their teeth. Since canine teeth contacting human skin is generally an unacceptable behavior, it's wise to redirect that play-bite urge to tug-of-war toys, complete with rules designed to make it a safe and rewarding game for both tug partners. Dogs should be free to engage in tooth-play with other dogs, as long as both dogs are willing participants.

And finally, dogs bite aggressively with their teeth. There are rare circumstances when this is acceptable behavior—for trained protection and police dogs, and for the untrained family dog who wisely bites a criminal intruder—but most companion dogs need to not bite humans if they want to live happily ever after. The best way to accomplish this is to go back to the socialization work of Top Thing #2 (How to Accept Intimate Contact).

Most aggression is caused by stress. A good socialization and positive training program reduces the number of things that might cause a dog to be stressed, thereby decreasing the likelihood that he will ever bite. All dogs are capable of biting, however, no matter how well socialized, if the situation is stressful enough—which is why the extreme stress generated by a stranger's attack on his human companion can cause even a very well-socialized and well-mannered dog to bite—as well he should!

7. How to Come When Called

A very reliable recall is the key to a dog's supervised freedom outdoors. While we would never counsel you to just open the door and turn your dog loose, if your dog has solid "comes when called" skills, you can have him with you off-leash in many suitable outdoor environments—gardening in your yard, hiking on dog-legal trails, playing in dog parks—without worrying that an errant deer will entice your dog into the woods and beyond your control. Very reliable recalls don't happen all by themselves. It takes a lot of training to end up with a dog who will turn his back on Bambi bounding across the meadow and return to you at a happy gallop instead.

One of the keys to achieving this milestone in dog training is to manage your dog so he doesn't have the opportunity to take off and romp in the woods with you screaming at him to come back. This means keeping him on a long line—and training him in the face of ever-increasingly enticing distractions—until you know his recall is rock-solid.

It takes an average of three years to train a dog to come to you in the face of extreme distractions. This means some dogs will get it sooner, and some will take longer, but plan on three years. Remember, that's three years of committed training, not just three years of sitting around waiting for the dog to get older!

8. How to Do an Emergency WHOA!

No matter how well trained, no dog is perfect. Even the most rock-solid recall may someday fail, and when it does, you'll be glad to have an emergency brake.

Train your dog to perform a long-distance down for emergency stops. Many dogs, while unwilling to turn their backs on a chase object and return to you, will happily drop to a down position, as long as they can keep their eyes glued to their prey. Once the prey is out of sight, the dog's arousal decreases, and she will be willing to return to you when you call her.

Some trainers use "NO!" or a "STOP!" in a loud roar to stop a dog from whatever behavior she is engaged in. This can work, but my preference is to tell the dog to do something rather than nothing.

9. **How to Walk Politely on a Leash**

Walking on leash, along with other important good manners behaviors such as "sit to greet people," can greatly enhance your enjoyment of your canine companion's presence. If he walks happily on a leash by your side instead of dragging you down the street, and politely greets people he meets on his outings, you are far more likely to take him places with you. The more places you take him, the more socialization and exercise he gets, and the better-behaved he is likely to be. The better-behaved he is, the more likely you are to take him places, proudly, as a well-loved and full-fledged member of your family.

10. **How to Play and Live with Other Dogs**

You may have only one dog, so what's the difference if he gets along with others? For one thing, dogs are naturally social animals, and you can enhance the quality of your dog's life if you socialize him with other dogs and provide him with opportunities to play with his dog pals at dog parks, doggie day care, or arranged play-dates in his own backyard. A day of dog play will eat up his excess canine energy and leave you begging for more play outlets. A tired dog is a well-behaved dog.

In addition, when you take your four-legged family member out in public, he will inevitably

It's simple. If a dog is fun to walk with, he'll get walked a lot. If he's not fun, he won't get walked, and he'll become less and less manageable—and perhaps less-loved.

encounter other canines. If he is well-socialized to dogs, he can handle these encounters with equanimity. Dogs who don't know how to act around other dogs may become fearful or overly excited—both of which can lead to aggression. Either way, if your dog acts out around other dogs you are likely to limit his exercise and socialization, which can give rise to other behavior problems, including destructive behavior and aggression.

Time to tally

So, how'd you and your dog do? If you checked 9 or 10 of the items, you should be proud of the work you have done with your dog, and the relationship you share.

If you have a lot of unchecked items, you'd better get a move on! Even if you are comfortable working around the gaps in your dog's knowledge, his lack of social or behavioral graces may be a source of friction between you and your roommates, spouse, or neighbors. Why not improve relations between the species, and teach him a few more vital skills? He'll be far safer and welcome in human society if you do.

Adoption Advice
Here's how to make your new dog's adoption work for life.

Adopting a new dog is an exciting, wonderful, and happy time. But bringing a new dog home is also an uncertain time. What will your dog be like? Will he be a good match for your family? Will he be everything you hoped for?

Bringing a new dog into the home can also, quite frankly, be a rather shocking time for you and your family. Suddenly your life will be compounded by the energy and needs of the new family member. Everyone will go through an adjustment—dogs and people alike.

Truthfully, some dogs come home from the shelter or other rescue situation and settle in with few problems; their adjustment period is brief and unremarkable. Many dogs are even on their best behavior—a honeymoon period—for several days or weeks. They may experience stress, but they deal with it by being cautious and responsive. But other dogs may deal with the uncertainty of being in a new home with other, more obvious stress responses. Some of those may include:

- Pacing and other overactive behavior;
- Attaching to one person in the family, but being very shy of others;
- Mouthing people, jumping up on them, barking, and chewing; and
- Trying to escape or hiding.

Don't panic if your new dog behaves in a less than desirable manner. In spite of the initial stress response, over the course of a few weeks or months, most dogs settle in and become wonderful companions. What happens in the first few days or weeks is not necessarily indicative of what life with the dog will be like long-term. But how you handle the stress response can certainly affect the long-term outcome.

As tempting as it may be to take your newly adopted dog to a park or crowded public events in the first few days following his arrival in your home, DON'T! He needs a few weeks of quiet walks with you, to learn what you expect and to develop a bond and trust with you.

Don't be shocked if your new dog does some "naughty" things in his first few weeks or months in your home. Help him out by limiting his opportunities to do the wrong thing. For example, keep your counters free of food!

Nice to Meet You! 10 Tips for Introducing a New Dog to Your Pack

Unless you have a bombproof canine pal who adores every other dog on earth, introducing your newest four-legged friend to other dogs can be a stressful experience at best. While dogs are genetically programmed to get along with pack members and the odds are therefore good that canines will be compatible, that doesn't necessarily mean instant warm fuzzies every time two dogs meet. If you are adding a new member to your personal pack, it is especially important that the introductions go well. Here are a few suggestions to tip the odds in your favor:

1. *Have a helper; don't introduce new dogs alone. You need to have at least one other adult there to help you in case there is trouble. Be sure your helper is comfortable and confident with dogs, and let her know, step-by-step, exactly what you plan to do and what you want her to do. Do not have children with you when you are doing introductions.*

Introduce dogs outdoors. Territorial issues are less likely to erupt outdoors than indoors, and the "great outdoors" provides more space and fewer traps.

2. *Introduce dogs on neutral ground. This is especially important if one or more of your dogs tend to be territorial. A neighbor's fenced yard, unused tennis court (if dogs are allowed), or other securely enclosed area works well.*

3. *Introduce dogs outdoors. Territorial issues are*

less likely to erupt outdoors than indoors, and the "great outdoors" provides more space and fewer traps—if the new dog feels threatened he can move away more easily in wide open spaces, not get stuck behind the sofa.

4. *Introduce dogs one at a time. If you are adding a dog to a home pack of several hounds, identify the home dog most likely to offer an easy greeting for the newcomer. When those two have hit it off, remove the first home dog and bring on the next most likely candidate. When the new dog has met each home dog individually, introduce pairs, again starting with the two most congenial home dogs. Keep adding one more dog at a time to the introduction groups until all the dogs are together.*

5. *Present dogs at a distance. Have your helper hold the new dog at the far side of the yard when you bring the home dog in the gate. Let them see each other from opposite sides of the yard. As long as there is no obvious aggression, release them so they can approach at their own speed, on their own terms, offering natural body-language signals.*

6. *Leave lightweight leashes attached to both dogs' collars. If there is a problem, you and your helper can each grab a leash and separate the dogs without putting your own body parts in harm's way. When it is clear that the dogs are getting along, usually after just a minute or two, remove the leashes so they don't get tangled around legs— yours and the dogs'—as the playmates begin to romp.*

7. *Ignore minor scuffles. A snap and snarl with minimal contact is one dog's way of telling the other to "Back off, Bub!" This is how they sort out their relationships and decide who can do what to whom. If you intervene in every scuffle, you make it more difficult for the dogs to figure each other out, and it takes much longer for them to become comfortable with each other.*

8. *That said, intervene when appropriate. If one dog is fearful and appears traumatized by the encounter, or is clearly getting trounced by the*

continued on page 36

continued from page 35

other(s) beyond a mild scuffle, then you need to step in, separate them, and rethink your introduction program. Have tools readily available to break up a fight if necessary.

9. *Be calm. If you are stressed, your dogs will read your body language and become more stressed themselves. Stress causes aggression. Speak calmly and cheerfully; move slowly and deliberately. Avoid sudden movements and loud verbal corrections, which can contribute to stress and aggression. If you need to intervene, use a cheerful positive interruption such as "Fido! Over here! Good boy!" rather than a verbal punisher such as "Fido! No! Bad dog!"*

10. *Be careful. If you are not confident about your introduction skills, or you have extenuating factors such as a huge size disparity (introducing a Great Dane to a Rat Terrier, for example) or a dog who has demonstrated aggression toward other dogs in the past, seek the assistance of a positive, professional trainer or behaviorist to help with your introductions. Also, remember that there may be space issues indoors that didn't occur outdoors. Watch your pack closely when you bring them inside. If necessary, manage behavior in the house in small groups until they are all more comfortable with each other.*

Equally important to remember is that while there may be a significant adjustment period, it is usually much shorter than the several years it takes to raise a puppy! And there is a whole lot you can do to make the transition easier. By being aware, modifying and redirecting any unwanted actions from the start, you can help your new dog become a good citizen.

De-stress!

In general, keep stress to a minimum for the first few days or weeks. How long depends on the dog's personality. Keep in mind that just the act of moving into a new home is stressful for most dogs—not to mention the stress he may have experienced before coming into your home. It can take several days or longer for the dog's stress hormones to return to normal levels once he feels safe and calm.

Take your time in introducing your new dog to friends, friends' dogs, and the local dog park. Remember that you will have this dog for the rest of his life; there is no rush! Give him time and space to settle in and bond with you before he is exposed to the world. Have him play and exercise in your yard and take him for walks in a quiet, low-stress area for the first few days or weeks.

Train for confidence

Basic training—sit, down, stay, come, and walking on a leash—can begin the day you bring your dog home. Use positive training methods such as clicker training. You can get started by referring to a book or video. Beginning training right away can help dogs understand that you will be taking care of them, and that they are safe. It will also help build confidence. For many dogs, training games will help them de-stress and settle in quicker.

Some dogs, however, will be "shut down" at first and may have a hard time learning a new behavior or even doing something they already know. Don't worry if your dog is not as responsive at first as you might like. If your dog seems reluctant, just make training games very easy, fun, and rewarding.

Try working with one simple behavior, like sit, and practice that until he seems ready to experiment with other behaviors. Or, if that seems too much, you can begin by simply hand-feeding a portion of your dog's meals to help him learn to trust you.

While training right away is beneficial, wait a few weeks before taking your dog into a class if he is stressed at all. For some dogs, you may even want to wait a little longer as training classes can also be very stressful.

If you need help right away, consider having a trainer come to your home instead of starting a class. Waiting to start a class until your dog has settled a little, and you have had time to bond, can help you both get the most from the experience.

With most dogs, bonding takes time. While a dog may form an attachment to a person quickly, he or she may not be bonded to the point of trusting that person to provide safety for several weeks.

Be patient

Give your newly re-homed dog more time than you think he needs to adjust. Wait until his stress hormones return to normal before taking him to places that may produce even more stress. Keep him on leash in open environments until he is trained and you are sure he will stay with you. Use your confinement area longer than you think necessary. Then slowly and carefully give your dog more freedom as he can handle it.

Imagine what your emotional state might be like if you were suddenly plucked from your current life (leaving everything you know and love behind), put into a shelter environment where you were forced to live with noise and uncertainty, then suddenly placed in a new family where you not only don't know anyone, but you don't know the rules or speak the language.

Be patient with your new dog. Give him the best start possible in his new home. And remember, with time and patience, everyone will settle in.

CHAPTER 2

Behavior and Training

Upper-Level Management
Training is not always the answer to solving your dog's problem behavior.

Every day, dog owners ask us questions—in person, on the phone, and online—about how to stop their dogs or puppies from doing something. The variations are limitless:

> "How do I stop him from going to the bathroom on the carpet?"
> "How do I keep her from chewing up my shoes (or books or furniture)?"
> "How do I make him stop stealing food from the counter?"

As simple as this seems, behavior management is the appropriate answer in probably better than 75 percent of the questions we are asked. In fact, management is key to preventing those behaviors from ever occurring in the first place! In many cases, management is necessary while the dog learns a new, more appropriate behavior. In others, management simply replaces unrealistic training expectations.

Here is a three-step formula for reprogramming or preventing unwanted behaviors:

1. **Rephrase.** That is, identify what you want the dog *to* do instead of what you want him *not* to do. In all the behaviors described above, the owner is asking how to get the dog to stop doing something rather than how to get to dog to do something.

2. **Manage.** Figure out how to *prevent* the dog from being rewarded for the unwanted behavior. This is actually the easiest part! Behaviors that are rewarded are reinforced—in other words, the dog

Baby gates are a cat's best friend. Dogs are denied the thrill of the chase when cats know they don't have to run.

is more likely to do them again. Chasing a cat is very rewarding to a dog—he gets a big adrenaline rush, and the cat runs away—what fun! Every chance your dog gets to chase a cat increases the likelihood that he will chase (and maybe eventually catch) the next cat he sees. If you don't want him to be rewarded by chasing cats, don't let him do it.

3. **Train.** Figure out how to consistently reward the dog for the desired behavior identified in Step 1. This is often the hardest part. Each of the training

programs for the behavior challenges listed above could be a full-length article of its own (and frequently, they have been; we'll refer you to relevant articles as we proceed).

Let's take a look at a number of problem behaviors and see how they can be addressed by our three-step formula, with particular focus on the management aspect:

How do I make him stop stealing food from the counter or table?

Rephrase: "How do I get him to only eat things that are in his bowl or on the floor?"

Manage: Prevent him from being rewarded for counter surfing. Clearly, the food that he finds on counters tastes good and is very rewarding. Use management tools such as doors (if food must be left out, shut the dog in another room so he can't have access to it); cupboards and the refrigerator; crates, pens, baby gates, leashes, and tethers (or other reasonable means of restraint to prevent his inappropriate access to food).

Train: Teach him a positive "Off!" or "Leave it!" cue and consistently reward him for ignoring food on

Stopping counter surfing is one of the easiest "problem behaviors" to solve: Simply put the food away! It might take a while to train the people in the household to put the butter away after making toast, but it can be done.

Few dogs would be able to resist the temptation to sniff at—or even snack from—a kitchen garbage can that is left out and unlidded. Imagine being locked in a candy store all night and not touching any of the goodies. Then put the garbage in a secure cabinet, or keep the doors closed to that room.

the counter and for keeping all four feet on the floor around food-laden counters and tables.

How do I stop him from peeing on the carpet?

Rephrase: "How do I teach him to go to the bathroom outside?"

Manage: Prevent him from being rewarded for peeing on the carpet. A full bladder causes discomfort. Urinating relieves that discomfort. Urinating on the carpet is more rewarding for an unhousetrained dog than suffering the discomfort of "holding it" until he can go outside.

The most important management tool is taking the dog outside so frequently that his bladder is never full to the point of discomfort (every hour on the hour, at least at first). Keep the dog under close supervision so you can notice when he is acting restless (a sign that he has to eliminate) and take him outside quickly, before he has a chance to pee on the carpet. And when you cannot supervise him, keep him crated, penned, or tethered (the latter only if you are home) to prevent him from being rewarded by peeing on the carpet when you're not paying attention. Keeping his crate—his den, as it were—unsoiled is more rewarding to most dogs than relieving even a moderately full bladder.

Train: Implement a full housetraining program that includes going outside with him regularly and rewarding him with praise and a treat immediately after he goes to the bathroom in the appropriate toilet spot.

How do I keep her from chewing up my shoes?

Rephrase: "How do I get her to chew on her own things and only her own things?"

Manage: Prevent her from being rewarded for chewing on inappropriate objects. Things like shoes, baby toys, and furniture have a nice firm-but-giving texture that feels good (is rewarding) to a dog's teeth and gums, especially to a puppy or young dog who is teething.

Pick up non-chew objects when the dog is in the room. Remove her from the room when non-chew objects must be left within reach (put her in a crate or pen if necessary). Supervise her closely and distract her attention from inappropriate objects. Tether her in the room with you to prevent her access to non-chew objects. Exercise her a lot; tired dogs tend to be well-behaved dogs.

Train: Provide her with irresistible chew objects and interactive toys such as stuffed Kongs, Buster Cubes, Roll-A-Treat Balls, and other safe items. If she is given the opportunity to chew only acceptable items she will eventually develop a strong preference for chewing on these things and your personal possessions will be safe.

How do I stop her from barking when she's outside?

Rephrase: "How do I keep her quiet when she's outside?"

Manage: Dogs usually become nuisance barkers because they are bored, lonely, overstimulated, or convinced that their job responsibilities include 24-hour sentry duty.

House confinement is the best management tool. Most dogs who are nuisance barkers spend too much time outdoors, which contributes to boredom, loneliness, overstimulation, and the perception that their jobs include constant sentry duty. Crates and pens indoors, if necessary, can help manage the dog's behavior while indoors. More exercise is also indicated; tired dogs tend to be well-behaved dogs.

Train: Teach her a positive interrupt—a gentle "Thank you, quiet!" (followed by a reward)—to acknowledge her for notifying you of something you should be aware of, and to let her know that you have everything under

Some dogs enjoy seeing what's going on outside; in this case, providing them with a safe place to do so may help relieve their boredom. However, if your dog gets excited or barks out the window, cut off his access to the room with the window altogether.

control so she can stop barking. Use this judiciously—do not expect it to work for a bored, lonely, overstimulated dog who is kept outside in the backyard all day and/or all night.

How do I keep him off the furniture?

Rephrase: "How do I teach him to sleep on his own bed?"

Manage: Control the environment to prevent him from being rewarded for getting on the furniture. The sofa is comfortable, so lying on it is its own reward.

Place boxes or upside-down chairs on the furniture to prevent his access. Lift up sofa and chair cushions so there's no comfy surface for him to lie on. Close doors to prevent his access to rooms with forbidden furniture in your absence. Use crates and pens to prevent his access to forbidden furniture in your absence. Provide him with his own *very* comfortable furniture to lie on.

Train: Consistently reward him for lying on his own very comfortable furniture.

Training yourself to manage

We could keep going—this list truly is endless—but you should be getting the idea by now. Any time you're faced with a behavior challenge, just apply these three simple steps—rephrase, manage, and train—to design your action plan for managing and/or modifying the inappropriate behavior.

A Classical Conditioning Primer

And now for the training part of that equation. Simple "treat-slinging"?
Look again; there's a powerful force at work here.

At its simplest, classical conditioning is learning by association. For example, if you run an electric can opener in front of a dog who had never eaten anything out of a can before, he may not respond to the sound in any way. But if you begin feeding the same dog canned food, he'll soon learn to associate the sound of the electric opener with the advent of his dinner, and begin to display great excitement whenever the electric can opener runs.

Classical conditioning happens everywhere, all the time, with or without our help or knowledge. Most of us have dogs that get excited when they hear the jingle of keys. A set of keys, by itself, has no special meaning for dogs. But when those keys are linked with walks or car rides, they can trigger as much excitement as the walks or car rides themselves.

While classical conditioning occurs naturally, we can also consciously use it as part of training and socialization. Classical conditioning is one of the most powerful (and often underutilized!) training tools available.

Shifting emotions

Classical conditioning differs from other types of training; in fact, it's not training, per se, although it can play an important role in a behavior modification program. The goal of training is to get the dog to exhibit certain behaviors—or cease to exhibit certain undesired behaviors—on cue.

Most training is accomplished through the use of *operant conditioning*, the use of rewards and/or punishment to encourage or discourage the dog from displaying certain behaviors. Praise, petting, or feeding a dog treats when he is sitting increases the likelihood of his sitting behavior; punishment such as ignoring the dog and turning your back on him will decrease his jumping behavior.

In contrast, classical conditioning doesn't change the dog's behavior directly, but acts as sort of a "backdoor" way to change his feelings about a given stimulus. You use classical conditioning to make the dog unconsciously *react* a certain way (this is called a conditioned reflex); your immediate focus is how the dog feels. The power of classical conditioning comes from its ability to help shift the emotional reactions that drive his behavior.

When using classical conditioning to change how a dog "feels" about certain stimuli, we simply pour on the treats, no matter what the dog is doing; his behavior doesn't influence our flow of treats. Eventually, he'll begin to associate good things with the formerly angst-producing stimuli. Petey, a former shelter dog, is a great candidate for the method. He becomes highly anxious when brought into a training facility.

Becoming a social animal

Behaviorist and author Jean Donaldson, who directs the behavior and training department at the San

Francisco SPCA, calls the use of classical conditioning in conjunction with early socialization "a puppy insurance policy." Each time you pair the presence of children with treats, for example, you are paying into an insurance policy that will protect you and your dog from behavior problems around children later in life. The more you put into the insurance policy, the bigger your protection! When you provide classical conditioning through feeding treats in the presence of children, the dog will not only learn to accept kids, but also will learn that when he is around kids, good things happen. If you also have the children actually feed your puppy treats or play his favorite game, he will learn that children not only equal good things, but also are the source of good things!

If you incorporate classical conditioning in all of your socialization efforts, you are more likely to have a dog who not only likes the things he's already encountered, but may also learn to simply enjoy new experiences.

If your dog's fears manifest in aggressive behavior, enlist the help of a knowledge-able behaviorist to guide you through the classical conditioning process.

Dispelling fears and aggression

Classical conditioning is a good tool for helping the dog to overcome most types of fears, including fear of people, noises, and new places. One of the great advantages of using classical conditioning to overcome a dog's fears is that you don't have to know *why* the dog is afraid. You just need to figure out what she is afraid of and then condition her to "like" that thing.

Fear and aggression are usually considered flip sides of the same problem. Dogs that respond to stressful situations with "flight" are considered fearful. Dogs that respond to stressful situations with "fight" are considered aggressive. But the underlying stress reaction may be similar. Classical conditioning is excellent for rehabilitating dogs who display fear-based dog-to-dog aggression.

Putting classical conditioning to work

Here are the steps to using classical conditioning with your dog. This process can help your dog form a positive association with something he has never experienced before. It can also help your dog overcome fears associated with other animals, people, or things. For brevity, we'll refer to the object, animal, or person you want your dog to like as the "scary thing."

1. **Identify the scary thing.** That is, determine exactly what it is that you would like to "condition." For example, a dog who exhibits fear of people may be afraid of all people, or just some people. If he is afraid of *some* people, figure out which people trigger his fear—it could be tall people, people with hats, children, men, women, or people with umbrellas.

2. **Pick something special to use for your conditioning "treat."** It can be anything your dog is crazy about—the more he likes it, the better. Food is a great choice. But if your dog loves balls or other toys, they can work, too. Ideally it will be something that is extra-special to your dog (like chicken chunks or roast beef) rather than pieces of his everyday kibble.

3. **Each time the scary thing appears, give your dog the special treat.** Here is the order:

    Scary thing appears; you give your dog the special treats.

    Scary thing goes away, the treats stop.

This is important. The scary thing must signal the beginning of the treats and the scary thing going away must end the treats.

4. **Give *lots* of the special treats in the presence of the scary thing.** You want the dog to be saturated with good things!

5. **Ideally, your dog should get this extra-special treat *only* in the presence of the scary thing.** This is especially true if you are working on a strongly ingrained fear. It's less important when conditioning your dog for general socialization or to condition something that is neutral to the dog.

6. **If possible, start with the scary thing at a distance or at a low intensity.** Ideally, you want your dog to notice the scary thing without it triggering a strong reaction. For example, if you are working on a fear of people and your dog is okay with strangers at 20 feet but begins to show fear at 15 feet, start working with the people at a distance of 20 feet.

7. **Take your time.** Watch how your dog responds and use his reaction as the criteria for upping the ante. Look for this "breakthrough": when your dog notices the scary thing and then immediately, happily turns to you for the special treats. Depending on his level of fear, it may take a few repetitions or it may take many repetitions before your dog is happy about seeing the scary thing. *Be careful not to rush this part of the process.*

8. **Don't worry about how your dog is behaving when you give the treats.** With classical conditioning, your dog gets the treats just for the presence of the scary thing, not for his behavior. It doesn't matter if your dog is sitting, standing, or spinning in circles. Even if your dog is acting out, keep up the treats!

9. **Set up lots of opportunities to shower your dog with special treats around the scary thing.** The more you can do it, the better and faster it will work. Conversely, try to make sure your dog is not exposed to the scary thing when you are without treats to give him.

10. **Be patient!** When you use classical conditioning to create a positive association to something neutral—such as a clicker—your dog will make the association very fast. But if you are trying to create new, positive associations to something the dog already has a bad association with, it may take many repetitions before you see progress.

Practiced Calm
A positive training program for promoting peaceful paws.

Whether you have a pup with normal puppy energy or an obstreperous teenager who has good-manners lessons to catch up on, clicker training can be a magically effective and gentle way to convince a dog to calm down. No yelling, no physical punishment; just clicks and treats for any pause in the action.

The biggest challenge with a "hyper" dog is that any praise or reward may cause her to begin bouncing off the walls again. It is nearly impossible to deliver a treat to an excitable dog while she is still in the act of being calm. By the time you get the treat to her mouth she is once again doing her Tasmanian devil act. She may well perceive the treat as a reward for her jumping jacks rather than for the sought-after calmness that occurred briefly several seconds before. Fortunately, this problem is not insurmountable.

Timing and consistency are key to successful training. If you give a reward to your dog more than a second or two after she exhibits the desired behavior, she will lose the connection, and may even come to believe she was rewarded for whatever she was doing at the moment you gave her the reward. However, once a dog has learned the connection between a reward marker (we recommend using the *click!* of a clicker or a verbal "Yes!") and a *pending* reward, your timing can be impeccable. An instant of calm elicits a *click!*, and the treat can arrive several seconds later. An added advantage of the clicker is that once most dogs hear the *click!*, they pause in anticipation of the coming morsel, drawing out the relatively calm behavior even longer.

The "all is calm" program

The first element in an "all is calm" program is to provide your dog with *lots* of exercise. Wise dog trainers and owners know that a tired dog is a well-behaved dog. Often, when people think their dogs are at their worst, they are simply chock-full of energy, bursting to find an escape.

If this sounds like your dog, schedule at least three tongue-dragging sessions of fetch per day. Climb to the top of a hill or staircase and throw the ball down so she has to keep climbing back up to return it to you. Set up an obstacle course with lots of things to climb and jump over. Be careful not to send her into heat stroke, but definitely play until she is pooped. Keep the exercise breed-appropriate—an athletic Border Collie can handle lots more physical challenges than an English Bulldog.

Don't think that a walk around the block will do it. A walk on leash, even a long one, is nothing but an exercise hors d'oeuvre for a young dog. You may be tired when you get home from the walk, but your dog is just getting warmed up! If no one in the family has time to give her adequate exercise, arrange for a dog walker to come by a couple of times a day and wear her out, or take her to doggie daycare as often as possible.

Manage, manage, manage

While wearing out your dog should be part of your regular routine, there are other changes you can make in order to manage her inappropriate behavior. All living things repeat behaviors that are rewarding to them. The management answer is to control your dog's behavior physically, through the judicious use of leashes, pens, crates, and tethers. Use these management tools wisely to prevent your dog from rewarding herself with your attention (at times you do not want to give it to her).

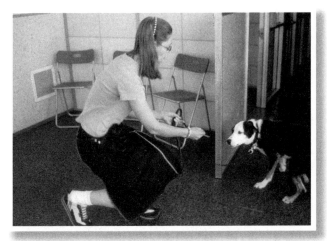

Petey acted very frightened when first brought into the training room. Kirsten leaves the door open at first, reducing the intensity of the scary stimuli (the enclosed space). She doesn't ask Petey to do anything, but simply begins doling out a steady supply of delicious treats. Initially, Petey retreats to the end of the leash after he takes each treat.

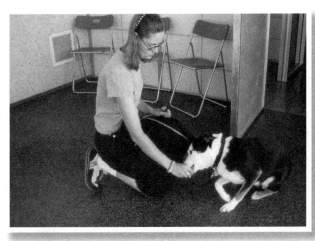

Gradually, Petey stops retreating between treats, crouching in one place by Kirsten. Bit by bit, he stops glancing around nervously and begins to focus only on Kirsten's treat hand. His gains in confidence are enough to indicate that Kirsten can ever-so-slowly increase Petey's exposure to the scary stimuli by moving further into the room.

Great strides are being made! The longer he samples the goodies that Kirsten keeps offering, and the more confidence he gains in the scary room, the higher he gets off the floor!

Petey still wants to leave the training room. No problem! He has improved in just one session. His expression is much brighter and his posture is more confident. It would be ideal, however, if Petey's owner could repeat this exercise several times before taking a class here, to give Petey more time to realize that this is a GOOD place.

Be quick with the click!

As soon as you have laid the foundation with exercise and management, you can begin an effective clicker-training program. Don't procrastinate; you can accomplish this on Day One of your "all is calm" program.

Start by "charging the clicker"—officially known in behavior circles as "conditioning the reward marker."

Begin by clicking the clicker in your pocket, to avoid startling her with the sharp sound. *Click!* the clicker, feed your dog a treat. *Click!* and treat. *Click!* and treat. As she begins to associate the sound with the

This is the first view most people get of Buster: A flat-out blur of a well-muscled projectile coming straight at them. He is wagging his tail and grinning, but still! Ouch!

Ah! That's better. A vigorous game of fetch with a tennis ball takes the edge off. Alison, Buster's trainer, has him fetch until he returns at a normal trot. Now he's ready for a training session.

At first, all Buster wants to do is to jump up and romp around Alison. She ignores this, simply turning away from him . . .

. . . until she sees Buster with *most* of his feet on the ground. Click! and treat. Buster is not yet sure why he has gotten the treat.

treat, bring it out of your pocket and click it in a more natural position at your side or your waist.

Your dog doesn't have to do anything special to get the *click!* and treat, as long as she isn't doing something unacceptable, like jumping on you or chewing the corner of the coffee table. If necessary, use one of your management tools to keep her out of trouble while you *click!* and treat. Most dogs catch on pretty quickly that the *click!* means a treat is coming. When your dog's ears perk and her eyes brighten at the sound of the *click!*, you knows she's getting it. Now you can use your "charged" clicker for training.

The goal of clicker training is to get your dog to understand that *she* can make the *click!* happen by offering certain behaviors—in this case, calm.

At first, you can't wait for long, leisurely stretches of calm behavior to click; some families report that their dogs *never* stop whirling around like a tornado,

Suddenly, the light bulb goes on! Buster lets out a woof! of happiness for the treat he *knows* he's about to get for keeping his feet planted on the ground. He gets it!

Gradually, Alison gives Buster fewer rewards for standing. When he happens to crouch, as if to sit, she clicks and treats.

Yes! Buster has figured out how to make Alison give him a Click! and treat. All he has to do is sit down firmly! Good dog!

at least when people are paying attention to them! Instead, begin by giving your dog a *click!* and treat just because all four feet are on the floor at the same instant. Be quick! You want her to understand that the behavior she got rewarded for was pausing with all four feet on the floor, so your timing needs to be sharp, and the *click!* needs to happen the instant all four feet are down.

If your timing is good and you catch her with four-on-the-floor several times in a row, you will see her start to stand still deliberately, in order to *make* the clicker go off. Lightbulb! A door has opened in her brain, and you can see her thinking. You now have a very powerful tool in your little plastic clicker box. You can use it to reinforce any behavior you want, any time it happens, and your dog will quickly start repeating that behavior for you.

Okay, back to calm. How does "pausing briefly on all four feet" translate into a calm dog? *Very gradually.* You are going to "shape" the pause into longer and longer periods of stillness, by extending the time, in milliseconds at first, that you wait as she is standing still before you *click!* and treat. If you err and she starts to jump around again, just wait. Eventually there will be another pause that you can *click!* and then start the shaping again.

As your dog gets better at being calm for longer and longer periods, be sure to reinforce randomly—sometimes for shorter pauses, sometimes longer. If you just keep making it harder and harder—longer and longer—she may get frustrated and quit playing the game.

Each training session should be relatively short, to avoid frustration for both of you, but you can do several in a day. You will have the most success, at least at first, if you practice working on calmness right after one of her exercise sessions, when she is tired anyway. As she gets the idea that "calm" is a very rewardable behavior, it will work even when she has more energy.

When your dog can hold still for several seconds at a time, add the verbal cue of your choice—something like "Easy . . ." that you will eventually be able to use to cue her for calmness. Over time, you will be able to phase out the *click!* and treat and use petting and praise as a reward instead of food. Keep your voice and body language calm and soothing to reflect and support her own growing calmness. Petting should be done as a massage— slow kneading or stroking, not vigorous patting or thumping.

"Forced" Calm Techniques May Cause More Harm Than Good

We have heard numerous reports of puppies or dogs who began showing aggressive behavior when their handlers used a certain training technique. In several of the cases, the dog owners were confused and upset, because they were using a training method that had been suggested to them by their veterinarian. In each case, the owners had been attempting to get their puppy or dog to "calm down" by either flipping it upside down and holding it to the floor (often referred to as an "alpha roll"), or by holding the pup upside down on their laps.

Be aware that the alpha roll can cause a puppy's aggressive behavior, however mild it may be. The alpha roll can greatly exacerbate aggression and, in fact, cause aggression to occur where it otherwise would not have. While some dogs don't take offense at being rolled over or held down, many others will respond out of fear or resentment, and will begin to fight back in self-defense. The more these dogs are physically forced to behave in a certain way, the more likely they are to display aggression.

Please: Forget what you have heard or read about dominance, "making the dog submit," and "letting the dog know who's the boss," because the suggested methods of accomplishing this don't always end with a useful result. Even if the alpha roll doesn't trigger a dog's defense mechanisms, it doesn't teach her to behave calmly on cue. Some dogs may think of their handlers as "the boss" after being flipped, but so what? It's more likely that the dog will come to regard her handler as unpredictable and scary. You also stand a good chance of extinguishing his interest in and willingness to participate in the training.

Just Rewards

One dog's pleasure is another dog's pain; rewards are an individual thing.

A dog's decisions in life, and his resulting behaviors, are based on whether a particular behavior yields something he likes (a reward) or something he doesn't like (a punishment). Training is simply a matter of manipulating the rewards and punishments in a thoughtful manner . . . . But you have to know your dog—be thoroughly aware of his likes and dislikes—and be conscious of your *own* behavior to make "training" work for you.

In the 1950s, behavioral scientist B. F. Skinner developed a number of principles that are applicable to all living things with a central nervous system. He found that animals are likely to repeat behaviors that are enjoyable (rewarding) to them, and not likely to repeat behaviors that result in something unpleasant (punishment). Neutral stimuli—things that don't matter to the animal—don't have an impact on behavior one way or the other.

Skinner demonstrated that humans can use these simple principles to modify an animal's behavior. Rewards are the most reliable way to deliberately increase an animal's offered behaviors; conversely, punishment decreases those behaviors. We use these behavioral principles in dog training with great success.

Keep in mind that the practical application of "rewards" and "punishments" varies from dog to dog, even though the definition doesn't. A reward is anything a particular dog likes. A punishment is anything that dog doesn't like.

We frequently use food treats as our reward in training because we can almost always find *some* food that a dog will value highly enough that it can serve as an irresistible reward, but food is not the *only* reward available to us. Remember, a reward is anything a dog likes. It could be a pat on the head (but not for dogs who don't like to be touched), verbal praise, a game of tug-of-war, a chase after a stick or tennis ball, a walk on leash, a car ride, or permission to jump up on the sofa.

When the average inexperienced dog handler hears the word "punishment," he generally thinks of overt forms of physical punishment, such as smacking, pinching, or jerking on the leash. We do not recommend or use physical punishment, as it endangers the handler, damages the relationship with his dog, and can destroy the dog's enthusiasm for training. Fortunately, physical punishment is not the only way to eliminate an unwanted behavior.

Remember, behaviorists define the word "punishment" as anything that causes an animal to *decrease* a certain behavior. In the case of dogs who don't like being touched, a pat on the head after they perform a straight sit could make them *stop* performing straight sits.

"Positive trainers"—people who have made a commitment to train without the use of pain, fear, force, or

Hearing the phrase that gives this water-loving Golden Retriever permission to jump into the lake is both a cue ("Go get it!") and a high-value reward. Hearing the same cue may be torture to a dog who doesn't really like to get wet!

Trainer Pat Miller works with her terrier-mix, Josie. The alert and engaged expression on Josie's face clearly conveys her enthusiasm for working with Pat.

intimidation—often use certain forms of "punishment" (in the behavioral sense) to accomplish their training goals. For example, when a dog who craves physical contact and attention jumps all over the trainer, she will turn her back on him and step away, removing both her attention (eye contact and interaction) and the possibility of physical contact with the dog. These are the rewards that the dog is seeking by jumping up. When the dog's jumping behavior keeps resulting

You can tell from the expression on this dog's face that she's not enjoying this training session. The verbal praise that her handler meted out for her correct down/stay has not brightened her expression or increased her eagerness to continue the training game. More valuable rewards are in order.

in the loss of something he wants badly, he will stop jumping—especially when this "punishment" is paired with the "reward" of attention, treats, and petting for sitting quietly.

What actually constitutes a punishment or reward to any given dog, then, is an individual matter; in behavioral terms, context is everything.

Unintentional training

Training, therefore, is the intentional use of rewards and punishments to purposefully manipulate a dog's behavior. What is sometimes difficult to remember is the fact that dogs are learning all the time, whether or not we are paying attention. Dogs do what works for them; they don't do things unless they get something out of it.

Whole Dog Journal does not advocate the use of shock collars in training. Positive trainers may use a limited amount of gentle negative reinforcement in the form of mild physical pressure, but generally consider shock collar training to be unacceptable.

Dogs do things that we consider "inappropriate behavior" because it's fun, it feels good, or it tastes good. From a dog's perspective, behaviors that are unacceptable to us (such as getting in the garbage, chasing cats, or sleeping on the sofa) are very enjoyable to them!

Frustrated owners frequently say, "He *knows* he's not supposed to do that! I punish him when he does, but he still does it. Why?" Sometimes, the enjoyment

What Is Positive Training?

There is no generally accepted textbook definition of positive training. Some trainers who use coercive tools such as choke chains and shock collars still call themselves "positive," because they include positive reinforcement as one of the tools in their arsenal, although not the primary tool.

When we use the term "positive training" in Whole Dog Journal, we are referring to a training philosophy and method that relies heavily on two of the four principles of operant conditioning, as defined by behavior scientist B. F. Skinner, who developed the following behavior principles in the 1950s. Dr. Skinner asserted that these principles were applicable to all living things with a central nervous system.

Positive reinforcement: The dog's behavior makes something good happen. "Positive," in behavioral terms, means something is added. "Reinforcement" means the behavior increases. So, for example, when your dog sits, you feed him a treat. His behavior—sitting—made something good happen; something was added—the treat. As a result, your dog is more likely to offer to sit again, so the behavior increases. Positive trainers use positive reinforcement a lot. Dogs who are positively reinforced learn to offer behaviors, searching for ones that we like in order to get rewarded.

Positive punishment: The dog's behavior makes something bad happen. (Positive means something is added; punishment means the behavior decreases.) For example, when your dog jumps on you with muddy paws you knee him in the chest, hard. He gets off. His behavior—jumping up—made something bad happen; something was added—your knee in his chest. As a result, your dog is more likely to think twice before jumping on you again. "Positive trainers" do not use positive punishment very much, if at all. Positive punishment can work and does with many dogs, but dogs who are positively punished may learn to fear the punisher, can become aggressive, may simply shut down in training, and are often reluctant to offer new behaviors for fear of being punished.

Negative punishment: The dog's behavior makes something good go away. (Negative means something is taken away; punishment means the behavior decreases.) Back to our jumping up example. When your dog jumps up on you with muddy paws, you turn your back on him and step away. As long as he keeps jumping you keep stepping away. When he stops jumping and has four paws on the floor, or even better, sits, then you reach down to pet him and feed him a treat. His behavior—jumping up—made something good, your attention, go away. Then you followed with positive reinforcement; his behavior of sitting made something good happen—you paid attention to him. Positive trainers do use negative punishment as a nonviolent means of providing a negative consequence for an unwanted behavior.

Negative reinforcement: The dog's behavior makes something bad go away. (Negative means something is taken away; reinforcement increases the behavior.) Say a trainer uses a shock collar to teach a dog to come when called. He calls the dog, and then pushes a button, holding it down and causing the dog to experience an unpleasant sensation until the dog has returned to him. Then he releases the button. The faster the dog returns, the quicker the shock stops. The dog's behavior—coming quickly when called—makes the bad thing, the shock, go away.

Our definition of positive is: Training that primarily uses positive reinforcement to reward desirable behaviors, and less frequently negative punishment (dog's behavior makes a good thing go away) when a negative consequence is needed. It may also include rare and very mild applications of negative reinforcement and positive punishment.

Who's Training Whom? Human Training Secrets Revealed

Is your dog training you? Don't laugh; it's pretty common. Scruffy, an Australian Cattle Dog, had his owner beautifully trained to open the door to let him in or out whenever he barked—every 20 minutes or so, all day. Lots of dogs have turned their humans into on-call petting machines by teaching them to reward an endearing nudge of the nose or tap of the paw with a placating scratch behind the ear. Not until the bark-

Dogs who have been trained with positive methods from puppyhood tend to show more volunteerism; they raptly observe their handlers, looking for opportunities to offer behaviors that may be rewarded.

ing, nose-nudging, or paw-tapping gets annoying does the owner try to make the dog stop, and by then it's too late—the dog fully expects the owner to respond appropriately and gets upset when the human doesn't perform the desired behavior.

Any time you and your dog are together, one of you is training the other. Dog–human relationships are generally most successful when the human is the trainer and the dog the trainee—at least the majority of the time! You need to be aware when your dog is doing something to try to modify your behavior, and cooperate only if you are sure it's a behavior you want to encourage. If not, you must ignore the dog's behavior so he stops trying to get you to perform (behaviors that aren't rewarded in some manner will eventually extinguish) and be sure to reward an incompatible behavior in its place. For example, rather than petting your dog when he nudges you, make it a point to pet him when he is sitting or lying quietly at your feet.

This is easiest to do when your dog first offers a behavior. Behaviors that are well-established are harder to extinguish than embryonic ones. Scruffy had long ago discovered that if his owner had any thoughts of not letting him out, all he had to do was bark louder and longer and she would eventually give in. This creates a very long schedule of reinforcement,

the dog gets from the behavior outweighs the owner's "punishment." A dog who is highly aroused by the experience of chasing a cat over the backyard fence may not care a bit about getting yelled at for it.

In other cases, the "punishment" may actually be rewarding to the dog. For example, a boisterous Labrador who gets yelled at, hit, or even kicked for jumping up on his owner may not have any clue that the yelling, hitting, and kicking is supposed to be a punishment. To dogs who *crave* attention and *love* physical contact with people, this rough treatment is simply an invitation to play an enjoyable (rewarding) game.

Also, dog owners may fail to realize that they often unthinkingly punish a dog for doing the right thing. If you do this frequently enough, you will inadvertently "train" your dog to *stop* offering the behaviors you want.

Consider the woman whose dog is enjoying a good romp with some canine pals at the dog park. It's time to leave, so she calls her dog to her. He immediately leaves his play pals and races to her. "Good dog!" she exclaims, and snaps his leash on, taking him from the park. In her view, the verbal praise was ample reward, and leaving the park has no connection to the recall. But here's how the dog sees it: "Mom called, I came,

It may take time to teach dogs to walk quickly, but if you consistently reward them with your attention when they speed up and ignore them when they slow, they'll soon learn to adjust their pace to a reasonable jog.

to perform—barking louder, poking harder with his nose, or digging unmercifully at you with his paw. If you could read your dog's mind, you might hear him saying, with much irritation, "Darn you, you stupid human! You know how to do this behavior, we've worked on it for years! Why are you being so stubborn?"

In the long run, it's much easier to make it a point to be aware of what your dog is trying to teach you, and to be sure you are the trainer more often than you are the trainee.

which means that if you are going to try to make an established behavior go away by ignoring it, you may have to ignore it for a very long time. It becomes a test of stamina—both yours and the dog's!

You may even have to suffer through an "extinction burst." Sometimes, shortly before the dog finally gives up, he will try really, really hard to get you

> **Caution:** *If you give in during an extinction burst you will create an even longer reinforcement schedule and reward a very strong manifestation of the behavior, which will make it even harder to stop the next time you try!*

and the fun's over. When I come to Mom, a bad thing happens—the fun stops." He is likely to think twice about coming the next time she calls while he is playing with friends!

Many people have lots of trouble training their dogs to come reliably when called. Perhaps they haven't given enough consideration to what happens to the dog *most of the time* after he does come. It doesn't take a canine Einstein to realize that coming when called is a bad idea if something "bad" consistently happens to him immediately afterward—say, he gets stuffed into the basement or locked away from all the guests in the kitchen, or tossed outside in the cold rain.

Training may also break down when the reward isn't valuable enough to motivate the dog to bother trying to get it. You must program an automatic response to the "come" cue with a high-value reward in the absence of enticing distractions *before* you try to apply it in the face of dashing squirrels. Few dogs will leave a squirrel hunt in order to come and earn a piece of dry kibble! Many positive trainers use a variety of enticing rewards and mix them up. Then the dog is never sure how big the "payoff" for his good behavior will be; he just knows it will be good.

If you doubt that mixing small rewards (such as verbal praise, a pat, or a piece of dry kibble) with larger rewards (such as pieces of fresh meat, chasing a ball, or being released to run free) is a powerful motivator, consider the slot machine. As long as it pays out a mixture of no rewards, small rewards, and only an occasional jackpot, human gamblers will continue to sit there and pull the handle, long past the time that it makes sense to do so!

Timing is key

It is important to a successful training program to understand what your dog likes and doesn't like, and to use those rewards and punishments effectively. In order to be effective, consequences—good or bad—must be delivered in close proximity in time to the behavior you are trying to influence.

Behaviorists agree that a reward or punishment must be delivered within three seconds, preferably one second or less, of the behavior you are trying to increase or decrease. This is a pretty small window of time, and underscores the value of using a clicker or other reward marker (or no-reward marker) to mark the instant of desired (or inappropriate) behavior. If you say "Oops!" the instant your dog jumps up and you turn away, you are teaching your dog a no-reward marker, which you can use to communicate to your dog which behavior it was that made the good thing go away (negative punishment). If you *click!* or say "Yes!" the instant your dog sits, he will come to understand that the *sit* earned the reward, even if it takes several seconds for you to get the treat into his mouth, and even if he gets up from the sit before you manage to deliver the treat.

The Crossover Challenge
Understand your dog's behavior as you switch to positive training.

Until you use only "dog-friendly" training methods, you won't as clearly see the difference between a "crossover" dog—one who was initially trained with force-based methods and then switched to positive-only training—and a dog who had *never* experienced scary, hurtful, or force-based training. They are, as the saying goes, completely different animals.

Many crossover dogs, in contrast, seem anxious about doing the "wrong" thing and being punished for it. These dogs don't generally "volunteer," instead needing to be lured or guided into new behaviors.

One of the biggest differences is that, when faced with a unique training request, crossover dogs tend to do nothing, or offer a safe behavior that they already know. In contrast, dogs who have been encouraged since infancy to "offer" novel behaviors in response to new training requests joyfully go to work trying to solve the puzzle. The modern methods of training teach, foster, and capitalize on this initiative; the dog's volunteerism is what makes it works so well.

In positive training, the goal is to help the dog do the right thing and then reward him for it, rather than punish him for doing the wrong thing. If he makes a mistake, the behavior is ignored, or excused with an "Oops, try again!" to encourage the dog to do something else. Using "Oops!" as a "no-reward marker" teaches the dog that the behavior he just offered didn't earn a reward, but another one will. So he tries again, and learns to keep trying until he gets it right, without fear of punishment.

In early training, he only needs to get it a "little bit right" to earn a *click!* and reward; the goal is always to help the dog succeed, to keep him confident and willing to play the training game. In the beginning, for example, the dog is rewarded for walking in the general area of "heel" position, in order to learn to walk politely on his leash. If competition heeling is desired, this can be "shaped" later for more precision by clicking closer and closer approximations to "perfect" heel position. He learns where he needs to be to make good stuff happen through repetition or rewards, and volunteers to be there because he likes good stuff.

In contrast, force-based training teaches the dog to heel by administering a sharp jerk (or pop) on the leash any time the dog steps out of heel position. He learns where he needs to be in order to avoid bad stuff through repetition of punishment, and stays in heel position because he doesn't want to get hurt.

Both methods can teach dogs to be well-behaved. The force-trained dog learns to watch and read people, in large part in order to avoid the negative consequences that occur when he makes a mistake. The praise and rewards that sometimes follow a correction are rarely enough to overcome the learned caution of trying some new behavior that might be punished. The positive dog also learns to watch and read the humans around him, so that he can take advantage of opportunities to offer good behaviors that are likely to result in good stuff. He has no fear of offering behaviors, because he has no anticipation of a painful consequence.

Crossing with your dog

We're not the only ones who have witnessed the vast differences between crossover dogs and those started from scratch with positive training. The phrase "crossover dog" was actually coined in the 1990s as a result of the large influx of trainers who found themselves switching over from old-fashioned methods to more positive training. In her landmark book, *Don't Shoot the Dog*, former marine mammal trainer Karen Pryor introduced the dog-training world to the exquisite method of positive training known as clicker training. As dog trainers learned about the effectiveness of the techniques, many of them, too, "crossed over" to positive training methods. As Pryor has said, "In the early '90s, I could count the number of clicker trainers on one hand. Now there are thousands of us!"

Size Matters
Secrets to training your small dog.

Once you adopt a small dog you realize that, safety concerns aside, there are some huge advantages to sharing your life with a mini-canine.

For example, they don't take up as much room as your large dog—you can have several in the same space as one Great Dane. They share your bed without hogging it. They sit on your lap and still leave room for the newspaper. They don't eat as much, so they are less expensive to feed, even with the best foods available. You can get by with smaller yards, and often lower fences. They require comparatively less grooming. Little dog poops are tiny and inoffensive, even in the house—you can pick up their mini-feces with a tissue and flush them down the toilet. As a corollary, the small dog is much more realistic to litter-box train than a Mastiff, if that suits your fancy.

Of course, there are some disadvantages as well. Little dogs *do* break more easily. Because of their small size, they can be mistakenly perceived as good pets for children. Some of them *can* be, but they are not automatically; it depends on the dog, good socialization, and the child's ability to respect the dog's small size. Their reputation as yappy and snappy is not entirely undeserved; they can become defensively aggressive if they feel threatened, and it's easy to feel threatened when you are surrounded by human giants who are anywhere from 10 to 60 times your size. And because the dogs are small, owners tend to be permissive and overprotective, overlooking and excusing behaviors that larger dogs could never get away with. Which brings us to the topics of training and behavior management.

Small-dog house manners

For optimum quality of life and relationship, it is every bit as important for the small dog to be trained as the large one.

Let's arbitrarily define the "small dog" as one who is 25 pounds or less. This encompasses a wide range of breeds, from the tiny three-pound Chihuahua to the short and sturdy Scottish Terrier. It includes dogs with such varied personalities as the independent Jack Russell Terrier, amiable Pug, aloof Basenji, work-oriented Welsh Corgi, and the relatively phlegmatic French

Bulldog, to name just a few. That doesn't even take into consideration the infinite permutations of small mixed-breed dogs.

So forget any stereotype you may be holding of the "small dog" personality. The training challenges that small-dog trainers face mirror to a large degree those faced by big-dog trainers, and the same positive training methods work just as well.

There are some differences, however. The conventional wisdom that small dogs can be harder to housetrain is often a reality. There are several reasons why they are more likely to soil in the house, although it is *not* because they don't have the instinct to keep their dens clean; they most certainly do. If your little dog's housetraining is giving you headaches, it may be because:

- Small-dog signals are harder to see. If a Rottweiler sits and stares at your face while you are reading the paper, you probably notice. If a Pomeranian sits and stares at your ankle, it's easy to miss.

- Big-dog owners may be more motivated. A tiny Yorkshire Terrier puddle behind the guest bed may not be discovered for weeks or months (or maybe never). The Great Dane in the kitchen is impossible to miss.

- Small dogs have smaller holding capacities. Although you would expect their organ capacity to be proportionate to their size and intake, the bottom line is they do seem to need to go out on a more frequent potty schedule.

- Small-dog owners are more likely to supervise less, use crates that are too large (in which the toy puppy can poop and pee in one end and sleep and play happily in the other), or not crate at all. A little pup can't possibly be as much trouble as a big one, can she? (Wrong!) And besides, we want Midge to sleep with us!

- Small-dog owners are more likely to paper-train and continue to rely on paper-training, sending a mixed message about inside elimination versus outside elimination.

Training a small dog is easiest when you are closer to her level, as demonstrated by trainer Sandi Thompson, of Berkeley, California. Thompson was a "big-dog person" until she met Tater, a Chihuahua-cross; she immediately became a "small-dog person."

- Small dogs are more likely to have had their den-soiling inhibitions damaged by overcrating and dirty puppy mill conditions. If a dog is required to live in her own excrement and urine, she comes to think that living in filth is normal, and she won't make an effort to "hold it" until she has access to a more suitable environment.

The answer to housetraining the small dog is scrupulous management. Maintain constant supervision, through the *appropriate* use of leashes, crates, tethers, direct supervision, and regular trips to the outdoor bathroom spot—every hour on the hour, at first, if necessary. Pay close attention so you don't miss your dog's signals. All of the other regular housetraining tips also apply, of course: Feed regular meals instead of free-choice feeding; pick up water before bedtime; change crate substrate if necessary; and *clean* soiled spots with enzyme-based animal product cleaners.

Good manners come in all sizes

The small-dog owner often overlooks other house manners as well. Jumping up is easier to accept when the dog is 5 pounds than 50, so lots of small-dog owners don't bother to teach a polite greeting. This can be accomplished with a small dog just as it is with a big dog, by preventing her from being rewarded by the behavior you don't want, and consistently and generously rewarding the behavior you *do* want with treats, toys, or a nap on the sofa.

This means turning your back on the jumper and petting her (and/or giving a treat) when she sits. She will soon learn to sit to get your attention. Be sure you give it! It also means body-blocking your dog when you see the "sofa gleam" in her eye—by moving into the open sofa space and/or not making your lap available—until she sits, and then inviting her up (assuming she is allowed up). Be sure to notice when she sits, and invite her up when she does; as small as she is, she is easy to overlook when she is sitting politely.

Your small dog also needs to be well socialized. Treat her like a dog! Lots of positive experiences from early puppyhood will help dispel the aggressive "arm-dog" caricature. Your little dog needs to have her feet on the ground a good part of the time so she can learn to go up and down stairs, get into cars, and walk on grass, dirt, gravel, carpeting, wood, and tile floors.

Take her hiking. Have her meet lots of friendly people—all ages, shapes, sizes, and races—armed with lots of tasty treats in lots of controlled circumstances. A good rule of thumb for socialization is to expose your pup to at least 100 *different* settings and types of people before she is four months old.

Basic small-dog training

It is true that there are lots of little dogs who strain on their leashes, don't come when called, and who think "sit" is something their owners do so the human can bend over and pet the dog. Yet the small dog is every bit as capable of learning basic and advanced training behaviors as the big dog—and it is just as important for his long-term well-being and safety.

Positive training techniques are the same for all size dogs—they all have canine brains that respond similarly to the four principles of operant conditioning. There are some considerations for small-dog owners that can make the relationship-building and training process more successful. Whether your goal is a well-mannered house dog or competition titles, if you keep the following concepts and tips in mind you and your small dog can both have more fun playing the training game together.

1. **You are very big.**

   Primate body language (direct approach, looming over, eye contact, assertive gestures and voice) is intimidating to any dog who has not learned to

---

Do train your small dog. You may not mind his tiny transgressions, especially while in the thrall of your early relationship, but a well-behaved dog is more fun for others to be around, regardless of size.

Use training treats that are especially small and tasty. Bits of cooked chicken, boiled egg, or cheese work well.

Work at your dog's level, sitting or kneeling on the floor, or with the dog up on a table or bed.

---

read and interpret "human." In the dog world, these behaviors are considered rude and offensive. The smaller the dog, the more threatening our natural human body language can be. When you are training your small dog, at least at first until she learns to read and trust you, be very conscious of using soft eye contact, making your gestures and voice small and soft rather than large and effusive, turning slightly sideways to her, and squatting instead of looming over your dog to interact with her.

2. **Your dog's stomach is very small.**

   Any dog owner should use small pieces of food treats and perhaps cut back on the size of the dog's regular meals, to prevent filling up before training is over and to avoid unwanted weight gain. Small-dog treats must be *very* tiny; you may even need to eliminate some of the dog's meals.

3. **Work on the floor.**

   If you always train your little dog when you are standing up, you are guaranteed to end up with a sore back. Exercises like "puppy pushups" and luring them down can be especially backbreaking from full height. In the beginning, especially when teaching stationary exercises, sitting on the floor with your dog will save your back, and at the same time make you less intimidating to her. You can also work with your small dog while you sit in a chair, or you can put her on a raised surface where she is comfortable, such as a table, sofa, or bed.

4. **Stand up and use a target stick.**

   You also need to train your dog while you are standing up—at least some of the time. She should learn to walk politely with you; even a small dog can damage her throat if she constantly strains at the leash. The better her leash manners, the more fun it will be to take her places, and the less likely she will become an arm-dog. You can teach her to target and then use your target stick to help her learn to walk with you, *without* having to bend over. Simply put the target stick where you want

If you're uncomfortable sitting on the floor with your small dog, you can conduct your training sessions with the dog on a bed or table; it's much easier on your back.

her to be. (See page 121 for more on target training.) You can also attach a soft treat to the stick for delivery to the little dog without having to bend over, or just drop treats on the floor.

5. **Use appropriate-size training tools.**

   Little dogs need lightweight collars and leashes. It's easy to underestimate the impact of a standard-weight leather leash if it accidentally bumps into your dog's face, or, worse, if you drop your end and it falls on her. Her training tools and toys should be scaled appropriately to her size; pet suppliers have gotten wonderfully creative with small-dog products like toy-dog-size tennis balls and narrow, lightweight nylon leashes.

Play it safe and smart

One of the reasons little dogs sometimes get an attitude about big dogs is that owners tend to panic when they see a big dog approaching. The owner's stress transmits to the small dog, who then becomes anxious herself. If you grab your dog every time another dog approaches, it will increase her stress and the potential for a confrontation.

Little dogs sometimes do get savaged by big dogs because their owners forget to think. "Be smart" means don't take your little dog places that you know are frequented by large, uncontrolled dogs. Only use your local dog park if there is a separate fenced area for small dogs.

If you are walking your dog on the street and you see someone approaching with a large dog, take evasive action—calmly cross the street while you practice good heeling so you can pass at a safe distance. If you see a loose dog approaching, look for an escape route—a place of business or fenced yard you can step into for safety. Carry an aversive spray such as Direct Stop that can thwart a persistent canine visitor. Only as a last resort should you pick your dog up—doing so also puts *you* at risk for injury if the approaching dog is intent on attacking.

Not that the risk of injury would stop any of us "small-dog people" from protecting our beloved little ones. Like any dog owner worth her salt, our own safety is the last thing we think about when our canine family members are threatened. Their diminutive size only heightens the protective instinct that would cause us to risk life and limb for them.

Go ahead, big-dog people, scoff at us if you want. It's only a matter of time before you meet the small dog who steals your heart.

Super-Sized
Keeping and training extra-large dogs can be a big challenge.

Newfoundlands. St. Bernards. Irish Wolfhounds. Great Danes. They are the giants of the canine world, and it takes a special kind of person to appreciate their extra-large appeal.

We think of a "big" dog as one whose normal weight exceeds the 100-pound mark. In addition to the above-mentioned breeds, this includes many of the

Most Mastiffs are good-natured, somewhat sedentary dogs. However, they still need regular exercise and socialization to keep them physically and emotionally healthy.

Mastiff-type dogs, the Great Pyrenees, Scottish Deerhound, some (but not all) Rottweilers, and more. The only requirement for membership in this club is size. Everything about them is big, from their appetites (and by-products thereof) to the crates, collars, and other training equipment that they use, as well as the toys that they play with. Pet supply companies offer giant-size Kongs, tennis balls, tug toys, and just about every other canine accessory you can think of. They know there's a "big" market out there.

Vet bills can be bigger too, since most surgeries are charged at least in part by the dog's weight. Larger dogs generally need more anesthesia.

Even finding a home can be more of a challenge for big-dog humans. Many landlords and hotels, if they allow animals at all, accept pets who are 25 pounds or less. The next socially acceptable size-increment seems to be around 70 to 75 pounds. Much bigger than that, and non-dog people tend to think you really are some kind of serious dog nut, to want to share your life and home with a dog who outweighs many of the family members.

Finally, sadly, many of the giant breeds tend to have short life spans; a 10-year-old Great Dane is pretty ancient, while lots of 10-year-old small dogs are still in excellent condition and can look forward to 5 to 10 more years of life.

The big challenge

The awe-inspiring size of these dogs presents their human companions with a long list of training and management challenges not encountered by keepers of smaller dogs. Some are simple logistical challenges. Exactly how big a vehicle do you have to have to accommodate a couple of Great Dane crates? We could be talking motor home here, just to run to the local training class! Not to mention the extra space you need in your master bedroom if you plan to crate a few Newfies in your personal den. And imagine the ease with which a Wolfhound's tail can clear a coffee table, or swipe expensive porcelain statuettes from their display shelves.

Everything we have said in the past about prevention through management and training goes triple for big dogs. Teaching good manners when your wee one is a mere 15 to 20 pounds at age 10 weeks gives

> The bigger the dog, the more people are likely to be intimidated. Extra training can help your dog be appreciated by all.
>
> Use training tools that are up to the job. Collars and leashes should be sturdy enough for an extra-strong dog. Head halters are especially useful for these dogs.
>
> Resist any impulse you may have to train these dogs with force or intimidation; this is a lose/lose proposition.

you a huge advantage over those who wait until 12 months, by which time the untrained, out-of-control, 150-pound Presa Canario may already be gearing up to maul an innocent neighbor. These dogs' forbidding size demands an early course in juvenile good manners. While your visiting aunt may be willing to tolerate the petite paw prints of a Pomeranian on her pants, she is likely to frown on plate-sized mud-covered Wolfhound feet on the front of her sweater.

Socialization is another critically vital part of a large dog's educational experience. Many giant breeds have strongly developed guarding instincts. A poorly socialized, poorly trained large dog is a significant risk to the safety of the community. A well-socialized and -trained dog will be able to turn on his protection behaviors if needed but, no matter his size, will be safe to have around your friends and family. A poorly socialized small dog is just as sad a statement about pet-owner irresponsibility as an unsocialized large dog, but is less of a risk to the community; a kamikaze Chihuahua can do far less damage on his worst day than a scud missile Neapolitan Mastiff on a minor bender.

Tall training tips

There are a number of good-manners behaviors that are particularly important to teach your large dog while she is still small. Pay special attention to these if you have a big dog:

- **Polite Greeting**

  As mentioned above, jumping up to greet humans is rude behavior for any canine, and especially intolerable for a large dog. Start when your baby giant is small by avoiding the temptation to pick her up and cuddle her. (Cuddling teaches her that "up" is a very wonderful place to be.) Instead, designate a spot on the floor as "cuddle space," and get down on her level to do snuggle time. Teach "sit" as a greeting and default behavior by consistently and generously rewarding your puppy for sitting, and turning and stepping away any time she jumps up. Insist that family members, visitors, and people on the street greet her only when she is sitting politely.

- **Loose Leash Walking**

  If you begin teaching polite leash walking to your young pup, you will never find yourself being skijored down the street behind your Rottie as she takes off after an unexpected skateboarder. The keys to teaching good leash walking are a high rate of reinforcement (lots of *click!*s and treats) and *very* high-value treats, so that it is more rewarding for your dog to pay attention to you than her surroundings. If you've already missed out on teaching this while your pup is small, consider using a head halter to maintain gentle control of your big dog while you retrain her leash behavior.

- **Say Please**

  Also known as "no free lunch" or "nothing in life is free," a "say please" program teaches your dog to ask for all good things in life by offering a sit in order to get what she wants. This prevents her from learning that she can push people around by virtue of her sheer weight and size. You can initially train and ask for the sit behavior, but your ultimate goal is for your dog to offer sits without being asked. If she is allowed on the furniture, she sits and waits to be invited, rather than just

In this variation of a "Leave it!" exercise, chunks of tasty cheese are placed on the ground, and the owner walks her dog close by, without *quite* enough leash to reach the cheese. She does *not* say "Leave it!" She only resists the dog's pull toward it.

After a moment's hesitation, the dog turns away from the tempting cheese. As she turns away, or, better yet, looks toward her owner for direction, her owner says "YES!" to "mark" the desired behavior, and then gives the dog an equally good treat.

This exercise teaches the dog that it is *more* rewarding to turn away from a desired activity toward your owner. And because the owner does *not* give a verbal "Off!" or "Leave it!" cue, the dog learns to make this decision on her own — self-control.

helping herself to the empty space on the sofa next to your visitor. Want to go outside? "Sit" makes the door open. Ready for dinner? "Sit" makes the dinner bowl descend to the floor.

- **Down**

Teach your dog that "lying at feet" is a highly rewardable behavior. Give her attention and treats on a variable schedule (sometimes close together, sometimes with longer pauses in between) when she lies down quietly. Give your guests a container full of treats and instruct them to reward the dog on a random schedule, too. Be sure to ignore any demand behavior, such as whining or barking, so the dog learns that the only behavior that gets rewarded is calm "lying at feet."

- **Off or Leave It**

It stands to reason that giant breeds have easier access to food-bearing surfaces such as tables and kitchen counters. One chance encounter with a roast beef sandwich can turn a dog into a dedicated counter surfer. In addition to managing your big dog so she never has the opportunity to learn to counter surf, a well-installed "Off" or "Leave it" cue, which tells the dog to back away from whatever she is looking at, can avert disaster when she has that "Mine!" gleam in her eye and is closer to the holiday turkey than you are.

- **Sharing with Others**

Like so many other things, resource guarding by a large dog can be infinitely more disastrous than the same behavior presented by her smaller counterparts. When your pup is small, teach her that having humans approach when she is eating or otherwise occupied with a high-value possession makes *more* great stuff happen. When she is eating from her food bowl, occasionally approach and drop a few exquisite goodies into it. Before long she will *want* people to be around when she is eating.

• **Go to Your Spot**

A useful behavior for all dogs, this one is especially helpful when you have guests who don't appreciate super-sized canines. By repeatedly luring your

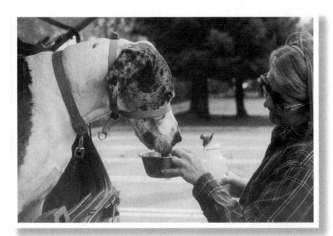

Head halters — or head collars, as they are sometimes called —are especially useful for handling giant breeds. Properly fitted, the halters are comfortable for the dog, and do not impair his ability to drink, accept treats, pant, or carry a toy. However, they also prevent the dog from dragging his handler in case he takes off after a cat or bird!

dog to her "spot" or using targeting to send her to it, you can program a gentle "Go to your spot" cue that tells her to go lie down in her corner. If you use a portable throw rug to mark her "spot" you can take it with you—to the dining room during meals, the den for videos, even to your friends' houses when you and your big dog go visiting.

• **Give**

The last thing you want to do is get into an argument with a big dog over something she has in her mouth. Take the time to teach your dog "Give" by trading for treats.

Most people make the mistake of only taking "forbidden objects" away from their dogs, which can teach the dog to object, since she learns that she'll never get it back. If you practice "Give" as a regular training exercise with a "legal" toy or chew object, you can repeatedly return the object in question after the dog gives it up for a treat. This way, she learns that she gets *two* rewards—the first for giving up the valuable object, the second when she gets the valuable object back again. Then, if she occasionally has to give up an "illegal" object that you can't return to her, it won't outweigh the positive impact of all the two-reward trades you have done with her.

• **Bite Inhibition**

Dogs bite. It's a natural canine behavior. Chances are that at some time in your dog's life, she may feel compelled to bite. If and when that happens, good bite inhibition could make the difference between a dent in the skin and plastic surgery. It could also determine whether your dog lives or dies, since dogs who bite and cause serious injury tend not to live long—especially *big* dogs who bite.

You can instill good bite inhibition in a pup by gradually diminishing the force of her bite rather than punishing all bites. A puppy naturally learns to control the force of her teeth through playing with her siblings. If she bites softly, without causing undue pain, the other puppies will keep playing with her. If she bites too hard, the pup she is biting may yelp and run away, refusing to re-engage in play for a time.

You can do the same thing. If your giant puppy bites softly, continue playing with her. If she bites hard enough to cause pain, give a high-pitched "Ouch!" or "Oops!" and walk away from her. After a short time, begin playing with her again. She will learn to control her bite so that the fun can continue without interruption.

- **Think Positive**

If you think it's a good idea to force confrontations with your large dog, think again. First, it's not necessary, and second, the bigger the dog gets, the more likely you are to lose. In old-fashioned force-based training, owners were advised to dominate their dogs, and if the dogs offered to fight back, increase the level of human aggression until the dogs submitted. Dogs who refused to submit were labeled "vicious" and "incorrigible," and were euthanized.

It takes two to fight. If you train with positive methods, you never set the dog up for conflict, and you teach her to willingly and happily respond to your behavior requests because good things happen when she does.

Big bother?

If big dogs are such a challenge, why even bother with them? Some people like the look and feel of a big, solid dog by their sides. Many of these folks don't consider a canine to be a real dog unless it is at least 75 pounds. There is something very comforting about the bulk of an impressively large canine, especially if you live alone in a remote location, travel through an unsavory

Big Ideas to Keep in Mind

- *When you own a big dog, you must be ultra-responsible. Make sure you are prepared for the added responsibility of a super-sized dog before you bring one home. Don't be lured by the novelty of owning a giant breed unless you are honest with yourself about what you are getting into.*
- *Train and socialize early and often. Socialization must be reinforced throughout a dog's life, especially for dogs who are protective by nature. Training is more than a six-week beginner class; even old dogs can learn new tricks.*
- *Manage, manage, manage. Big dogs can get into bigger trouble than small dogs. Make a strong commitment to manage your dog's behavior so he doesn't get reinforced for undesirable behaviors, especially those that might put others at risk.*
- *Respect the feelings and fears of other people. Not everyone loves large dogs, and some people are terrified of them. Don't let your dog approach people unless and until you know that they are comfortable being greeted by a dog who may outweigh them.*

part of town, or take your dog for a late night walk in Central Park.

There is also much to be said for big-dog personalities. As a general rule, they are calmer than many of their smaller brethren—it's a lot of work to haul around that much bulk. Besides—a St. Bernard–size dog with a Jack Russell Terrier's energy level probably wouldn't be around long—who could live with that?

If you want to think big, by all means go for it. Big rewards go along with those big challenges. Just be sure you are ready for the extra-large responsibilities that go along with sharing your home and your heart with a super-sized canine.

Remedial Housetraining for Adult Dogs
All healthy adult dogs can be housetrained, but you'll need commitment.

Adult dogs can have a variety of explanations for their housetraining failures. Many come from kennels or shelters, but even dogs who have been in stable homes since puppyhood can have trouble with housetraining.

Some of the most common reasons that dogs fail to learn when and where to eliminate include:

- **Having a medical problem.** If you have a dog that was reliably housetrained and suddenly has housetraining problems, consider the possibility of a medical issue. Infections, certain illnesses, and some medications can all contribute to house soiling.

- **Not truly understanding the "house" rules.** For example, a dog may understand that he should go outside and will do so when he has free access (such as a doggie door), but not understand that he needs to hold it when he does not have free access.

- **Not having generalized the rules from one place to another.** A dog may have been housetrained in a previous home, but not know that the same rules apply in a new home. Or, a dog may know to go outside at *his* house, but not understand that he also needs to go outside when visiting a friend's house or staying in a hotel.

- **Being asked to "hold it" for too long.** Some dogs can easily go all day without eliminating. For other dogs, holding it all day is very difficult or even impossible. This can be especially true for dogs who are small, young, elderly, or who have a medical problem.

- **Having learned that eliminating in their living space is acceptable.** Dogs who have spent much of their lives in kennels often lose their natural inhibition about eliminating where they eat and sleep. In addition, dogs with a history of "accidents" in the home because of an illness, poor management, or other factors may simply learn that it is less stressful to go inside than to try to "hold it."

Getting down to business

The process for housetraining your adult dog is identical to that for training puppies. You must supervise your dog at all times when he is inside, except when he is crated or otherwise confined. This means keeping your attention focused on the dog so as to prevent *any* opportunity for the dog to make a mistake, or, at the very least, to be able to interrupt him "midstream"—a good opportunity to rush him outside and then praise him for going in the "right" place.

The best way to accomplish this, when you are not actually looking at the dog or playing with him, is often referred to as the "umbilical cord" method. If you are watching TV, working on your computer, washing dishes, or otherwise occupied, clip a leash onto your

Crates, X-pens, and baby gates will be your biggest allies in the campaign to housetrain your dog. Access to the entire house must be earned, slowly, as the dog exhibits reliability.

Is It a Housetraining Problem? Or Something Else?

When talking about housetraining for adult dogs, it's important to understand that not all house soiling is a housetraining problem. Other physical and behavior issues can contribute or cause a dog to eliminate in the house. If you suspect your dog may have any of these issues, please consult with a behavior counselor or qualified trainer.

- **Submissive or excitement urination.** *Dogs who leak urine during greetings, when meeting new people, when you first come home, or during play may be exhibiting submissive or excitement urination. This is a confidence issue (and is often outgrown as a young dog matures), not a housetraining issue!*
- **Marking.** *When we think about territory marking, most of us think only about male dogs. But male and female dogs can mark territory with both urine and feces, outside and indoors.*

- **Separation anxiety.** *Dogs suffering from separation anxiety may eliminate shortly after you leave your home, often within just a few minutes. (If you are not sure the accidents are happening shortly after you leave, try returning home after a half hour to find out.) Consult with a behavior professional to help you resolve your dog's separation anxiety.*
- **Fears and phobias.** *Thunderstorms, fireworks, and other fear-inducing noises can cause some dogs to urinate or defecate in the home.*
- **Health issues.** *Any onset of house-soiling behavior in a previously housetrained dog, urination during sleep, or other loss of bladder and bowel control should be evaluated by a veterinarian. Urinary tract infections, certain illnesses, and some medications can contribute to house-soiling problems.*

dog's collar, and tie the other end around your waist or belt loop. It should be long enough to allow him to sit or lie at your feet, but short enough to prevent him from making a move to eliminate without your knowledge.

If your dog regularly eliminates in his crate or other confined space, and your veterinarian has ruled out all health problems as the cause, try changing your confinement area. If you have been using a crate, for example, change to an exercise pen in a different part of the house. Start by feeding your dog in her new confinement space and leaving her alone there for only short periods.

If your dog has been eliminating on her bedding, change the type of bedding you use, too. If she's been sleeping (and eliminating!) on a blanket, switch to a flat, thick bed of newspaper, or a fleece pad. The idea is to create a new "living space" with no former associations for your dog as a place to eliminate. Continue to use the crate as a living space for longer periods until

you have established the new confinement area as a living space.

A routine helps adult dogs as much as it helps puppies. What goes in on schedule comes out on schedule. Establish regular feeding, sleeping, and waking times. Take your dog out, at minimum, upon waking, after eating and drinking, before leaving home, immediately after play, when you first arrive home, and before bedtime.

Make sure you teach your dog where to go! This is an important and often overlooked step. Pick a spot to which you regularly take your dog. Don't just put him outside; go with him. When your dog goes in the appropriate spot, immediately reward the behavior with praise and a treat. A dog who is rewarded for going in a specific spot will be more motivated to go in that place and may also begin asking to go to the place (offering the behavior) because it earns rewards.

Read your dog's signals. Look for clues in his behavior that tell you he needs to go outside. Dogs

The crate or X-pen where your dog will spend his unsupervised time should be comfortable and cozy.

won't always go to the back door. Some common signs include acting restless, "bugging" you, pacing, and just before the act, circling. But sometimes the behavior is more obscure, so be observant.

In addition, try to anticipate your dog's needs. Does he always need to go outside immediately after waking? When someone comes to the door? After playing?

When accidents happen, don't punish! If you actually catch your dog in the act—not one second after—it's okay to interrupt with a clap or noise and then rush the dog outside. Be sure to reward your dog when he finishes up outside. If you discover the act afterward, even immediately afterward, don't punish your dog. It really won't help, and could set back the process by making your dog afraid to go in front of you. Simply clean up the accident well with an enzyme-neutralizing cleaner.

Patience pays off

How long will it take? The answer is, "It depends." It depends on the dog, the situation, and you. There is no magic formula or specific amount of time.

People often want it to take a lot less time than is realistic. Think about all of the steps the dog needs to learn—to go in a specific place, to hold it for a period of time, to ask when he needs to go out, to apply these rules to all inside areas. Be patient! This is a lot for a dog to learn. Plan on a few months at minimum, and a year or more for a dog with a longer history of house-training problems.

Of course, that doesn't mean you have to deal with your dog actually eliminating in the house for months! Remember the first two steps: supervise and confine. With diligence, you can establish a routine that will help you avoid most accidents within a few weeks, if not sooner.

Crate Training Made Easy
Teaching your new dog these critical lessons will pay off all his life.

The crate is a sturdy plastic, fiberglass, wood, metal, or wire box just big enough for a dog to stand up, turn around, and lie down in comfortably. It can be used with the door open, at your convenience, or with the door closed when mandatory confinement is called for.

When the crate is properly introduced using positive training methods, most dogs love their crates. Canines are den animals and a crate is a modern den—a dog's personal portable bedroom to which he can retire when he wants to escape from the trials and tribulations of toddlers and other torments. He can take it with him when he stays at boarding kennels, and when he travels with you and sleeps in hotels and motels.

Owners love crates because they generally make housetraining a breeze and prevent damage to the house, furnishings, and personal possessions. They can give a new puppy owner peace of mind when Baby Buddy has to be left home alone. They can be used for a positive time-out when visitors tire of Buddy's antics, or when he insists on begging at the dinner table.

The crate is also a great tool for convincing owners of backyard dogs to bring their hounds into their homes (where they belong). By bringing the dog indoors but keeping him confined, at least at night, hesitant owners can ease their fears about mayhem and ruined rugs while at least partially integrating the deprived dog into the family.

Many dog owners have discovered that dog crates can serve double duty as sturdy end tables and comfortable safe havens for your canine pals!

We often recommend that owners use food-filled toys (such as a Kong, seen here) to keep a dog busy and content in his crate. This practice should be discontinued, though, if the treat triggers any guarding behavior.

Not a prison

A crate is not a place of punishment. Never force your dog or puppy into a crate in anger. Even if he has earned a time-out through inappropriate behavior, don't yell at him, throw him in the crate, and slam the door. Instead, quietly remove the dog from the scene and invite him into his crate to give both of you an opportunity to calm down.

Nor is a crate appropriate for long-term confinement. While some puppies are able to make it through an eight-hour stretch in a crate at night, you should be sleeping nearby and available to take your pup out if he tells you he needs to go.

Crate Difficulties

Overcrating

Some people are horrified of the concept of crating a dog. Often, however, the negative crate perspective stems from concerns of "overcrating." Apparently some owners crate their dogs all day while they're at work, let them out for a couple of hours when they come home, and then crate the dogs all night while everyone is sleeping. This is too much time in a crate for a dog's physical and mental health.

Alternatives to crating include finding other confinement options, arranging for multiple bathroom breaks, or finding a daycare situation of some kind.

One nonalternative is leaving your dog outside in a fenced yard during the day. This does allow him total freedom to poop and pee at will, but it also leaves him vulnerable to threats from the environment—theft, poisoning, accidental escape, snakes, raccoons, skunks, coyotes. Outdoor confinement also leaves the dog free to practice inappropriate behaviors such as digging, escaping, and barking, and exposes him to the extremes of weather.

Crate-soiling

If Spot eliminates in his crate even when not overcrated, your first course of action is to rule out medical problems. Loose stools, a urinary tract infection, or other incontinence problems make it impossible for a dog to hold it for normal periods of time. Assuming all is well, there are several other possible causes of crate soiling. Your approach to Spot's crate-soiling behavior depends on the cause.

If he has learned to soil his crate, it may help to change his bedding, or remove bedding altogether until he's retrained. Bedding that absorbs fluids, such as a blanket, can make it more comfortable for your dog to be in his soiled crate. His current bedding also may have become his preferred substrate. Instead, try newspaper, a square of heavy-duty compressed foam rubber (the kind used for flooring), or no bedding. A tether may be a reasonable alternative to nighttime crating.

Make sure his crate is the correct size—big enough for him to stand up, turn around, and lie down comfortably. If it's too large he can potty in one end and sleep in the other.

Perhaps you're just not making sure Spot eliminates outside before you crate him. In your morning rush to get to work on time, you let him out in the backyard and assume he empties before he comes back in. That may be an incorrect assumption. If it's cold or rainy, he may have huddled on the back porch, waiting to be let back in.

Go out with your dog on leash before and after he eats his breakfast to make sure he's empty when you crate him. If he's reluctant to go out in inclement weather, create a sheltered potty spot, so he doesn't have to eliminate with rain or snow dumping on his head, or strong winds buffeting him.

If he's determined to go on grass, it's the dead of winter, and there's no grass available, you may need to scrape snow away from the grass in his sheltered potty spot or provide indoor-grown grass until you can teach him a new substrate preference. Maybe Astroturf would work!

Refusing to go into the crate

Dogs who refuse to enter their crates may have never been crate-trained, or the crating process was somehow abused. He may have been overcrated and now resists entering a den he fears he'll be forced to soil. Perhaps someone previously used his crate as punishment, or he may have had a bad experience in a crate. Whatever the reason, you'll need to embark on a program of counter-conditioning and desensitization to change his association from bad to good, and retrain his crating behavior.

Start by scattering yummy stuff around the outside of his crate, placing a couple of tidbits just inside the door so he can stick his head in to get them. Gradually toss more yummies inside the crate to entice him further in. When he's going in easily, start hand-feeding tidbits while he's inside, to encourage him to stay in. If you use a clicker, you can now begin to click! and give him a treat for going into the crate.

When he'll go in and stay calmly inside the crate while you feed treats, close the door gently, feed treats through the door, and then let him out. Gradually increase the length of time you keep the door closed, until he's quite comfortable with this step. Then take a step away from the crate, click! and return to give him his treat. Continue this process until he is happy to enter and stay in his crate.

You can play another crating game to motivate your dog to "kennel." Take something scrumptious, like a meaty knucklebone, and put it in the crate. Show it to your dog, then close the door with him outside the crate. Let him spend some time trying to get into the closed crate to get at the bone, then open the door allowing him to zoom in (and back out, if he wants) to claim his prize.

To keep crating fun for your dog, be sure to practice crating games often, not just when he's going to be crated for extended periods. You can also give him food-stuffed Kongs and other interactive toys to keep him happy in his crate.

If your dog absolutely refuses to enter the crate, get one that comes apart. Take the top off, then start the counter-conditioning process.

Panicking in the crate

Some dogs, particularly many of those with separation anxiety (SA), can't tolerate the close confinement of a crate. They experience a full-blown panic attack, and frantically try to escape from their prison.

A panicked dog's efforts to escape from his mental and emotional anguish may include hysterical, non-stop barking and howling, for hours and hours without pause; frantic attempts to bite and claw his way out, often breaking teeth and ripping out nails in the process; and stress-induced urination and defecation, which he proceeds to paint all over the walls of his crate as he thrashes around.

You cannot subject a panicked dog to these conditions. You must address the SA problem through behavior modification, and may someday be able to use a crate with your dog, if you are successful in modifying the SA. In the meantime, look for doggie daycare-type management solutions.

During the day, a puppy should not be asked to stay in a crate longer than two to four hours at a time; an adult dog no more than six to eight hours. Longer than that and you risk forcing Buddy to eliminate in his crate, which is a very bad thing, since it breaks down his instinctive inhibitions against soiling his den. Dogs who learn to soil their dens can be extremely difficult, sometimes nearly impossible, to housetrain.

Training do's and don'ts

Remember that the crate should be just large enough for your dog to stand up, turn around, and lie down comfortably. He doesn't need to be able to play football in it. If you want to get one large enough for your puppy to grow into, block off the back so he has just

enough room, and increase the space as he grows. Cover the floor of the crate with a rug or soft pad to make it comfortable and inviting, and you're ready to begin training.

Start with the crate door open, and toss some irresistibly yummy treats inside. If he is hesitant to go in after them, toss the treats close enough to the doorway that he can stand outside and just poke his nose in the crate to eat them. If you are training with a clicker or other reward marker, each time he eats a treat, *click!* the clicker (or say "Yes!" if you are using a verbal marker).

Gradually toss the treats farther and farther into the crate until he steps inside to get them. Continue to *click!* each time he eats a treat. When he enters the crate easily to get the treats, *click!* and offer him a treat while he is still inside. If he is willing to stay inside,

In some homes, all the dogs sleep in their own crates, putting an end to middle-of-the-night "arguments" over the fluffiest cushions or another dog's toys.

keep clicking and treating. If he comes out that's okay too, just toss another treat inside and wait for him to re-enter. Don't try to force him to stay in the crate.

When he enters the crate to get the treat without hesitation, you can start using a verbal cue such as "Go to bed" as he goes in, so that you will eventually be able to send him into his crate on just a verbal cue.

When he happily stays in the crate in anticipation of a *click!* and treat, gently swing the door closed. Don't latch it! *Click!* and treat, then open the door. Repeat this step, gradually increasing the length of time the door stays closed before you *click!* Sometimes you can *click!* and reward without opening the door right away.

When your dog will stay in the crate with the door closed for at least 10 seconds without any signs of anxiety, close the door, latch it, and take one step away from the crate. *Click!*, return to the crate, reward, and open the door. Repeat this step, varying the time and distance you leave the crate. Don't always make it longer and farther—intersperse long ones with shorter ones, so it doesn't always get harder and harder for him. Start increasing the number of times you *click!* and treat without opening the door, but remember that a *click!* or a "Yes!" *always* gets a treat.

It's a good idea to leave the crate open when you aren't actively training. Toss treats and his favorite toys in the crate when he's not looking, so he never knows what wonderful surprises he might find there. You can even feed him his meals in the crate—with the door open—to help him realize that his crate is a truly wonderful place.

If at any time during the program your dog whines or fusses about being in the crate, *don't let him out until he stops crying!* This is the biggest mistake owners make when crate training! If you let him out when he is fussing, you will teach him that fussing gets him free.

If, however, he panics to the point of risking injury to himself, you must let him out. You may have a dog with a separation anxiety challenge. A crate is generally not recommended for dogs with separation anxiety, since they tend to panic in close confinement. If you believe your dog has a separation anxiety problem, stop the crate training and consult a behaviorist or a trainer who has experience with this behavior.

Instead of letting your dog out whenever he fusses or whines, wait for a few seconds of quiet, then *click!* and reward. Then back up a step or two in the training

As a first step with dogs who are reluctant to go in their crates, lock away their favorite toy or treat inside. Let their anticipation build before opening the door to let them go in and get it.

program until he is again successful at the task you've set out for him. When your dog is doing well at that level again, increase the difficulty in smaller increments, and vary the amount of time, rather than making it progressively longer. For example, instead of going from 5 seconds to 10 to 15, start with 5 seconds, then 7, then 3, then 8, and so on.

Maintaining success

Sometimes dogs and often puppies can do the whole crate training program in one day. Some will take several days, and a few will take weeks or more.

Once your dog is crate-trained, you have a valuable behavior management tool for life. Respect it. If you abuse it by keeping him confined too much, for too long a period of time, or by using it as punishment, he may learn to dislike it. Even though he goes to bed

Don't respond to your dog when she barks for attention in the crate. You'll quickly teach her to bark louder and longer if you do.

willingly and on cue, reward him often enough to keep the response happy and quick. Keep your verbal "Go to bed" cue light and happy. Don't ever let anyone tease or punish him in his crate.

Greetings and Salutations

The process of teaching your dog to greet people calmly starts at home.

Consistency is the cornerstone—and the bane—of training success. Consistent reinforcement of polite doggie greetings is reasonably easy. The tough part is ensuring that impolite greetings are consistently *not* reinforced. Even if *you* are very good at not reinforcing your dog's jumping-up behaviors, the entire rest of the world is pretty crummy at it. If jumping up is reinforced randomly, it's very difficult to extinguish.

Greeting family members

The process sounds easy in principle. It's not always so easy in practice. You're most likely to encounter problems with greeting immediate family members, guests in your home, and people in public.

In theory, teaching family members to correctly play their parts in the training process should be the easiest, since they should be committed to helping you change the behavior. In reality, we know how hard

Use a tether to prevent your dog from jumping up on guests when they arrive. Generously reinforce his calm behavior.

those darned humans can be to train! But remember that positive reinforcement works well with primates, too!

You can try several different approaches with family members. First, all must agree to stop reinforcing your dog for jumping, and must all understand that *any attention at all* is reinforcement. Making eye contact with your dog when he jumps up is reinforcing him. By pushing him off, you've touched him—reinforcement! Asking him to "Off!" gives him attention by speaking to him. Reinforcement! In fact, just the fact that his paws touched you can be rewarding to your dog, even if you do nothing else.

To avoid reinforcing your dog for jumping up, he needs to get the opposite response. Rather than eliciting attention, a jump should make all attention go away. When the dog starts his lift-off, say "Oops!" as you turn your back on him and step away. If he jumps again, turn and step away again. Keep an eye over your shoulder, and when he stops jumping (and, we hope, sits), turn back toward him and give him treats and/or attention.

Meanwhile, use a tether to *teach* him a more appropriate greeting. You can secure your dog with a leash, but a more durable tether consists of a four- to five-foot piece of plastic-coated cable with sturdy snaps on both ends.

With your dog on his tether, approach from a distance. If he's leaping about in greeting, stand still until he's calm, then move forward. Anytime he starts to jump, stand still, or even take a step back. When you are close enough to reach out and touch him (but he still can't jump on you), stand still and wait for him to sit. You can help him get the idea by holding a treat at your chest a few times, but you'll want to fade the treat (stop using it) quickly so he learns to offer a sit in

Teach your family not to reinforce the dog when he jumps up—to quickly turn away.

greeting without being lured. By the same token, don't *ask* him to sit—wait for him to offer it. You want him to volunteer the sit in greeting, not wait to be asked for it.

When he sits, mark the polite behavior with a "Yes!" or the *click!* of a clicker, feed him a treat, and give him attention. Repeat this exercise until he sits promptly as soon as you head toward him.

Many dogs will immediately resume jumping up when petted, especially if they have been allowed to greet people boisterously in the past. If your dog starts to leap up as you reach for him or pet him, simply stand up, take a step backward (out of his range), and wait for him to sit again. You may have to withdraw and return several times in rapid succession before he realizes that leaping up makes the thing he wants (attention) go away, and sitting firmly on his bottom makes it return.

Now have the rest of the family practice, all the way down to the toddler.

Of course, your dog won't always be on a tether, but when he has learned this exercise he'll be much

quicker to offer you (and others) that highly reinforced "sit" behavior in other scenarios as well.

Perhaps the most aroused greetings occur when you return home after a long day away. He's clearly thrilled to see you, and it can be hard to turn your back on such a sincere display of love. If you are reluctant to squelch your dog's welcome-home enthusiasm, redirect it to a game you both can enjoy. Stash your dog's favorite toy—or several—in a box just outside the door. Walk into the house with the toy in your hand, and toss it for him to fetch. Even better, reinforce polite greetings by waiting for a sit before you toss. The "welcome-home fetch game" allows your dog to be happy about your return, lets you reciprocate, and still keeps his energy controlled and directed into a productive and polite outlet.

You may have a family member who insists that he *wants* the dog to be able to jump on him. Promise this person that he can teach the dog to jump up on cue—*after* the dog has learned to greet politely. That might motivate him to help with, rather than sabotage, the dog's training. Then, when the two of you are ready to teach "Jump up!" be sure you select verbal and body-language cues that are very distinctive, and not likely to be offered by accident by an unsuspecting dog greeter.

Greeting guests in your home

Of course, it's too much to expect that visitors will know enough to turn their backs on your dog when he jumps up on them, so it's incumbent on *you* to make sure he doesn't have the opportunity. Your tether will come in handy here. When the doorbell rings, calmly clip him to his tether station, feed him a yummy treat, then go greet your guests. You don't have to worry about a door-darting dog, or one who blithely ruins your guest's nylons. Peace of mind. Over time, your dog may even come to learn that the doorbell is the cue to go to his tether and wait for treats!

As your guests enter, hand them a few treats, and ask them to approach your dog on his tether. Be sure they understand that they can feed him the treats and pet him *only when he is sitting*. Then supervise to be sure they follow directions.

When your dog's initial excitement subsides, you can release him to greet your guests off leash. By then, you will have had time to instruct them on how to properly reinforce his polite greeting, and how to avoid reinforcing him if he does try to jump.

You can also choose to play the "welcome fetch" game with visitors. Put a large sign on your door instructing visitors to take a toy from the box, bring it in the house with them, and throw it for your dog when he sits. Dog-loving visitors will enjoy this immensely.

Greeting people in public

In public, your leash is the tether. Hold the leash, giving your dog only about three feet of slack. As people approach, keep your distance and the leash at a length that prevents your dog from lunging forward and jumping up on the passerby. You can, of course, reinforce your dog if he offers a sit. If the approachers

> Impress on the entire immediate family the importance of being consistent about reinforcing polite greetings and preventing inappropriate greetings from being rewarded.
>
> Have the family agree on which training and management techniques you will use with your dog.
>
> Enlist the aid of friends and strangers to provide lots of reinforcement to your dog for appropriate greeting behavior.
>
> Be assertive about not allowing friends and strangers to reinforce inappropriate greetings.

appear to have dog-petting on their minds, ask (*insist!*) that they wait for him to sit first. If they say, "That's okay, I don't mind if he jumps up," politely but firmly tell them that *you* mind, and that they need to wait until your dog sits. If they ignore your instructions, turn and walk away with your dog, with a cheery "Oops! Sorry!"

If they are willing, you can hand them a couple of treats to feed when your dog sits. If they seem really interested, ask them if they'll help you train. Give them a handful of treats and ask them to do several approach-sit repetitions to give your dog more practice at greeting strangers politely on the street.

Fearful greetings

So far, we have presupposed an overenthusiastic greeter, whose behavior is best addressed with positive reinforcement and negative punishment principles of operant conditioning, where the dog's behavior (a polite sit) causes a good thing to happen (attention), and jumping up causes that same good thing to go away.

Some dog owners have the opposite problem: the dog who launches a volley of defensive fear barking at the sound of the doorbell or the approach of a stranger on the street. This behavior is best modified through the use of counter-conditioning: changing the dog's association with visitors and strangers from "Bad! Scary!" to "Yay, treats are coming!"

You might begin by ringing the doorbell yourself, and immediately follow the sound with several tidbits of canned chicken (or something equally succulent and delicious), delivered to your dog's waiting jaws, *even if he's barking*. Repeat this exercise until the sound of the doorbell generates a "Yay! Where's my chicken?" response instead of wild barking.

Then have someone else ring the doorbell—someone your dog knows. Repeat the doorbell-chicken sequence until you're getting the positive response.

Then have the person ring the bell and open the door. This is likely to elicit another round of defensive barking. Feed chicken. Then repeat, and continue repeating until the doorbell/door opening sequence consistently generates the "Where's my chicken?" response from your dog. Then have the person ring the bell, open the door, and step into the room.

Continue the progression, one small step at a time, feeding chicken at each step until you get the positive response at that level, then take the next step. When he's fine with the person he knows, try someone he doesn't know, or at least doesn't know as well, until he can maintain calm when anyone enters the house.

You can do a similar exercise with people on the street. Set yourself up a distance off the sidewalk so people aren't walking directly at your dog. The instant he notices someone walking in your direction, start feeding him bits of chicken. When the person has passed by, stop. Over time, as he associates people approaching with yummy chicken, his response should become calmer.

Important note: Do *not* have the *other* person feed treats to a fearful dog. His desire for the treat may overcome his caution, temporarily, but when the treat is gone and he realizes he's too close to a person who scares him, he may bite. You need to first change the association by feeding your dog the treats yourself. When your dog is happy to have visitors and strangers in close proximity, *then* you can ask the other person to drop treats, or offer them gently using very non-threatening body language: kneel sideways to the dog, hold the treat out to the side, don't make direct eye contact or any overt moves to reach for the dog.

If you are consistent and persistent, your dog can learn to greet people politely. In fact, he will soon run up to you and *sit* as hard and as fast as he can, with as much enthusiasm as he now displays when he jumps up on you.

Sit Happens—The Magic of Clicker Training

After you learn how easy the positive approach to training really is, you'll never push a pup's butt to the floor again!

Nowhere, perhaps, is the difference between positive and compulsion training more beautifully obvious than with the "sit."

Sitting on cue is one of those basic behaviors that every dog should know, and happily, it is an absurdly simple behavior to teach. Remember, dogs already *know* how to sit—it's just the "doing it on cue" part that we have to work on!

The key to positive training is remembering to notice and reward the dog when he does something right. A dog sits dozens of times a day, all on his own. If we make it a point to reward him a good percentage of the times when he does, he'll do it even more, because *all living beings repeat behaviors that are rewarding to them.*

Positive trainers use treats as rewards because food is a primary motivator—all living things need food to survive—and because a dog can quickly eat his treat and get back to the fun of training. It is *possible* to train without reward markers and treats by using toys, play,

petting, and/or praise as rewards; but in my experience, it's less effective and less efficient.

We also recommend using a "reward marker," a word or a sound that tells a dog the instant he has exhibited a desirable behavior. Clickers are commonly used as reward markers because the *click!* sound is so distinctive and consistent. Reward markers can also consist of the word "Yes!" (or any other word you choose), a "mouth click," the click of a ball-point pen, or any other consistent, distinct sound. The *click!* or "Yes" (or other reward marker) is a *promise* to the dog that a treat is forthcoming, and every *click!* earns a treat.

Magic marker

Start out with a generous supply of delicious treats and a clicker in hand. *Click!* the clicker (or say "Yes!" or use another reward marker) and immediately feed

Trainer Sandi Thompson begins a session by freely doling out tasty treats while clicking a clicker. The puppy begins to associate the reward marker (*click!*) with the treats.

The puppy's full attention is now riveted on Sandi. She then stops the flow of food. When will he get another treat? He stares, waiting for another delicious morsel . . .

Finally he gets tired of craning his neck to look up. He sits for a more comfortable view, and Wow! Sandi clicks and gives him a treat.

the dog an irresistible (and small) treat. *Click!* and treat several more times. Usually, it takes no more than a half-dozen treats to convince the dog to rivet his attention on you.

Once this happens, stop the constant flow of treats, and hold one up near your chest. Often, the dog will try to jump up for the treat. If he does, simply whisk the treat out of sight and turn away, without making eye contact or paying him any attention. Eventually he will sit, because it's easier to look up at you (and the treat) when he's sitting. The instant he does, *click!* and treat.

It takes most dogs less than three minutes to become sitting machines, offering sit after sit in order to make the *click!* happen and earn the treat reward; this is the secret of the "magic marker." The dog learns that *he* makes the *click!* and treat happen. Trainers jokingly call this the "Helen Keller moment." Once we open that door, the dog is ready for training.

Putting sit on cue

At this point, notice that you have not yet *asked* the dog to sit. With operant conditioning, we get the behavior first, *then* we add the verbal cue. There is no point in using a word to ask the dog to do something when he has no idea what it means. Once we know we can get the dog to offer the behavior, then we add the word so that he can start to make the association between the word and the behavior.

This is easy with the sit. Take a step backward. Your dog will get up to follow his newfound treat machine. Stop, and he'll sit to make the *click!* happen. As his bottom touches the floor, say "Sit!" then *click!* and treat. You are telling him—in verbal shorthand—that the behavior he just did is called "Sit." Repeat this several times, and then start saying "Sit" just *before* he sits. By watching his body language, it's easy to predict when he is about to sit. Now you are teaching him that the

He has not "refused" to sit on cue; he simply didn't understand the slightly different context. Don't nag at him with several repetitions of the "Sit" cue. Rather, get his attention, and when you can see that he is ready to sit, say the word.

Sandi "shapes" the puppy's movement into a proper "Down" by waiting for him to lower himself further and further before he gets a "Click!" and treat.

Sandi begins teaching the puppy to lie down by luring him down from a sit with a treat. She clicks and gives him a treat as he makes a forward and down motion.

Highly motivated by food, this puppy learns the "down" exercise VERY quickly. "Fading" the lure might take a little longer for such a devoted chow-hound.

"Sit!" sound precedes his sit behavior. *Click!* and treat every time.

An uneducated observer would think that the dog was responding to the verbal cue when he's really not. At this point, you are still *predicting* the dog's sit behavior with the word. He does not yet understand that the word is his prompt to sit.

You can test this assertion by asking your dog to sit at a time when his body language tells you he is not about to sit—when he is distracted, sniffing the floor, or looking away. Lo and behold, he doesn't sit!

Downhill from here

Teaching the down is not quite as easy as the sit, since dogs are less apt to "offer" the down behavior in a training session than a sit. Once again, a food-treat motivator comes in handy. You can lure your dog into a down by putting a treat in front of his nose and moving it slowly toward the ground. Lots of dogs will follow the lure easily and end up in a perfect down on the first try. *Click!* and treat!

Some dogs won't, however. They may not understand what you want them to do, and so they stand up when you try to lure them down. Some dogs are reluctant to lie down because they feel more vulnerable in the down position. In these cases you can "shape" the behavior. Shaping means breaking the final desired behavior into small steps and clicking and rewarding the dog repeatedly at each step along the way. Here is one way to shape the down:

1. Have the dog sit facing you. Hold the treat in front of his nose and move it two inches toward the ground. *Click!* and treat. Repeat several times until he shows no sign of trying to stand when you move the treat.

2. Have the dog sit. Hold the treat in front of his nose and move it five inches toward the ground. *Click!* and treat. Repeat several times until he shows no sign of trying to stand when you move the treat. If

he does get up, say "Oops!" in a cheerful tone of voice, and try again. If he consistently gets up, go back to two inches, and when he can do two inches without getting up, try *three* inches. (When your dog has trouble with the transition from one step to the next, make the steps even smaller.)

3. Keep moving the treat closer to the floor until your dog's nose is touching the ground. Now move the treat away from his nose along the floor, toward you, a few inches. *Click!* and treat when he follows it with his nose. Gradually move the treat farther and farther away from his nose, clicking and treating as he follows without getting up. Eventually he will move one paw forward as he follows the lure. *Click!* and treat, then continue to lure him with the goodie until he is all the way down. *Click!* and jackpot! Give him several treats, one after the other, while you tell him what a wonderful dog he is.

Bingo—you've done it! Or rather, the dog has done it. Once. Fortunately, it's usually much easier the second time. Keep practicing until he will lie down for you easily when you lure him, and then start adding the verbal cue, "Down," *as* he does it. Remember, you're not asking him to "Down" yet, you're telling him that the behavior he is doing is called "Down."

As soon as your dog has had an opportunity to hear the word *with* the behavior a half-dozen times or more, you can use the word first, then lure to help him lie down.

Fading the lure

Now comes the real challenge—getting your dog to lie down on the verbal cue *without* the lure. You must "fade" the lure—that is, reduce his (and your) dependence on the treat to get the "Down."

Have your dog sit facing you, and hold the treat behind your back. Say "Down" in a cheerful tone of voice. He probably will sit and look at you, since he doesn't know what the word means yet. Give him several seconds to think about it, then put the treat in front of his nose and lure him down. *Click!* and treat. Then do it again.

Watch him closely when you say "Down." If he looks at the ground or makes a tentative motion as if to lie down, it's almost as if he's asking you if that's what he's *supposed* to do. Tell him "Good boy!" and quickly lure him the rest of the way down for a *click!* and treat. If you encourage his tentative movements, you will speed up his response to the verbal cue.

Another way to fade the lure is to use smaller and smaller motions toward the ground with the treat until you're not moving it at all. Or, motion toward the ground with your empty hand; *click!* when he goes down and feed him the treat.

How quickly you accomplish the verbal down depends on the dog *and* you. A dog may go down on a verbal cue in as few as three repetitions, or still need the lure at the conclusion of a six-week class. Timing and persistence are key. If you frequently forget to pause after the verbal cue before you lure, your dog will focus on the lure, and won't learn the cue.

Formula for learning

Remember that the more complex a behavior is, the more likely it is that you will have to shape it. The better you are at breaking the behavior into small steps, the easier it is for your dog to understand what you want.

Once he figures out that *he* makes the *click!* happen, you can use the same training formula to teach *any* behavior. Figure out how to get the behavior, *click!* it, and put it on cue. Simple. Not always easy—but simple.

The most valuable aspect of this training method is that it teaches a dog *how to learn.* This is a skill that the two of you can rely on for the rest of his training career—whether for formal competition, or to perform new tricks to impress your friends. His ability and interest in learning behaviors that please you will also help make him a more enjoyable housemate and companion.

Come to Me, Run to Me

To teach your dog perfect recalls, use praise, practice, and more practice!

When it comes to learning to come when called, not all dogs are created equal. Some dogs learn the "recall" very easily. They seem to know instinctively that coming when called is to their advantage. Others will come when called most of the time, perhaps more reluctantly. For some dogs, however, coming when called is the most challenging behavior they will ever learn—especially when faced with choosing between complying with the request and distractions like squirrels, cats, balls, or other dogs.

Teaching a dog to come when called (also known as the "recall") is not as difficult as you may think. It takes time, enthusiasm, and lots of practice, but even the most reluctant dog can learn to perform a reliable recall in most situations.

Make it enjoyable for your dog to come to you when you call him. If, more often than not, coming to you equals unenjoyable consequences, he'll quite sensibly decide that coming when called is not very high on his list of priorities.

Getting started

In brief, for your dog to have a reliable recall, you will need to follow these steps:

- Teach your dog the initial behaviors (coming when called is really a series, or chain, of behaviors).
- Make your dog think coming when called is the best thing that happens in life.

- Practice, practice, practice.
- Increase distractions gradually, so that your dog learns that coming to you is always more rewarding than anything else.
- Continue reinforcing (with variable rewards) *for life*.

Always use the highest-value rewards when teaching "Come." Try chicken, liver, cheese, sardines, and other smelly, yummy, soft treats. From the start, make recall practice the highlight of your dog's day.

Chain, chain, chain

Because coming when called is actually a chain of behaviors, it works best to teach each part of the chain separately first.

1. **Charge up the cue.** This simple step will give you a head start on the rest of the training. Go into a low-stimulation environment where you and the dog can be alone (like the bathroom or bedroom). Say

the word you have chosen for your cue (in these examples, we'll use the word, "Come!") and then give your dog a treat. Repeat this 10 to 20 times. Do this exercise several times over two or three days. You are essentially supercharging the cue.

2. **Teach your dog the beginning behavior by capturing it, using a food lure, or both.** To "capture" the behavior, simply set your dog up for success. When your dog is about to come to you anyway (what trainers call "offering" the behavior), say "Come!" just before he gets to you, then use your reward marker (in most cases, a *click!* of a clicker or the word "Yes!") and give your dog a reward.

For example, you can say "Come!" when your dog is on his way to you to get his dinner, when you are about to go for a walk, or when you are getting ready to toss his favorite ball.

If you want to use a treat lure to get started, simply put the treat in front of your dog's nose, and as he sniffs it, take several steps backward. When he follows the treat toward you, *click!* a clicker (or say "Yes!" or use another reward marker) and give him the treat. Repeat this several times.

Once your dog will easily follow the treat, add the cue "Come!" It's important to quickly "fade" or eliminate the treat lure, going to a *click!* and treat as soon as possible. Practice in your living room, bedroom, backyard, and other low-stimulation environments.

3. **Practice the "quick turn" and "sit" on (leashed) walks.** Surprise your dog on your walks by suddenly calling him and taking several steps back. When he turns to follow, *click!* or say "Yes!" and give him a treat. Tell him what a great dog he is!

After a couple of practices, add in the sit and/or a collar touch. For example, say, "Jesse, come, sit!" With a few dozen repetitions most dogs will begin automatically sitting.

4. **Increase the distance and speed.** If you have practiced a recall only across the length of your living room, don't expect your dog to be able to come from a distance of the length of a park or field. You'll need to practice with gradually increasing distances first.

Start by just calling him a few feet, then a few more until you can call him through your house and across your backyard. Practice away from home in fenced areas, or in an open area using a long line for safety.

How can you get your dog to run to you? Practice calling during ball games or tug games, using the continuation of the game as the reward. Try running in the opposite direction when you call (he'll race after you to catch up), or calling him back and forth between two people.

5. **Teach your dog to pay attention when you ask, separately from teaching "Come."** It is difficult to get a dog to come when you can't get his attention! Work "attention" games into your everyday life with your dog. For the next 10 days or so, every time your dog looks your way (even just a quick glance to "check in" with you), reward her with praise, affection, a favorite game, or a *click!* and treat. Do this throughout the day whether you are at home or out in the world.

At first your dog may check in more at home than in other places. That's okay. Just keep rewarding at home, and your dog will begin to look at you more when you are out in the world as well. After a couple of days of rewarding the natural check-in, start occasionally saying your dog's name and rewarding her when she looks your way.

6. **Put it all together.** When your dog has learned all the individual pieces, you can start putting the behaviors together. This is the time to practice the recall as the whole chain of behaviors—responding to your request for attention, coming to you quickly, sitting or accepting a collar touch, waiting for the release.

Practice at various times during the day in low-distraction environments. It is critical at this stage to set up your dog for success; only use your cue for the recall when you are 99 percent certain he will come. Don't bother calling him when it's very unlikely that he will comply; for example, right after you enter the dog park and take off his leash, or right as one of his family members or best friends enters your front gate.

Also, keep your practice sessions light and fun! If you turn your training sessions into a big bore, with too many repetitions and not enough fun, he well decide to quit "playing" with you.

Praise only

When you first teach your dog to come, try to avoid four very common human errors that can set back your training.

1. Be careful not to put your dog into a situation where he or she will learn that *not* coming is rewarding! For example, if you ask your dog to come, and he runs the other way (and has fun doing it!), then he has just been rewarded for not coming. At this stage in training the recall, it is essential to use good management! Let your dog off leash only when it is very safe and when you will be able to go and get him when you need to.

2. Do not use "Come" to end a play session or other fun times, or to call your dog to you to perform a distasteful task (like pulling off burrs or clipping nails). This teaches your dog that coming to you could be a bad thing.

3. Be careful not to fall into the "bribe" trap. Let's say you blew it (we all do!) and called your dog at a time when he wouldn't come. At that point, don't show him a treat or a ball to get him to come. This teaches your dog to come only when you have an obvious reward. Instead, go and get him, make it easier (say, by asking him to come to you on leash), and try again.

4. *Never* scold your dog when he comes to you, no matter what terrible thing he was doing just before he came to you. He *stopped* doing what he was doing and came to you! That's great! So be sincere and enthusiastic. Your body posture, tone of voice, and energy will all make a difference. A sensitive dog will often circle or sniff (rather than come) if you bend over at the waist, or call with a stern voice. If your dog is starting to come, but hesitates, encourage her with happy praise.

You should *never* admonish your dog when he has come to you. Doing so is the quickest way to ensure he will *stop* coming. It *can* be very difficult to resist, especially when you're angry with your dog for doing something naughty. But coming back to you was *good*, so make sure you greet him warmly and reward him.

Party time!

This can't be said too much: *Make recall training the highlight of your dog's day. Use the best treats and toys as rewards. Vary the rewards. And most importantly, always keep it fun!*

Make a list of your dog's top rewards. Along with treats, use natural events in your dog's life as possible rewards, such as playing with other dogs, walks, dinnertime, and playing fetch. Consider anything your dog loves to do as a reward! Mix them up.

For example, if your dog loves chicken, playing with other dogs, and tug games, reward the recall sometimes with chicken, sometimes with a surprise

Always follow a recall with one of your dog's favorite things—food, Frisbee, or playing with another dog.

When your dog is distracted, time your "come" cue for the moment the dog can most easily disengage from his other activity, for example, when he turns away from the other dog he just greeted.

Avoid repeatedly calling your dog when you know he won't or can't come. Go get him instead.

While you are teaching him to come, never end your dog's play or fun by calling him to you.

Always be enthusiastic and upbeat when your dog comes to you, no matter what he was doing before he came.

tug game, and other times with a release to play with dog friends. Make recall training part of other fun activities, like walks and fetch, too.

Practice and distractions

Of course your dog will come to you when it's all about fun and games. But what about when it really counts: in the face of serious distractions or in a life-or-death situation? How do you make sure your dog will turn away from something really interesting to come to you?

The key is to train with *systematically and increasingly difficult* distractions. This is possibly the most important step for teaching your dog to come reliably in almost all situations.

But what does it mean? It means, quite simply, that you have to practice, practice, and practice some more. It means that those practice sessions must be full of heavily rewarded recalls. And it means that you must practice with distractions—and with distractions that are at a level your dog can handle. Increase the difficulty of those distractions only when he can successfully handle it. This takes time, effort, and some planning, but it will pay off big time when you really need your dog to come!

In order to train with increasing distractions, you will need to have thought through the things your dog finds distracting. Because this varies from dog to dog, try writing down what distracts *your* dog. A puppy might be engaged by a leaf blowing across a lawn. Some dogs are enthralled with balls. Others lose concentration when they see other dogs playing or a neighborhood cat. Write down everything your dog finds distracting, then rank them according to how big a distraction it is for your dog. Pick at least 10 different locations you can practice in. New places are distracting, too.

Set up a training plan to remind yourself to stick to a regular practice schedule. Then, keep track of your practice sessions and your dog's progress; these notes can help you decide when to go to the next level of distractions.

Increase the distractions when your dog is enthusiastically coming at least 9 out of 10 times at your current level. What if your dog is making a lot of mistakes? If you have two mistakes in a row, make the exercise easier for your dog; help him be successful.

Train for life

Please keep in mind that there is no such thing as a 100 percent reliable recall. Dogs will always be dogs! What that means is that they are living, thinking, decision-making beings who will always make their own choices. No matter how much you train or practice, and no matter how well your dog responds, you will always need to use good judgment when your dog is off leash.

Recognize the types of situations that will make it difficult for your dog to come reliably. Is it chasing birds, visiting with other dogs, or the scary sounds of thunder that make it most difficult for your dog to respond? Know and respect your dog. Don't expect her to be someone she is not!

But when you take the time to really train your dog's recall, you may be surprised and even impressed with just how reliably she will come. While teaching your dog to come can be done over the course of several weeks or several months, keeping your dog's recall strong will mean continuing to train and reward it throughout her lifetime.

For a young dog (or a dog for whom coming is particularly challenging) continue practicing a couple of times a week at various locations and with various distraction levels for months after your dog has the basics down. For all dogs, integrate your recall practice into your daily life. Play with it on off-leash walks. Call your dog to you several times on your walk, then send him back off to play.

Keep rewarding your dog for great recalls, but use varied rewards, such as treats, toys, praise, or freedom.

Walk This Way

Teach your dog to walk on a loose leash to make your walks more fun.

Walking politely at your side doesn't seem like it should be so difficult to teach a dog, but it often proves to be the most challenging behavior for dog owners to achieve.

Why do so many dogs pull on leash? Because they can. Many dogs learn, from the time they're wee pups, that pulling on the leash gets them where they want to go. They pull, owner follows. There are a number of other reasons that dogs pull:

1. We are slow and boring, and the world is infinitely exciting and rewarding. If you take your dog for a hike in a safe place *off leash*, chances are good he'll run several miles for every mile you trudge on your pathetic two human legs.

2. Leash walking is not a natural behavior. Rarely do dogs plod sedately side by side. They dash, dart, gallop, romp, run, and trot, but rarely do they plod, unless you have a senior citizen who's feeling his years.

3. Lack of consistency. Although owners may understand the concept of polite leash training and would like their dogs to be a pleasure to walk, most owners are *also* eager to get where they're going, sometimes. If you insist on a loose leash most of the time, but allow your dog to pull when you're in a hurry or your attention is elsewhere, pulling is likely to be his first behavior choice when he really wants to get somewhere.

4. Behaviors that are intermittently reinforced are very durable. If a dog has learned to pull and is occasionally rewarded for this (by getting to reach what he is pulling toward), he will continue to pull whenever the opportunity arises.

5. Sometimes the dog pulls because the owner never gives him slack in the leash. Many owners suffer from "Floating Arm Syndrome"—no matter how

Not every dog will pay such rapt attention to you (rather than his environment) in hopes of earning a treat, but you might be surprised at how much your dog will improve his polite walking skills if he gets tasty treats occasionally when he's walking by you.

many times you remind the owner to keep her arm at her side in order to keep slack in the leash, that arm mysteriously levitates to shoulder height, and the leash tightens, *even when the dog is walking politely by her side.*

6. If someone attaches a rope to your belt and pulls, you're likely to pull back. If they push, there's a good chance you'll push back. This is the "opposition reflex," a natural response that enables us to maintain equilibrium and stay upright. Dogs have it too, and it kicks in when the leash tightens on their collar—they pull against it.

7. It's not important enough. Some owners rarely put a leash on their dogs because they rarely take them anywhere. For these owners, it's just not a high-priority behavior to practice—so they don't.

Polite walking versus "Heel"

Old-fashioned training classes assumed that everyone aspired to the level of precision required for obedience ring competition. We taught students to bark the "Heel!" command and stride forward, using leash "pops" or "corrections"—both euphemisms for punishing the dog with a sharp jerk on the choke collar if he dared stray an inch out of perfect heel position.

If your dog starts to rush ahead of you, try just stopping. *Click!* and treat when he turns back to you and slacks the leash.

Start your dog's on-leash lessons *OFF* leash. This gives him the freedom to discover the location of the most rewarding position for him to walk by you, without interference from the leash.

Feed him the treats from the side on which you want him to walk. Offer them with your hand behind your knee to keep him from crossing in front of and tripping you to reach the treats.

You can still find similar old-fashioned training classes today, but increasingly you'll encounter pet dog training classes, where a cheerful "Let's walk!" cue replaces the "Heel!" command, and clicks and treats for reasonably polite walking replace physical punishment for minor missteps.

"Heel" means "Walk precisely beside me." However, a growing number of positive trainers are earning obedience and rally titles for their dogs with enviably high scores by teaching their dogs to walk precisely by their sides without ever jerking on a collar. Rather, sits, heel position, and other required exercises are all taught by shaping, clicking, and positive reinforcement—treats, play, and praise, with the trainer gradually fading the use of clicks and treats before setting foot into the show ring.

Whether your goal is winning trophies and titles in competition or strolling around the block in harmony with your canine pal, you can use the following dog-friendly training techniques and avoid potentially spine-damaging yanks on your dog's collar. It's best to practice in short sessions, perhaps 5 to 15 minutes apiece, and to quit while you're ahead—when you're having some success and you and your dog are both enjoying the training game.

Free walking

Start with your dog off leash in a safely enclosed area, indoors or out. Have a good supply of tasty treats, and your clicker or other reward marker handy.

Start walking around the enclosed area. Any time your dog is within three feet of you, *click!* (or use another reward marker, such as the word "Yes!") and give your dog a treat. Your dog will discover that it's very rewarding to stay near you and begin to walk with you, at least some of the time. Use a high rate of reinforcement—lots of clicks and treats—accompanied by cheerful praise, to convince your dog you're more fun and rewarding than the world around him.

When your dog starts to "hang" with you as you walk, pick which side you want him to walk on and start clicking only if he's on that side. At first, *click!* and treat whenever he's closer to your chosen side. As he begins to spend more time on that side, *click!* and treat for positions that come closer and closer to your goal walking position. This is called "shaping"—breaking a desired behavior into small steps and reinforcing *approximations* of the final behavior, gradually tightening the criteria until you eventually have the final goal behavior.

You can use other reinforcers besides food. Pairing your *click!* and treat with cheerful praise will give your dog a positive association with voice rewards, and help you eventually fade (get rid of) the need for the *click!* and treat. You can also use toys and play as rewards. Hide a small squeaky toy or tug rope in your pocket, and after a stretch of exceptionally nice walking, whip it out, squeak and toss, or play a bit of tug as your dog's reward. Keep him guessing!

Choosing one side for polite walking will keep your dog from crossing back and forth in front of you and tripping you up. Traditionally, dogs are taught to walk on the left side—possibly a carryover from the time when owners routinely carried and used rifles in their right hands while hunting with their dogs. While some dog sports still hold with this tradition, notably obedience and rally, others, such as agility and canine

freestyle (dancing with your dog), ask the dog to work on both sides. Choose the side that works for you and your training goals, and later you can train to the second side as well, if you desire.

When your dog is frequently walking by your side, it's time to add the leash.

Leash walking

You can start with the leash attached and skip the free-walking exercise if you want, but practicing off leash first helps you avoid falling victim to many of the reasons dogs pull on leash. Neither you nor your dog can pull on the leash if it's not there!

Remember that your dog's leash is not a steering wheel or handle. It's a safety belt, intended to prevent your dog from leaving. It's not to be used to pull him around. To position him by your side to begin walking, rather than dragging him there, use treats and body language to show him where you want him to be.

For left-side walking, start with your dog sitting by your left side. Hold the leash and clicker in your left hand (same side as the dog) and have a good supply of treats in your right hand. Make sure there's enough slack in the leash so it stays loose when your dog is in the reinforcement zone you've identified for polite walking. You can also use a waist belt or otherwise attach your dog's leash to your body, as long as he's not big enough to knock you down and drag you.

Use your "Let's walk!" cue in a cheerful tone of voice and start walking forward. The instant your dog begins to move forward with you, *click!* and treat. At first, *click!* and treat very rapidly—almost every step. When your dog is attentively focused on his new, generous, treat-dispensing machine (you!), you can gradually reduce the rate of reinforcement.

Careful! If you reduce the rate too quickly or too predictably, you'll lose the behavior. As you *gradually* reduce the rate of reinforcement, be sure to *click!* and treat *randomly*—so your dog never knows for sure when the next one's coming. If he knows you're going to reinforce every tenth step, he can quit paying attention for nine steps, and zero back in on you on the tenth. This phenomenon is called an *interval scallop*. We humans are creatures of habit, and easily fall into predictable patterns. Our dogs are masters at identifying patterns.

The manner in which you hold and deliver your treats is critical to success with polite walking. When you walk, have the treats in your right hand but hidden behind your right hip. If you hold them in your left hand where your dog can see or smell them, it will be harder to fade treats later on. If you hold them in front of you in your right hand, your dog will keep

Retractable Leashes: Not Good for Dogs Who Pull

Retractable leashes are leashes that extend up to a distance of 15 to 30 feet or so when the dog pulls away from the handler, and then retract into the plastic handle when the dog returns. They are very popular with dog owners, who see them as a way to provide their canine pals with more exercise and a wider territory in which to range, while still complying with leash laws and preventing their dogs from ranging too far.

However, most training classes and many leash laws specify a maximum six-foot leash length for good reason. There are a number of drawbacks to what may initially appear to be a very cool tool:

- *A dog who is regularly walked on a retractable leash learns that pulling on the leash allows him to keep going farther away—the exact opposite of what we want him to learn.*
- *A retractable leash can't be shortened when the dog is pulling against it.*
- *The farther away from you that your dog is allowed to range, the less control you have of him.*
- *Unless you are paying perfect attention, and are very skilled at pushing the button to stop the leash from feeding out, the retractable leash gives your dog the ability to dart in front of a moving car, get tangled around another dog's leash, or charge hot on the heels of a wayward cat.*
- *The buttons that stop these leashes from playing out to their maximum length sometimes jam or "pop" out of the locked position, especially when a dog makes a quick bolt. With a strong, unpredictable dog, they simply cannot provide a secure, close restraint 100 percent of the time.*

- *These leashes are not appropriate for walking on sidewalks, where your dog should rightfully be restricted to no more than a six-foot radius around you (and oftentimes even less). Your dog should not have the freedom to use other people's front yards as toilets, even if he is on leash.*

We're not saying that you should never use retractable leashes. Just use them after your dog is fully trained not to pull on his leash, and after you have good enough voice control to stop your dog in midcharge if he spontaneously charges after something.

Dogs enjoy exploring their environment to a greater degree, and retractable leashes allow and thus reward this roving and ranging. That makes the pulling behavior self-reinforcing to the dog—the opposite of what we usually want.

stepping in front of you to watch your hand (with the treats), and you'll keep stepping on him.

To deliver treats, wait for a second or two after the *click!* as you keep walking, then bring your right hand across the front of your body and feed the treat just behind your left knee. Quickly move your hand behind your right hip as soon as you've delivered the treat. Feeding the treat where you want your dog to be—on your left side—reinforces that position. If you feed the treat in front of you, you'll reinforce *that* position, and you'll be stepping on him again.

Remember to *click!*, *then* treat after a brief pause. If you begin to move your treat hand toward him *before* the *click!*, he's just thinking about *food* rather than what he did to make you *click!* the clicker. For the same reason, you want to lure as *little* as possible during leash walking. Luring will keep him in position, but it interferes with his ability to think. Your goal is to get him to realize that walking in the desired reinforcement zone makes you *click!* the clicker and earns him a reward.

If your goal is a show-ring heel, continue to shape for a more precise position as previously described, until your dog will walk reliably with his shoulder in line with your leg. Then change your cue from "Let's walk!" to "Heel!" so your dog can distinguish between "now we're going for a relaxed stroll," and "now we're working for that perfect 200-point score."

The lure of the lure

Of course, it's not always that simple. There will be times when your dog forges ahead of you and tightens the leash, or stops to sniff something of interest as you walk past him. There are positive solutions for those challenges as well.

When you have to pass a very tempting distraction, use a lure, briefly, to get your dog past the distraction. Put a tasty treat at the end of his nose (the more tempting the distraction, the higher-value the treat must be)

and walk him past. As his polite walking behavior improves, your need for luring should diminish.

About face

Direction changes can be very useful in teaching polite leash walking. When your dog starts to move out in front of you, before he gets to the end of his leash, turn around and walk in the opposite direction.

Do this gently; you don't want him to hit the end of the leash with a jerk if he doesn't turn with you! As you turn, use a cheerful tone and a kissing noise to let him know you've changed direction. When he notices and turns to come with you, *click!* and offer a treat behind your left knee. He's now behind you, so you'll have ample opportunity to *click!* and treat while he's in the zone as he catches up to you.

> Commit to teaching your dog polite leash walking so you'll enjoy taking her more places and doing more things with her.
>
> Be consistent about reinforcing loose leash walking and *not* reinforcing leash pulling.
>
> Insist that everyone who walks your dog on leash follow the same procedures you use to properly reinforce polite leash walking.

An easy remedy for leash pulling

There will be times when your dog pulls ahead of you on a tight leash. This is a great opportunity to play "Be a tree." When the leash tightens, stop walking. Just stand still—like a tree—and wait. No cues or verbal corrections to your dog. Be sure to hug your leash arm to your side so he can't pull you forward.

Eventually, he'll wonder why his forward progress

has stopped, and look back at you to see why you're not coming. When he does, the leash will slacken. In that instant, *click!* and feed him a treat *behind your left knee.* The *click!* marks the loose leash behavior, and he'll have to return to the reinforcement zone to get the treat. Then move forward again, using a higher rate of reinforcement if necessary, until he's again walking politely with you.

Penalty yards

If "Be a tree" is not working, add "penalty yards." Your dog usually pulls to get somewhere—or to get to something. If he won't look back at you when you make like a tree, back up slowly—with gentle pressure on the leash, no jerking, so he's moving *farther* away from his goal. This is *negative punishment*—his pulling-on-leash behavior makes the good thing go farther away. When the leash slackens, *click!* and treat, or simply resume progress toward the good thing as his reward.

Go sniff!

Sniffing is a natural, normal dog behavior. If you *never* let your dog sniff, you're thwarting this hardwired behavior. He may become frustrated and aroused if he's constantly thwarted, so when you're doing polite walking together, you can sometimes give him permission to sniff.

If he stops to sniff, keep walking, putting gentle pressure on his leash to bring him with you, giving him a *click!* and treat as soon as he moves forward. When you know you're approaching a good sniffing spot, however, you can give him permission by saying "Go sniff!" Give him enough leash to reach the spot without pulling, even running forward with him if necessary. You can also use "Go sniff" as a reinforcer for a stretch of nice leash walking!

Proofing

Proofing is the process of solidifying polite leash-walking behavior in the presence of distractions. This works best with controlled distractions, starting at a distance where the temptation is not strong enough to compel your dog to investigate.

Practice his leash-walking behavior at a distance that works, then gradually bring the distraction closer. Increase the rate of reinforcement or the value of the reinforcer as needed, but try to avoid bringing the distraction so close you have to use a lure to get your dog past it. As you practice with various temptations at closer distances, your dog will learn to keep working with you and you'll be able to reduce the rate of reinforcement again.

It's up to you to decide whether you want your dog to walk politely on leash or heel precisely at your side. Dogs want good stuff, and they do what works to make it happen. If walking on a loose leash makes good stuff happen for your dog, the two of you will stroll happily side by side into the future together.

Behavior and Training

Oh, Baby!
Expecting a child? Don't wait until she arrives to work with your dog.

Even if children have never been a consideration for you, you should still strive to make sure your dogs are good with children. If you don't even have kids, why?

Because children exist.

Wherever you go in today's world, there are likely to be young humans. Unless you plan to keep your dog cloistered in your own home, shut away when friends with children visit, you need to help her be comfortable with children. Your dog's very life could depend on it.

At one time, our culture was far more tolerant of dog bites than it is today. Thirty years ago, if a dog bit a child, Mom's response was, "So, what did you do to Nipper to make him bite you?" Children were expected to learn how to respect a dog's space, and if Johnnie acquired a few nicks from a dog's teeth in the process, so be it. Today, one bite, even a minor nip, can be a death sentence for a dog. Of course, in the "old" days, Mom and Dad didn't risk losing their homeowner's insurance over a minor dog bite or two, either.

Children are the most frequent victims of dog bites in this country. That's no accident. From a dog's perspective, babies and children are weird; unpredictable; noisy; move erratically; make long, hard, direct eye contact; often cause pain; and don't respond appropriately to a dog's appeasement, deference, or self-defense signals.

Since most children aren't allowed to learn by experience that when a dog stiffens, growls, and curls his lip, the next thing that usually happens is a snap or bite, kids tend to be oblivious to the various levels and intensities of a dog's warning signals. No wonder dogs perceive children as threatening!

The best insurance against future dog bites to humans, young *and* old, is puppy socialization. If it's

If your adult dog was not well-socialized to babies and children when *she* was a puppy, start preparing her to live with a baby as soon as you know you are pregnant.

too late for puppy socialization, it's not too late to start playing catch-up with remedial socialization. If you already have a baby, are planning to have one soon, have distant plans for children, or don't ever intend to have human puppies, now's the time to start your personal kid-bite insurance program.

Puppy socialization time

Many young couples acquire a puppy early in the relationship, long before the advent of the first baby. The puppy is a surrogate child, and the couple dotes on him—taking him everywhere, allowing him to sleep on the furniture, even share the marriage bed. For several years the dog enjoys his status as an only child. The couple tends to socialize with other childless adults, and the dog rarely sees human babies. Then the couple decides it is time to have a baby. Now they have a problem.

Puppies go through a critical learning period in the first few months of their lives. During this time, usually between the ages of four weeks and four months, they learn which things in the world are safe and rewarding, which ones are painful and dangerous and should be avoided, and which have no consequence. Anything not experienced during this critical period tends to automatically fall into the "dangerous" category. Read the section on The Case for Kindergarten in chapter 1 on the importance of socializing and how to socialize your pup.

Adult-dog kid conditioning

Maybe it's too late to socialize your dog to babies and children during her critical learning period. Is it too late to teach her to live with children? Not necessarily.

If your dog's experiences with children up until now have been neutral and she's otherwise well-socialized, seek out gentle children and have them feed her treats. Watch her closely. If she seems cheerful and happy, continue to find opportunities for her to have positive experiences with kids.

If your dog is tense or nervous with children, take it more slowly. Let her see babies and kids at a distance, and *you* feed her treats. Select a very special treat, like steak or chicken, and feed it to her only in the presence of children and babies. When she notices a child in the distance, steak starts raining from the heavens—tiny tidbits, nonstop. When the child leaves, the flood of steak stops. Every time a child appears, the steak starts. When the child leaves, the steak stops. You want your dog to think that children and babies, and *only* children and babies, make steak happen.

When your dog looks at you happily for her steak when she sees a child in the distance, you know she's starting to perceive children as reliable predictors of steak. Your goal is to convince her to like them close up

as well, through the continued association with really wonderful food.

Gradually move closer to the children, repeating the exercise, always watching your dog's body language to be sure she's comfortable.

This is critical: *Never* punish your dog for showing signs of discomfort or even aggression, such as growling, when children are around. The growl is a critically important warning sign. It's your dog's way of telling us she's not comfortable around kids. If you punish her, she may learn to suppress the warning sign, making her far more likely to bite a child one day, severely and *without warning*.

Think about it: *You can't punish your dog into loving children!* You have to use positive conditioning and reinforcement to convince her that kids are good to have around.

The older your dog is, the longer she's been uncomfortable around children, and the stronger her response to them is, the longer this process (known as counter-conditioning and desensitization or CC&D) will take.

Of course, you'll always supervise her around children, even if she loves them. If your dog is merely tolerant of children, you'll have to supervise much

No matter how well they get along, you must actively supervise your children and dogs when they are together. Dogs can get scared or hurt by even a small child, and reflexively take defensive action.

If Dad plans to walk the dog while pushing the stroller, have him practice walking with an empty stroller long before he tries it with Baby on board. That way, he can concentrate on the dog, making a positive outcome far more likely.

more closely. If she's truly uncomfortable with them, you'll need to confine her in a safe place where children aren't permitted, such as her crate in your bedroom, whenever you cannot actively supervise their interactions.

Getting your dog ready for the new arrival

When a baby—and eventually a child—is coming to live at your house, your task is more daunting, *and* more vitally important. As soon as you know Baby's on the way, start helping your dog get ready.

Whatever changes are going to occur in her routine should happen long before Baby arrives, so she won't associate them with the arrival of the new family member. Ideally, you'll keep her as much of a full-fledged member of the family as she is now, finding ways to incorporate her presence into your daily baby routine rather than excluding her.

Here are some suggestions for helping the baby's introduction to the family positive for your dog:

- **The nursery:** If this is now the dog's room, don't wait until the final countdown to repaint and restrict her access to it. Redecorate as far in advance as possible. Put a soft cushion for your dog in one corner of the room and teach her a "Go to your bed" exercise. Whenever you're puttering in the nursery, reinforce her with treats for lying there quietly. You can give her a food-stuffed Kong there. When you're not in the room, use a baby gate across the doorway to keep your dog out.

- **Restricted access:** If you plan to restrict your dog's access to other rooms after the baby is born, do it now, using baby gates and closed doors, and positive reinforcement to reward her for staying in approved areas. Try to allow her access to as much of the home as possible.

- **Your dog's routine:** Anticipate any changes in your routine that will change your dog's. If Mom walks her three times a day and Dad will be taking over dog walking for a while, start making that switch now. If Dad will become your dog's primary caretaker, have him assume those duties as soon as possible. Plan to include Baby's presence in as many of your dog's activities as possible, so she thinks Baby makes all the fun stuff happen.

  If you intend to hire a pet sitter to provide some dog care, integrate him or her into the routine several months before Baby arrives. If Mom plans to walk the dog while pushing the stroller, practice this while Mom is still active and agile, so she can figure out the logistics of managing leash, dog, and stroller without tipping Baby onto the sidewalk. In fact, if your dog doesn't already have good leash manners, start training immediately by standing still when she pulls on the leash and consistently rewarding her for walking with you.

- **Greetings:** If your dog hasn't already learned how to greet people politely, give yourself several months to teach and reinforce polite greetings.

Reward her with treats and attention for sitting in front of you. If she jumps up, turn your back and step away from her. Be consistent! If you sometimes reward her for jumping up, she won't understand that it's inappropriate to jump up when Mom or Dad's arms are full of Baby.

- **Doorways:** If your dog doesn't already know how to wait before going through a door, there's no time like now to teach her. You don't want her to knock over a pregnant Mom as she comes and goes, and you certainly don't want to worry about chasing an escaped dog down the street while Baby lies unattended on his blanket on the living room floor.

- **Leave it:** Teach your dog a positive "Leave it" cue so she'll happily respond (and be rewarded for it) when you ask her to stop kissing the baby, or to drop the pacifier that will inevitably fall on the floor.

- **Escape route:** Before you know it, Baby will be crawling around after your dog on the floor. Even dogs who love kids need a getaway plan. Provide your dog with an escape route, such as a low barrier she can jump over or an elevated surface she can jump on so she can escape from Baby's grasp when she's had enough. Show your dog how to use it, and practice until she's skilled at the maneuver. Dogs who are cornered by small tormenters without a way to escape may feel compelled to bite in self-defense.

Homecoming

When Baby arrives, your dog will be excited to see Mom after she's been away. The day before Mom and Baby come home, have Dad bring home a blanket that's been wrapped around Baby, to pick up his scent. Show the blanket to your dog. Let her sniff it, and feed her yummy treats. Then put the blanket in her bed. When Baby comes home the next day, his scent will already be familiar to your dog.

When you all get home, have Dad hold Baby outside while Mom goes in to greet your dog. If the dog forgets her polite greeting manners in her excitement, she won't hurt Baby, and she won't get yelled at. You don't want her first introduction to Baby to be negative! *Then* have Dad come in with Baby, while Mom has treats ready to reward the dog for greeting Dad and the human puppy nicely.

Rather than banishing the dog to the backyard while everyone settles in, encourage her to lie calmly on her rug, or if necessary, use a tether to keep her out of the midst of chaos until things calm down. Have Mom sit on the sofa with Baby while Dad rewards the dog's good behavior on her rug with treats, praise, and a Kong stuffed with irresistible goodies.

If you've done your homework well, your dog will soon love Baby as much as you do, and you'll have successfully set the stage for a long and happy relationship between your dog and your child.

The Value of Training the Kids

Junior's work with the family dog nurtures empathy, strengthens bonds.

One of the things that parents almost always say when they decide to add a dog to the family is, "It will help teach the kids about responsibility." That's the hope, anyway.

Those of us who are committed to teaching non-force, positive dog training see another important opportunity for growth that may arrive with the dog. Many pet dog trainers today are using modern, dog-friendly methods that teach students—children and adults alike—that it is *not* appropriate or necessary to use pain or physical force to make another creature to submit to their will. These trainers teach kids how much more powerful (and enjoyable) it is to use kindness, patience, and intellect to communicate and solve problems with their dogs.

Kids can learn a lot from participating in positive dog training—and you benefit because the dog will behave better, too.

Natural talent

Kids are not necessarily accustomed to being as competent as Mom and Dad. But dog training is one field where they can really shine, and even eclipse their parents' abilities.

While dedicated dog-loving kids can train their dogs to do just about anything dogs *can* do, they should start with the basics. The following are some easy exercises that will cultivate your child's ability and desire to build a positive relationship with the family dog.

Team-clicking: "Charging" the clicker

Kids love clickers. Many adult students hate the idea of training with a "gadget," but kids are sold from the first *click!* They can't wait to get their hands on that little plastic box and start clicking the dog. The toughest part is making them understand that the clicker is not a

Older kids can work together to "charge the clicker" (these boys are nine years old). You may have to assist a younger child in this task, where one of you clicks the clicker, and the other gives the dog a treat immediately afterward. Sally, a German Shorthair Pointer, quickly learns to look to Brendan for her treat every time Eli clicks the clicker.

toy—*every time they click the clicker, they have to give the dog a treat!*

With younger children (age three to seven) or kids who need work on impulse control, you can team-click: You *click!* the clicker, and they dole out the treats. If you have a canine youngster with needle-sharp puppy teeth, let your child do the clicking while you work on softening the puppy's bite, and have him drop treats on the floor when it's your turn to *click!* If your dog already knows how to take treats gently, you can take turns, with one of you on the clicker while the other one feeds treats from the hand. Older children can usually handle both tasks themselves, with some supervision from you.

Your child's first training exercise is "charging the clicker," known more formally as "conditioning the dog to the reward marker." This exercise simply teaches the dog that the sound of the clicker (or the word "Yes!" if you don't have access to a clicker) means that a treat is coming. It's the easiest exercise you will ever do, and a breeze for a kid.

One of you clicks the clicker. The other feeds the dog a treat. *Click!* Treat. *Click!* Treat.

Occasionally a dog is afraid of the click! *sound. In this case, you can use a softer marker, such as the* click *of a ball-point pen or your tongue. Kids are usually pretty good at tongue clicks!*

In this initial exercise, the dog doesn't have to do anything at all. The only caution is that you don't want to *click!* when your dog is doing an unwanted behavior, such as jumping up. Most dogs get the concept pretty quickly. You'll know when you see the dog's eyes light up and start looking for the treat the instant she hears the *click!* Let your child tell you when he

Michael lures Carly into a sit, then clicks the clicker and gives her a treat. At this stage, Michael does not say "Sit," he just waits for her to offer the behavior.

thinks your dog has it figured out—it will teach him to start watching and understanding the dog's body language, which is an important part of a successful canine-human relationship.

Sit happens

Your dog may start offering sits while the two of you are charging the clicker, especially if you remember to hold the treat up at your chest, because it is easier for her to sit and watch the treat than to crane her neck back while standing. Encourage your budding trainer to hold the treat up at his chest, while you look for opportunities to *click!* the dog when she happens to have her bottom on the ground. If you and your child consistently *click!* when the dog is sitting, she will eventually conclude that sitting *makes* the *click!* happen, and she will start sitting on purpose to make you *click!* the clicker. The next exercise, sit, will be a breeze for her to learn, because she's already doing it!

You will both need to remember not to ask your

Even after Carly seems to understand what she should do when someone says "Sit," she doesn't seem to get it when Brendan tells her to "Sit" when he himself is in a sitting position! Again, you may have to build "generalization" by backing up a step or two and repeating the process in each new setting. Brendan has to lure Carly into a sit a few times before she realizes "Sit" applies here, too.

If you have more than one kid—and especially if you have more than one dog!—you can hold fun training contests. Give a prize to whoever can get the dog to do the most sits and downs in one minute. Then switch dogs and hold the contest again (remember, in positive training, you want *everyone* to win!).

dog to "Sit" until she is already sitting. Novice trainers, including kids, forget that dogs aren't born knowing English. Just because you tell the dog to sit doesn't mean she will, and since you're not going to force her to sit, there's no point in wasting your breath. Instead, tell your child to wait for the dog to sit, or to help her sit by holding the treat to her nose and moving it back over her head, then *Click!* and treat when she does.

When the dog is sitting easily for your child, then he can start saying "Sit" *when the dog is already sitting*.

After the dog has had the opportunity to hear the word "Sit" a number of times *while sitting*—a dozen to two dozen times, perhaps, depending on how fast she learns—your child can say "Sit!" just *before* the dog sits, when he can tell by watching the dog's body language that she is about to plop her bottom on the ground to make the clicker go off. *Click!* and treat. At this point it may appear that the dog is sitting because your child asked her to, but in reality, she is sitting because she has been practicing this routine, and she knows if she sits when your child holds the treat up to his chest, it will make the clicker go off. Your dog probably doesn't understand the word yet—you may need to give her a little more help. If your child says "Sit!" and the dog doesn't do it, lure the dog into a sit by placing the treat in front of her nose and move it over her head. Remember that it doesn't help to keep repeating the word—you don't want to teach her that the cue for sit is "Sit! Sit! SIT!"

The general idea

When your dog can perform the "Sit" reliably for your child at home, take the pair of them to practice at other locations.

Dogs do not generalize well. That means that if you always work with your dog on "Sit" in the kitchen, three feet in front of the refrigerator, she may well conclude that "Sit!" means "Sit in the kitchen, three feet in front of the refrigerator." The first time your child asks your dog to sit in the living room, she may not do it, because there's no refrigerator there!

You will have to back up a step in training, and use the treat lure to show the dog that "Sit!" means "Sit wherever you are, not just in the kitchen." You can also teach her that "Sit" means "Sit by my side, sit when my back is toward you, sit when I am sitting on a chair, sit when I am lying on the floor." She also needs to learn that "Sit!" means "Sit when there are visitors in the house, sit when you see another dog, and sit even if a

Top 10 Reasons Why Your Child May Make a Better Trainer Than You

The following list includes a number of generalizations about normal, dog-loving kids and normal, kid-loving dogs. Little of what we present here is applicable to kids who don't like dogs or are deeply fearful of dogs, or dogs who are deeply fearful of children. If your dog and kids have relationship problems—if there is any aggression being perpetrated upon each other—we would suggest that you consult a professional, positive trainer to help you with socializing them.

Confident kids who love their dogs may be in the best position to accomplish training miracles with the family dog, thanks to:

1. **One word: Food!** *Most dogs recognize quickly that kids dispense treats at a very high rate of reinforcement. Kids are always eating, and they often drag their food around with them—in the car, on the sofa, in the yard, and so on. And they love to share! Even the tiniest toddlers quickly learn that dogs pay more attention to them when they are eating—and sharing. Trainers want their canine pupils to watch them, and to regard them as the source of delicious treats . . . so kids have that going for them without even thinking about it.*

2. **Kids are closer in size to dogs** *than adults, and therefore are less intimidating. Their faces are within licking range and their hands are closer, more likely to dole out petting. Dogs who are threatened by even a quiet, gentle adult towering over them will often regard even a pushy youngster as a trusted playmate.*

3. **Most kids have higher-pitched voices** *than adults, and they tend to speak with more animation. This elicits an excitement response in many dogs. In fact, adult trainers sometimes have to cultivate a high-pitched tone of voice to keep dogs playing the training game. Kids already have it!*

4. **Kids are more physically exciting** *to dogs. They are human kinetic wonders, moving unpredictably, wiggling and squirming, and they are just as likely to jump up and down as throw themselves on the floor. As a predatory species, dogs find movement irresistible; they automatically train their attention on things that move. (And face it: compared to kids, adults are boooo-ring!)*

5. **Kids are more likely to try to cajole or "trick" the dog into doing something than to physically force him** *(unless they have been exposed to people who use compulsive training). While their methods may be unorthodox—luring a reluctant dog into the car by waving their Beanie Baby at him, for example—they often have more success with the dog than Mom or Dad do. Many family dogs regard the adult as the "enforcer," the person who grabs the dog, puts the leash on, picks him up, or otherwise makes him do what he doesn't want to do. As a result, dogs tend to regard the kids as being "safer" to be around.*

6. **Kids have more time!** *We know that some kids are very busy, what with school, homework, soccer, and so on. But training is best accomplished in numerous, short sessions. Kids can ask the dog to perform a behavior, such as "sit," 20 or 30 times a day while they pour their cereal, brush their teeth, and tie their shoes. If they are packing their lunches or eating a snack, they can ask the dog to do a "down" or two in exchange for a few treats. Two-minute television commercial breaks are perfect opportunities to train the dog.*

7. **Kids can really relate to a dog's philosophy of life:** *"What's in it for me?" Explain it to them this way: "You know how much more fun it is to get a treat or a prize after you've done something good? That's how dogs are! And you know how bad you feel when you've done something really good and no one notices at all? Dogs feel like that, too!" Explained simply, most children will immediately appreciate the importance of praise and rewards for the dog.*

8. **Kids tend to be more observant of the dog's subtle body language than adults.** *Perhaps as*

a result of spending more "bonding" time with the dog (or maybe it's from watching thousands of hours of cartoon animals who are fully equipped with human attributes and powers of communication), it's often the kids who first notice that the dog is feeling sick. That he "smiles" when he's really happy. That he walks a certain way when he needs to go to the bathroom. Praise your child when she accurately assesses the dog's "message," and help her interpret the finer points of behavior.

Eli lures Sally into a down. Like many short-haired dogs with thin skin, Sally is reluctant to allow her body to come into contact with the concrete. Working on this behavior in a more comfortable location would improve her response.

For example, a dog who is feeling confused may turn his head away or lick his nose; a dog who really "gets" what you want him to do may bump you with his nose or paw to invite you to keep playing the game.

9. **Kids may handle the dog's "failures" better.** *Most kids are accustomed to feeling less effective than adults. Frequently, when adults can't get their dogs to do what they want, they get frustrated and sometimes even punitive. Kids are more accustomed to not being able to get others to do what they want; they tend to take it less seriously when the dog ignores their "orders." Teach your children to ignore the dog's "wrong" responses, and to focus chiefly on rewarding the dog for everything he does right. It will keep the dog's training on the fun, fast track. And speaking of fun . . .*

10. **All that dogs and kids want to do is have some fun.** *A love of play is something they share. Kids can capitalize on the fact that they are desirable playmates for the dog, and reward him for good behavior with a good romp. Conversely, when training turns into a long, boring chore, kids and dogs will bail. Remind your kids to keep their training sessions short and fun, and kids and dogs alike will continue to come running when you call, "Training time!"*

cat runs by." Then you will know that your dog *really* understands the word "Sit!"

Four-step training formula

You and your children just followed a four-step formula for teaching your dog "Sit." Guess what? Your budding trainers can follow the same steps for teaching your dog everything else they want to teach her:

1. Get the dog to do the behavior, using the treat to show her what you want, if necessary. *Click!* and treat when she does it.

2. Repeat Step 1 until she does the behavior easily.

Kids are closer in size to dogs than adults, and therefore are less intimidating. Their faces are within licking range and their hands are closer, more likely to dole out petting.

Then add the word you want to use to cue the behavior the instant she does it. *Click!* and treat.

3. When she has had time to hear the word in relation to the behavior, say the word just *before* she does the behavior, and then help her with the treat, if necessary.

4. As soon as she seems to have made the connection between the word and the behavior, help her generalize the behavior to other locations. Take the training crew to practice at parks, on walks around the block, in parking lots, and in stores that allow dogs. A good positive training class is another great place for your child to practice working with your dog around distractions.

Off Limits

10 steps to teach your dog to leave anything alone.

The "Off" exercise can be one of the most useful behaviors you can teach your dog.

"Off" means "Whatever you are paying attention to right now, I want you to leave it alone." It can be applied to the roast on the counter, the snacks on the coffee table, the dead skunk beside the trail, the neighbor's cat darting across the yard, or frail 93-year-old Aunt Martha. It's one of our favorite exercises for

Cynthia places some kibble under her foot and says "Off." Cayenne says, "No problem!"

Cynthia says "Yes!" and rewards Cayenne with a cube of hot dog from her hand.

Cayenne advances to the challenge of "hot dog on my paw." Cynthia has to cover it once.

When he looks away from the hot dog on his paw, Cynthia feeds Cayenne three other pieces.

Blue easily respects the "Off" cue when applied to food she shouldn't eat. But the ball-crazy Border Collie has a harder time "hearing" the cue when applied to a tennis ball.

Mardi holds the tennis ball firmly to the ground with her shoe. It's critical to wear shoes that offer protection from your dog's best efforts. Blue tries everything to dislodge the ball . . .

Finally Blue gives up. She takes a step backward and gives Mardi a quizzical look. Mardi says, "Yes!" and gives Blue a piece of tasty cooked chicken. The ball stays under her foot.

Mardi could have produced *another* ball and given it to Blue as a reward. But by using a treat, she ensures that Blue doesn't think she got the forbidden ball after all.

After several successes with the ball covered, then uncovered, Mardi moves farther away. She delivers the treat right to Blue's mouth when she says "Yes!", lest Blue dive for the ball.

Buoyed up by her successes (and the chicken), Blue ignores the ball even as she jogs past it. A "real-world" challenge might entail having a helper roll or bounce a ball past her.

watching a dog's brain at work as she grasps the concept of "leave it alone." Best of all, it's fun and easy. You can do the exercises all in one session if your dog is an "Off" whiz, or it may take several.

1. Hold up a highly desirable "forbidden treat object" such as a cube of freeze-dried liver so your dog can see it. When she shows interest, say "Off!" in a cheerful tone of voice and place the object on the floor. Be sure to use a pleasant tone, not an intimidating one. You are giving her information, not scaring her away from the treat.

2. Quickly, before she can grab it, cover the treat with your foot. Let her dig, claw, bite, and lick to her heart's content. Wear sturdy old shoes—do not do this with bare feet or sandals, or your shiny Sunday best. Do *not* repeat the "Off" cue. Just wait.

3. Sooner or later she will lose interest in the forbidden object, or be distracted. The *instant* she looks away from your foot, *click!* the clicker (or say "Yes!") and reward her with a treat *of equal value* from your hand. Do *not* feed her the treat under your foot.

4. If she eats the reward and immediately goes back to digging at your foot, wait until she looks away again, then *click!* and reward. Keep doing this until she is no longer paying any attention to the treat under your foot. Use a high rate of reinforcement (lots of clicks and treats) until she realizes that it is more profitable to "not look" at the treat under your foot.

5. If she eats the reward and does not immediately go back to your foot, *click!* and reward her so she quickly figures out she does not have to repeatedly try to get the object and then stop, in order to make the *click!* happen. Your goal is to get her to leave it alone completely, not keep going back to it.

6. After several repetitions, pick up the forbidden object, show it to her again, say "Off!" and place it on the floor, again covering it with your foot. Each time you start the exercise fresh by picking up the object and placing it on the floor, say "Off" one

time, and only one time. Do *not* keep repeating the "Off" cue if she keeps trying to get it from under your foot. You want her to understand that once you say "Off!" it means *forever.*

7. When she seems to understand that she should leave your foot alone, uncover the treat slightly. Be prepared to cover it again quickly with your foot if she dives for it! Keep clicking and rewarding her for looking away from it, until she will leave it alone even when it is uncovered. You will be amazed by how quickly she learns this.

8. As she becomes more reliable about leaving it alone with your protector foot nearby, gradually move farther away from the treat until you can stand three to four feet away and she still honors the "Off." Err on the side of caution; if she grabs the forbidden object, she will have been rewarded for the exact *opposite* of your behavior goal. If this happens, you must back up in the program and repair the damage.

9. When she is reliably honoring "Off" with you standing four feet away, attach the leash to her collar, set up the "Off" with the forbidden object on the floor, and move three feet off to one side. Keep the leash just barely taut but not tight, so you can restrain her if she moves toward the treat.

   Now call her to you. She should honor the "Off" cue and come to you rather than lunging forward to get the treat. When she does, *click!* and jackpot! (Give a handful of treats, one by one, as an extra big reward.) If she moves toward the treat, simply restrain her with the leash—don't say "No!" or repeat "Off." Just wait for her to give up and turn back to you. Then *click!* and treat.

10. Now you can apply this to real life. With your dog on leash, walk past piles of treats you have laid out on the floor, or other natural enticements, such as a bowl of chips on the coffee table. As soon as she makes eye contact with the enticement, say "Off" *one time* in a cheerful tone of voice and stand still, restraining her, with the leash short enough that

she can't reach the object. Wait until she gives up and turns back to look at you. *Click!* and reward.

Repeat until she understands that "Off" applies to real-life encounters. When she will reliably and routinely honor the "Off" cue without even tightening the leash, you are ready to try it off leash.

On your first off-leash attempt, use relatively boring enticements such as a pile of dry cookies, and be sure to have wonderful rewards to give her when she turns back toward you in response to your cue. Warm her up on leash, then take off the leash and give it a try. Be confident and visualize success, so you don't pause and tense up near the item, and she'll likely reward you with a perfect performance.

CHAPTER 3

Difficult Dogs

Living with a Difficult Dog
Coping strategies for when you get "more dog" than you bargained for.

"She's a wonderful dog at home. But I can't take her anywhere because she simply goes crazy when she sees another dog."

"I was asked to leave my agility class because my dog kept barking and lunging at the other dogs. We have to channel her energy somehow. What are we going to do now?"

"I just don't know if I should keep him. He's a great dog with us, but he's so wild around other animals and people. I'm afraid he'll hurt someone or get into a serious dog fight."

Does this sound like your dog? Every dog gets "wild" sometimes. But some of us live with dogs who exhibit difficult or wild behaviors every day.

It might help you to learn that many dogs who exhibit "difficult" behaviors such as hyperactivity, aggression, and destructive separation anxiety do so as a result of stress. The behaviors that we find so troublesome—barking, overenthusiastic greetings, dragging us around on leash, destructiveness—are all efforts by the dog to relieve his stress.

By your own standards, your dog's life may not seem all that stressful—after all, he doesn't have bills to pay, does he? But when you apply the more scientific definition of the word—anything that alarms or excites him, triggering his sympathetic nervous system into action and flooding him with the "fight or flight" chemicals adrenaline and noradrenaline—you may be

The Labrador Retriever in this photo is a good dog—affectionate, playful, and smart—but he's also a difficult dog. He jumps up, he whines and barks in the car, he pulls like crazy on leash, and he has no "recall" whatsoever.

able to see how many seemingly unrelated things in his environment actually contribute to his "misbehavior."

Again, the triggers could be anything the dog sees as exciting or threatening. For some dogs, this may be strange people or dogs. For others, visual stimulation such as the sight of squirrels or cars going by out the window could trigger stress. Auditory cues such as trains, sirens, or garbage trucks might set off their internal alarms. For emotionally needy dogs, being left home alone might trigger a stress reaction.

And imagine how difficult it must be not to act out in some physical way while being flooded with adrenaline.

There is hope

Dogs whose stress results in behavior issues like non-stop barking or even aggression are often labeled "difficult" dogs. Living with a difficult dog can be unpredictable and sometimes even frightening. Simple things—like friends or family coming to dinner, going for a walk in the neighborhood, even taking him to the vet—can be an ordeal.

There is hope. The answer may not be one single solution, but rather a holistic approach. By integrating a positive attitude, lifestyle changes, training, and behavior modification, life with a difficult dog can become much easier.

First, prevent emotional overload

Before implementing any training or behavior program with a difficult dog, you will need to figure out a short-term management plan to help prevent the emotional overload that leads to stressful outbursts. A stressed dog can't learn and a stressed person can't teach.

Management means controlling your dog's environment to the extent that he doesn't have the opportunity to become hyperreactive, anxious, or aggressive—at least long enough for you to help him learn new coping skills. Management may involve confinement, head halters, changing routines—anything to help prevent the dog from acting out. Remember, each time a dog has the opportunity to act out, he stands a good chance of being rewarded for doing so, increasing the likelihood that he will act out again in the future.

Consider this example: Muffin and her human companion are walking down the street. Muffin sees another dog coming her way. Perhaps Muffin is worried and unsure how to behave. She barks and lunges in hopes that the other dog will move away. The human companions of both dogs cooperate, by moving the dogs to opposite sides of the street. For Muffin, her

Adrenaline drives over-excited greetings like this; counter by ignoring the dog until he's calm.

When this dog is not allowed to pull away and explore a new environment, he vents his frustration by vocalizing loudly in a whiny howl. Asking him to perform some active tasks, such as spinning or catching a ball, will engage his brain *and* release nervous energy.

Focusing on the Positive

Changing your attitude about your dog is the first and possibly the most difficult step in developing a saner life together. It probably seems obvious that a positive outlook can make a huge difference. But when you live with a dog who sometimes behaves in a frightening way (like snarling at other dogs), it's hard to remember his wonderful qualities. It's also hard to have faith that things can and will get better.

Focus on your dog's good traits. Every dog has traits we see as positive and some we see as negative. By identifying your dog's good traits, you'll begin laying a foundation for strengthening those traits and bringing out the best in your dog. Try writing down all of your dog's good qualities. Post them on the refrigerator or somewhere else where you will see them often.

Take some time to reframe the negative traits, too. If your dog is overly protective and aggressive toward other dogs, it's easy to see her behavior as a "problem." However, think about your dog's breed or breed mix.

A cattle dog mix, for example, might see her family as her "flock" and keeping other dogs away might be her instinct-driven "job." A hyperactive nature, which is difficult to cope with in a small home with a small yard, would lend itself to endless hours of herding. Even her relentless hunting of small furry creatures (like rats, gophers, and squirrels) would most likely be appreciated in a rural setting where it is important to control the vermin population. Your difficult dog, in another setting, might be a prized dog!

Identifying the aspects of your dog's nature that are natural and normal can help you understand that your dog is not being bad—or even difficult—but just being true to her genetically inherited nature.

Of course, that doesn't mean you can just ignore these natural behavioral traits that present problems. But by looking at your dog's positive qualities, and reframing the challenging behaviors, it may be easier to appreciate who your dog is, and not expect her to be someone she isn't.

---

barking and lunging just successfully resulted in the other dog moving out of her space. While she may not have been given a single treat, Muffin was definitely rewarded for her behavior.

Of course, from the human perspective, if a dog is acting aggressively toward another dog while on a walk, crossing the street is a perfectly reasonable solution. So how can you avoid rewarding a dog like Muffin for aggressive behavior?

If possible, do not give her the opportunity or place her in a situation where she is likely to be aggressive. Hypervigilance on the part of Muffin's human companion could be the initial management strategy. By turning corners, walking the other way, or crossing the street when another dog came into sight, before Muffin had a chance to bark or lunge, Muffin's human could successfully prevent Muffin's angry outbursts. Walking her earlier in the day, before the prime dog-walking hours, could also help.

In addition, it would help to use a head halter on Muffin for all her walks so that her head could easily be turned away when she did see other dogs.

Train for the brain

According to James O'Heare, executive director of the Academy of Canine Behavioral Theory, the best strategy to get a dog through a stressful event is to focus the dog's attention on a specific cognitive task. In other words, give him something to do—engage his brain. A dog whose brain is engaged is much less likely to react emotionally in any given situation. (Conversely, a dog who is in an emotional state generally cannot think or focus on a specific task.)

Teaching a dog an incompatible behavior is one of the first courses of action and will help both in physically managing the dog and with gradually

It's Important to Rule Out Physical Causes

When dealing with any behavioral issue, it is always a good idea to consider possible medical conditions that could contribute. You may want to consult with a veterinarian and/or a veterinary behaviorist.

- **Thyroid problems** *can be a factor in dogs who exhibit aggressive behavior. In one study of more than 600 dogs with behavior problems, thyroid dysfunction was found in 62 percent of the aggressive dogs. The seasonal effects of allergies to grass, fleas, or other substances can also contribute to behavior issues. Pain of any sort can contribute to stress and the related acting-out behaviors. Certain medications have side effects that influence behavior.*

- **Diet** *may impact how your dog acts. Sensitivities to foods or food allergies certainly contribute to behavior issues. Eliminating certain grains, raising or lowering protein levels, increasing or decreasing carbohydrates, feeding fresh cooked or raw diets—all lay claim to helping both a dog's health and behavior. Talking about your dog, his issues, and his diet with a knowledgeable veterinary nutritionist or behaviorist may help you determine if dietary changes will make a difference.*

- **Consider the serotonin connection.** *Serotonin is a chemical in the brains of dogs (and people) that affects moods. According to James O'Heare, executive director of the Academy of Canine Behavioral Theory and the author of several books including* Canine Neuropsychology *and* The Canine Aggression Workbook, *serotonin deficiency or inactivity has been linked to hyperactivity, aggression, and general anxiety disorder in dogs. O'Heare believes for dogs with low serotonin, increasing serotonin levels in the brain may significantly help stress, anxiety, and*

aggression issues. Antidepressant drugs—such as Prozac, Clomicalm, and Elavil—are one option, and may be particularly effective when used in conjunction with behavior modification. But they do pose the risk of serious side effects.

- **Boost dietary tryptophan.** *Certain changes in the diet may boost the level of tryptophan, an amino acid that helps the body use serotonin. Those changes ideally would include eliminating all corn from the dog's diet because corn's high level of another amino acid, tyrosine, works as a sort of anti-triptophan. In addition, giving a dog pure carbohydrate meals (like rice and vegetables) with Vitamin B6 within two hours of a small serving of kibble may help increase serotonin.*

- **Consider nutritional supplements.** *Supplementing with the amino acid tryptophan (which is marketed as ProQuiet, and can be ordered through a veterinarian) can help the body synthesize serotonin, and thus increase serotonin levels in the brain. The over-the-counter supplement 5-HTP (available in health food stores) also aids in serotonin synthesis and may be an alternative to tryptophan. Talk with a knowledgeable behaviorist or veterinarian about how much to give your dog if you consider using one of these supplements.*

- **Exercise to reduce stress.** *A well-exercised dog is always a better-behaved dog. But daily endurance-type exercise—such as 15 minutes or more of trotting or swimming—can also help raise serotonin levels in the body. In addition, endurance exercise stimulates the body to release endorphins, which contribute to an overall lower stress level. Endurance exercises may produce better results than short, explosive exercises like playing ball, as these may actually produce a stress response.*

desensitizing him to the stimulus that sets him off. For example, teaching your dog to watch you while heeling can be a terrific management tool for dogs with compulsive greeting problems or on-leash aggression. If the dog is watching you, he can't lunge at that other dog!

In addition, develop a repertoire of fun and engaging behaviors to help your dog de-stress. These should not be control exercises, but rather, active behaviors that are strictly for fun and play. For some dogs, catch games with a ball or toy work very well to de-stress. Use these fun activities to help your dog unwind after a stressful event.

For example, if you are walking down the street and pass a strange dog, have your dog heel and watch you, keeping her engaged and offering plenty of great treats until you are well past the other dog. Then, let loose with a few fun games to help you both let go of any residual stress. Are there specific behaviors your dog does well and enjoys doing? Make the behaviors you love in your dog the highlight of your training. This can, in and of itself, help defuse stress-related behavior.

Coping strategies for unexpected events

For those of us who live with dogs that have problems with stress-related "bad" behavior, the best strategy is to avoid situations that our dogs cannot handle while working on training and behavior modification. But in the real world, we aren't always completely in control of our environment. What can you do, in the moment, when you are caught off guard?

First, if your dog has not reacted yet, engage him! Have him sit, down, heel, spin, shake hands—pretty much any easy trick that will keep his mind busy and keep you tossing treats, rapid-fire, in his direction. If you can keep him engaged, he may not become emotional. If you feel yourself losing his engagement, get yourself and your dog out of the situation as quickly as you can.

If he is already reactive—no longer responding to you or your cues—increase the distance between your dog and his trigger. Turn around and walk the opposite way, as fast as you can. Move far enough away from the "prompt" that triggers your dog's stress until he (and you!) visibly calms down.

This can be a difficult thing for many people. In stressful situations, humans often want to stop and make their dogs behave. This absolutely will not work once the dog's emotional response is activated. You must create enough distance from the stress trigger to enable your dog to "think" rather than react.

Finally, imagine the most common "caught off guard" situations, and then plan and practice what you will do if you are ever caught in those situations. This will help you both "automatically" do the right thing when the unexpected happens. Remember, asking your dog to do an "active" behavior (such as spins, shaking hands, high-five) is better than a "control" behavior (sit, down, or stay). And be prepared to give your dog a huge jackpot of tasty rewards any time he does manage to keep cool and remain attentive to you in the face of an unexpected trigger.

Demolition Dogs
Don't get mad when your dog destroys your stuff; get busy!

You arrive home from work, dreading what you are going to find. Your fears are realized as you walk through the door and discover tufts of sofa-cushion stuffing scattered in snow-like drifts across your living room floor. Your 10-month-old Border Collie, Darby, grovels at your feet, obviously aware that she's been a very bad dog. You knew she was going to get even with you for leaving her home alone all day. Right?

Wrong!

Owners often misunderstand their dogs' motives for destructive behavior and misinterpret their dogs' responses when the damage is discovered. The result of this lack of understanding is often the inappropriate application of verbal and/or physical punishment, which, ironically, can make the problem even worse.

Dogs are normally destructive for one or more of five reasons, none of which involve spite, malice, or "getting even." The five reasons are:

1. **Stress:** Physical activity relieves stress. A stressed human may pace the floor, go jogging, chew her fingernails, or tap a pencil on the table or a foot on the floor. Chewing, digging, and other destructive behaviors are stress relievers for dogs. Stress-related destructive behavior can be relatively mild, or can turn into full-blown separation anxiety.

2. **Teething:** A young dog can be in mild to somewhat severe discomfort when his new teeth are pushing through the gums, and until they are fully emerged at 18 to 24 months. Chewing helps relieve teething pain, which is one of the reasons puppies and adolescent dogs are such dedicated chewers.

3. **High jinks:** Dogs explore the world with their mouths, and young dogs are particularly driven to explore the world around them, as so much of it is new and exciting. Does this taste good? Does this feel good? Is this fun to play with? In addition, puppies and juveniles tend to have high energy levels,

and sometimes go on a rampage in a burst of feel-good energy, similar to a teenager who trashes the house with a keg party when his parents unwisely leave him home alone for a weekend.

4. **Boredom:** Busy dogs need something to do. The herding breeds especially can be workaholics; if you don't give them a job, they'll create one, and it may not be one that meets with your approval.

5. **Habit:** If a dog is poorly managed and allowed to repeatedly engage in destructive behavior during his formative months (the first one to two years) he may develop destructive behavior habits that can continue throughout his life. In contrast, if he is well managed for his first two years, he is unlikely to pick up destructive behaviors later in life—unless his environment changes drastically and causes him undue stress.

Not guilty

Whatever the underlying cause of your dog's destructive behavior, it's important to realize that dogs don't do things out of spite. Their brains simply don't work that way.

When you come home to a dog-trashed house and your dog grovels at your feet, the most likely explanation is that she can see by your body language that you're upset, and offers deferent signals—ears back, submissive grin, crawling on the floor, rolling on her back—in an attempt to divert your wrath away from her. She doesn't know why you're upset, but she can tell that you're about to be dangerous.

Even if you haven't seen the damage yet, your tension over the anticipated destruction you might find could well be enough to induce her to go belly-up, especially if she is a "soft," non-assertive dog.

If you are convinced your dog "knows" he is guilty

of wrongdoing when he gets into the garbage, try this experiment: Strew trash around the kitchen yourself, out of your dog's sight. Then let him into the kitchen and ask him if he made the mess. Chances are he'll display his classic "guilty" behaviors, even though he had nothing to do with the garbage on the floor.

Self-control

It's understandable to feel frustrated and angry if you come home after a hard day at work to a house that looks like it's been hit by a tornado. However, any punishment you issue at this point is totally useless and ineffective in altering your dog's behavior. She probably ripped up the sofa cushions hours ago. Dirty looks and stern words may make you feel better in the moment, but will do nothing to change your dog's behavior, other than teaching her to associate your return home with bad stuff.

Physical punishment is inappropriate. If you're going to use it (which we don't suggest) it must happen within a few seconds of the undesirable behavior in order for the dog to be able to make the connection. You can't do that when the behavior occurred hours earlier.

At worst, you might calmly invite Darby into her crate so she is out of harm's way while you clean up the mess and vent your wrath with broom and mop on the unfeeling kitchen floor.

Tame the tornado

The solution to Darby's destructive behavior is management, not punishment. As always, prevention is far simpler than cure, so crate training is an invaluable puppy lesson that can help your dog avoid destruction that arises from stress, teething, and high jinks, and can prevent her from having the opportunity to develop destructive habits.

If you missed the opportunity to crate-train your dog as a pup, it may not be too late. Many adult dogs can easily learn to love their crates. It may take your adult dog longer to accept the crate than a puppy, but if you take the time to convince her that the crate is a wonderful place to be, she will probably decide that being crated is okay. (See Crate Training Made Easy in chapter 2 for more on using a crate.)

There are exceptions. Many dogs with separation anxiety (SA) cannot tolerate being crated—the confinement causes them to panic, and they often injure themselves in their desperate and sometimes successful attempts to escape. If your dog is easily stressed but not displaying classic signs of SA, be extra careful about not adding to her stress with forceful crating techniques. In addition, any displays of your displeasure can move a moderately stressed dog toward the "full-blown" end of the SA scale.

Some adult dogs who don't suffer from anxiety are also unwilling to experience the joys of crating. Options for destructive dogs who can't be crated include dog-proofing a room or kennel run for her to stay in where she can't do damage; taking her to a doggie daycare center; or leaving her in the custody of a friend, neighbor, or family member who is home all day and willing to dog sit. Some lucky owners are able to take their dogs to work with them. If you are one of these, be sure to supervise your canine shark closely at work so she doesn't destroy things at the office—or you may lose your dog privileges.

Spending all day alone is a scary thing for dogs, who are genetically programmed to seek comfort and security in a "pack" of family members. Problem behaviors such as chewing and digging are effective methods of relieving the stress of being alone.

Dogs with SA can often be helped with behavior modification in combination with Clomicalm, a drug used to lower their stress levels and help them be more able to cope. Check with your behavior consultant and/or veterinarian if you think this might be appropriate for your dog.

Work it out

Along with management, exercise can be an important element of your destruction reduction program. Exercise reduces stress and eliminates one of the primary causes of high jinks behavior—those high energy levels. Even teething and habit-related chewing can be diminished with a good exercise program. A tired dog is a well-behaved dog.

Structured exercise of some kind is best; it keeps the dog focused and minimizes out-of-control arousal. Play fetch with a ball, toy, stick, or Frisbee, and require that she sit politely each time before you throw. Play tug of war, and insist that she play by the rules, which include that she give the tug toy to you when requested, and not grab it again until invited.

Remember that a walk around the block on leash is not sufficient exercise for any young dog; it's a mere exercise hors d'oeuvre. Try a long hike in the hills—off leash if legal and your dog is under control, and on a long line if he's not yet ready for off-leash hikes. As you watch your dog run circles around you, you'll realize why a leashed walk barely puts a dent in his energy. Other people may find it's easier to find a professional dog walker to exercise and thoroughly tire out the dog. Some dog walkers offer half- or full-day outings to the beach or other open spaces.

Mind games

Boredom chewing can often be resolved by giving the dog something to do. Create games that will exercise her mind. The Buster Cube and the Roll-A-Treat Ball,

available from most pet supply stores and catalogs, are perfect for this. You place treats inside the ball or cube, and your dog must push the object around the room to make the treats fall out.

Training is another way to exercise your dog's brain. A good positive training class makes dogs think, and they have to think hard. Dogs generally come home from a training class and sleep like logs—and then you practice at home all week, encouraging him to work that brain every day. If you are looking for fun training ideas, purchase a copy of the game My Dog Can Do That, which will keep you and your dog occupied for hours on end learning creative new behaviors.

"Find It" is another great brain game to play. Before you leave, hide treats all over the house, in reasonably easy-to-reach places. Don't hide them under the sofa cushions or in other in places that will encourage your dog to dig or chew—you're trying to make that behavior go away, remember? Your dog can spend hours looking for all the treats!

Final tips

If your dog is under the age of two and still doing teething-related chewing, you'll be wise to keep valuable objects out of her reach and supply her with plenty of chewable objects. A stuffed Kong is a good choice. Even adult dogs enjoy a good chew now and then, so keep that Kong around—or several, if you have a multi-dog household.

If destructive behavior happens while you are home with your dog, you need to ratchet up your supervision program so she doesn't have the opportunity to get into things she shouldn't. Crates, leashes, tethers, and baby gates are all useful management tools.

There are lots of Demolition Darbys out there. With good management, your dog doesn't need to be one of them.

Canine Social Misfits

For their own safety and for yours, dogs need to be exposed—early and often—to a variety of "outside world" experiences.

Dogs aren't born full-fledged "man's best friends." As with all baby animals, there is a period of time in their lives when they must learn about the world in order to survive. This critical period is a window of opportunity for socialization—a time when puppies learn what is safe and good and what is not. Opinions differ as to how long the window is open, but it falls somewhere in the period between 4 and 20 weeks. After the window closes, anything not previously identified as safe will automatically fall into the unsafe category. Dogs must be socialized to the human world during this time, or they will forever be fearful of—or, at the very least, anxious about—new people, sights and sounds.

Dogs who are well socialized receive lots of gentle human contact and handling from the time their eyes open on into adulthood. Guide Dogs For The Blind and other service dog organizations who must produce the calmest, most socialized dogs possible send their puppies to live with 4-H families, where the participants try to take their service puppies with them everywhere they go. As they get older (8 to 20 weeks) they are given careful exposure to other stimuli, such as visits to the vet hospital and groomer; walks in town; rides on elevators and escalators; sounds of cars; motorcycles and skateboards; people of different ages, sexes, and ethnicities; people who dress, talk and move in strange ways; people with umbrellas, crutches, and wheelchairs.

Dogs that are raised outside and/or with little contact with a wide variety of humans and human experiences may always be anxious and fearful with people.

Proof positive

Have you ever marveled at the ability of service dogs to remain calm and responsive to their handlers' requests in the midst of a noisy, bustling environment? Then you have witnessed proof that such a thorough, positive exposure to the outside world really does result in a more confident and well-adjusted dog, and one who will easily accept new stimuli, even without prior exposure to that specific experience.

Unfortunately, there are many poorly socialized dogs around us. Some of them are the result of benign neglect—dogs whose owners didn't anticipate the need for them to be socialized (such as routine or emergency medical care, or even emergency re-homing, if something happened to their caregivers).

Look for people of every description to help you socialize your dog. This wise owner recruited well-mannered kids to feed his dog some treats, thus helping her associate kids with "good things."

Most unsocialized dogs are ordinary dogs whose owners simply never knew about or bothered with this important aspect of their dog's care and training, such as dogs who live with elderly people and freak out and bite when the grandchildren visit, or dogs whose families raise them in the country and then move to the city, where they overreact to the bustle of urban life and the neighbors complain about their incessant barking. An unsocialized dog is a canine social misfit, and a tragic story waiting to happen.

An ounce of prevention

The easiest way to avoid this problem, as with most serious dog behavior challenges, is through prevention. While your veterinarian, concerned about diseases, may caution you against exposing your new puppy to the real world, failure to do so can result in a poorly socialized adult dog. And, in the long term, lack of socialization can be a bigger threat to your puppy's well-being than the risk of disease.

The answer to this dilemma is to expose a properly vaccinated young dog to a controlled social environment. Take her to a well-run puppy class, where she can meet lots of different people and lots of healthy puppies. Invite friends of all ages and races over and have them dress up in odd clothes, hats, umbrellas, or sunglasses. Invite children over to play gently with her and to feed her treats.

The more positive encounters a dog experiences while her socialization window is open, the more well-adjusted, confident, and gregarious she will be as an adult.

A positive pound of cure

But wait, you say: I'm the owner of an unsocialized adult dog. Don't despair. Frequently, steps can be taken to make the world a less terrifying place for unsocialized dogs. The quality of their lives can be improved with desensitization, and with training that gives them confidence and helps them make sense of the world around them. It takes a lot of work and a patient owner, but it can be done.

It should come as no surprise that the methods used to rehabilitate an unsocialized dog must be posi-

The goal: Happy, friendly, confident dogs that you can take anywhere, anytime.

tive ones. It's important to always remember that your unsocialized dog is not acting out of spite or malice. She is truly afraid, even terrified, of the things that she reacts to. Don't blame her. It's not her fault. Be patient, and help her to learn slowly that the world is not such a frightening place after all.

Progress is slow in the best of circumstances, and once she starts taking tentative steps to emerge from her shell, the tiniest correction can send her scurrying back to safety. Each dog will progress at her own pace. Pushing an unsocialized dog too quickly can destroy weeks, even months, of painstaking progress.

Here are the steps to take to encourage courage in an unsocialized canine:

1. **Teach your dog "a bridge," or reward marker.** A bridge is a word or a sound that tells your dog that she has earned a reward. The clicker, a small plastic box that makes a clicking sound when pressed, is often used as the bridge in dog training. Your unsocialized dog may be sound sensitive. If so, you may want to start with a one-syllable bridge word, such as "Yes!" instead of the clicker. "Good dog!" is not a good choice for a reward marker. It's too long. A dog can do several behaviors during the time it takes to say two syllables. Which one is getting rewarded? Besides, we tend to say "Good dog!" to our dogs all the time just because we love them. We need a marker that only means "a reward is coming."

To teach your Timid Tess the bridge, just say "Yes!" (or *click!* the clicker if she tolerates the sound), and immediately feed her a small but very tasty treat. She doesn't have to do anything special to get the "Yes!" and treat at first, but do try to avoid marking and treating if she is doing something you don't want her to do, like jumping on you.

If Tess is unsocialized even to you and won't come close enough to eat treats out of your hand, you can toss the treats to her at a distance or scatter treats all over the ground, and say "Yes!" or *click!*

every time she picks one up. Once she knows that the marker means "Treat!" you can, for the rest of her life, *click!* (or "Yes!") and treat her every time she does something good; this will reinforce that behavior and increase the likelihood that she will do it again.

> ## Don't "protect" the dog
>
> *You must avoid coddling your skittish dog through this process. As tempting as it may be, do not allow yourself to coddle and comfort her. You will be rewarding and reinforcing timid behavior, not giving her confidence, like you might think. If you act concerned, she will be even more convinced that there is something to be afraid of. You'll do better to act matter-of-fact, jolly her up, and let her know there's nothing wrong. The target object works really well in place of coddling.*

2. **Reward-mark her entire meal.** Let this be the only way Tess gets to eat—by being in your company and eventually, when she's brave enough, by eating out of your hand. She needs to learn that you are the source of all good things. Reward-marking won't work as well for a free-roaming feral dog—she will have access to other food sources and won't have to tolerate your presence to find food. *Please note—we absolutely do not advocate starving a dog in order to get her to take food from you.* You will need to find an environment where Tess feels comfortable eating in your presence—if necessary, a large enough room or yard that she can be fairly far away from you at first while she picks up treats off the ground and gets marked.

3. **Reward-mark her for calm behavior around others.** Once Tess knows that the bridge means "Treat!" you can "Yes!" or *click!* and treat anytime she is being brave. If she is normally afraid of children and she sits quietly next to you on a park bench while a child walks by, "Yes!" and reward. Look for

very small, rewardable behaviors. If she glances at a child and doesn't react, "Yes!" and reward.

4. **Make a list of her fear triggers.** You probably have a good idea of what things frighten Tess. These are her "fear triggers." Make a list, and include everything you can think of. Ask other family members to help. Then prioritize your list. Now decide which trigger you want to start with in her desensitization program. Start with something achievable. For your dog's sake and for yours, it's important to have small successes throughout the process. You might need to take a big trigger and figure out how to break it down into smaller pieces.

For example: if her Number 1 Trigger is tall men with beards and cowboy hats, you might start with tall, clean-shaven men. Start leaving cowboy hats around the house in conspicuous places, and occasionally put one on yourself. Other family members and people who are well-liked by Tess can do the same. Once she accepts tall men, you can advance to clean-shaven tall men with cowboy hats. Meanwhile, work at desensitizing her to short men with beards. Then try tall men with beards without cowboy hats. When you have desensitized her to all of the pieces, then you can finally put them together as tall men with beards wearing cowboy hats.

This takes time and patience. If you skip steps you may undo all of your painstaking training progress and have to start over.

5. **Use counter-conditioning and desensitization.** Desensitization is the process of gradually acclimating a dog to the things she is afraid of. Counter-conditioning means replacing her undesirable reaction—fear—with a more desirable one that is incompatible with fear, such as the eager anticipation of a tasty treat.

Let's say Tess is afraid of strangers. Since we can't control a stranger's behavior, we need to create a stranger who will work with us. Get a friend whom Tess does not know to act as your stranger, and brief him ahead of time. Set up a system of simple hand signals so you can let him know if you want him to stay where he is, come closer, go farther away, or move to the side. If your dog's fear threshold is 30 feet—that is, if she starts acting stressed or scared when strangers are 30 feet away—start with your stranger at 35 feet.

In order for desensitization and counter-conditioning to work you need to be very good at recognizing your dog's signs of stress. The book On Talking Terms With Dogs: Calming Signals, by author Turid Rugaas, is an excellent resource for learning how to read your dog's body language signals.

You should be sitting comfortably, with Tess on a leash next to you in a controlled environment. You don't want some real stranger to wander through and mess up your carefully staged training session. While your dog is calm about the stranger's presence just beyond her threshold, feed her lots of tasty teats. Handfuls! Then have your stranger gradually move closer . . . very gradually . . . a few inches at a time if necessary.

It helps if your "stranger" is talented enough to act natural, not be furtive or suspicious. Also, he should avoid making any eye contact with the dog. A direct stare is a threat in canine body language, and is especially threatening to a dog who is already stressed.

If the dog starts to get nervous at 29 feet, signal the stranger to stop. Feed Tess more treats until she relaxes, and then end the session. Have the stranger walk away (another huge reward for Tess's good behavior). Schedule another session for the next day.

During the second session you might have your stranger move laterally at a distance of 29 feet to vary the experience. If Tess continues to stay relaxed as the stranger moves around and approaches, give her lots of rewards and stop the session at a reasonable distance before she gets stressed. Don't push it. Success in slow increments is the key. You want Tess to know that the presence of strangers makes good things (lots of treats) happen.

6. **Reward-mark while others feed treats.** If Tess is more tolerant of people than in the scenario described in Step 2, you can have other people feed her treats when you reward-mark, or they can reward-mark and treat. The ultimate goal is to have Tess believe that people are safe and good, not scary and dangerous. The more she will accept treats from others, the more she can associate them with good things, not just you.

7. **Teach her to target.** "Targeting" is teaching your dog to touch a target with her nose on cue. It's easy to do, and it's a great confidence builder for timid dogs.

To start, hold a target object—such as your hand, a pencil, or a short (two- to three-foot) dowel—in front of you. Use something that won't frighten her. When she touches it with her nose, *click!* or say "Yes!" and feed her a treat. (If she won't touch it, rub a meaty-flavored treat on it so it smells irresistible.) When she is eagerly touching the target, add the cue word "Touch!" as she does it. Continue to *click!* and treat. In short order she will be eager to touch the target when you ask her to.

Dogs love this exercise. It's like a treat vending machine—they push the button, they get a treat. By placing the target, which they love, near something that they are leery of, you can get them to approach the scary object. When they get clicked and treated for touching the target near the object, they soon decide that the scary thing isn't so bad.

Obsessive-Compulsive Dogs
Hope for dogs who display repetitive (and often self-destructive) behavior.

There are a number of repetitive behavior syndromes from which dogs may suffer. One is fly-snapping, when a dog compulsively snaps the air until driven into a frenzy. Other such behaviors include spinning, tail-chasing, freezing in a particular position or location, self-mutilation (biting or licking), and flank-sucking. Some behaviorists also include pica—the ingestion of inedible objects such as rocks, sticks, socks, and who knows what else—in the compulsion syndrome family.

While these behaviors are very similar to the condition known as obsessive-compulsive disorder in humans, many behaviorists believe that the term canine compulsive disorder is more appropriate to describe the behaviors in dogs.

In human psychology, obsessions are persistent, intrusive thoughts that cause extreme anxiety and that the patient tries to suppress or ignore. Compulsions are repetitive behaviors that the patient performs in order to prevent or reduce the anxiety. Behaviorists argue that because we don't know whether dogs actually have obsessive thoughts (although Border Collie owners could argue this!), we should omit the word "obsessive" and use the term "canine compulsive disorder" (CCD) to describe the syndrome in dogs.

Clinical signs, causes, and treatment

Very little research has been done into CCD—much of what we know about the syndrome is based on anecdotal evidence, and even that is relatively rare. The primary cause is believed to be a situation of conflict or frustration to which the dog must try to adapt. The disorder often begins as a normal, adaptive response to the conflict or frustration. Eventually the response

Given the opportunity, this Jack Russell Terrier would spend hours each day compulsively licking his favorite toys. His eyes glaze over, he drools, and he loses interest in all other activities.

becomes removed from the original stimulus and occurs whenever the dog's stress or arousal level exceeds a critical threshold.

Strong evidence exists that genetics play a role in at least some compulsive behaviors. There is a higher-than-average incidence of tail-chasing in Bull Terriers and German Shepherd Dogs, fly-snapping in Cavalier King Charles Spaniels, and excessive licking (acral lick dermatitis) to the point of causing a lesion (lick granuloma) in many large breeds, including the Doberman Pinscher, Golden Retriever, Labrador Retriever, and German Shepherd Dog. Flank-sucking is an often-seen compulsive behavior in Dobermans as well.

Trainers and behaviorists suspect that CCD is probably underdiagnosed, as very few veterinary schools give their students thorough training in animal behavior, and many owners don't recognize or don't report compulsive behaviors. A behavior falls into the compulsive category when it becomes a stereotypy—a repetitive and unvarying pattern of behavior that serves no obvious purpose in the context in which it is performed. Compulsive behaviors often evoke a

Know your dog. Chasing soap bubbles helps this energetic JRT burn off excess energy, but she calms down afterward and does not persist in running or snapping. Other, more compulsive dogs might generalize this behavior into snapping at imaginary bubbles or repetitive spinning—without any bubbles present.

response from the owner, and thus may be unwittingly reinforced as a result.

Treatment program

Treatment consists of both environmental and behavioral modification, and, often, pharmacological intervention. Here are 10 steps to a successful treatment program:

1. Intervene as early as possible.
2. Have your veterinarian conduct a complete physical examination and evaluation to identify and eliminate any medical conditions that may be contributing to or causing the behavior.
3. Identify and, if possible, remove the cause or causes of the dog's stress, conflict, or frustration.
4. Avoid rewarding the compulsive behavior. Remember, it can be rewarding for the dog simply to have his owner pay attention to him.
5. Eliminate any punishment as a response to the compulsive behavior.
6. Provide sufficient exercise on a regular schedule.
7. Consult with an alternative practitioner to apply alternative modalities—such as massage techniques, herbal therapies, acupressure, and acupuncture—to help relieve the dog's stress.

CCD has been shown to have a genetic component. Compulsive fly-snapping is found in a number of Cavalier King Charles Spaniel families.

Conflict and Frustration

Certain environmental conditions are known to contribute to the development of stereotypic behaviors in dogs, especially those who are otherwise already predisposed to compulsive disorders. These include:

- **Physical restraint:** *Dogs who are kept in the very stressful environment of a shelter or kennel for extended periods of time often begin spinning in their kennels, many of them to a very marked degree. This compulsive behavior may or may not diminish when the dog is removed from the kennel and placed in or returned to a calm home environment. Constant chaining or confinement in the home can also elicit spinning and other CCDs, especially when the dog is constantly stimulated by the environment.*

- **Stimulation with inappropriate toys or activities:** *Some people find it amusing—at first—when dogs display certain repetitive or manic behaviors, and encourage the dogs in such activities as spinning in circles or chasing the light from a flashlight or laser pointer. Unfortunately, some dogs seem to get "hooked" on these activities, with their new passion for the activities resulting in obsession with the games or similar preoccupations. Due to the risk of developing CCD, this sort of game should be avoided with dogs who have a predisposition for compulsive behavior.*

- **Unpredictable environment:** *Inconsistency in the environment (inconsistent training methods or application of punishment or rewards, lack of training, ineffective training methods) can frustrate the dog, as can a dog's inability to control or avoid aversives such as thunderstorms or punishment. A poorly socialized dog will also be stressed and frustrated by changes in the environment, even minor, seemingly insignificant ones.*

- **Conflicting motivations:** *Two equally strong motivations that are in conflict with each other (approach and withdrawal) can elicit canine compulsive syndrome. For example, a dog who is both fearful and territorial may be in conflict when a stranger approaches his territory. A fearful dog who is constantly called upon to defend his territory may develop stereotypic behaviors. A non-visible electronic fence that provides no physical protection or blockage of visual stimuli for the enclosed dog may also be a contributing factor.*

- **Lack of appropriate outlet for normal behaviors:** *Dogs are very social animals, highly motivated to interact with others. A dog kept in isolation has no outlet for these important hardwired social behaviors, and may develop compulsive behaviors to cope and compensate. Puppies deprived of the opportunity to suck may also exhibit stereotypic behaviors such as excessive licking and flank-sucking, as well as sucking on other objects such as cushions and toys.*

---

8. Interrupt the behavior when it occurs and replace it with an alternative behavior using positive reinforcement training methods. For instance, teach a dog who licks his paws excessively to lie with his head on the floor between his paws, then reward him consistently for this behavior. Work with a qualified behavior consultant to implement an appropriate behavior modification program.

9. Manage the behavior to the extent possible. For instance, you can use an Elizabethan collar on the licking dog when you are not present to supervise his behavior.

10. Utilize appropriate drug therapy as needed, using serotonin-related drugs such as clomipramine (Anafranil) and fluoxetene (Prozac) rather than phenobarbital. Remember that these drugs are not

Dogs who are typically confined all day run a higher risk of developing CCD.

ian and behavior consultant. If done too suddenly, there may be a rebound effect, and the compulsive behavior may reappear more strongly than ever.

Good prognosis

There is hope for dogs with CCD. A study conducted in 1997 at the behavior clinic of the Ontario Veterinary College (now Purdue University) by A. U. Luescher, DVM, PhD, Dipl. ACVB, resulted in successful behavior modification for approximately two-thirds of the dogs participating. The remaining third included owners with poor compliance as well as owners who chose not to participate in the treatment program. An analysis of the cases in that study found that the longer the duration of the behavior, the less positive the outcome, thereby confirming the importance of early treatment in cases of CCD.

a cure, but rather are intended to be used in conjunction with a behavior-modification program. The goal is to eventually wean the dog off the serotonin reuptake blockers. This must be done very gradually, in consultation with a veterinar-

Relieving Anxiety
Many dogs with separation anxiety can improve with training and management.

You are at your wit's end. You were gone for less than an hour, and when you returned home, your dog Maxx had already destroyed your new sofa, defecated on your antique Oriental rug, and inflicted deep gouges in the just-repainted front door frame.

You have tried leaving him in the backyard, but he chewed through the fence and got picked up by animal control. You tried crating him, but he scraped his toenails bloody and broke a canine tooth trying to dig and chew through the crate door. When you left him in the garage he tore everything within reach to shreds. When you left him in a covered chain-link dog pen on the back patio, you got complaints from three different neighbors about his nonstop barking and howling. You've even tried showing him the damage and punishing him for it, but it hasn't helped. You hate to think of giving him up, but you don't know what to do with him. If he would only behave himself when you are away from home.

Maxx has separation anxiety—a behavior problem that results from a dog's natural instincts to want to be near other members of his pack. It is a normal survival instinct, but one that can often be derailed early in a pup's life through proper conditioning. For you and Maxx, however, it's too late for the proper early stuff. Mad Maxx already has a full-blown case of separation anxiety, and now you need to try to fix it.

Conditioned response

It won't be easy. Separation anxiety is a panic attack—your dog's classically conditioned response to the terror of being left alone. When you walk out the door,

Exercise your dog well before you leave. A tired dog has less energy with which to be anxious and destructive.

Maxx doesn't sit around and muse about whether or not to eat the sofa. Separation anxiety behavior is not a conscious choice—it just happens.

In fact, his anxiety begins before you even leave the house; your dog can tell from your morning routine whether this is a get-up-and-go-to-work day (which leaves Maxx home alone) or a relax-and-stay-at-home day. As soon as Maxx determines that it's a work day, he starts to worry, and every step in the routine increases his anxiety. The 5 A.M. alarm clock. The rush to put Maxx out to potty and then toss him his food dish. The shower and shave. The suit and the shiny shoes instead of blue jeans and sneakers. Coffee and a banana instead of bacon and eggs. The grab for the briefcase and car keys, the pause at the front door for dramatic hugs and kisses to Maxx, and the fervent admonitions to behave himself while you're gone.

Phew! By the time the door closes in his face and you rush down the sidewalk to the car, Maxx is already worked up into a high state of arousal. He makes no conscious decision to go on a destruction binge—he is simply stressed to the max. Effective ways for him to relieve his stress include chewing, digging, urinating, defecating, and vocalizing.

Anxiety or high jinks?

Most separation anxiety behavior happens within 30 minutes of the owner's departure and within a similar period before the owner's anticipated return. This is one of the keys to determining whether Maxx's behavior is truly an anxiety reaction or simply a bout of puppy high jinks.

If you can leave and come back in an hour to an unscathed home but four hours puts Maxx over the top, chances are you're dealing with boredom, excessive energy, or a housetraining issue rather than true separation anxiety. (Some dogs will become destructive in their efforts to go outside to relieve themselves if they are very committed to not soiling the house.)

If, on the other hand, your dog displays immediate signs of anxiety upon your exit, he's a candidate for SA

Counter-conditioning and desensitization teaches the dog that it is rewarding to stay calm in the face of stress.

retraining. If you can just get the anxious dog through the first half-hour or so, and avoid raising his anxiety level at homecoming time, you are usually home free. Simple—but not easy.

This task is best accomplished through a program of counter-conditioning and desensitization (CC&D)—fancy terms to describe getting Maxx to like something he now intensely dislikes or fears. In this case, the "something" is being left alone.

The challenge with using CC&D for separation anxiety is that ideally you start with a very low-level stimulus that the dog can tolerate, associate it with something wonderful (like the dog's favorite treats), and gradually work up to a level of normal stimulus, while taking care not to trigger the unwanted response during the process.

If you are desensitizing a dog to loud noises, for example, it is relatively easy to prevent his exposure to noisy environments between training sessions. It's considerably more difficult for the average pet owner to design a schedule that leaves Maxx alone for no more than a few seconds at first, then minutes, then hours, during the weeks or months that it takes to build his tolerance to being alone. If you are truly committed to working through the problem, and have the time and energy, you can get through this.

Managing Maxx

So, where do you start when you can't confine him, you can't trust him loose in the house or yard, and you can't punish him? What are you supposed to do with a Mad Maxx who is rapidly wrecking everything you possess? You need to do two things:

1. Manage his environment while his behavior is being modified so he can't hurt himself or destroy the things around him.
2. Using counter-conditioning and desensitization, teach Maxx that it is safe for him to be alone.

Let's start with the easy one: managing the environment. This means not leaving Maxx alone until he has decided that being alone is okay. You might be able to find a friend, neighbor, or relative who is home during the day, where Maxx can stay and be safe. Perhaps you are fortunate enough to work in a place where your dog could come to the office with you. It never hurts to ask!

Doggie daycare is another excellent option. Commercial daycare centers are thriving in an increasing number of communities around the country; there might be a good one near you. Be sure the daycare operator knows that Maxx has separation anxiety and understands how to deal with it—that he can't be left alone and must not be punished for anxiety-related behavior.

Sometimes, although only very rarely, getting another dog can help. If you are considering this, you should only get a second dog because you want one and are committed to keeping the newcomer whether it helps Maxx's problem or not. Be careful—you could end up with two dogs with separation anxiety and destructive behavior!

Finally, there are pharmaceuticals that have appeared on the market relatively recently that purport to help with resolving a multitude of canine behavior problems. Clomicalm (clomipramine hydrochloride) is the one most commonly prescribed for separation anxiety, but must be used in conjunction with a good behavior modification program in order to be truly effective; the drug alone will not solve the problem.

Maximized training

A behavior modification program will help your dog understand that he can survive being left alone. Depending on the severity of the problem, this may happen relatively quickly, or it may take a long time and never be completely resolved. If you have a Velcro dog who can't even tolerate you being in the next room,

---

Companion Exercises

There are a number of other steps you can take to help reduce your dog's separation anxiety behavior. These are things that can help prevent the problem as well as help modify the already existing anxiety behavior:

- *Exercise your dog well before you leave. A tired dog has less energy with which to be anxious and destructive. Be sure to end the exercise 20 to 30 minutes before you go, so he has time to settle down.*
- *Five minutes before you leave, give him a food-stuffed Kong to take his mind off your imminent departure.*
- *Make your departures and returns completely calm and emotionless. No huggy and kissy "Mummy loves you!" scenes. If he gets excited and jumps all over you when you return, ignore him. Turn your back and walk away. When he finally settles down, say hello and greet him very calmly.*
- *Defuse the pieces of your departure routine by also doing them when you are not leaving. Pick up your car keys and sit down on the sofa to watch TV. Dress in your business suit and then cook dinner. Set your alarm for 5 A.M. on a Saturday, then roll over and go back to sleep.*
- *Mix up your departure routine when you are leaving, so your dog's anxiety doesn't build to a fever pitch. We are creatures of habit, too, so this is hard to do, but can pay off in big dividends. Eat breakfast before you shower instead of after. Pick up your keys and put them in your pocket before you take your dog out for his final potty break. Put your briefcase in the car while you are still in your bathrobe. Make the morning ritual as unpredictable as possible.*

---

you will need to start with very small steps. Here's one program for working with separation anxiety:

1. Teach your dog to accept a tether with you standing right next to him. When he is comfortable on the tether, take one step away, say "Yes!" before he has a chance to get upset (or *click!* your clicker, if he is clicker-trained), then step back to him and feed him a treat. Repeat this step until he shows no sign of anxiety when you are one step away. Be sure that you remain very matter-of-fact about stepping away. If you get excited or emotional, so will he.

2. Now, gradually increase the length of time that you remain one step away before you "Yes!" (or *click!*) and return, until he will tolerate your one-step distance for a full minute or longer. Vary the longer times with shorter ones, so he doesn't start to get anxious about the exercise getting harder and harder each time. You want him never to know how long you will be gone, and at the same time you are teaching him that you always return.

3. Now take two steps away, say "Yes!", and immediately return to feed him a treat. Repeat at this distance until he is comfortable with you being two steps away, then again gradually increase the time at this distance.

4. Very gradually increase the distance, repeating the exercise at each new step until he is calm, then increasing the time at each new distance. If he panics at any point, you have moved too quickly— go back to the previous distance and work there again until he is calm. The take another half-step, if necessary, to avoid triggering his panic.

5. When he will remain calm while you walk to the other side of the room, sit down, and read a magazine, you are ready for the next phase. Start the exercise as before, but this time walk to the doorway of another room, step outside briefly, say "Yes!" and step back into the room before he has a chance to get upset that you are out of sight. Return

and reward. Repeat this until he is calm about you stepping out of the room, and then gradually increase the length of time that you remain out of sight.

6. Now, sometimes close the door as you step out of the room, briefly at first, then for longer periods.

Do the same exercise with each of the doors leading from the room, including the door that leads to the outside. Sometimes leave the door open, sometimes close it. Be sure to return and reward each time before your dog goes into panic mode. If he starts acting anxious at any time, slow down, and go back to a part of the exercise that he can tolerate. Then, when he is calm, proceed more slowly to the step that upset him.

7. Now take him off the tether and repeat Step 6, closing the door each time to prevent him from following you out of the room. Keep the departures very brief, so he doesn't have time to start digging at the door.

8. Gradually increase the length of time you are out of the room, but remember to intersperse the longer ones with short ones so he never knows how long you will be gone. Remember, too, to remain calm yourself.

9. When he is comfortable with you stepping outside for several minutes, start adding bits of your departure routine to the exercise. Pick up your keys, step outside briefly, return, "Yes!" and reward. Then put the keys down. Go outside, open and close the car door, then come back inside. "Yes!" and reward. As he gets better with pieces of the routine, add more pieces.

10. Assuming that you drive a car to work or school, the next step is to actually start the car engine, then come back inside and reward. Start the car engine, then vary the amount of time you wait before coming back in to reward. Drive down the driveway, then drive back to the house, come back in and reward. Your goal is to gradually increase

the length of time you can be outside to 30 minutes or more. If you can hit the magic 30-minute mark, you are well on your way to success.

Pacing is key

Be sure to proceed through these 10 steps at a pace that your dog can tolerate. Short, successful sessions at first (5 to 10 minutes), are better than long, frustrating sessions that end in failure. You may be able to proceed through the steps in a week or two if your dog's separation anxiety is mild, but it is more likely that it may take you several weeks, or months, to work up to 30 minutes. If you aren't making any progress at all, talk to your veterinarian about adding Clomicalm to the equation.

Fixing separation anxiety is hard work, and it's easy to get frustrated with your dog's destructive behavior. Remember that he's not choosing to do it out of spite or malice—he is panicked about his own survival without you, his pack, there to protect him. It's not fun for him—he lives in the moment, and the moments that you are gone are long and terrifying.

If you make the commitment to modifying his behavior and succeed in making him brave about being alone, you will not only have saved your home from destruction, you will have enhanced the quality of your dog's life immensely, and perhaps saved him from destruction, too.

Hyper Hounds

Diagnosing and (more importantly) dealing with overactive dogs.

The explosion of apparently "hyper" dogs in our world can be traced to several factors:

- The popularity of breeds that are (when well-bred) genetically programmed to have enhanced environmental alertness, vigilance, and high activity levels. While high activity levels are distributed across all breeds, they are especially prevalent in the sporting breeds (Labrador Retrievers, Golden Retrievers) and herding breeds (Border Collies, Australian Shepherds).
- The puppy-milling and retail sale of those popular breeds that results in poorly bred, poorly socialized pups ending up in the hands of owners underprepared to care for and train them.
- Unreasonable expectations of dog behavior by owners who have a poor understanding of their dogs' needs and behaviors.
- Lack of adequate exercise and socialization.

Paws is a highly active dog—you *have* to say that about a dog who romps on a trampoline all by himself!—but he can demonstrate great powers of attention and concentration when properly motivated. He exhibits his best "manners" after really hard workouts.

Overdiagnosed

It's true that hyperactivity does exist in dogs. It is, however, also true that it is greatly overdiagnosed. Hyperactivity, otherwise known as "hyperkinesis," can be defined as displaying frenetic activity, abnormally short attention spans, and high impulsiveness. Such dogs can also demonstrate overbearing attention-seeking behavior. It is truly a canine form of attention deficit hyperactivity disorder (ADHD). Like some children who are prescribed Ritalin or some other stimulant, it seems that some dogs who are truly hyperkinetic can benefit from the administration of stimulants to help them focus and pay attention.

What differentiates a normal, high-energy dog from one who has ADHD? Dogs with ADHD demon-

Many people are attracted to certain breeds of dogs because of certain traits, such as a Labrador's genial temperament and athletic prowess. They conveniently forget that the dogs also frequently come with an intense desire to hunt and fetch.

strate exceptionally short attention spans and a high degree of impulsiveness that make it impossible for them to focus on one task for long. They are easily distracted.

In contrast, most high-energy dogs can focus very quickly on the click-and-treat game. They are normal, active dogs who haven't learned how to control their own behavior—but they can, if you show them how. In fact, owners are often amazed by the undivided attention their previously intractable canine companions will offer—as soon as the dogs are given a reason to focus, when they learn that focused attention makes good stuff happen. The truly hyperactive dog can't focus even if she wants to; everything she encounters, regardless of how trivial or irrelevant, is given equal and minimal, active but fleeting interest.

Hyperactive dogs also tend to be especially sensitive to sudden environmental changes—overreacting to the presence of a strange person or animal, and apparently unable to adjust to the new stimulus. In addition, they seem to have an intolerance for boredom and an exaggerated need for novelty and variety. They don't do well with repetitive tasks (such as basic obedience drills), but may excel in situations requiring creative solutions, such as the Border Collie who often must think for himself and make his own decisions about how to move the sheep.

Hyperactive dogs also are likely to get into everything (because they are bored and looking for creative opportunity), can be destructive, and are often emotionally unstable. They can become almost unmanageable if physically restrained, and may exhibit uncontrollable rage-like aggression if frustrated.

Causes and effects

Like so many other behaviors, hyperactivity is believed to result from a mix of genes and environment—nature versus nurture. Certainly, the high-energy breeds are more prone to develop true hyperactive behaviors, but a dog's genes are just the canvas on which his personality is painted by life, training, and socialization experiences. Hyperactivity can be minimized or exacerbated from puppyhood on, depending on social and environmental factors.

Excitable dogs can often be identified early. They are frequently the puppies who continually bite at hands and fight any attempt to restrain or control them—not with just a mild struggle, but with violent resistance. An excitable puppy placed into a calm, structured environment, with an owner who provides adequate exercise, socialization, and training, has a good chance of growing up to be a well-behaved, albeit active, canine companion. In the wrong environment, this pup is a disaster.

Exposure to overly active and playful children can feed hyperactivity—just one of many reasons that interactions between children and dogs should be very closely supervised. Excitable children tend to do exactly the wrong things in response to an excitable puppy's inappropriate behaviors—hitting back, restraining, running, or screaming—all of which are guaranteed to escalate the pup's level of excitement. Even a pup with a moderate activity level can be induced into hyperactivity in the wrong environment.

Social isolation also makes a significant contribution to hyperactive behavior. An owner might promise to bring Rex into the house as soon as Rex learns to be well-behaved, but Rex can't learn to be well-behaved when he is experiencing the activity-increasing effects of social deprivation.

Most terriers love to play fetch, and spend an inordinate amount of time shaking the fetch item vigorously. If the toy were an animal, this action would break its neck.

A 1961 study conducted by Waller and Fuller found that puppies raised in semi-isolation exhibited excessive social contact behavior when given limited access to other puppies. When kept with their litters, the number of social contacts reduced by 75 percent. One conclusion of this study is that dogs may possess a biological need for a certain minimum amount of daily social stimulation and activity, and if that need is not met, a dog compensates with excessive activity when placed in a social situation.

It is likely that the minimum amount of social stimulation needed varies from one dog to the next. When faced with a dog who has higher-than-anticipated social needs, some owners resort to routine isolation of the dog in order to deal with the unwanted behaviors. This results in inadequate attention, insufficient exercise, and excessive confinement, adding fuel to the fire and creating a vicious cycle. When the dog is released from his confinement his behavior is worse than ever, which results in more isolation, and further decline of behavior. His chances of ever becoming a house dog grow dimmer.

Some physiological conditions are believed to play a role in canine ADHD as well. In a study published in 1999 by Dr. Jean Dodds and Dr. Linda Aronson, in collaboration with Dr. Nicholas Dodman and Dr. Jean DeNapoli of Tufts University, 634 dogs were evaluated for thyroid dysfunction as it related to various behavior problems. Of those dogs, 42 were determined to be hyperactive; 31 percent of the hyperactive dogs (13) were diagnosed with thyroid dysfunction.

Of 95 dogs in the study whose behavioral responses to thyroid therapy were evaluated, 81 dogs (85.3 percent) showed at least a 25 percent improvement in their behavior. Thirty-four of the dogs (35.6 percent) showed better than 75 percent improvement. Of 20 dogs treated with conventional methods and modification techniques over the same time period, only 11 (55 percent) improved by at least 25 percent.

Chronic lead poisoning is also a potential cause of hyperactivity in dogs. Two common sources are destructive chewing on old linoleum or on surfaces painted with lead-based paints.

There is also evidence to suggest that inadequate nutrition, especially early in life, may permanently affect activity levels throughout the remainder of a dog's life. This means that the importance of proper nutrition during puppyhood cannot be overstated. Breeders must be sure that puppies in large litters or those born to mothers with insufficient milk receive adequate nutrition from other sources, and that the mother's dietary intake can meet the demands of a nursing litter. It has been suggested that a diet high in protein, or containing elements to which a dog is allergic, may also contribute to hyperactive behavior.

Although the scientific jury is still out on the role that food additives and colorants play in hyperactive behavior, and, in fact, many studies have not found a direct correlation, a 1980 study did find a sharp decrease in hyperactive symptoms when dogs were put on a 28-day additive-free diet.

Working with "normal" high-energy dogs

Say you determine that you have a high-energy dog, rather than a hyperactive one. That may be good news, but you still need to deal with your out-of-control canine. Here are some tips to help you turn your Wild Willy into a Gentle Bill:

- Increase the structure in his environment. Teach him to "say please" (sit) to make good things happen. Have him sit for his dinner bowl. Have him sit for his leash to go for a walk. Have him sit to make the door to the backyard open. Have him sit to be petted, or to get a cookie for coming back inside.
- Increase his exercise. Whatever he gets now, give him more, and make it quality exercise. Tossing him out in the backyard is not quality exercise. Go out with him. Throw sticks or balls, play tug-of-war, get

Conduct a 10-Minute ADHD Test

How can you tell if you have a "normal" high-energy dog or one with ADHD? The proof is in the Ritalin. Your veterinarian can administer a low dose of an appropriate amphetamine after measuring your dog's respiration, heart rate, and reaction to restraint. Some 30 to 120 minutes after the amphetamine is given, most hyperkinetic dogs will show a marked decrease in excitement and activity level as well as a measurable drop in respiration and heart rate, and greater acceptance of restraint. A normal-but-active dog will have the opposite response, with an increase in excitement, activity, heart rate, and respiration, and a decreased tolerance of restraint.

First, however, you might want to try an ADHD experiment at home. Make sure your high-energy dog hasn't eaten for at least four hours. Take him out for a good hard romp in a safely enclosed area to take the edge off—but don't run him into exhaustion. Then leash your dog, grab your clicker and a treat bag full of very high-value treats, and take him to a place with minimal distractions (indoors) for some clicker-testing fun:

1. *"Supercharge" your clicker, using a very high rate of reinforcement and tiny treats for one minute (30 to 60 treats per minute). Click! the clicker, and then feed the dog a smidgen of chicken for each click. Click!, treat. Click!, treat. Your dog doesn't have to do anything but focus on you; don't ask for sit, down, stay, or any other behavior. If he tries to jump on you, turn away, but keep clicking and giving him treats. Be sure to deliver the treats at his nose level so he doesn't have to jump up to get them. If he's grabby, toss the treats on the floor in front of him.*

2. *After one minute, reduce the rate of reinforcement to 15 to 30 clicks and treats per minute. Start moving the treat over his head to lure a sit. If he does sit, briefly increase the rate of reinforcement by three to four clicks, then slow down again. Do this for two minutes.*

Start out by "supercharging" a clicker—clicking the noise-maker and following each *click!* with a treat. This quickly teaches a dog that the *"click!"* sound always precedes "something good."

Next, begin reducing the "rate of reinforcement," that is, the number of times per minute that you *click!* and deliver a treat. A dog with ADHD may begin to lose his focus at this point.

3. For the next two minutes, continue at a reinforcement rate of 10 to 20 clicks and treats per minute, but now, if he sits, click! the clicker but hold off delivering the treat for two seconds at first, gradually increasing the delay of the treat's delivery by up to four or five seconds.

4. For two more minutes, click! and treat on a variable, random schedule of reinforcement. That is, vary the number of seconds between clicks and treats, sometimes doing several clicks and treats rapidly in a row (remember to treat after each click!) sometimes pausing for one second, or five, or three, or seven, between clicks. Try to keep it random; we humans are very good at falling into patterns!

5. Now, stop clicking for 30 seconds.

6. After 30 seconds, click! the clicker only if he looks at you. If he keeps looking at you, keep clicking and treating, using the random reinforcement schedule in Step 4. If he looks away, stop clicking.

If he looks back at you or looks in your general direction, click again. Do this for 2½ minutes.

Time's up—the test is over!

If your dog was willing to play this game with you for the entire 10 minutes with only occasional minor attention lapses, you probably have a normal high-energy dog. It's time to increase his exercise, socialization, and training programs.

If, however, you lost your dog's attention totally somewhere between Steps 2 and 4, there's a good chance you really do have a hyperkinetic dog. Time to call your vet to schedule that amphetamine test, and while you're there, have a full thyroid panel done as well as a blood test for lead poisoning. Remember that thyroid results within the clinically normal-but-low range can be a contributing factor to behavior problems.

If your dog can stay focused even when the rate of reinforcement slows, and when the delivery of the treat is delayed for several seconds after the click, he probably does not have ADHD.

Just as with humans who have ADHD, dogs who display this syndrome can excel at "jobs" requiring activity and/or quick responses, such as agility, sheepherding, or tracking.

him to swim in a pond, take him to the dog park. And add structure to his exercise. Have him sit politely for you to throw the ball. Make sure he will give you the tug toy when you ask him to. Have him sit before you open the gate into the park.

- Increase his socialization time. If you've been leaving him outside because he's too wild, grit your teeth and bring him in. Use leashes, tethers, crates, and baby gates as needed to preserve your sanity while integrating him into the family.
- Increase his training time. If you've already taken him to a basic training class, sign up for a Level Two. Or a tricks class, or agility—anything that will keep the two of you active and learning together. Keeping his brain occupied and busy is just as important as occupying his body.

The ADHD difference

What do you do if you conclude that your dog has ADHD? In some cases, these dogs exhibit behaviors that are so intrinsically driven by organic causes that behavior modification and positive training alone can't help. Fortunately, a high percentage of ADHD dogs can be helped with the judicious use of stimulants in combination with a behavior modification program. Hyperactive dogs tend to be very responsive to positive reinforcement shaping procedures in conjunction with brief time-out periods.

Think back to the results of your 10-minute ADHD test. At what step did you start to lose your dog? If he was with you through Step 2 and you lost him at 3, you know that he does well with a continuous schedule of reinforcement at a fairly high rate.

Go back to the step where he did well (Step 2), and work toward Step 3, breaking your "gradually" into even smaller increments—perhaps a half-second rather than a full second—so you don't lose him with too big a leap.

Keep your expectations low. Shape most of his behaviors in very tiny increments with a high rate of reinforcement. Keep your training session brief (five minutes, maximum), with a short time-out to calm him before you start another brief session.

Sample task for ADHD dogs

With many dogs, lure-shaping a down is a simple matter, accomplished in short order by moving the treat toward the floor and clicking the dog for following into a down position. We often have success in just three or four clicks, as we hold the treat at the dog's nose and he focuses on it (*click!* and treat), we move it halfway to the floor and he follows (*click!* and treat), three-quarters of the way and his feet are sliding forward (*click!* and treat), and he's down (*click!* and a jackpot of treats!).

In contrast, the hyperkinetic dog may require 20 or even 100 clicks, over several sessions, before you reach your final behavior goal. Teaching "Down" to this dog might require the following:

- The dog is sitting. You hold a treat in front of his nose and he focuses on it. *Click!* and treat.
- He stays focused on the treat. *Click!* and treat.
- Lower the treat a half-inch. His nose follows. *Click!* and treat.
- He stays focused. *Click!* and treat.
- Lower the treat another half-inch. He follows. *Click!* and treat.
- Lower another half-inch. He follows. *Click!* and treat.
- He stays focused. *Click!* and treat.
- Release him from the sit, tell him he's a great dog, and both of you take a five-minute brain break.
- Start with the sit again. As soon as he focuses on the treat, *click!* and treat.
- Lower the treat an inch. His nose follows. *Click!* and treat.
- Lower the treat another inch. He follows. *Click!* and treat.
- He stays focused. *Click!* and treat.
- Lower the treat another inch. *Click!* and treat.

- He stays focused. *Click!* and treat.
- Lower the treat another inch. *Click!* and treat.
- Take another brain break.

You get the idea: slow and steady. Anytime you increase the increment, say from one inch to two inches, make sure he stays with you. If you lose him between one and two inches, go from one inch to one and a half inches. Take frequent brain breaks, and don't make your total session more than about 15 minutes. If you lose his attention a lot, you are expecting too much. Use smaller increments, a higher rate of reinforcement (*click!* him often just for staying with the game), and more breaks.

You never know, with patience, in the right positive environment, your "hyper" pal may turn out to be a great agility, herding, tracking, or drug-sniffing dog!

Predatory Dogs

Few people want their dogs to act on their inherited predatory drives.

Dogs' predatory instincts are one of the things that makes them fun to play with. When you throw a ball or a stick and he chases it, you are triggering his natural predatory desire to chase things that move. In fact, some behaviorists argue that predatory behavior should not be called aggression at all—that it is more appropriately interpreted as a form of food-getting behavior.

Indeed, the motivation to chase prey objects is vastly different from other forms of aggression, which are based on competition for resources and/or self-protection. It is distinguished from other forms of aggression by a marked absence of "affective arousal" (anger), and is a social survival behavior, not a social conflict behavior. Predatory behavior is indicated by distinct behaviors: hunting (sniffing, tracking, searching, scanning, or waiting for prey); stalking; the attack sequence (chase, pounce, catch, shaking kill, choking kill); and post-kill consuming. The underlying motivation for chasing things that move is to eat them.

Dogs who challenge, bark, snarl, and chase skateboarders or joggers who pass the house are generally believed to be engaging in territorial aggression—individual predators don't usually openly advertise their intent by making lots of noise (although anyone who has ever followed a pack of baying hounds knows that group hunting can be quite noisy!). Dogs who hide in ditches or behind bushes and silently launch their attacks on unsuspecting passers-by are exhibiting more classic predator behavior. However, the frustration of restraint on a chain or behind a fence combined with constant exposure to the trigger of rapidly moving prey objects can push a dog from predatory behavior to real aggression. Both behaviors, of course, are dangerous.

Just because predatory behavior is natural doesn't mean that it's acceptable in its inappropriate manifestations. Predatory behavior has been responsible for the deaths of many unfortunate pet cats, rabbits, chickens, sheep, goats, and other livestock, and even humans. While it often can be expressed in harmless, even useful outlets such as games of fetch, retrieving ducks, and herding sheep, chase behavior can be dangerous to dog and prey alike. It is our responsibility, as caretakers for our canine companions, to be sure their natural predatory instincts don't get them into trouble.

Manage, manage, manage

As with so many other undesirable dog behaviors, if your dog has a strong prey drive, your first line of defense is management. Make sure you have a secure fence from which your dog cannot escape. Don't leave him in the yard unattended if he will be constantly tantalized by lots of fast-moving prey objects, such as squirrels, deer, skateboarders, or small children running and playing.

Use a leash or long line to prevent your dog from taking off after deer, rabbits, and squirrels when you are on walks and hikes. Especially keep him on leash at dawn and dusk, when the deer and the antelope—and other small, wild things—are most likely to play. Look for ways to minimize his visual and physical access to prey in his own yard—a solid fence will prevent him from seeing things moving by quickly, and will prevent many potential prey animals (including small children) from entering easily. A non-visible underground electronic fence will not. Nor will it prevent him from leaving the yard if he is highly motivated to chase prey.

A muzzle can also be useful on a limited basis. Since muzzles restrict a dog's ability to drink water and pant normally, you cannot leave one on your dog while you are away all day at work. But if he's devastating the squirrel population in your backyard, or you want to give a litter of baby bunnies a chance to grow up and get wiser and faster, you can put a muzzle on him for brief fresh-air and potty trips to the yard. Be sure to take time to desensitize him to wearing a muzzle first, by associating it with yummy treats while you put it on him for gradually longer periods of time.

Training

You will never train most herding dogs not to chase things that move, given the chance. Similarly, you'd be hard pressed to convince many terriers not to go after rats and other small creatures when the opportunity arises. Their brains are hardwired to chase, and you can't change that.

A slightly less imposing goal is to change the predatory response into an incompatible behavior response. For example, you could teach your Border Collie that the appearance of a deer is the cue to lie down. She can't "down" and chase the deer at the same time. For your terrier, the appearance of your kitten could be the cue to sit at your feet. This type of training can be difficult because the dogs are so highly motivated to chase—it is quite a challenge to convince them that they'd rather do something else. You must find something highly rewarding in order to make it work. This might be food, or the opportunity to chase a tennis ball—after she lies down—instead of the deer.

This approach works best in your presence, and only if you practice it regularly rather than just expecting it to work in the heat of the moment. You might not ever be able to expect that your Border Collie will leave the deer (or the skateboarders) alone if she is outside, unrestrained, and left to her own devices.

A solid foundation of good manners training can also be helpful, combined with vigilance on your part.

The frustration of being able to see passing people, dogs, bikes, cats, etc., but not being able to chase them, can grow over time and result in a dog who becomes fixated on attacking the "prey," given the chance. Blocking the dog's view will help.

If you are out hiking with Bess and see the deer before she does, you can call her to you and snap the leash on. Even if she sees it first, a really reliable recall will bring her back to your side, especially if you call her pre-launch, before she is headed hell-bent-for-leather after the fleeing deer.

A well-trained emergency "Down!" can also save the day, even if your dog is in full stride. Many dogs will "Down!" even when they won't "Come!" because they can still watch the prey. Stopping the charge gives the dog's arousal level and adrenaline time to recede, and you may be able to call her back from the "Down" or calmly walk up to her and snap her leash on her collar.

What About the Baby?

One of the very real concerns expressed by new or soon-to-be parents is that of the family dog's predatory behavior being elicited by the baby. There is some evidence to support the belief that at least some dogs may view an infant more as a prey object than as a little human. New babies move strangely, and make funny noises that can resemble prey distress sounds.

The Centers for Disease Control in Atlanta, Georgia, published figures from the 25 dog bite–related fatalities in the two-year period from 1995 through 1996. Of those 25 deaths, 20 of the victims were children (80 percent). Three of the children were less than 30 days old, one was under five months, and ten were from one to four years old. The remaining six child victims were under 11 years old.

It is likely that the three neonates and perhaps the five-month-old baby were victims of prey-related behavior, while the others were at least as likely to have somehow elicited a true social conflict or aggression attack.

We strongly recommend that all parents-to-be, but especially owners of dogs with strong predatory behavior who plan to bring an infant into the home, work with a trainer or behaviorist to desensitize the dog to the sights and sounds of a baby, and to create a good training and management plan to ensure that Fido and Junior will be comfortable with each other.

There are CDs and audio tapes of baby noises available to help with this process, which can be used to teach the dog that a baby's cries are the cue to lie down on his bed—or do a Lassie trick and go get Mom or Dad.

It goes without saying that dogs should never be left alone with infants and young children, but that warning goes triple for dogs who have demonstrated any propensity toward predatory behavior. A family dog mauling or killing a child is a horrible tragedy that just doesn't have to happen.

Dangers of thwarting

Dogs who have strong, hardwired behaviors are usually happiest if they are allowed to engage in those behaviors in some form. Greyhounds chase mechanical rabbits on the track—and while the abuse that is rampant in the Greyhound industry is abhorrent, there is no question that the dogs love to run and chase. Jack Russell Terriers are in heaven when they get to play in earthdog trials.

In fact, if hardwired behaviors are constantly thwarted (prevented from occurring), you risk having your dog develop compulsive disorders (see page 122).

If you are the owner of a dog with strong predatory inclinations, it behooves you both to find an outlet for the behavior rather than simply trying to shut it off. Encourage your dog to chase and fetch balls, sticks, and toys, and take the time to engage in several fetch sessions with him per day.

Use these strong reinforcers to incorporate training in your play sessions and strengthen your dog's good manners. If your dog rudely jumps up and tries to grab the Frisbee from your hand, whisk it behind your back until he sits, then bring it out again, and only throw it if he remains sitting until you throw. You are using two of the four principles of operant conditioning here. The dog's behavior—jumping up—makes the Frisbee go away, which is "negative punishment"—the dog's behavior makes a good thing go away. When he sits and stays sitting, you throw the Frisbee. This is "positive reinforcement"—the dog's behavior makes a good thing happen. Works like a charm.

If you have a terrier, provide an outlet for his prey-seeking behavior by creating a digging spot—a box filled with soft soil or an area you have dug up where he is allowed to dig. Bury his favorite toys and encourage him to "Find it!" Toys that squeak and wiggle are especially suited to terrier games.

Come chase with me

One of the most useful applications of chase behavior is in conjunction with teaching your dog to come when called. Lots of dog owners make the mistake of moving toward their dogs—or even chasing after them—when they won't come. In dog language, a direct frontal approach is assertive, even aggressive, and dogs naturally move away from it.

It's much more effective to do the exact opposite—run away from your dog! Start playing chase and recall games when your dog is a pup. Get excited, call your pup, and run a short distance away. Let him catch up to you while you are still facing away from him, then turn sideways, kneel down (don't bend over him), praise him, feed him a treat or play with a tug or fetch toy, and pet him (if he enjoys being petted; not all dogs do). If your dog is no longer a pup, you can still play this game to strengthen his response to the "Come!" cue.

Teach your dog from early on that "Come!" means "Chase me and play," keep up the games as he matures, manage him so he doesn't get to practice inappropriate predatory behavior, and find acceptable outlets for his natural chase behaviors. Using these tactics, you'll have a much better chance of eliminating those incompatible behaviors later on when you are faced with the challenge of competition from real prey.

The Incessant Barker
How to prevent (or at least manage) your dog's nuisance barking.

While dogs are primarily body-language communicators, they also use their voices to share information with other members of their social groups. Compared to their wild brethren, however, our domesticated dogs use their voices far more—a tendency we have genetically encouraged. We've created herding breeds, including Shelties, Border Collies, Welsh Corgis, and others, who use their voices when necessary to control their flocks. We've bred scent hounds to give voice when they are on the trail of prey.

We've also created a lot of breeds whose predilection for barking is a side effect of their main purpose. For example, we created many terrier breeds for hunting small rodents. These dogs are often notoriously barky, perhaps from generations of excited pursuit of their prey. Likewise, many of the toy breeds are known to be "yappy," serving double duty as door alarms as well as lap warmers.

Contrary to popular (human) belief, dogs generally have good reasons to bark. Addressing their grounds for vocalizing may well stop the noisemaking.

For what it's worth, we've also produced breeds that have a reputation for quiet. Many of the guarding breeds tend not to announce their presence, but instead carry out their duties with a quiet intensity. Chows, Akitas, and Mastiffs are more likely to escort you off the property with a low growl or a short warning bark rather than a canine chorus. And of course, Basenjis don't bark at all; they scream when they are displeased.

Types of problem barking

We'd probably all be pleased if our dogs limited their barking to those situations for which they were bred to give voice, but of course they don't. Those who have inherited a propensity for using their voices freely in one situation are highly likely to use them freely in others as well. And so, we end up with "nuisance" and "problem" barking.

Problem barking comes in a variety of flavors, each with its own unique triggers and solutions. Your dog might bark in several different situations, requiring a multi-pronged behavior modification program.

Whatever the cause of your dog's barking, don't make the mistake of yelling "Quiet!" (or worse) at your dog. This is likely to increase his excitement and arousal, adding to the chaos rather than achieving the desired effect of peace in the kingdom. Even if you do succeed in intimidating him into silence, you risk damaging your relationship with him, as he learns to be quiet through fear.

Instead, use your human brain to figure out how to manage and modify your dog's penchant for pandemonium. Fortunately, with a commitment of time, effort, training, and management, most barking can be controlled. Start out by identifying the type of barking your dog practices most frequently and apply the appropriate solution.

Boredom barking

The largest category of nuisance barking is caused by boredom. Boredom barkers are the dogs who are left out in their yards all day, and sometimes all night, with nothing to do but patrol their territory and announce the presence of anything and everything. Sometimes it seems they bark just to hear themselves bark; perhaps they do.

Boredom barking often has a monotonous tone, and can go on for hours. The greatest numbers of barking complaints received by animal agencies are generated by boredom barkers.

The Fix: Fortunately, there's an easy fix for outdoor boredom barking. Most of these dogs, if left inside, are happily quiet in their human's den. The complicating factor is the length of time a dog can be safely left alone in the house. Crates and exercise pens are good management solutions for dogs who haven't yet learned good house manners, and dog walkers can be enlisted to provide midday potty breaks if owners work long hours. (Dog walkers need not be professionals; you can often enlist the help of a friend, family member, or a neighbor.)

Boredom barking can also be reduced by enriching your dog's life, by increasing his physical exercise and mind-engaging activities. A good, tongue-dragging, off-leash run or fetch and some interactive games and toys such as stuffed Kongs, Iqubes, and Egg Baby Turtles, daily, can minimize the tedium of a lonely dog's day.

Play barking

These are the dogs who can't handle too much fun. They are the canine equivalent of cheerleaders, run-

Remove the barker from the playing field when others want to engage in fetch or chase-me games.

ning around the edges of the game giving voice to their arousal while others play. Herding dogs are often members of this group. Bred to keep livestock under tight control, they often experience an inherited compulsion to control anyone or anything that moves.

The Fix: This is such a hardwired behavior that it's difficult to modify. You do have several options:

- Accept and allow the behavior. Determine a time and place where the barking is least objectionable, and let the dog do it.
- Manage the behavior. Remove the barker from the playing field when others want to engage in rough-and-tumble or chase-me games.
- Use "negative punishment," a gentle, nonviolent form of punishment that can be effective if applied consistently. Negative punishment is the behavioral term for any situation in which the dog's behavior makes a good thing go away. If your dog is playing (an activity he enjoys) and starts barking (the thing you don't want), you remove his opportunity to play. Use a cheerful "Oops, time-out!" and remove him from the game for a brief (perhaps one- to five-minute) session in the penalty box (say, another room).
- Teach a positive interrupt (see sidebar). Use it

An Incredibly Useful Training Tool: The Positive Interrupt

The positive interrupt is a well-programmed, highly reinforced behavior that allows you to redirect your dog's attention back to you when she's doing something inappropriate, like barking. Ideally, you want your dog's response to the "Over here!" cue to be so automatic—classically conditioned—that he doesn't stop to wonder whether what he's doing is more rewarding or interesting than turning his attention toward you and running to you for a treat. He doesn't think—he just does it, the way your foot automatically hits the brake of your car when you see taillights flash in front of you on the highway.

Here's how to program a positive interrupt:

1. Install the cue in a low-distraction environment. Use a phrase such as "Over here!" or "Quiet please!" as your interrupt cue. Say the phrase in a cheerful tone of voice when your dog is paying attention to you, then immediately feed him a morsel of very high-value treat, such as a small shred of canned chicken or sardines. Repeat until you see his eyes light up and his ears perk when you say the phrase.

2. Practice with the cue in a low-distraction environment. Wait until your dog is engaged in a low-value activity, such as wandering around the room, sniffing something mildly interesting. Then say your interrupt phrase in the same cheerful tone of voice. You should see an immediate interrupt in his low-value activity, and he should dash to you for his treat. If he doesn't, return to Step 1, perhaps with an even higher-value treat.

3. Practice with the cue in a low-distraction environment with minor distractions. Still in the low-distraction environment so you can control the distraction level, add moderate distractions—one at a time—and practice the interrupt. For example,

sit in your kitchen (low-distraction environment) with a helper such as one of your friends or family members. Give your helper a bag of chips. At your cue, ask your helper to help themselves to a chip or two; this should be a fairly minor distraction. Gradually increase the intensity of the distraction. Your helper can noisily crunch the chips, or get up and walk around—and eventually hop around while crunching chips.

Gradually move up to major distractions in your low-distraction environment while practicing the positive interrupt. If you lose your dog's automatic response at any step, return to the previous step.

4. Move your lessons to an environment with real-life distractions. Go for a walk around the block with your dog on leash. Use the interrupt when he becomes preoccupied with a mild to moderate real-life distraction, such as an interesting bush he would like to sniff or a fast-food bag on the sidewalk he'd like to check out. If a major distraction presents itself, including a stimulus that causes him to bark, give the interrupt a try! Don't get discouraged if it fails to work in a challenging situation; just keep practicing in less-difficult surroundings. And make sure the treat you use is irresistibly delicious.

5. Use the positive cue to interrupt barking. When your dog automatically turns his attention to you in response to your cue when confronted with major real-life distractions, you have a valuable tool for interrupting his barking. Be sure you practice occasionally with mild distractions as well, to keep the cue "tuned up," and remember to thank him and tell him what a wonderful dog he is when he stops barking on your request.

when he barks to invite him to come to you and briefly stop the barking, then release him to go play again.

- Encourage him to carry his favorite toy in his mouth during play. A mouth full of highly valued toy makes it difficult to bark, or at least muffles the sound. Caution: This is not a good option to select if your barking dog also "resource guards" his toys from other dogs.

Demand barking

This is less annoying to neighbors, but it can be very irritating to you. Your dog is saying, "Bow wow, give it to me *now!*" Demand barking may be encountered in the early stages of positive training, as your dog tries to figure out how to make treats, play, and attention happen. It often starts as a low grumble or soft "whuff," and if not nipped in the bud can turn into a full-scale, insistent, persistent bark.

The Fix: It's easy to derail demand barking when it first starts by ignoring the dog. When your dog barks for treats, attention, or to get you to throw his ball, simply turn your back on him until he is quiet, then say "Yes!" and return your attention to him. His goal is to get you to give him good stuff. Your goal is to teach him that barking makes good stuff go away.

At first, you'll need to say "Yes!" after just a few seconds of quiet, but fairly quickly extend the period of quiet so he doesn't learn a behavior chain of "Bark, be quiet for a second, get attention." At the same time, you'll need to reinforce quiet when he doesn't bark first, again, to prevent the behavior chain.

It's more challenging to extinguish demand barking when your dog has had lots of reinforcement for it. Remember, any attention you give him reinforces demand barking. Eye contact, physical contact, verbal admonishment—all of these give him what he wants: attention!

The process for modifying the behavior of a veteran demand barker is the same: remove all reinforcement. However, be prepared for an extinction burst—a period when the behavior gets worse rather than better. The behavior used to work, so the dog thinks if he just tries harder, surely it will work again. If you give in during an extinction burst, you reinforce the more intense barking behavior, and guess what happens next time? Right—your dog will offer the more intense behavior sooner, and it gets even harder to extinguish the barking. Oops!

Alarm barking

This is Lassie's "Timmy's in the well!" bark. It means something is seriously wrong—or at least your dog thinks so. The alarm bark usually has a tone of urgency or ferocity that's absent in most other barks. Because your dog's judgment as to what constitutes a serious threat may differ from yours, after many false alarms you may fall into the trap of asking him to stop barking without investigating the cause. Don't! This may be the time a fire is smoldering in the kitchen.

The Fix: Always investigate. It could just be the UPS driver leaving a package on the porch, but it might be something serious. Sometimes Timmy really is in the well! Investigate, use a positive interrupt to stop the barking, and then reinforce the quiet. You can also thank your dogs for letting you know something important was happening.

Greeting barking

Your dog may be giving an alarm: "Danger! Intruder at the door!" Or he may be barking in excitement: "Huzzah! Dad's home!" His tone—ferocious versus excited—will tell you the difference.

The Fix: If you have guests arriving, the management and modification program is complicated by the fact that you have to answer the door! Ideally, a second person answers the door while you use the positive interrupt to halt the barking. If there is no second person available, use the interrupt, secure your dog in another room or tether him, then go greet your guests. (You may want to put a note on your door asking guests to be patient if it takes you a minute or two to come to the door.)

Before adding a new dog to your family, take into consideration your tolerance for barking, and select a type of dog whose genetic propensity for vocalizing matches your tolerance level. Appreciate your dog's voice as a useful communication tool and teach her how to control and use it appropriately. Don't reward—purposefully or accidentally—any type of barking that you wouldn't want to live with indefinitely.

You can also help minimize greeting barking by remaining calm when the doorbell rings, because otherwise, your dog may get excited and bark at your excitement. In families with children, you may have to spend some time training the kids not to rush excitedly to the door, too!

Often, people unwittingly train their dogs to bark when they come home, by greeting the dog in a boisterous manner. It's human nature to enjoy it when another being seems glad to see us. But it's one thing to be greeted by a wagging, wiggling dog, and another to be greeted by a cacaphony of loud, maniacal barking. And with some dogs, one often leads to the other.

If your dog is barking as you approach your door, wait outside until he is quiet for at least a few seconds. Then enter the house, remaining very calm and quiet yourself. If your dog starts barking as you enter, ignore him until he is quiet, then greet him calmly. After you have been home a little while and he is calm, you can initiate a play or affection session.

Frustration barking

Frustration barking can be identified by its tone of shrill insistence. It is a close relative of demand barking, but is more likely to occur when you are a distance from the dog, or when it is directed at something other than you.

The Fix: Handle it the same way as demand barking. Ignore the behavior you don't want (the barking) and reward the behavior you do want (quiet). A reward marker such as the *click!* of a clicker or a verbal "Yes!" is very useful to mark the quiet, since you are often at a distance from the dog when the barking and the moment of quiet happen.

As with demand barking, the more your dog has been rewarded for frustration barking in the past, the more committed and consistent you'll need to be to make it go away, and the more likely you'll have to work through a significant extinction burst.

Anxiety barking

Hysterical vocalization is just one of several manifestations of separation anxiety (SA), often accompanied by destructive behavior, extraordinary efforts to escape confinement, and/or inappropriate urination and defecation. Separation anxiety is a complex behavior—a full-blown panic attack. To modify SA barking, howling, or screaming, you must modify the entire anxiety complex.

The Fix: While it can be modified through a program of counter-conditioning and desensitization, SA barking usually requires the intervention of a professional trainer or behavior consultant, sometimes with the assistance of behavior modification drugs. If your dog's barking is related to anxiety, we suggest you contact a good, positive trainer or behaviorist to help you with the complex and difficult anxiety behavior.

Not all barking is bad

A dog's voice can be a useful thing, especially the bark that lets us know a dog needs to go outside, or is ready to come back in. Some service dogs are trained to bark to alert their owners. Dogs warn us of intruders and tell us of pending emergencies.

While your dog's shrill voice might make you grit your teeth, remember that there may be times when she will use that same voice to tell you something important, and you'll be glad she has a voice to use.

The "Gift" of Growling
Why you should never punish a dog for growling.

It may seem intuitive to punish growling. Growling leads to biting, and dogs who bite people often must be euthanized, so let's save our dog's life and nip biting in the bud by punishing him at the first sign of inappropriate behavior. It makes sense, in a way—but when you have a deeper understanding of canine aggression, it's easy to understand why *it's the absolutely wrong thing to do.*

Punishing the dog for growling teaches him to NOT give any warning when he's uncomfortable.

Communication efforts

Most dogs don't want to bite or fight. The behaviors that signal pending aggression are intended first and foremost to warn away a threat. The dog who doesn't want to bite or fight tries his hardest to make you go away. He may begin with subtle signs of discomfort that are often overlooked by many humans—tension in body movements, a stiffly wagging tail.

"Please," he says gently, "I don't want you to be here."

If you continue to invade his comfort zone, his threats may intensify, with more tension, a hard stare, and a low growl.

"I mean it," he says more firmly, "I want you to leave."

If those are ignored, he may become more insistent, with an air snap, a bump of the nose, or even open mouth contact that closes gently on an arm but doesn't break skin.

"Please," he says, "don't make me bite you."

If that doesn't succeed in convincing you to leave, the dog may feel compelled to bite hard enough to break skin in his efforts to protect self, territory, members of his social group, or other valuable resources.

Caused by stress

What many people don't realize is that aggression is caused by stress. The stressor may be related to pain, fear, intrusion, threats to resources, past association, or anticipation of any of these things. An assertive, aggressive dog attacks because he's stressed by the intrusion of another dog or human into his territory. A fearful dog bites because he's stressed by the approach of a human. An injured dog lacerates the hand of his rescuer because he's stressed by pain.

When you punish a growl or other early warning signs, you may succeed in suppressing the growl, snarl, snap, or other warning behavior—but you don't take away the stress that caused the growl in the first place. In fact, you increase the stress, because now you, the dog's owner, have become unpredictable and violent as well.

Worst of all, and most significantly, if you succeed in suppressing the warning signs, you end up with a dog who bites without warning. He has learned that it's not safe to warn, so he doesn't.

If a dog is frightened of children, he may growl when a child approaches. You, conscientious and responsible owner, are well aware of the stigma—and fate—of dogs who bite children, so you punish your dog with a yank on the leash and a loud "No! Bad dog!" Every time your dog growls at a child you do this, and quickly your dog's fear of children is confirmed—children do make bad things happen! He likes children even less, but he learns not to growl at them to avoid making you turn mean.

You think he's learned that it's not okay to be aggressive to children, because the next time one passes by, there's no growl.

"Phew," you think to yourself. "We dodged that bullet!"

Convinced that your dog now accepts children because he no longer growls at them, the next time one approaches and asks if he can pat your dog, you say yes. In fact, your dog has simply learned not to growl, but children still make him very uncomfortable. Your dog is now super-stressed, trying to control his growl as the child gets nearer and nearer so you don't lose control and punish him, but when the scary child reaches out for him he can't hold back any longer—he lunges forward and snaps at the child's face. Fortunately, you're able to restrain him with the leash so he doesn't connect. You, the dog, and the child are all quite shaken by the incident.

It's time to change your thinking.

"Help!"

A growl is a dog's cry for help. It's your dog's way of telling you he can't tolerate a situation—as if he's saying, "I can't handle this, please get me out of here!"

Your first response when you hear your dog growl should be to calmly move him away from the situation, while you make a mental note of what you think may have triggered the growl. Make a graceful exit. If you act stressed you'll only add to his stress and make a bite more, not less, likely. Don't worry that removing him rewards his aggression; your first responsibility is to keep others safe and prevent him from biting.

A professional dog trainer or behaviorist can help you learn to see and interpret the signals your dog uses to try to tell you that he is uncomfortable, so you can remove the stressor—or at least, remove the dog from a stressful situation.

Once you learn the triggers that make your dog uncomfortable, you can try to keep them at a distance.

If the growl was triggered by something you were doing, stop doing it. Yes, your dog learned one tiny lesson about how to make you stop doing something he doesn't like, but you'll override that when you do lots of lessons about how that thing that made him uncomfortable makes really, really good stuff happen.

This is where counter-conditioning comes in. Your dog growls because he has a negative association with

Make sure your dog's discomfort with you touching his paw is not related to pain. If it hurts when you touch him there, counter-conditioning won't work. It's a good idea to get a full veterinary workup if there's any chance your dog's growling may be pain-related.

something—say he growls when you touch his paw. For some reason, he's convinced that having his paw touched is a bad thing. If you start by touching his knee, then feeding him a smidgen of chicken, and keep repeating that, he'll come to think that you touching his knee makes chicken happen. He'll want you to touch his leg so he gets a bit of chicken.

When you see him eagerly search for chicken when you touch his knee, you can move your hand slightly lower and touch there, until you get the same "Where's my chicken?" response at the new spot. Gradually move closer and closer to his paw, until he's delighted to have you touch his foot—it makes chicken happen! Now practice with each foot, until he's uniformly delighted to have you touch all of them. Remember that the touch comes first, so it consistently predicts the imminent arrival of chicken.

If at any time in the process—which could take days, weeks, or even months, depending on the dog and how well you apply the protocol—you see the dog's tension increase, you've moved too quickly. Back up a few inches to where he's comfortable being touched and start again. Or, there may be other stressors present that are increasing his tension. Do an environment check to be sure nothing else is happening that's adding to his stress. Have the rowdy grandkids leave the room, give him a little time to relax, and start again.

Remember, dogs can't tell us in words what's bothering them, but they can communicate a lot with their body language and canine vocal sounds. Pay attention to what your dog is telling you. Listen with heart and compassion. Be gentle when your dog tells you he needs help. Come to his rescue. Treasure his growl.

Once Bitten

It's not the end of the world if your dog bites—but you must take action.

There are few things quite as disconcerting as having your own dog bite you. Despite the horror stories of free-roaming Pit Bulls mauling children as they walk to school, the majority of bites occur in the owner's home. The majority of bite victims are friends or members of the owner's family. Of all dog bites, 61 percent occur in the home or a familiar place, and 77 percent of bite victims are family members or friends, according to a Web site run by attorney Kenneth Phillips, who specializes in dog bite cases (www.dogbitelaw.com). A relatively small percentage of bites are inflicted by errant stray dogs. This means that most bites leave a shocked owner feeling betrayed by his loyal canine, and wondering whether he can ever trust his four-footed friend again.

Your dog might seem to love being around your children—and still be at risk of biting one of them. It depends on what her specific stressors are. You need to know what her stressors are, and manage her environment carefully.

Why dogs bite

All dogs can bite, and given differing circumstances, all dogs will. Although we humans regard any bite as aggression, for dogs, biting is a natural and normal means of canine communication and defense. It's actually surprising that our dogs don't bite us more often than they do!

Aggression is generally caused by stress, which can come from a variety of sources. Some dogs have high bite thresholds—it takes a lot of stressors to make them bite. Some have low thresholds—it doesn't take much to convince them to bite. A dog with a high bite threshold may seem like the best choice around kids. This is often true, but if noisy, active children are very stressful to the dog, even a high-threshold dog might bite them. Conversely, a dog who has a low bite threshold may be a fine child's companion if children are not

one of his stressors, and if he is kept in an environment that is free of the things that are stressors for him.

Pain, fear, anxiety, arousal—any kind of threat to the dog's well-being can be considered a stressor. A timid dog whose space is trespassed upon will retreat, but if prevented from retreating, he will bite out of fear. A mother with pups whose space is trespassed upon may feel threatened by the intrusion, and bite. A resource guarder bites because he is offended (stressed) by his perception that the human might take a possession. The bite often resolves the situation for the dog and relieves his stress, which is why a dog may bite in one instant and seem fine the next. When the resource guarder bites, the human (generally) withdraws; with the threat to his food bowl gone, the dog is perfectly calm and happy again.

Wounds to the human victim's skin often heal far more quickly than the breach in the relationship between dog and human. This is unfortunate, because the majority of bites are perfectly justified—from the dog's point of view—although often misunderstood by the human.

If humans better understood dogs, we would realize it's about behavior, not trust. Many biting dogs could easily remain in their homes and lead long and happy lives, with a low risk for a second bite, if their owners only understood how to identify and minimize their dogs' stressors.

> *If your dog growls or snaps frequently, you need to take notice. He is telling you that there are lots of stressors pushing him toward his bite threshold. If you don't take action, chances are good that he will eventually bite. Dogs who bite tend to have short life spans.*

The wrong thing to do

The most dangerous course of action—for the dog and the human—is also the one taken by most uninformed owners of dogs who bite. Many people react to their dog's bite by physically and sometimes severely punishing the dog into submission. Some dog trainers even recommend this method, to be employed at the dog's first sign of aggression. A warning growl or snarl is met with a harsh verbal correction and a leash jerk, followed by more serious measures such as hanging (holding the leash so high that the dog's feet leave the ground, choking off his air until he submits) or helicoptering (spinning the dog around while he's hanging) if the dog continues to resist. While this method does

manage to "whip" some dogs "into shape," others will escalate their resistance, fighting back until dog, human, or both are seriously injured or even dead.

If your dog bites

If your dog bites, you have at least four options. You can:

1. Manage his behavior to prevent him from ever having the opportunity to bite again. While difficult, this is possible. It means greatly restricting his movements so he has no access to humans, other than adult family members. If company comes over, the dog is crated in a closed room. If the grandkids visit, he is crated or sent to a kennel that is equipped to safely handle a biting dog. Even if he adores the grandkids, the fact that he has bitten puts them at unacceptable risk. Unless you are 100 percent confident that you know what his stressors are and can prevent them from occurring during the kids' visit, you cannot take the chance.

   Of course, selecting this option means a reduced quality of life—no more walks in the park, on or off leash; no more rides in the car; and no more spending hours on his own in the fresh air and sunshine in the fenced backyard.

2. Manage his behavior to prevent him from biting while you implement a comprehensive behavior modification program. This requires a serious commitment. If your dog's behavior is relatively new and mild, you may be able to accomplish this on your own. (See "Modify aggressive behavior," on page 153.)

   Most owners, however, need the (sometimes costly) help of an experienced, positive behavior counselor or behaviorist to help them succeed. The behavior professional will help identify your dog's stressors, and set up a program to use desensitization and counter-conditioning to convince him that the things he now perceives as "bad" (stressors) are really "good." If he changes his perception, they will no longer cause him stress, and they won't push him over his bite threshold.

This doesn't happen overnight. The longer your dog has practiced his aggression responses, the longer it takes to modify them. The more committed you are to working with him, the more opportunities he will have to reprogram his responses and the faster it will happen. Meanwhile, he must be crated or kenneled while visitors or grandkids are at the house, and not be taken for walks or car rides, nor left to his own devices in the backyard.

3. Re-home him with a new owner who is willing and able to do one of the first two. This is a long shot. Depending on the circumstances of the bite and the dog's general nature, some dogs who have bitten may be accepted into training programs for government drug- or bomb-sniffing dogs, or as police K9 units. Your average adoption home, however, is no better equipped than you to make the commitment necessary to safely keep a biting dog. Most rescue groups will not accept dogs who have a history of biting, and shelters that do accept them will often euthanize, rather than take the risk (and the liability) of placing them in a new home.

If you re-home him yourself, you risk having the dog fall into the hands of someone who will punish him severely for biting, or otherwise not treat him well. You may even continue to bear some liability, moral if not also legal, should the dog do serious damage to someone at his new home.

There are millions of dogs looking for homes who haven't bitten anyone. You love your dog and are trying to re-home him. What are your chances of finding someone to adopt him who is willing to take the risk of bringing home a biting dog?

4. Have the dog euthanized. This is never a happy outcome. Still, you need to think long and hard about this dog's quality of life. If you can only manage his behavior, will he be happy, or miser-able, being shut out of the activities he loves? Can you guarantee that the home you find for him will treat him well? What if he bites again?

If you can manage and modify, and still maintain your own quality of life as well as his, by all means, that is the best choice. But if not, remember that aggression is caused by stress, and stress is not an enjoyable state of being. If the dog is so stressed that you can't succeed in managing and modifying his behavior and he is a high risk for biting someone else, he can't be living a very enjoyable life. Nor can you! As difficult as the decision may be, it is sometimes the right and responsible one for the protection of all of your loved ones, including the dog.

What you should never do is close your eyes and hope and pray that he doesn't bite again. You are responsible for protecting your family as well as other members of your community. Denial will only result in more bites.

Modify aggressive behavior

Aggression is a classically conditioned response. Your dog does not generally take a seat and ponder whether he is going to bite the next time you try to clip his nails or remove him from the bed. When a stressor occurs,

Because the risks associated with a failed program for aggression are high, it is strongly recommended that you work with a competent positive behavior professional to implement a CC&D program. The following program is not intended to take the place of professional guidance.

it triggers an involuntary reaction—the dog's brain screams, "Nail clipping—BAD!" and the dog bites. If you want the dog to stop biting when you clip his nails, you have to change his brain's reaction to "Nail clipping—GOOD!"

You will use food, a very powerful positive reinforcer, to change the way your dog's brain responds to a stressor, using "counter-conditioning and desensitization" (CC&D). Here is one possible program for a dog who bites during nail trimming, as an example. You can change the steps to fit any situation that typically causes your dog to bite.

1. Write down every step of the process you normally go through for nail trimming (or whatever situation your dog has problems with). Your list may look something like this:

    a. Set the nail clippers on coffee table.

    b. Grab dog.

    c. Drag dog to coffee table; keep stranglehold of dog's collar.

    d. Grip dog in unbreakable headlock.

    e. Pick up clippers.

    f. Pick up dog's right front paw with left hand while maintaining headlock.

    g. Move clippers toward paw.

    h. Touch paw with clippers.

    i. Clip first nail.

    j. Clip second nail, etc., all the way through all the dog's nails.

2. Determine how to separate different elements of this procedure into separate goals for CC&D. Separate goals might look like this:

    a. Develop positive association with clippers.

    b. Teach dog to sit quietly and accept paws being held.

    c. Convince dog to allow nail clipping.

3. Create a mini-CC&D program for each separate element. Work on each program separately but concurrently so you can put them all together later.

    a. Develop positive association with clippers. Purchase several nail clippers. Leave them around the house next to his dinner bowl, on the coffee table, and in other visible places. Carry them in your hand as you go about your daily routine. Feed the dog treats while you are holding the clippers. Teach him to touch the clippers with his nose for a high-value reward. Pet him

Develop a positive association with nail clippers.

with the clippers in your hand and feed him treats.

b. Teach your dog to accept paw holding. Have your dog sit quietly with you. Touch him at a point that does not elicit tension—perhaps the top of his head. Feed him a high-value treat. Repeat several times, giving him a treat each time, then move your hand slightly down his neck and feed him a treat.

Repeat this process, giving him treats all the while, very gradually moving down to his elbow, his knee, his paw. It may take several sessions just to get to his elbow. If at any time you elicit signs of aggression—a growl, snarl, or snap—you have moved too quickly. An ideal CC&D program never elicits the behavior you are trying to eliminate. Continue this gradual process until you can lift each paw and hold it longer and longer without resistance.

c. Convince the dog to allow nail clipping. Your dog now thinks that nail clippers are good and paw holding is good. You must now convince him that the actual clipping is good as well.

Do this gradually. Hold the clippers in one hand while you repeat the paw desensitization step (Step 3b) with the other, to show him that paw touching in the presence of clippers is also good. Be generous with your high-value treats. Then use the hand with the clipper to repeat Step 3b until he is happy about having you touch his paws with the clipper. Continue by closing the clippers near his toenail, then against his toenail, then by actually clipping the very tip off one nail.

4. NOW STOP! If he handled this much well, it is tempting to go on to the next nail, but it is important that you stop here. One nail clipped without resistance is a huge success. Don't spoil it by pushing him into feeling stressed, and undoing your work.

Repeat the process the next day, and if all goes well, clip the next nail. The third day, if he still does well, try clipping the next two nails. Eventually, when he is comfortable with the whole process, you can sit down and clip all his nails in one session, without risk of being bitten.

To minimize your dog's other stressors, make a complete list of all you can identify, then create and apply a program such as the one above to desensitize and counter-condition him to each. There may be some stressors for which this is impossible, but remember that the more stressors you desensitize him to, the more likely it is that he will spend the rest of his life bite-free.

Rage without Reason

Idiopathic aggression is (thankfully) quite rare, but also quite dangerous.

The term "rage syndrome" conjures up mental images of Cujo, Stephen King's fictional rabid dog, terrorizing the countryside. If you're the owner of a dog who suffers from it, it's almost that bad—never knowing when your beloved pal is going to turn, without warning, into a biting, raging canine tornado.

The condition commonly known as rage syndrome is actually more appropriately called "idiopathic aggression." The definition of idiopathic is: "Of, relating to, or designating a disease having no known cause." It applies perfectly to this behavior, which has confounded behaviorists for decades. While most other types of aggression can be modified and reduced through desensitization and counter-conditioning, idiopathic aggression often can't. It is an extremely difficult and heartbreaking condition to deal with.

The earmarks of idiopathic aggression include:

- No identifiable trigger stimulus or stimuli.
- Intense, explosive aggression.
- Onset most commonly reported in dogs one to three years old.
- Some owners report that their dogs get a glazed, or "possessed" look in their eyes just prior to an idiopathic outburst, or act confused.
- Certain breeds seem more prone to suffer from this condition, including Cocker and Springer Spaniels (hence the once-common terms—Spaniel rage, Cocker rage, and Springer rage), Bernese Mountain Dogs, St. Bernards, Doberman Pinschers, German Shepherd Dogs, and Lhasa Apsos. This would suggest a likely genetic component to the problem.

Glimmer of hope

The good news is that true idiopathic aggression is also a particularly uncommon condition. Discussed and studied widely in the 1970s and '80s, it captured the imagination of the dog world, and soon every dog with episodes of sudden, explosive aggression was tagged with the unfortunate "rage syndrome" label, especially if it was a spaniel of any type. We have since come to our senses, and now investigate much more carefully before concluding that there is truly "no known cause" for a dog's aggression.

A thorough exploration of the dog's behavior history and owner's observations often can ferret out explainable causes for the aggression. The appropriate diagnosis often turns out to be status-related aggression (once widely known as "dominance aggression") and/or resource guarding—both of which can also generate very violent, explosive reactions.

An owner can easily miss her dog's warning signs prior to a status-related attack, especially if the warning signs have been suppressed by prior physical or verbal punishment. While some dogs' lists of guardable resources may be limited and precise, with others it can be difficult to identify and recognize a resource that a dog has determined to be valuable and worth guarding. The glazed look reported by some owners may also be their interpretation of the "hard stare" or "freeze" that many dogs give as a warning signal just prior to an attack.

Although the true cause of idiopathic aggression is still not understood, and behaviorists each tend to defend their favorite theories, there is universal agreement that it is a very rare condition, and one that is extremely difficult to treat.

Theories

A variety of studies and testing over the past 30 years have failed to produce a clear cause or a definitive diagnosis for idiopathic aggression. Behaviorists can't even agree on what to call it!

Given the failure to find a specific cause, it is quite possible that there are several different causes for unexplainable aggressive behaviors that are all grouped under the term "idiopathic aggression." Some dogs in the midst of an episode may foam at the mouth and twitch, which could be an indication of epileptic seizures. The most common appearance of the behavior between one and three years of age also coincides with the appearance of most status-related aggression, as well as the development of idiopathic epilepsy, making it even impossible to use age of onset as a differential diagnosis.

Some researchers have found abnormal electro-encephalogram readings in some dogs suspected of having idiopathic aggression, but not in all such dogs they studied. Other researchers have been unable to reproduce even those inconclusive results.

Another theory is that the behavior is caused by damage to the area of the brain responsible for aggressive behavior. Yet another is that it is actually a manifestation of status-related aggression triggered by very subtle stimuli. Clearly, we just don't know.

The fact that idiopathic aggression by definition cannot be induced also makes it difficult to study and even try to find answers to the question of cause. Unlike a behavior like resource guarding—which is easy to induce and therefore easy to study in a clinical setting—the very nature of idiopathic aggression dictates that it cannot be reproduced or studied at will.

Treatment

Without knowing the cause of idiopathic aggression, treatment is difficult and frequently unsuccessful. The condition is also virtually impossible to manage safely because of the sheer unpredictability of the outbursts. The prognosis, unfortunately, is very poor, and many dogs with true idiopathic aggression must be euthanized, for the safety of surrounding humans.

Document your dog's episodes of unexplainable, explosive aggression so you can describe all the details to a trainer or behaviorist, including all environmental conditions you can think of.

Don't despair, however, if someone has told you your dog has "rage syndrome." First of all, he probably doesn't. Remember, the condition is extremely rare, and the label still gets applied all too often by uneducated dog folk to canines whose aggressive behaviors are perfectly explainable by a more knowledgeable observer.

Your first step is to find a skilled and positive trainer or behavior consultant who can give you a more educated analysis of your dog's aggression. A good behavior modification program, applied by a committed owner in consultation with a capable behavior professional, can succeed in decreasing or resolving many aggression cases, and can help you devise appropriate management plans when necessary to keep family members, friends, and visitors safe.

If your behavior professional also believes that you have a rare case of idiopathic aggression on your

The Evolving Vocabulary of Aggression

Different behaviorists and trainers have used and continue to use different terms for what was once commonly known as "rage syndrome." The confusion over what to call it is a reflection of how poorly understood the condition is:

Rage syndrome: *This once popular term has fallen into disfavor, due to its overuse, misuse, and poor characterization of the actual condition.*

Idiopathic aggression: *Now the most popular term among behaviorists; this name clearly says "we don't know what it is."*

Low-threshold dominance aggression: *Favored by those who hold that idiopathic aggression is actually a manifestation of status-related aggression with very subtle triggers.*

Mental lapse aggression syndrome: *Attached to cases diagnosed as a result of certain electroencephalogram readings (low-voltage, fast activity).*

Stimulus responsive psychomotor epilepsy: *Favored by some who suspect that idiopathic aggression is actually epileptic seizure activity.*

Here are some of the newer terms now in use to describe various types of aggressive behavior:

Status-related aggression: *Once called dominance aggression, a term still widely used. Modification of status-related aggression focuses on getting the confident, high-ranking dog to behave appropriately regardless of status; old methods of dealing with dominance aggression often focused on trying to reduce the dog's status, often without success.*

Fear-related aggression: *Once called submission aggression. A dog who is fearful may display deferent (submissive) behaviors in an attempt to ward off the fear-inducing stress. If those signals are ignored and the threat advances—a child, for example, trying to hug a dog who is backing away, ears flattened—aggression can occur.*

Possession aggression: *Previously referred to as food guarding and now also appropriately called resource guarding, this name change acknowledges that a dog may guard many objects in addition to his food—anything he considers a valuable resource, including but not limited to toys, beds, desirable locations, and proximity to humans.*

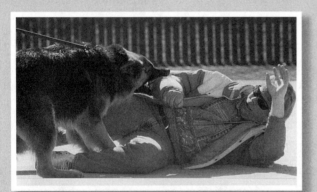

True idiopathic aggression is a particularly uncommon condition.

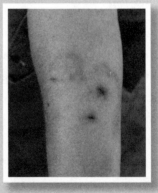

In the rare case of true idiopathic aggression, euthanasia is the only humane solution. Because the aggressive explosions are truly violent and totally unpredictable, it is neither safe nor fair to expose yourself or other friends and family to the potentially disfiguring, even deadly, results of such an attack.

Difficult Dogs

hands, then a trip to a veterinary behaviorist is in order. Some dogs will respond to drug therapies for this condition; many will not. Some minor success has been reported with the administration of phenobarbital, but it is unclear as to whether the results are from the sedative effect of the drug, or if there is an actual therapeutic effect.

In many cases of true idiopathic aggression, euthanasia is the only solution. Because the aggressive explosions are truly violent and totally unpredictable, it is neither safe nor fair to expose yourself or other friends and family to the potentially disfiguring, even deadly, results of such an attack. If this is the sad conclusion in the case of your dog, euthanasia is the only humane option. Comfort yourself with the knowledge you have done everything possible for him, hold him close as you say goodbye, and send him gently to a safer place. Then take good care of yourself.

Reform School
The latest developments in remedial classes for reactive dogs.

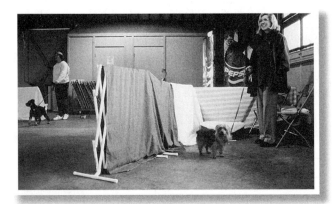

In today's "difficult dog" classes, the focus is on gradually teaching dogs new and more appropriate responses to increasingly proximate contact with other dogs. Pupils begin learning new skills behind visual barriers, which help prevent triggering relapses.

We used to call them growl classes—a term that, in hindsight, was perhaps a poor choice, likely to intensify feelings of apprehension in the human member of the training team before dog and owner even walked through the door into the classroom for the first session. These were classes designed for dogs whose aggressive on-leash reactions to dogs or other environmental stimuli made them inappropriate candidates for regular companion-dog classes; they were simply too disruptive, even dangerous, to be in mixed company.

While the term "growl class" may have mostly gone by the wayside, fortunately the concept of a class for difficult dogs has not. It is a tribute to dog owners of today that many of them are unwilling to give up on their canine companions, even when faced with behavior challenges that can shake the foundations of the dog–human bond. It's as much a tribute to the modern dog training profession that trainers continue to seek out and develop innovative, positive, and effective solutions for owners who are committed to helping their dogs "be nice." From East Coast to West,

trainers are increasingly offering classes that now go by friendlier names, such as "Feisty Fido," the goal of which is to help owners help their difficult dogs be more manageable in the real world.

Do you have a Feisty Fido?

Candidates for difficult dog classes are generally those who tend to react more intensely than the situation calls for. They may bark aggressively at other dogs on leash, lunge uncontrollably after joggers, or claw at car windows when someone passes by. While some of this is normal dog behavior (chasing things that move is a hardwired canine response), difficult dogs are distinguished by their owners' sense of frustration and helplessness—they have tried all the remedies that worked just fine for their friends' and neighbors' dogs

Oops! These dogs have gotten a little closer than is comfortable for them at this stage. Both stiffen and begin to "wind up" into an aggressive confrontation. Their owners stay calm (very important), keep the dogs from actually being able to touch, give a calm "Off!" cue, and offer a tasty lure to lead the dogs away from each other. It works beautifully, and the owners lavish praise and treats on the dogs as they retreat.

At the Marin Humane Society in Novato, California, instructor Trish King walks a strange dog past an opening in a students' alcove, as the owner rewards her dog for staying calm.

Later in the class, students walk their dogs—at a distance that does not set them off—past other students, rewarding the dogs for maintaining focus on their handlers.

to no avail. Fido is still intimidatingly feisty. If you are reluctant to take your dog to a training class because of his embarrassing or frightening behavior, or the two of you have been excused from a regular class for the same reason, then you are good candidates for a canine "special education" class.

Most trainers who offer classes for Rowdy Rovers agree that, while dog–dog aggression is an allowable behavior problem for class participants, dog–human aggression is not.

Different Classes for Different Types of "Rowdy Rovers"

Like most trainers who provide this type of service, Trish King agrees that owner education is a vital part of the program. She offers three different types of classes for dogs with challenging social behaviors, to create positive learning environments for the humans that are most conducive to addressing their dogs' specific behaviors:

- **Difficult Dogs:** *For dogs who are seriously aggressive toward other dogs.*
- **Feisty Little Fidos:** *For difficult dogs who weigh 25 pounds or less.*
- **ADD Dogs:** *For young adult dogs who are displaying "Adolescent Dog Disorder"—frustration or aggression on leash as a direct result of their strong desire to go play with other dogs.*

The goals are similar but different for each type of class. For the Difficult Dogs, the aim is to increase the owner's level of confidence and control, as well as modify canine behavior so their dogs are safe and civilized around other dogs. There is no expectation that these dogs will come to love and frolic with each other by the end of the eight-week program.

Feisty Little Fidos are also expected to learn to be civilized around others, although because of their smaller size, actual physical control is less of an issue.

ADD dogs are the group most likely to learn how to "play well with others" by the end of their classes. Their inappropriate behavior is driven by the thwarting of their strong desire to socialize, as opposed to truly agonistic motives. When owners are taught how to appropriately redirect and reward their dogs' focus and attention, the frustrated arousal recedes. Owners in this class are often gratified by the ultimate miracle of seeing their dogs romping happily together with no signs of aggression.

Methods and tools

Overwhelmingly, trainers use positive training and behavior modification tools and methods to work with Feisty Fidos. Owners bring their dogs' soft beds to class, and the dogs relax in them in between more active parts of class, giving the dogs a chance to "practice" calming down from an aroused state, even in the presence of other dogs. Treats, toys, and touch are used to reward dogs for their progress; these also work to classically condition the dogs to form more positive associations with being around other dogs.

Finding a class near you

Once a rarity, difficult dog classes can now be found in many communities. You can go to the Web site for the Association of Pet Dog Trainers (apdt.com) and click on its "Trainer Search" button. The site allows you to search by city and state for trainers near you, and while not all APDT members may fit our definition of a positive trainer, and not all of them offer classes for Rowdy Rovers, it's a good place to start.

Not just any class, though . . .

Once you have located a class near you, you will need to investigate further.

- Observe a class in progress. If a trainer won't let you observe a class, don't bother to pursue it any further.
- Listen to the trainer speaking. She should discuss the science of behavior and learning, and explain concepts such as counter-conditioning, desensiti- zation, and stress levels. She should not just tell people what to do with their dogs, but how, and especially why.
- Be absolutely sure the training is all positive. Handlers should be using buckle collars, leashes, harnesses, treats, and clickers. Anything that applies force is counterproductive. No choke chains, no prong collars, no shock collars.
- Be sure the instructor is experienced at teaching difficult dog classes. Everyone has to learn some- how—usually as an assistant or apprentice—and you don't want yourself and your dog to be guinea pigs.
- Look for safety controls throughout the class. Dogs and owners should be set up to succeed safely. Equipment, methods, exercises, and environments should all be designed to ensure safety; anything in the environment that puts dogs or humans at risk is not acceptable.

Patricia McConnell's booklet, *Feisty Fido*, is included as a textbook by many trainers who teach difficult dog classes, and is an excellent adjunct to the information in this article. While hands-on assistance from a skilled trainer in the nurturing environment of a group class of owners facing the same challenges you are with your Rowdy Rover is ideal, McConnell's book is a great backup tool that can start you in the right direction while you track down a suitable class.

Finally, don't despair. You are not alone, and your dog's behavior is probably not beyond all hope and help. Find yourself a good Feisty Fido class, and you just might be pleasantly surprised to find that it's easier and far less painful than you thought to turn your difficult dog into a reliably good canine citizen.

CHAPTER 4

Nutrition

How to Choose a Food
You are uniquely well-qualified to select the best food for your dog.

No one is in a better position than you are to decide which food you should feed your dog. That may not be what you wanted to hear. You may have been hoping that someone would reveal to you the name of the world's healthiest food, so you could just buy that and be done with it.

But dogs, just like people, are individuals. What works for this dog won't work for that one. A Pointer who goes jogging with his marathon-running owner every day needs a lot more calories than the Golden Retriever who watches TV all day. The diet that contains enough fat to keep a sled dog warm through an Alaskan winter would kill a Miniature Poodle who suffers from pancreatitis.

Every food on the market contains different ingredients, and each one has the potential to cause

Should you set up blind taste tests for your dog? Ask your vet what to feed your dog? Go with what your dog-walker suggests? Choose whichever product WDJ says to feed? The answer to every one of these questions is NO!

symptoms of allergy or intolerance in some dogs. Every food contains a different ratio of macro-nutrients—protein, fat, and carbohydrates—and you have to learn by trial and error which ratio works best for your dog. Each product contains varying amounts of vitamins and minerals, and though most fall within the ranges considered acceptable by the Association of American Feed Control Officials (AAFCO), some may be in excess of, or deficient to, *your* dog's needs.

So how do you choose?

The starting place

Well, you have to start somewhere, and you undoubtedly have. Your dog is eating *something* already. First you must learn how to identify the foods with the best-quality ingredients—whole meats, vegetables, fruits, and grains, and high-quality sources of dietary fat—to get you into the right "ballpark" in terms of quality. Then you have to start individualized feeding trials on your dog.

Start by assessing your dog's health. Take a sheet of paper and make a list with two columns: one for health problems, and one for health assets. Any conditions for which she receives veterinary care or medications go in the "problems" column. Other conditions that should be listed here include bad breath; teeth that are prone to tartar buildup; chronically goopy eyes; infection-prone or stinky ears; a smelly, greasy, flaky, or thinning coat; itchy paws; excessive gas; recurrent diarrhea, constipation, or incontinence; repeated infestations of worms or fleas; low or excessive energy; and a sudden onset of antisocial or aggressive behavior.

In the health assets column, list all the health characteristics that your dog has in her favor, such as fresh breath, clean teeth, bright eyes, clean ears, a lack of itching, a glossy coat, problem-free elimination, a normal appetite and energy level, and a good attitude.

If there are a lot more assets on your list than problems, and the problems are very minor, you may have already found a diet that works well for your dog. But if your list reveals a lot more problems than assets, your dog is a good candidate for a change of diet—in addition to an examination and some guidance from a good holistic veterinarian!

Now take a look at the food you are currently feeding your dog. Note the food's ingredients, as well as its protein and fat levels, and its caloric content. *Write all of this down*, so you can make logical adjustments if need be.

Nutritional management of disease

Just two decades ago, it was considered fairly radical to propose that canine diseases could be treated, at least in part, by manipulating the patients' diets. Today, the increasing availability of "prescription" diets is the big story in the pet food industry. As stated by the editors in the preface of the fourth edition (2000) of *Small Animal Clinical Nutrition* (the nutrition bible for most veterinarians):

> This is truly an exciting time for those involved in the discipline of clinical nutrition because of the veterinary profession's increased understanding of the role of nutrition in health and disease management, pet owners' continued interest in receiving the best nutritional information for their pets and the recent proliferation of commercially available therapeutic

> **Keep a Health Journal for Your Dog**
>
> *Nobody likes to do it, but if your dog suffers from chronic or intermittent health problems, keeping a record of his diet and symptoms will be invaluable for determining whether there is a link between his diet and his condition. Then, periodically look through the data for trends. Did your dog's energy and coat quality go down when you switched to that "diet" food? He probably needs a food with a higher percentage of fat. Did some types of food seem to trigger diarrhea that persisted for days, and only went away when you switched to another food? Look for ingredients or macronutrient levels that these problem-causing foods have in common, and adjust your next dog food purchase accordingly.*

foods. Our ability to improve the quality of life for pets and their owners is great.

If your dog has any sort of disease or an inherited propensity for disease, ask your veterinarian about the benefits of nutritional therapy to help treat or prevent the disease. *Don't* settle for the suggestion of a commercial "prescription" diet; most of them are formulated with lower-quality ingredients. Instead, ask what *specifically* in the diet has been manipulated so as to be beneficial for your dog. Then, see if you can find a product that offers the same benefits *and* better-quality ingredients. The best example is a "kidney" diet for dogs with kidney failure. The goal is to feed these patients a diet with a moderate level of *very* high-quality protein and low amounts of phosphorus. An intelligently formulated home-prepared diet can do a *far* better job of accomplishing these goals than the commercial diets on the market.

You should also do some research on your own to determine what dietary changes might help your dog. A good starting place is Donald R. Strombeck's *Home-Prepared Dog & Cat Diets: The Healthful Alternative* (available by order in bookstores, and from Amazon. com and DogWise.com). Dr. Strombeck details strategies for changing the dog's diet to treat and/or prevent gastrointestinal, skin, skeletal and joint, renal, urinary, endocrine, heart, pancreatic, and hepatic disease.

Other diseases that can be improved with dietary management include:

- **Allergy or intolerance.** There are a number of breeds that are particularly susceptible to food allergies, including Cocker Spaniels, Dalmatians, English Springer Spaniels, Labrador Retrievers, Lhasa Apsos, Miniature Schnauzers, and more. Again, it's important to keep a record of what foods you feed your dog, what they contain, and how your dog looks and feels. If your records indicate that one or more ingredients trigger bad reactions in your dog, seek out foods that do not contain those ingredients in any amount.

- **Cancer.** High-fat, low-carbohydrate (or carb-free) diets are ideal for cancer patients. Cancer cells use carbs for energy, and don't easily utilize fat, so you can effectively "starve" the cancer cells while providing extra energy to your dog with a diet rich in a high-quality fat sources.

- **Inherited metabolic disorders.** Some breeds are prone to diseases with a strong dietary influence. For example, the West Highland White Terrier and the Cocker Spaniel have an inherited tendency to suffer from copper buildup in the liver; these dogs should eat a diet that is formulated with low levels of copper. Malamutes and Siberian Huskies can inherit a zinc-metabolism disorder, and require a high-zinc diet (or zinc supplements).

Ask your veterinarian (and reliable breeders) about your dog's breed-related nutritional requirements. And contact the manufacturer of your dog's food for the expanded version of the food's nutrient levels. Pet food makers are not required to print the levels of every nutrient on their labels, but should make this information available to you upon request.

If your dog is overweight, you may have to cut her daily ration considerably to prevent her from getting fat. If she responds to forced dieting with begging, counter surfing, and garbage raiding, you may have to seek out a high-fiber, low-calorie food—one that may not necessarily contain the highest-quality protein or fat sources on the market—to keep your dog feeling contentedly full without getting fat.

Caloric considerations

Another thing you have to consider is the caloric content of the food you choose. If the food you select for your dog is energy-dense, and your dog is a couch potato, you may have to cut her daily ration considerably to prevent her from getting fat. Some dogs respond to forced dieting with begging, counter surfing, and garbage raiding. If your dog is one of these, you may have to seek out a high-fiber, low-calorie food—one that may not necessarily contain the highest-quality protein or fat sources on the market—to keep your dog feeling contentedly full without getting fat.

Dogs exhibit a wide range of energy requirements. You may have to find a higher- or lower-calorie food based on the following attributes that can affect your dog's energy needs:

- **Activity level.** The more a dog exercises, the more energy he needs to consume to maintain his condition; it's that simple.

- **Growth.** Growing puppies have higher energy requirements than adult dogs. A food with a higher protein level, but a moderate (not high) fat level, is ideal. Obese puppies are far more prone to degenerative joint disease—especially in large and giant breeds—than puppies with a normal or slim physique.

- **Age.** The age at which a dog becomes a senior citizen varies from breed to breed, with larger dogs considered geriatric at earlier ages. Older dogs typically require fewer calories to maintain their body weight and condition, partly because they tend to be less active than younger dogs.

- **Environmental conditions.** Dogs who live or spend much of their time outside in severe cold temperatures need from 10 percent to as much as 90 percent more energy than dogs who enjoy a temperate climate. The thickness and quality of the dog's coat, the amount of body fat he has, and the quality of his shelter have direct effects on the dog's energy needs.

- **Illness.** Sick dogs have increased energy needs; it takes energy to mount an immune response or repair tissues. However, dogs who do not feel well also tend to be inactive, which lowers their energy needs.

- **Reproduction.** A pregnant female's energy requirement does not increase significantly until the final third of her pregnancy, when it may increase by a factor of three.

- **Lactation.** A nursing female may require as much as eight times as much energy as a female of the same age and condition who is not nursing.

- **Neutering.** It is generally accepted that neutered (and spayed) dogs have reduced energy needs. However, there are actually no studies that conclusively prove that neutered dogs require fewer calories simply as a result of lower hormone levels. It has been suggested that these dogs gain weight due to increased appetites and/or decreased activity levels.

- **Other individual factors.** Other factors that can affect a dog's energy requirement include its temperament (nervous or placid?) and skin, fat, and coat quality (how well he is insulated against weather conditions).

Choosing a food for your dog can be daunting. Don't stress! Just read the labels, choose one, and see how your dog responds. If his response is poor, try another. There are many top-quality foods available today.

Human factors

Finally, there are the human factors that may influence your dog-food purchasing decision, such as cost and local availability. Understand that there *is* a connection between the quality of an animal's food and his health, and do the best you can do.

It's also worth considering the reliability, responsiveness, and availability of the manufacturer's customer service people. It can be frustrating and costly if a company makes terrific food, but you can never reach them, your direct-ship order is regularly late, or the customer service people are either rude or unhelpful. Today, there are too many companies doing a good job and making good food to put up with this.

The Right Stuff

How to identify the healthiest dry dog foods on the market.

Top-quality food starts with top-quality ingredients. To mix a metaphor, you really *can't* make a silk purse out of sows' ears, chicken heads, bovine tumors, restaurant grease, rendered fat from animals that died on farms, and cheap grain by-products left over from the human food manufacturing industry. Many people say, "Oh, for goodness sake, they are just dogs! Why can't they eat guts and stuff?" Well, they *can*, of course, and most dogs *do!* The vast majority of pet food produced in this country is made with what we would consider to be poor-quality ingredients.

For optimal health, every credible *human* nutrition expert in the world advocates eating a balanced, varied diet of fresh, top-quality foods. There is no biological reason to expect dogs (or any other animal) to be any different. Pet bird experts now realize that an all-seed diet is unbalanced and inadequate for avian health; birds also need access to fresh plant material (fruits, vegetables, and green foods such as sprouts) to thrive. People who keep rabbits as pets now know that alfalfa pellets alone don't sustain rabbits as well as a diet that includes a variety of fresh hay, root vegetables, and green, leafy vegetables.

Dogs are just the same. A balanced, home-prepared diet of a variety of fresh, healthy ingredients is optimum; a commercial diet made with the same ingredients is leagues better than a commercial diet made with cheap fats discarded from restaurants, inexpensive carbohydrates produced as waste from the brewing industry, and plant proteins such as corn gluten meal (animal proteins have a much more complete amino acid profile than plant proteins).

Of course, the best ingredients cost a lot, and a reliable supply may be difficult to find. Pet food makers who are committed to producing foods for the top end of the market have to continually hunt for ingredients that meet their standards—and be prepared to reject shipments that fail to pass their inspection.

Ingredient quality is *the* key to a dog food's quality, as well as the criterion that is easiest for the average consumer to judge, based on a simple review of the ingredients listed on the label.

Good manufacturing practices

Ingredients aren't the *whole* story, of course. A company that spends the lion's share of its budget on the ingredients for its foods, but, as one example, expends few resources on laboratory testing to confirm the product meets its label guarantees, may cause the food to flunk inspection by state feed control officials and stop its sale.

Tough standards (and top compensation) for employees, good employee management, superior packaging, proper storage, reliable transportation, smart marketing, education of sales staff at retail locations, knowledgeable and responsive customer service and support . . . these are all areas where a company needs to shine to garner the long-term support of consumers who will pay top dollar for top-shelf products.

Manufacturers who neglect even one of these areas are just asking for trouble. If plant employees don't read well or communicate well with their supervisors and coworkers, they may fail to properly inspect a load of corn that arrives at the plant, allowing toxin-laden grain into production; or accidentally contaminate production equipment with an improperly diluted cleaning agent; or add a dangerously high amount of the mineral supplement to a batch of food, which can cause a life-threatening overdose in exposed dogs.

Most hazards to the wholesomeness of a pet food

can be controlled through rigorous planning and management. However, a company must have the resources and commitment to expend those resources to continuously maintain vigilance over the product management from ingredient purchasing to consumer support.

Consumers have few resources available to determine whether dog food makers have "the right stuff" in these areas. One of the best indictors of a company's commitment to quality is reflected in its ability to respond quickly and intelligently to consumer questions and concerns. Noncompulsory manufacturing certifications are another way a company can unequivocally demonstrate its commitment to quality.

How to Select Dry Food

- **Look for foods that contain a lot of high-quality animal proteins.** It would be great if manufacturers disclosed the approximate percentage of meat, poultry, or fish in their food, but they rarely do, so look for foods that *appear* to have lots of animal protein. Ingredients are listed in order of their weight, so ideally a food will have one or two animal proteins in the first few ingredients.

When a company offers a number of "special formula" products, you must read the labels to determine how (or if!) the products differ in any significant way.

Understand that whole meat (such as chicken, beef, and lamb) contains a lot of water weight. If a food list starts out with chicken, and there is no other animal protein listed until seventh or eighth on the list, the food does *not* actually contain a lot of animal protein. But if it starts out with chicken, and chicken (or another animal) "meal" (essentially dehydrated chicken) is second or third on the list, chances are the product contains an admirable amount of animal protein. Animal proteins tend to be more digestible and palatable than plant proteins and offer a wider array of essential and nonessential amino acids.

- **Reject any food containing meat by-products or poultry by-products.** It's just about impossible to ascertain the quality of by-products used by a food manufacturer. There is a much wider range of quality in the by-products available for pet food manufacturing than there is for whole meats. Whole meats are expensive, and because they are expensive, dog food makers insist on their quality to an extent that is unreasonable when buying bargain-basement by-products. So, because the quality cannot be confirmed, avoid foods that contain by-products.

- **Reject foods containing fat or protein not identified by species.** "Animal fat" is a euphemism for a low-quality, low-priced mix of fats of uncertain origin. "Meat meal" could be practically anything.

- **Look for the use of whole grains and vegetables.** That said, some grains and vegetables have valuable constituents that accomplish specific tasks in a dog food formula. The more vegetable fragments and grain by-products on the ingredients list, and/or the higher they appear on the list, the lower-quality the food.

- **Eliminate all foods with artificial colors, flavors, or preservatives** listed on their ingredients panels. Note: Some ingredients—usually fats, and some fish products—arrive at the pet food factory containing artificial preservatives; these do not have to be disclosed on the ingredient list, since the maker did not add them.

- **Eliminate all foods with added sweeteners.** Dogs, like people, enjoy sweet foods. Like people, they can develop a taste for these nutritionally empty calories.

Also look for these elements on the label:

- A date code or production code that is easy to find, read, and interpret.
- More than just the required nutrients (fat, protein, fiber, moisture) listed on a product label's "guaranteed analysis" (GA).
- The caloric content of the food listed on the label.
- *All* of the food maker's contact information listed on its product labels (and their product literature and Web sites).
- Certified organic ingredients.

In addition, some manufacturers have pursued and obtained noncompulsory manufacturing certifications, including:

AIB certification. The American Institute of Baking (AIB) is a nonprofit educational foundation that offers the most comprehensive and well-accepted standards and inspection for good manufacturing practices in grain-based food production, including pet food production.

Manufacturers pay for the voluntary inspection of their plants and their program documentation. The inspection results in a score from 0 to 1,000; if the score is 800 or higher, the inspected facility receives a certificate of achievement or recognition. A score of 900 or more receives a "Superior" rating; a score of 800 to 899 receives a rating of "Excellent," and a score of 700 to 799 receives a "Satisfactory" rating. Current and/or subsequent high AIB ratings confirm a manufacturer's commitment to excellence.

APHIS registration. A company that alleges to use top-quality meat sources (sometimes claimed as "human quality," though no such legal definition for this term exists) in its products should be able to prove it with registration numbers for all its meat suppliers from the United States Department of Agriculture's Animal and Plant Health Inspection Service (USDA APHIS).

ISO 9001:2000 rating. The International Organization for Standardization (ISO, and yes, that's the order in which they put their initials) is a nongovernmental organization that promotes quality and standardization in management as a tool for improving any entity that supplies a product or service. The ISO standard that can be applied to the production of pet food is called ISO 9001:2000. The process of readying a company to qualify for an ISO 9001:2000 rating is expensive, time-consuming, and perhaps only worth the effort to a fairly sizeable company.

Organic certification. In 2002, the United States Department of Agriculture (USDA) National Organic Program (NOP) created a seal (and accompanying rules to govern its use) that qualifying pet food makers could put on their products to indicate they were made with organic ingredients in a plant that passed a rigorous inspection by an organics program certifying agency. In 2004, the USDA attempted to disallow pet food makers to represent their products as being in certified compliance with USDA's NOP standards, because pet foods were not regulated by the USDA in the first place. (The regulation of pet food production is conducted by states.) The USDA backed down in mid-2005, allowing pet food producers who met the requirements to continue carrying the organic seal, but appointed an ad hoc task force committee to develop organic labeling standards tailored for pet food.

Can? Do!

The best canned dog foods offer myriad benefits for your dogs.

Selling the entire concept of canned food to diehard kibble fans is an uphill battle. "It's expensive," dog owners frequently complain. "It smells bad. It's not very convenient. It has to be kept in the refrigerator once it's opened. When you have big dogs, you have to open too many cans to make a meal!"

These may be valid points. But have you ever noticed how dogs are *crazy* for the stuff?

The line of really good canned dog foods gets longer every day as mainstream pet food makers explore the top end of the market, and those who have years of experience making these foods expand their lines. Our dogs are the winners in the competition.

It's possible that dogs like canned food simply because it smells strong. But it may also have something to do with the fact that canned dog foods usually contain much more meat—sometimes twice as much or even more—than dry dog foods.

Canned foods also retain their nutritional value better than dry foods. Further, the nutrients contained in the food ingredients suffer less damage in the cooking process than the nutrients in the ingredients of kibble. (Note that vitamin/mineral mixes are added to *all* commercial foods, to ensure the finished products contain minimum levels of a range of nutrients needed by dogs—the canine equivalent of the "recommended daily amount.")

The amount of protein and fat in a food before and after it is canned are virtually unchanged. Neither does the canning process affect most vitamins. It has been said that vegetables can lose more vitamins by lying in a refrigerator for a week than in the canning process.

Canned foods usually contain far fewer chemical additives than dry foods, if any at all. It would be wasteful to use artificial flavors in canned products; because of the moist, fragrant nature of the meat-based contents, artificial flavoring and other palatants are not needed to entice dogs.

To destroy any possible bacterial contaminants, cans are subjected to heat processing after they have been sealed. This obviates the need for preservatives to keep the food from spoiling. (This does not mean the foods are entirely free of preservatives; some ingredients have preservatives added to them before they arrive at the pet food plant. As long as the maker does not *add* preservatives, this "hidden" ingredient does not have to be declared on the food label.)

Thanks to the oxygen-free environment, canned food is prevented from degrading for at least several years. Note that because it lacks added preservatives, canned food *must* be kept refrigerated after opening, and, like fresh meat or poultry, is best consumed within a day or two.

It's the water

The most obvious difference between canned and dry dog foods is the moisture (water) content. Most canned foods contain about 78 percent moisture.

Canned dog foods contain so much water for two reasons. The most important one is because water helps facilitate the production process; without added water, the mixed ingredients would be too thick to flow through the mixing and filling machines in the manufacturing process. (This is why water is often described on the list of ingredients of many canned foods as "water sufficient for processing.")

By the way, eating a food that is so high in moisture is helpful for dogs with cystitis or kidney disease. The high moisture content can also help a dog who is on a diet feel full faster.

Moisture-laden ingredients such as fresh vegetables and, especially, fresh or frozen meats are most efficiently used in canned foods. In the production of *dry* food, moisture has to be removed from these ingredients, which uses energy and costs money. Because water-filled ingredients can be used so efficiently in wet foods, they *are*. This is another reason canned foods, even lower-quality examples, tend to contain more fresh or frozen meat and fresh vegetables than their dry counterparts.

When a mix of good-quality, fresh or frozen animal products is used in a canned food, the resulting food will often contain the amounts of protein (and range of constituent amino acids) and fat required by law; all that is needed to make it "complete and balanced" is a vitamin/mineral supplement, and sometimes some ingredients to correct the calcium-phosphorus ratio. With dry foods, most manufacturing equipment can't tolerate mixtures that contain more than 50 percent meat, while canned foods may contain as much as 95 percent meat.

Further, meat—and by this we mean all animal proteins, including poultry, pork, fish, lamb, and beef—is *the* most palatable ingredient that pet food makers have at their disposal. Funny how dogs like what's good for them.

How to choose a canned food

Like every type of dog food, only a small percentage of canned products are of the utmost quality. The bulk of the market pursues high-volume sales of low-cost foods. Only a few manufacturers have trained their sights on the top end of the market, where dog owners expect only the best ingredients and utmost performance from the food—healthy, happy companion dogs; show dogs with great coats, teeth, and eyes; breeding dogs with perfect production records.

There is no legal definition of a "premium" or "super-premium" food, so what it means when manufacturers describe their products with those words is anybody's guess. Some justify the appellation with the explanation that their products are extremely high in protein or fat. However, a high protein and fat content does *not* make a food "better." You can definitely feed a dog too much of either one.

The following is *Whole Dog Journal*'s selection criteria for a top-quality wet food:

- Eliminate all foods containing artificial colors, flavors, or added preservatives.
- Reject foods containing fat or protein not identified by species. "Animal fat" and "meat proteins"

If your dog needs to lose weight, you can use canned foods as part of his ration to help him feel full faster. Look for low-fat varieties, however.

Consider feeding canned foods if your dog is at risk for, or is suffering from, any sort of cystitis or kidney disease.

Buy products that list a whole meat product first on the ingredients panel.

Look for products that contain whole meats, vegetables, and grains (if any).

Expect to pay for quality. Top-quality food is not inexpensive.

Puppy, Adult, Active, Senior, Lite . . . Does It Make a Difference?

When a pet food maker offers 5 or 20 varieties of its dog food, how do you choose one for your dog? Does he have to eat a "senior" formula now that you have celebrated his seventh birthday? Must you buy "small bites" if your dog is tiny? Is feeding "lite" food better than feeding a smaller amount of regular food?

There are no uniform answers to these questions. You must read the labels to determine how the products differ, and to guess whether the differences are significant enough to warrant buying something other than the regular "adult" variety.

Compare the ingredients lists and the guaranteed analyses of two varieties. Ask your vet to suggest target fat and protein levels for your dog, and look for a food that meets those targets, regardless of the type of dog for which it is ostensibly formulated.

are euphemisms for low-quality, low-priced mixed ingredients of uncertain origin.

- Reject any food containing meat by-products or poultry by-products. There is a wide variation in the quality of the by-products that are available to dog food producers. And there is no way for the average dog owner (or us, for that matter) to find out, beyond a shadow of a doubt, whether the

by-products used are carefully handled, chilled, and used fresh within a day or two of slaughter (as some companies have told us), or the cheapest, lowest-quality material found on the market. There is some, but *much less* variation in the quality of whole-meat products; they are too expensive to be handled carelessly.

- Eliminate any food containing sugar or other sweetener. A food containing quality meats shouldn't need additional palatants to entice dogs.

- Look for foods with whole meat, fish, or poultry as the *first* ingredient on the food labels. Ingredients are listed on the label by the total weight they contribute to the product. Fresh or frozen whole meats contain lots of water, but in lower-quality products, water may be the first ingredient.

- Look for a nutritious meat, poultry, or fish broth used in place of water. Broth is obtained by cooking meat, fish, or poultry bones, part, and/or muscle tissue, and must be at least 95 percent moisture.

- If grains or vegetables are used, look for the use of *whole* grains and vegetables, rather than a series of reconstituted parts e.g. "rice," rather than "rice flour, rice bran, brewer's rice."

- Speaking of grain . . . there is nothing that says a canned food has to contain *any* grain. Grains are less expensive, and have lower-quality amino acid profiles than meat and poultry. And, unlike humans, dogs do *not* need carbohydrates to live; they can do fine with just protein and fat. Look for foods with small amounts of grain (or none).

When Foods Go Bad

Know how to protect your dog from commercial food disasters.

The extensive pet food recalls of early 2007 shook the industry to its core. If there was an upside to the disaster, it's that America woke up, started looking at its pet food labels, and had a few questions. Every pet food company in this country was *buried* in calls, letters, and e-mails from pet owners who wanted to know how the disaster had happened—and what the makers of their dogs' foods were doing to prevent it from happening again. That's a *good* thing.

Nevertheless, dog owners need to stay aware of the fact that commercial pet food (or human food!) is not infallible. As we learned in 2007, ingredients can be adulterated with impurities and toxins. In addition, errors in formulation, production, storage, and transport can result in tainted or unhealthy food. Labels can be inaccurate, for a variety of reasons.

If you are aware of the potential dangers of tainted dog food, and know how to prevent them or rapidly respond to them, your dog should be safe from harm.

Manufacturing problems

Every pet food maker has war stories to tell about disasters they averted (sometimes at great cost) and smaller-scale quality-control failures that cost them clients. A partial list of the most common things that can go wrong in the production of dog food include:

- Spoiled or tainted ingredients are used, including rancid fats, spoiled proteins, or moldy grains. Some molds excrete toxins (collectively called mycotoxins); some mycotoxins, such as vomitoxin, can make dogs very ill. Others, such as aflatoxin, can kill.
- Ingredients are included in excessive (toxic) amounts, including vitamin/mineral premixes, preservatives, or coloring agents.
- Ingredients that are not supposed to be in a formula are included by error (this is dangerous to a dog with a severe allergy to an ingredient that is not on the product label).
- Foreign object contamination: plastic, glass, metal, rodents, insects, pesticides, or cleaning agents.
- The food doesn't "cook" at adequate temperatures to result in a complete bacterial kill.
- The plant's equipment is not cleaned adequately or frequently enough, resulting in contaminated product.
- Kibble is inadequately dried, resulting in the growth of mold in the bags.

Pay attention if your dog is reluctant or slow to eat his food, and don't force him to eat it! It may be rancid—or contain a toxin.

If it doesn't *look* right . . .

First and foremost, it's important to withhold any food from your dog that doesn't look right. The presence of foreign objects, a coating of powdery or hairy mold, and even a significant deviation from the food's usual color can signify something amiss with the food's production.

If you see anything unusual about your dog's regular food, call the maker's toll-free number, printed on the bag or can of most commercial foods, and talk to a representative about it. (If the package does not list a phone number for the maker, call the retailer that sold you the food and enlist his help in reaching the manufacturer. Usually, the retailer will have a number for his salesperson, who will work quickly to put you in touch with his employer.)

The company should be able to provide an explanation and offer remediation. First, though, they will need to confirm that you do, in fact, have some of their food. To do this, they will need information from the product label so they can determine when and where the food was made. For this reason, you *must* have and keep each bag or can until you have fed all the product it contains.

The importance of this cannot be overstated. "Without the date-code information (from the label), the manufacturer is totally blind," says Russell Armstrong, president and cofounder of VeRus Pet Foods, of Abingdon, Maryland. In fact, he adds, every food maker has had the experience of trying to deal with a dog owner who insists their pet became ill after eating the company's food, but who can provide no proof of ever having purchased it.

If, in contrast, an owner is able to provide a food maker with the date-code information from the food in question, the maker can check its database for any other reports of problems with that batch. If an investigation is needed, the maker can even go to its storehouse of samples from that batch and have them examined and/or tested for the irregularity seen by the dog owner.

"I require my manufacturers to pull samples from every 1,000 pounds of product," says Frank Cook, vice president of Natural Balance Pet Foods Inc., of Pacoima, California. "Usually, for our products, our co-packer [contracted manufacturer] runs about 80,000 pounds [in a batch]. I have them pull two samples every 1,000 pounds. One is tested, and one is shelved for the life span of the product. Should there be any problem with that product down the road, we always have a sample to test."

Often, in the case of a foreign object in the food or food that is suspected to have made a dog ill, the maker will ask the consumer to send the remainder of the product back to the company for testing and analysis. This needs to be done, but the consumer should be a little cautious, warns Armstrong. "I think it's important to send the manufacturer some of the food—or the foreign object, if that's what the trouble is. But you should realize that once you send it away, you don't have it anymore, and if a legal problem arises, you are going to wish you had your evidence back," says Armstrong.

His recommendation is to send just some of the suspect food back to the maker. In the case of a foreign object, take pictures or other documentation. "That way, if the manufacturer fails to test it, or reports that everything was perfectly fine, and you are skeptical or concerned whether you are getting the right answer, at least you have some product that you could send out for testing yourself," Armstrong advises.

Armstrong takes the approach that well-informed customers are the happiest and safest customers, so he encourages owners to let the company know about any anomaly seen in VeRus's products. In the best case scenario, he says, a call to the maker will calm the consumer's fears and educate them a little more about their dog's food.

"Even small things are worth a call to the maker," he says. "For example, if you notice discoloration in the product—it could be indicative of mold or rancidity, or it could be something innocuous. A change

Buy fresh food. Check the "best if used by" date on the bag.

Visually inspect the food—it shouldn't be dusty or moldy. Smell it—it shouldn't smell rancid. Discuss any irregularity with the maker before you decide whether to feed it.

Store dry food in its original bag, in a cool, dry place. Ideally, keep the bag in an airtight container.

If your dog has an adverse health event that could *possibly* be related to the food, withdraw the food immediately. Contact the manufacturer and report the event as well as the product's date code. If the symptoms are serious, get your dog to a vet, fast, and put your vet in contact with the manufacturer.

Pay attention if your dog is reluctant or slow to eat his food, and don't force him to eat it! It may be rancid or oxidized.

from winter wheat to summer wheat (or vice versa) can cause minor coloration changes; switching from dark meat to white meat can cause a kibble to change in color. Even changing the die on the extruder that shapes the food can make the appearance of the kibble change in size and color. Manufacturers should be able to give answers to those sorts of questions easily," he says.

Ceasing to feed the suspect food and contacting the manufacturer can also help the maker identify a lethal problem more quickly, potentially saving dogs' lives. L. Phillips Brown, DVM, technical advisor for Newman's Own Organics, of Aptos, California, says that all reputable pet food makers maintain a database of information about every report made by a client.

As the keeper of the "adverse events" database for Newman's Own Organics, Dr. Brown is in the perfect position to detect any trend that develops with a defec-

tive product, and take immediate action to analyze the problem. "The faster people contact us and let us know about problems, the quicker we could solve them, if need be," he says.

If it doesn't *smell* right . . .

If a food *looks* fine but *smells* bad when you open it—and, especially, if your dog seems reluctant or slow to dig into it—it's likely that the food's preservative and antioxidant agents have not performed as well as they should. The fats in the food may be rancid, making it unappealing, but not necessarily unhealthful. Oxidation of the fats in a food reduces the absorption of essential fatty acids and fat-soluble vitamins—defeating the purpose of buying that costly nutritious diet!

If it doesn't smell right, don't feed it. Your dog probably won't eat it anyway.

Proper storage is important

No matter what type of preservatives are used in your dog's food, it can quickly turn rancid if exposed to oxygen and hot temperatures. Every dog owner should know proper food storage procedures, but very few take the time to locate (or allocate) a storage space in their homes that won't expose the food to dangerously high temperatures. Dog food is supposed to be stored "in a cool, dry place." That's *not* the garage, in many parts of the country.

Plastic containers seem to be the bane of dog food manufacturers. Every representative we spoke to had horror stories that shared elements of plastic storage containers and sick dogs. They recognize that storing the food and scooping from the bag can be a hassle, especially with big bags, but suggest that the bag is the best, safest place for the food.

"Dog food bags were designed to prevent anything from either entering into the food or exiting from the food," explains Armstrong. "And the wrong type of plastic can actually speed the decay of the food. Some plastics can actually absorb much of the vitamin C out of the food; it leaches out and is sucked right into the plastic material. This, of course, affects the shelf life of the food; with the low levels of antioxidant vitamin C, the fat starts to oxidize and this accelerates the spoilage."

Cook emphasizes the hazard of unwashed plastic containers. "Many people dump new, fresh food on top of the remnants of old, rancid food. Those remnants of oxidizing old food can speed the oxidation of the new food," he warns. Cook also prefers that owners keep dry food in its original bag, but if they have a food-grade plastic container, he recommends that they wash it out well and allow it to dry thoroughly before putting fresh food in it.

According to Armstrong, metal containers (such as trash cans) don't necessarily cause spoilage, but they can affect the taste of the food. "It's always best to leave the food in the bag, even if you keep the bag in a metal can to prevent rodents from getting in it," he says. Plus, this solution keeps the date-code information handy.

What you should expect from the food maker

"Honesty." That's what Armstrong says is what an informed consumer should expect from a company to whom they are reporting an adverse health event possibly linked to its food. "The company should be as straightforward with the dog owner as possible. If they have received other reports similar to the one the consumer is making, they should tell the owner about the other reports," he says. Comparing information may help the owners' veterinarians treat affected dogs.

In return, however, Armstrong expects the consumer to be able to report critical data about the food in question. "First, we need the date code from the

bag of food," he says. "If it's a date code we've had any complaints about, we'll let them know. Next, we'll want to know where they bought the food—which store exactly, so we will be able to contact that store and alert them to possible problems. We'll also need to know how long they've had the food, how much they have fed to their dog, and what the dog's symptoms are. If they took their dog to the veterinarian, I need to know the vet's name and phone number because I need to contact them."

After gathering all the needed information, and asking for some of the suspect food (if needed), Armstrong tells the dog's owner what he is going to do about the problem. "I let them know we're going to send the food out for testing with the comparative product samples, and that I'll let them know what the findings were. If they would like to return that bag to their retailer and exchange it, I encourage them to do so, but I ask them to please retain some of the product and the date-code information."

Sometimes the problem is obvious, and tests are not needed to identify the cause of distress in the dogs that ate affected product. This was the case in one of the largest adverse events in the pet food industry, the Nature's Recipe vomitoxin affair in 1995. Frank Cook, now vice president at Natural Balance Pet Foods, Inc., was then the vice president of Nature's Recipe. "We identified the problem immediately," he says. "It wasn't difficult to recognize it as vomitoxin (a toxin excreted by a mold growing on grain) because vomitoxin makes the dog vomit. And our consumers were all saying, 'Hey, my dog is throwing up!'"

Cook and the other executives at the company announced a massive recall of the food—some 16,000 tons of food that were scattered all over the United States, Asia, and Europe—at a total cost of more than $20 million dollars. They also hired a public relations firm (actually, the same outfit that helped Johnson & Johnson get through the Tylenol tampering murders in the early 1980s) to help them handle the resolution of the problem. The PR firm suggested that Nature's

Recipe should vigorously protect its good name by rushing uncontaminated product to every consumer who might possess affected product. "Every time someone called in with a complaint, we FedExed them a fresh bag the very next day," says Cook. "It was very costly, and the event set the company on its heels, but it survived, and I think the reason it did was because we reacted so rapidly."

Cook wryly admits that being an executive at the company during the event wasn't the high point of his career, but adds, "We learned so much—and the whole industry learned with us. We learned a lot about the value of customer service, and how people will stick with you if you make things right as quickly as possible."

The incident is undoubtedly why Cook is such a stickler for pulling so many samples from his current company's production line, and why Natural Balance's date-codes include a *time of day* in addition to the date. "If you pull a sample only from the beginning, middle, and end of a run, there is a lot of room for error in between," he points out.

Variety Is the Spice of Life . . .

. . . so change your dog's food occasionally. Feeding the same kind, year after year, can cause health problems.

Nutrient imbalances

In the veterinary literature, there are many documented cases of animals with nutritional deficiencies (or excesses), and in virtually every one, the problem arose (or was discovered) because the animal was kept on one food for a long period of time.

Cats, being rather odd creatures with strange dietary requirements, have been the unintended victims more frequently—taurine, copper, vitamin E, and potassium deficiencies have turned up in cats on some foods. Dogs, whose metabolism is more adaptable, haven't had as many problems, though zinc and fatty acid deficiencies have occurred in certain poor-quality foods. An excess of zinc in a commercial dog food sickened author Ann Martin's dogs and started her on a course of research into commercial pet food manufacturing and regulation, resulting in her book, *Food Pets Die For* in 1997.

But wait a minute . . . aren't we talking about "complete and balanced" foods? How can a complete and balanced food have deficiencies or excesses of nutrients? Unfortunately, even for the best commercial dog food, there are several places along the road to the store shelf where the food's nutritional value can go astray:

- First, the standards by which the food is made aren't perfect. Animal nutrition is an evolving science, and we don't yet know all there is to know about it (if we ever will!).
- Second, the exact amounts of nutrients in a given ingredient may not be known, or may be inaccurately assessed. A batch of cornmeal might be assumed to have a certain nutritional composition, based on past batches of cornmeal, but depend-

Although feeding a *mixture* of commercial foods is not recommended, it's good to vary your dog's diet by switching commercial brands and varieties.

ing on the weather where the corn was grown, the soil conditions, and the type of fertilizer used, the exact amounts of each nutrient in any one batch can vary quite a bit.

- Third is supplier error. A vitamin/mineral premix added to the food may guarantee minimum levels of each item, but if the quality control on that premix was poor (as it may have been in the food Ann Martin's dogs ate, which tested very high in zinc), the finished dog food will compound the error.

- Also, because of the nutritional standards themselves, which specify *minimums* for most nutrients but not *maximums*, pet food makers may not test for the probability that their finished product is too high in some nutrient. Excesses of certain minerals, for example, can wreak havoc on dogs' health. Even a wide divergence between the stated and actual amount of something like protein or fat can cause problems for some dogs.

  Say you choose a food for your dog, an older, sedentary spaniel with kidney problems, based on its stated protein content of 19 percent—a comparatively low-protein food. But the amount guaranteed on the food labels is a *minimum.* In other words, the label says the food contains *at least* that 19 percent protein; it may have much more. After all, some foods are produced on a "least cost" basis, and the ingredients may change significantly from batch to batch.

- On the other hand, some manufacturers develop a formula—a recipe, if you will—for making their food, and they will stick with that recipe no matter what. If their recipe results in a food that is typically at the very low or high end of acceptability for some nutrients, you can imagine that after years of feeding the same food, your dog's body will eventually exhibit the effects of that chronic over- or undersupply of those nutrients.

We think of the production of food, even pet food, as a fairly scientific affair, but the truth is, all pet food manufacturers make mistakes in formulation or production that result in nutrient excesses or deficiencies. Look through the state feed control reports from around the country; it becomes obvious that virtually every manufacturer—no matter how good, bad, or indifferent its reputation—at one time or another fails one or more tests for protein, calcium, magnesium, or other nutrients.

Intolerance and allergy

A very different pitfall of feeding a single food for years and years is the potential for your dog to develop an intolerance or allergy to one or more ingredients. Food intolerances and allergies can often cause similar symptoms, but there are significant differences between them.

A dietary intolerance is a reaction to something in the food, but this reaction does *not* involve an immune response. The list of suspects is a long one, and includes food ingredients, as well as additives such as flavoring agents, coloring agents, emulsifiers, humectants, stabilizers, thickeners, texturizers, and dozens more. Signs of gastrointestinal disturbances (especially vomiting and diarrhea) are far more likely to be caused by food intolerance than by a food allergy. A food intolerance can develop at any time in the dog's life.

True food allergies—immediate immune responses triggered by exposure to a certain food—are thought to be fairly rare. Food allergy usually causes skin reactions, such as papules, rashes, and ear infections (actually, the inflammation sets up the scene, and then bacteria and yeast that are normally present cause secondary infections). Histamine is part of this reaction; it is a pro-inflammatory chemical that affects the local cells and blood vessels and also summons other inflammatory cells onto the scene.

However, most skin reactions are due to atopy (*inhalant* allergies); only a small percentage turn out to be caused by food. It usually takes months to years of exposure to a food to develop a food allergy, and food allergies are usually caused by proteins. Proteins are found in animal products, of course, but also to some degree in cereal grains. Thus, switching foods every three or four months, from chicken and corn to lamb and rice, turkey and barley, or duck and potato, may help prevent your dog from becoming food-allergic in the first place.

Preventing fussiness

The last big reason to periodically change foods is to prevent finicky eating. Many pet food makers use palatability enhancers, products that transform otherwise unappealing processed food into irresistibly tasty nuggets. Consequently, a dog fed a single food may become "addicted" to one particular flavor. Most of us have heard of dogs who will eat nothing but one brand, or even one flavor made by one brand of food; if the owner runs out of that food the dog goes hungry until the distraught owner manages to find some of the flavor in question. It's best to have your dog develop more cosmopolitan tastes, and be willing to eat whatever you give her.

Making the switch

For all of the reasons listed above, it's a good idea to change foods occasionally—as often as every three to four months. There is some evidence in people that avoiding a particular "problem food" for four months may resolve the issue and the body will again tolerate it. Also, that's a short enough period that allergies are unlikely to develop.

But when you get ready to make the transition from one food to another, be sure to plan ahead. You don't want to run completely out of one food and just plunk down a bowl of something new in front of Rover's nose. If you've trained him right, he may not push it under the rug, but a sudden switch could cause tummy upset.

For most dogs, a four-day (or eight-day) change-over works best. Young dogs usually adjust quickly; older dogs may need a little more time. For the first day (or two), feed 75 percent of his old food mixed with 25 percent of the new food. After a couple of days, feed 50 percent each of old and new food; then 25 percent of his old food and 75 percent new food, and finally all new food. This gives the dog's resident gut bacteria time to gear up to handle the new ingredients properly.

For the first two weeks on a new food, monitor your dog's appetite, stool quality, and energy level, and watch for unusual symptoms—itchiness, runny eyes, diarrhea—that could indicate the food is not right for him. Eventually, you'll be able to settle on three or four different foods between which you can rotate. As always, your dog's skin and coat quality, activity level, and appetite are the best indicators of whether the food is contributing to his optimal health.

Getting a Raw Deal
Why and how to convert your dog to a raw food diet.

Raw revolution

Even the most rabid opponents of raw foods can't deny that dogs wouldn't even be here today if they couldn't thrive on an uncooked diet. Canines have eaten raw for a *whole* lot longer than they've eaten cooked foods! It's difficult to understand, in the face of this one fact, how any dog guardians (much less thousands of veterinarians) could deny that raw food diets are healthful for dogs. And while their wild cousins continue to dine on freshly captured prey, most American dogs and cats eat commercial pet foods from cans and packages or home-cooked grains and meats.

The result, say a number of veterinarians and nutritionists, is deteriorating health in our canine companions. In response is a growing trend toward home-prepared diets for our dogs, away from cooked food and toward more natural fare.

While commercial pet food companies developed and promoted their product lines in the 1940s and '50s, Afghan Hound breeder Juliette de Bairacli Levy fed her dogs raw meat, raw bones, raw goat's milk, raw fish, raw eggs, and a variety of raw fruits, vegetables, nuts, and oils. Supremely healthy and intelligent, her dogs won numerous championships. De Bairacli Levy described her "Natural Rearing" philosophy in a series of books, and gained a devoted following around the world.

Australian veterinarian Ian Billinghurst has converted many dog owners to raw food with his books *Give Your Dog a Bone* and *Feed Your Pups with Bones*. His well-known BARF diet (Bones and Raw Foods, or Biologically Appropriate Raw Foods) consists of raw meaty bones, occasional raw eggs or ripe fruit, small amounts of raw pureed vegetables, and other extras, such as kelp, herbs, and table scraps. Billinghurst does

This dog is enjoying a little dental exercise while trying to get the marrow out of this fresh bone. But chewing this sort of long, hard, and meatless bone fails to provide vital nutrients to the dog, and may even cause an aggressive chewer to crack or break a tooth. When feeding bones as part of an all-raw natural diet, most "raw feeders" rely heavily on raw chicken wings and necks as the primary, balanced source of minerals.

not use cooked grains, explaining that they contain relatively poor quality protein, interfere with calcium absorption, stress the pancreas, and contribute to mineral imbalances, allergies, and diabetes.

Making the switch

Although some dog owners have switched from cooked to raw in a single day without incident, such a drastic change can trouble some dogs. Here are some common-sense guidelines that help dogs and owners make a smooth transition to a new diet.

First, change your dog's feeding schedule. This is especially important if you've been leaving food out all day. In the wild, dogs hunt when they're hungry, gorge themselves when they catch prey, and go hunting again on an empty stomach. No animal in the wild lounges beside a food dispenser.

Feed your dog once or at most twice per day, wait 15 minutes, then pick up whatever is left over and put it away. Do this six days per week, and on the seventh day, give your dog only water. Young puppies, miniature or toy breeds, and dogs with certain illnesses should not be fasted for more than half a day (ask your veterinarian), but most dogs respond very well to this feeding cycle. They become more alert, attentive, and energetic—and no, it isn't because they are starving. Removing food between meals and fasting one day a week gives their digestive organs a well-deserved rest and sharpens the body's response to food.

The younger, healthier, and more omnivorous the dog, the safer a rapid change from commercial pet food to raw fare. The older, less healthy, or more finicky the dog, the more important it is to move slowly.

If you have any question about your dog's health before or during the transition, consult a holistic veterinarian or a breeder who has raised generations of your breed on an all-raw diet.

Start by adding new food to old, maintaining the familiar taste and texture for as long as necessary. For young, active chow hounds in good health, combine 75 percent old food with 25 percent new food for a few

Most dogs adapt rapidly to a raw food diet, and owners notice an improvement in their dogs' health and appetite.

days or a week, then feed half and half for a few days, and gradually reduce the old food to 25 percent or less, until the dog is eating all raw food. For older dogs, go more slowly. If your dog walks away from unfamiliar foods, hide a fraction of a teaspoon of raw meat in the middle of his dinner. After several days, add more. If your dog has a favorite treat, add it, too.

Introducing raw meaty bones

Most of the breeders and owners who feed a bone-based natural diet use whatever meaty bones are available at reasonable cost, such as lamb neck bones, chicken backs, and beef oxtails. To introduce a dog to raw bones, however, most experienced "raw feeders" use chicken wings or poultry necks.

"I recommend gradually switching dogs from cooked to raw foods and smashing or grinding raw bones until the dog is eating a completely raw diet, without any grains, yeast, milk, or dairy products," says Schultze. "If the dog has had digestive problems or has been on pharmaceutical drugs, especially antibiotics, within the past year, I would make the switch with the aid of digestive enzymes and non-dairy probiotics." Probiotics are beneficial bacteria such as acidophilus. Start with a fraction of the amount recommended on the label, gradually increasing to the recommended dosage.

Depending on his metabolism and activity level, a dog may need more or less, but 2 percent of his weight in raw meat and bones is a safe ballpark figure for a dog's total ration of food (1 pound for a 50-pound dog). To provide the stomach exercise that helps prevent bloating, meat should be whole or in large chunks, not minced or ground. De Bairacli Levy recommends that bones be fed last, after the raw meat and vegetables, so that they are cushioned in the stomach.

Dogs new to bones often experience temporary diarrhea, constipation, or both as their systems adjust, especially if they eat large quantities. Remember to

Switching Slowly but Surely

Most dogs make the transition to a raw diet without complications, but there are always exceptions. We've heard of individual dogs who have required medical attention following a dramatic diet change.

Hemorrhagic gastroenteritis is often blamed on a too-rapid change of diet, and a dog or puppy that is not equipped to deal with raw bones may find its system overwhelmed if they are suddenly provided.

When her mother's 10-year-old Labrador Retriever came to live with New York trainer Nancy Strouss, the Lab had been eating a supermarket kibble all her life. Strouss offered her everything she fed her Goldens, and within a week, Samantha's coat was shining, her eyes were brighter, and her gait improved. But then she started throwing up.

"There was no pattern to it," says Strouss. "Sometimes it was bile and sometimes undigested food; sometimes she vomited right after dinner and sometimes in the middle of the night or first thing in the morning. Because my Goldens stayed healthy, I knew there was nothing wrong with the food, and she still looked great and had lots of energy, so I hoped this symptom would pass as she adjusted." The vomiting stopped after seven days, but it was replaced by something worse: a week of uncontrollable diarrhea.

Samantha was experiencing the symptoms of too-rapid detoxification, which can happen when the diet is drastically changed. To help Samantha recover, Strouss drastically reduced the raw protein and for two weeks fed her cooked potatoes, rice, leeks, and boiled chicken with liver-supporting supplements.

Samantha responded immediately. Gradually over the next two weeks, Strouss replaced the cooked chicken with raw meat and the cooked potatoes with raw vegetables.

Today, four months after her arrival, Samantha eats all raw food, including meaty bones, and has no digestive problems. "She's almost 11, but she acts like a two-year-old," says Strouss. "She runs, jumps, and plays ball, her coat continues to improve, her eyes are clear, she has no ear infections, her arthritis has disappeared, and she never steals food, which she did on a daily basis in her old home."

---

feed small amounts at first, start with bones that are easy to chew, smash them with a hammer to help your dog digest them, feed them last, and give adult dogs a digestive enzyme during the transition to raw food.

Chicken wings and necks are perfect "first bones" for teething puppies. Ann Mandelbaum, who breeds Standard Poodles in Connecticut, introduced a recent litter of pups to raw chicken wings when they were four weeks old. "Every day I gave one wing to each pair of puppies and let them work on it together," she says. "At first they gnawed most of the meat off and left the bones. By the middle of the week, they were nibbling on the ends, and by the end of the week, the bones were disappearing."

In addition to their nutritional benefits, raw bones provide dental floss in the form of gristle and tendons. "You can always tell a bone-chewing dog," says holistic veterinarian Beverly Cappel, of Chestnut Ridge, New York. "They have the whitest, strongest, cleanest teeth."

Even when they appreciate the benefits of feeding raw bones, some owners are reluctant to provide them due to messiness (feed them outside!), because they have been frightened by veterinarians or another authority figure, or because they feel overwhelmed by the logistics of changing to a raw diet. Unfortunately, *not* including raw bones in a mostly meat diet may create nutritional imbalances that cause serious harm. Billinghurst warns against the use of substitutes such as heat-sterilized bone meal and calcium supplements, for they can disrupt the natural balance of minerals in growing bodies and can *cause*, rather than prevent, hip dysplasia and other structural problems. There are over a hundred important elements in raw bones, bone marrow, and connective tissue, all of which are vital to the health of joint cartilage, intervertebral discs, vascular walls, and other parts of the canine body.

Raw bones that are soft enough for your pet to bite through, swallow, and digest contain all of these nutrients. A small number of commercial supplements made from cold-sterilized raw bones contain most of them. If you are reluctant to feed your dog raw bones but want their nourishment, you can substitute either company's products or you can grind raw meaty bones in a meat grinder, keeping in mind that supplements and freshly ground bones cannot provide the tooth-cleaning benefits, hours of chewing pleasure, or stomach exercise that raw meaty bones provide.

What about bacteria?

Healthy dogs in the wild can eat just about any raw meat and survive, if not thrive. However, dogs on commercial food may not produce all the hydrochloric acid and beneficial bacteria they need for protection from pathogens.

If you are concerned about bacteria, you can disinfect large pieces of raw meat, raw bones, or eggs in the shell. Soak them in a solution of ½ teaspoon original formula Clorox bleach per gallon of water, OR several drops of 35 percent food-grade hydrogen peroxide in a

> Stay flexible and open-minded; let your dog decide what diet works best for him. It doesn't make any sense to stay tied to a feeding method because it makes theoretical sense if it doesn't work for *your* dog in practice.
>
> Read more about raw diets.
>
> If you are anxious about a certain diet, don't feed it to your dog, no matter what your friends, breeder, trainer, veterinarian, or Internet "chat" buddies say. What you feed your dog is up to you.

sink of cold water (enough to create small bubbles but not enough to change the meat's color), OR ½ teaspoon liquid grapefruit-seed extract in a sink of cold water. Let stand 5 to 10 minutes, rinse by soaking in plain water, and drain.

However, it should be mentioned that most raw feeders discontinue these disinfection practices as they gain confidence in their healthy dogs' ability to handle any bacteria that may be present in their raw food.

Some people buy their meat at the supermarket, while others arrange bulk shipments of organically grown meat and bones through holistic veterinarians, co-ops, dog clubs, and local hunters. For convenience, some manufacturers prepare raw food for dogs and freeze it for shipping.

"People are unnecessarily intimidated by raw-food diets," says pet nutritionist Pat McKay, author of *Reigning Cats and Dogs.* "That's unfortunate because it isn't difficult or time-consuming. In fact, if you spend more than 10 minutes a day feeding your dog, you either love to be in the kitchen or you're doing something wrong."

Best for *your* dog?

The decision really ought to be based on what your dog "says" about his diet. If, after a fair trial (perhaps three months?) on a complete and balanced raw diet, he has more health and/or behavior problems than he did before the trial, a smart owner should start a new trial including cooked foods.

Similarly, there is no use denying that some humans cannot bring themselves to prepare and feed raw foods. It doesn't really matter why they can't or won't, because if they don't believe in what they are doing and feel really good about it, their dogs are bound to experience trouble with the diet. And nothing good will result from trying to make them feel bad about their decision, or attempting to force or guilt them into a different course of action.

True holistic care for dogs is, by definition, tailored for the individual—and that's the individual dog *and* guardian. We strongly encourage guardians to think for themselves and do what they think is best: feed raw, cook, or do both; to observe their own dogs with open minds, staying alert to any improvement or decline in their dogs' condition; and to remain flexible and willing to change their approach in response to the evidence in front of them.

Pre-mixes

Beyond kibble and canned dog food, there is a less common (but no less worthy) type of commercial food. Here's a look at commercial products that make it easy to feed a home-prepared diet.

Some of these "pre-mix" manufactures produce a dog food "base" containing grains and vegetables, to which a dog owner adds fresh meat to complete the diet. Others contain dehydrated ingredients; water is added to rehydrate them.

Some of the products are intended to be cooked. The others served uncooked and are simply rehydrated with water and soaked before serving.

A few of these companies make products that can be fed alone for "complete and balanced" nutrition; they meet the nutritional profiles of the Association of American Feed Control Officials (AAFCO) *without* the inclusion of meat or anything else. These products are also the only ones that were formulated with the AAFCO nutrient profiles in mind.

Most of the products contain herbs; some contain just one or two, some contain quite a variety. A few of the products contain other novel ingredients such as bee pollen. Most of the companies use at least some organic ingredients; a couple use *all* organic ingredients, except for the vitamin/mineral supplement used

---

Practice safe steaks

One of the most frequently cited objections that veterinarians have to raw diets is the potential for bacterial contaminants present in the meat to infect and kill your dog, all his canine friends, and indeed, your hapless children and your elderly mother, too.

Well, it's true: meat infected with E. coli, *salmonella,* Campylobacter, *and* Listeria *sickens thousands of people every year. Does this mean that no one should eat meat? Perhaps! Or maybe it means that you should act as if all meat in your home is infected, and handle it accordingly: Employ scrupulous meat-handling and sanitation practices, and leave the consumption of raw meat to your healthy dog, who is naturally and exquisitely well-designed to deal with ingested bacteria.*

Handling raw meat in a safe manner is not rocket science. All of the normal precautions of handling the meat eaten by you and your family apply, including:

- *People with immune system disorders should avoid handling raw meat. Raw foods are not suited for immune-compromised dogs, either.*

- *Keep food frozen until you are ready to feed it. Then, thaw small amounts (only what your dog will eat within a day or two) in the refrigerator. Never, ever allow food to sit for long at room temperature—duh! If you need to thaw food in a hurry, seal it in a Ziploc bag and place it in warm water for not more than a few minutes.*

- *Wash your hands with hot water and soap immediately after preparing the dog's food.*

- *Promptly wash everything that comes in contact with the food with hot, soapy water: bowls, knives, grinders, countertops, and cutting boards. Periodically use a disinfectant, such as a mild bleach solution or sea salt and lemon juice.*

- *Discard any food your dog leaves in his bowl after eating. Don't allow him to "leave it for later." Don't even save it for later in the refrigerator!*

- *Don't forget to wash the dog's water bowl in hot, soapy water daily. Many dogs drink right after eating, and could conceivably contaminate their water with bacteria in their mouths after eating.*

in the pre-mix. Speaking of vitamin/mineral mixes, a few of the products contain these supplements. A few products require the addition of some sort of oil supplement.

Completely convenient

Commercial frozen foods make feeding a "natural" raw foods diet easy. Feeding a raw meat diet can be intimidating for the uninitiated. Fortunately, there are now companies that offer our dogs a source of food that has the convenience of a prepared diet, the nutritional benefits of a biologically suitable food, *and* confirmation of space-age laboratory testing that it contains all the nutrients a dog needs.

These diets all contain fresh meat—and here, we mean "meat" in its broadest sense; we're talking about muscle meat, organ meat, bones, fat, connective tissues—all that prey animals have to offer carnivorous predators. Animal proteins offer the most complete array of amino acids required by canines, and the other tissues almost perfectly complete the dog's nutritional requirements.

Lab tests confirm it: with a little added vegetable matter and some smart if minor supplementation, the best of these meat-based diets meet the nutrient profiles for "complete and balanced" canine diets established by the Association of American Feed Control Officials (AAFCO), *just* like most dry and canned foods do! Only, because they aren't cooked, leaving the heat-sensitive nutrients in their fresh ingredients intact, many of these products do not require the addition of a vitamin/mineral supplement to accomplish this feat.

Don't overlook the importance of raw bone in these formulas; the ones that don't contain it *must* contain an adequate substitute source of calcium and other minerals. Many people who feed BARF diets use whole, raw meaty bones such as chicken wings

Look for products that meet your needs: Organic? Complete and balanced or supplementary? Grains or grain-free?

Look for manufacturers with local retail outlets, or whose shipping schedule, range, and prices work well for you.

Discuss your dog's health status with the food company rep. He or she should be able to help guide your purchases based on your dog's needs.

Use safe meat-handling and sanitation practices at all times.

and turkey necks as the major source of calcium in their dogs' food. Most of these commercial raw diets include *ground* raw bones, to take advantage of their nutritional value without any of the hazards occasionally posed by bone consumption.

Ideally, you'll be able to buy one of these frozen diets from a retailer near you, enabling you to whisk the food home to your freezer. Somewhat less ideal is receiving the product via overnight or two-day delivery, packed in dry ice and/or a cooler.

But anyone who has ever had a birthday present or Amazon.com order arrive late knows that stuff happens. Planes are grounded, storms close highways, and so on.

Before you order any product, we suggest that you question the maker closely as to the company policy on shipping mishaps. Who will pay for meat that arrives at room temperature? Because you don't want *your* dog to eat it!

Most of the companies ship on a certain day of the week—only on Mondays or Tuesdays, for example—and give you ample notice as to the expected time and date of delivery. Then it's up to you to be waiting at the door for the delivery truck, so that costly package doesn't linger on a hot porch.

It's All in How You Make It

Great ways to prepare nutritious grains and vegetables for your dog (and you).

Traditional preparation methods increase the digestibility of many foods we share with dogs. These simple steps so dramatically improve the nutritional content of everyday foods that they reduce or eliminate the need for nutritional supplements.

In fact, the food-source nutrients that these techniques release are so easily assimilated that their effects are superior to those of any synthetic or laboratory-produced supplement. Improving the nutritional content of the food we give our dogs can significantly improve their overall health, endurance, skin and coat condition, joint flexibility, strength, digestion, wound healing, reproduction, and immune function.

Time and organization are the main ingredients in these techniques, but quality is a factor, too. Holistic veterinarians agree that today's dogs are adversely affected by industrial and agricultural chemicals and pollutants. Whenever possible, it makes sense to use organically grown, minimally processed, fresh, whole foods.

Any home-prepared diet can be improved without altering its basic ingredients or menus by using the following methods.

Lactic acid fermentation

Vegetables are important to canine health, and although advocates of home-prepared diets debate the quantity of vegetable matter dogs should consume, all agree that vegetables contain essential nutrients that are not provided by other foods.

Unlike animals that evolved on a vegetarian diet, dogs lack the ability to break down cellulose, a carbohydrate consisting of linked glucose units in plant cell walls. One way to help dogs digest vegetables is to

puree them. Blenders and food processors make this task easy, and pureed root vegetables like carrots and parsnips, leafy herbs such as parsley, and grasses like wheat grass or barley grass can be added to every meal with good results.

Today, food scientists are educating people in the art of preparing foods in ways that preserve and enhance the nutrients naturally contained in them. People who are committed to providing the healthiest foods for their families won't find it too difficult to extend these methods to the preparation of the family dog's meals.

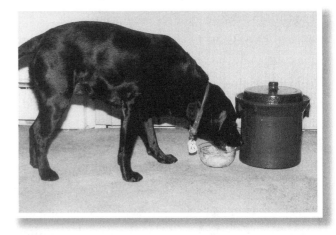

A Labrador dives right into a bowl of lacto-fermented cucumbers fresh out of a ceramic German pickle crock. Most dogs (and their families) relish the taste of vegetables prepared by this method.

Nutrition

There is another way to improve the digestibility of vegetables, and a growing body of research indicates that this method both prevents and helps cure cancer and other serious illnesses. Lactic acid fermentation is one of the simplest and oldest methods of food preservation.

There are two kinds of lactic acid. One is found in the blood, muscle tissue, and stomach; the other is produced by bacteria. During active exercise, pyruvic acid, a compound derived from carbohydrates, breaks down into lactic acid, which can accumulate in the muscles and cause cramps. Lactic acid consumed in foods such as yogurt and naturally fermented vegetables does not have this effect. It actually helps remove the harmful lactic acid from muscles.

Lactic acid that is generated through fermentation produces vitamin C, vitamin B12, enzymes that support metabolic activity, choline (which balances and nourishes the blood), and acetylcholine, which tones the nerves, calms the mind, and improves sleep patterns. Lactic acid is also a chemical repressor that fights cancer cells without harming healthy cells.

To make lacto-fermented vegetables, you don't need special equipment, although a plastic Japanese salad press or ceramic German pickle crock simplifies the effort. You can do it in a glass or ceramic bowl using a weighted plate as a press. The basic ingredients are vegetables, a pinch of salt, a few optional herbs, and time.

Cucumbers, the fastest to prepare, are ready in about two hours. Carrots and other root vegetables take a couple of days if they are sliced rather than shredded and a week or more if prepared in a large ceramic crock.

You may try this technique on your pet's behalf, but once you taste the results, lacto-fermented vegetables may become part of your own daily diet. The vegetables can be added to salads, served as side dishes, or used in recipes that call for raw vegetables.

As with any new food, introduce fermented vegetables gently and in small quantities. Many dogs love them at first bite, but if your dog needs coaxing, mix a tiny amount with her regular food and whatever oil you normally add, such as flax seed, coconut, or cod liver oil.

Some pet nutritionists recommend that vegetables make up as much as 20 to 25 percent of a dog's diet, while those who follow the prey model, in which vegetables represent the partly digested contents of a prey animal's digestive tract, use much smaller amounts. Whatever vegetables you now feed can be replaced with a slightly smaller amount, such as 10 to 15 percent less by volume, of lacto-fermented fare. Fermentation and pressing condense the vegetables and concentrate their nutrients. The resulting liquid, which looks like water but is really the vegetables' juice, is a rich source of lactic acid and other nutrients. It can be added in small amounts, such as 1 or 2 tablespoons at a time, to your pet's food and drinking water.

Use only glass, ceramic, stainless steel, or plastic pressing materials, not aluminum, tin, or copper. Keep all utensils meticulously clean.

For best results, use an unrefined sea salt such as Eden, Lima, or Celtic Sea Salt, all of which are sold in health food stores. These salts, which are manufactured in France by traditional methods, are gray in color, feel moist to the touch, and contain all of the minerals and trace elements found in unpolluted seawater. Wash vegetables thoroughly, but do not peel organically grown produce except for thick-skinned cucumbers; if the vegetables are commercially grown, reduce pesticide residues by washing well, removing outer leaves, or peeling. Then slice with a knife, shred with a grater, puree, or slice or shred with a food processor, discarding any tough stems or damaged portions. When feeding lacto-fermented vegetables that were shredded, thinly sliced, julienned, grated, or finely minced before pressing, monitor your dog's stool to see how thoroughly they are digested. If you see identifiable pieces of shredded carrot or minced greens, puree the lacto-fermented vegetables before feeding them next time.

Shred or finely mince any combination of greens or cabbage (Chinese, green, or purple cabbage; beet greens, turnip greens, or dandelion greens); grate, thinly slice, or julienne carrots, radishes, parsnips, beets, green peppers, parsley, and/or other colorful vegetables. Mix 8 cups firmly packed vegetables with 1 teaspoon sea salt. You can also add minced garlic (up to 2 cloves) and 1 to 2 teaspoons minced fresh herbs or ½ to 1 teaspoon dried herbs (such as sage, rosemary, thyme, dill, basil, oregano).

If using an open bowl, crush, knead, or mix until the vegetables begin to soften; fill the bowl as described above, and press until ready. If using a plastic salad press, simply stir to mix well, fill the press, fasten the lid, screw the top down tightly (but not so tightly that you break the mechanism), and after several hours, tighten it a bit more. The vegetables will compress as they ferment.

If brine does not cover the vegetables within two or three hours at normal room temperature (65° to 75°F), your vegetables need more crushing, more salt, or a heavier weight. Press up to 6 hours or overnight. In hot weather, the vegetables may be ready much sooner; in cold weather, press up to 24 hours.

Vegetables are "done" when they taste tangy and feel slightly soft. They keep in the refrigerator for several weeks, especially if stored in plastic bags from which you press the air before sealing, or store them in glass jars with their juice.

Want a preview? Too busy to make your own? Some health food stores carry lacto-fermented vegetables, including unpasteurized sauerkraut.

Making grains digestible

Although dogs are not designed to eat cooked food, they cannot digest raw grain, either. Pet nutritionists agree that the only grain that dogs can fully utilize has been predigested, such as by a prey animal's digestive organs. Cooked grains are more digestible than raw grains, but cooking does not digest grains. Microwave cooking, cooking in a pressure cooker, and the high heat and pressure used in extrusion processing (the method used to produce most commercial kibble) alter the protein molecules and fragile oils in grains.

In traditional cultures, grain was never used in its dormant state. Raw grain contains enzyme inhibitors that prevent sprouting until the grain absorbs enough moisture and warmth to support life. Lacking these conditions, grain remains inert.

In the industrial West, grain is taken from field to storage in a single day. This is very different from traditional methods, in which harvested grain was left in the field for days or weeks, during which rain and sunlight provided the conditions needed for germination. Partly germinated grain was stored whole, ground just before use, and soaked overnight before cooking. Gruels and porridges made from the grain were cooked slowly over gentle heat, and breads made from it were allowed to ferment for days before baking. All of these steps release vitamins, amino acids, and other nutrients while removing chemicals that interfere with digestion.

Soaking removes phytic acid, an organic acid in untreated grain that combines with calcium, magnesium, copper, iron, and zinc in the intestinal tract, blocking their absorption. According to Sally Fallon, this is why a diet high in whole grains can lead to serious mineral deficiencies and bone loss. You can

It's easy to grow healthy sprouts for your dog. Health food stores sell plastic sprouting lids for wide-mouth quart jars, or you can fashion a sprouting lid with cheesecloth and a rubber band.

Making Stock

To make a mineral-rich stock—a clear broth made from bones and vegetables—put 4 quarts cold, filtered water in a large stainless steel pan. Add 2 to 4 cups coarsely chopped carrots, celery, garlic, potatoes, parsnips, turnips, and other vegetables, or their peelings and scraps, plus a whole free-range chicken cut into several pieces or 2 to 3 pounds of meaty bones from chicken, turkey, beef, lamb, venison, or fish. The best fish to use for stock is low in fat and high in bone, like snapper or rock fish.

Add several sprigs of fresh thyme to turkey or meat stock. Add 2 tablespoons apple cider vinegar for chicken or turkey stock, ¼ cup vinegar for fish stock, or ½ cup vinegar for beef, lamb, or venison. Vinegar acidifies the broth and draws out minerals, especially calcium, magnesium, and potassium.

Let these ingredients stand for one hour before cooking. Then bring to a boil, remove the scum that rises to the top, cover, and simmer on the lowest heat setting for 12 to 24 hours. The longer stock cooks, the more nutritious it is.

About 10 minutes before finishing the stock, add 1 large bunch of chopped parsley, which will improve the stock's mineral content.

Remove from heat, let the stock stand until cool, then strain it through a colander. Store the strained stock in glass jars in the refrigerator. Chill well and remove any congealed fat. The stock can be frozen for long-term storage; refrigerated stock keeps well for one to two weeks.

When refrigerated, the stock should gel. This is the signature of a well-prepared, bone-dense stock that is rich in vitamins, minerals, and gelatin.

Stock can be used in place of water when cooking soaked or sprouted grains for maximum nutrition and digestibility. It can also be added to food. Suggested serving size: 2 to 4 tablespoons stock per meal for average-sized (30- to 40-pound) dogs.

---

prevent this adverse effect with overnight soaking in warm water, which, in addition to destroying phytates, neutralizes the enzyme inhibitors present in all grains, increases the production of beneficial enzymes, helps break down gluten (a difficult-to-digest protein found in most grains), and makes grains less likely to cause allergic reactions.

Unlocking nutrients

The process of germination or sprouting changes grains into living foods that are rich in vitamins, trace minerals, the carbohydrate-digesting enzyme amylase, amino acids, and other nutrients. Before-and-after measurements show as much as 25 times more vitamin K and 12 times more carotene in grain after it has sprouted. B-complex vitamins such as pantothenic acid typically increase up to 200 percent, vitamin B12 by over 500 percent, pyridoxine by 600 percent, and riboflavin by nearly 150 percent.

Use organically raised wheat, rye, spelt, kamut, barley, oats, millet, buckwheat, or other grains from a health food store, macrobiotic supply company, or sprout catalog. Rice is the only popular grain for which this process is not recommended.

Soak ½ to 1 cup grain in a wide-mouth quart jar of water to which you have added 10 drops of liquid grapefruit-seed extract, an all-purpose disinfectant. Soak the grain 10 to 12 hours or overnight. For increased mineral content, add a pinch of powdered or liquid kelp to the soak water.

Health food stores sell plastic sprouting lids for wide-mouth quart jars, or you can fashion a sprouting lid with cheesecloth and a rubber band. Sprouting lid in place, drain the jar well, then lay it on its side in a warm place away from direct sunlight. Ideal sprouting temperatures are between 70° and 80° Fahrenheit.

After 24 to 36 hours, you will see small white roots emerge from the grain. If you don't see this growth on almost every seed by the second day, your grain is not viable and should be discarded. Assuming that it's sprouting, let it grow another day, then puree the grain in a blender or food processor.

Add a tablespoon of raw honey (a source of carbohydrate-digesting amylase) and/or ¼ teaspoon of an enzyme powder containing amylase and let the mash stand at room temperature for an hour or two before refrigerating. This gives the amylase a chance to work, further breaking down and predigesting the grain.

To introduce predigested grain to your dog, start with 1 teaspoon per 10 pounds of body weight every other day and gradually increase the amount as desired.

Cooking grains

Many popular diets for dogs include large or small amounts of cooked grain. The nutritional content of any cooked grain can be improved by first soaking it in warm, filtered water and whey. For best results, soak 1 cup grain such as whole wheat, rolled or cracked oats, or a coarsely ground blend of wheat, millet, short-grain rice, barley, and oats, in 1 cup water plus 2 tablespoons liquid whey for at least 6 hours or up to 24 hours. Some grains, like rye, may need additional water and soaking time for complete hydration. The ancient grains teff and amaranth are best soaked for 24 hours.

To make a traditional porridge, add the soaked grain to 1 cup boiling water or stock (see "Making Stock," page 191), lower heat, cover, and simmer for 5 to 10 minutes. Soaking significantly reduces the cooking time of whole grains.

To make a simple whole-grain casserole, Sally Fallon recommends combining 2 cups sprouting grain with 3 cups beef or chicken stock. Bring to a boil and

---

A Delicious and Nutritious Vegetable Dish for Your Dog (and You!)

Cucumbers in an Open Bowl

Slice peeled cucumbers up to ¼-inch thick. Find a plate that will just fit inside the bowl; it will be your press. Fill a large glass jar with water; it will be your weight. Clean the plate and jar well, as they will be in direct contact with the vegetables. To each firmly packed cup of cucumber slices, add a pinch or two of sea salt. Stir gently to mix well. Fill the bowl almost to the top, cover with the plate, and weight it with the jar. If using a Japanese salad press, combine 8 cups cucumbers with 1 teaspoon salt, fill the press, attach the lid, and screw the pressing plate down firmly.

In about two hours (more or less depending on slice thickness and room temperature), juice will cover the plate and your cucumbers will be tangy, crisp, and ready to eat. Lacto-fermented cucumbers are best used within a week. Most dogs like them so much that they can be used as training treats.

---

skim. Add 1 teaspoon sea salt and ½ teaspoon each dried thyme, rosemary, and crushed green peppercorns. Boil vigorously until the liquid is reduced to the level of the grain. Transfer to a 250°F oven and bake for approximately four hours, or until the grain is tender.

Add digestive enzyme powder according to label directions when feeding cooked grain to help compensate for the enzymes destroyed by cooking.

Whole rice and millet contain lower amounts of phytates than other grains, and they are gluten-free, which makes them easier to digest even without presoaking. However, these grains should be cooked very slowly over low heat in a high-mineral, gelatinous broth to facilitate digestion.

Corn is widely used in commercial pet foods because it is inexpensive. It is also notoriously difficult for dogs to digest. In traditional cultures that utilized corn or maize, it was always soaked in lime water. Soaking in lime water releases the vitamin B3 in corn, which otherwise remains bound up, and it improves the amino acid quality of proteins in the corn's germ. Soaking also destroys corn's enzyme inhibitors.

To make lime water, place one inch of dolomite powder (sold as a supplement in health food stores) in a half-gallon (two-quart) glass jar. Fill the jar with filtered water, cover tightly, shake well, and let stand overnight. The resulting clear liquid will be lime water, which does not require refrigeration. To use, carefully pour off what you need without disturbing the settled powder. To replenish the jar, top it with filtered water, cover, and shake well.

Upgrading to Pasture-Fed
Are you ready to take the final step toward your dog's optimum diet?

The foundation of nearly every home-prepared diet for dogs is animal-source protein, such as beef, lamb, chicken, turkey, dairy products, or eggs. These foods are so abundant in our supermarkets that we take them for granted and assume they are nutritious. After all, our scientists, public health officials, and medical experts make no distinction between food produced by animals raised outdoors on open pasture and that of animals raised in confinement on factory farms.

But you are what you eat, as the saying goes, and the difference between the meat of factory-raised

The best way to pasture-feed chickens is to use mobile pens that are moved daily to a fresh, clean spot in the grass, such as this pen at Simply Grazin' in Hopewell, New Jersey.

Most cattle are raised on grass pastures and "finished" with a 60- or 90-day stay in a feedlot, eating a grain-rich diet (mostly corn) that is literally laced with antibiotics, to prevent illness caused by stress, overcrowding, and the unnatural diet.

animals and animals that dine on open pasture is dramatic. Many holistic veterinary health practitioners routinely recommend that their patients eat animal-origin products only if they are organic and pasture-fed or free-range.

Problems with factory farming

Almost 90 percent of America's farm animals live on factory farms, where, instead of green grass, they eat packaged foods that may contain ingredients they were never designed to consume, such as corn and soybeans—or, for roughage in the mixed feed, ground-up phone books, plastic pot scrubbers, or stale-dated chewing gum, complete with wrappers. Overcrowding, a lack of sunlight and fresh air, the routine application of drugs and pesticides, inactivity, and stress weaken their immune systems, make them susceptible to infections and chronic illnesses, soften their bones, and reduce the quality of their meat and eggs.

Feedlot cattle are routinely treated with dewormers like Dectomax, Ivermectin, and other systemic pesticides, which are supposed to leave the animals' bodies after six months, but residues of which can remain in their fat for much longer. Additional toxins migrate to fat cells, while others, such as heavy metals, collect in the bones.

The high-protein, grain-heavy diet fed to feedlot cattle causes a condition called "rumen acidosis," which, in turn, causes many cattle—12 to 32 percent is the commonly quoted figure—to develop abscesses on their livers, unless the precipitating condition is prevented with regular doses of antibiotics. Abscessed livers do not pass food inspection and represent a significant loss for the grower.

Virtually all animals raised in confinement are given antibiotics to keep them alive and to encourage weight gain, hormones to regulate their growth and reproductive cycles, seven-way combination vaccines, and steroids to stimulate growth. Drug residues concern health experts because they encourage the development of drug-resistant bacteria and can adversely affect human health. Athletes who consumed factory-farmed chicken have failed urine tests for steroid drugs, and medical journals have documented the adverse effects of hormone-treated chicken on children.

"Confinement operations could not make a profit if their animals were subject to strict health standards," says Sally Fallon, director of the Weston A. Price Foundation, an organization that advocates a return to nontoxic farming methods and the consumption of whole foods.

Factory-farmed hens suffer from "caged layer fatigue," a form of osteoporosis caused by a lack of fresh air and sunshine combined with the mineral-depleting demands of constant egg laying. Despite being fed calcium supplements, bone fractures and paralysis are common. Forced molting, in which hens are deprived of food and water to shock them into starting a new egg-laying cycle, is banned in Great Britain but common in North America.

Broiler hens are fed growth hormones, antibiotics, and animal by-products, including condemned and diseased parts. Animal health advocate Michael W. Fox, DVM, warns that intensive confinement systems produce food-borne diseases that ultimately affect humans and benefit only the pharmaceutical and medical industries.

Chickens and turkeys can be sold as "free-range" if they have USDA-certified access to the outdoors for five minutes per day. But the term "range," a synonym for pasture, has lost its meaning, as there are no criteria for the outdoor area's size, environmental quality, or space allowed per bird. All too often, factory-farmed free-range birds live in crowded conditions on gravel or concrete with no access to grass of any kind and little, if any, access to the outdoors. These birds are de-beaked (a procedure that impairs their ability to preen and eat normally) and live in unnatural social isolation rather than in family groups.

Cancer is so common that commercially raised animals are accepted for human consumption after their tumors are removed. Fewer inspectors and faster assembly lines make even the most cursory inspections difficult or impossible. Many supermarket chickens are infected with salmonella, and beef is frequently recalled because of *E. coli* contamination.

Federal officials respond to these problems by allowing drug manufacturers to supervise the testing of their own animal drugs in order to complete the approval process as quickly as possible, raising questions about safety and effectiveness. To treat salmonella, *E. coli*, and other pathogens in meat products, they recommend formaldehyde rinses, chlorine rinses, and irradiation. These treatments apply to meat and poultry sold for human consumption, the "best" that modern agriculture has to offer.

Where possible, try to find wild-caught game and fish from hunters and fishermen. (You may not want to tell them that you are interested in the food for your dog!

Everyone Benefits from Grass-Fed, Wild, or Truly Free-Range Meats

Benefits for the Consumer

- *The meat from grass-fed, grass-finished animals is lower in fat than meat raised in confinement, and it's higher in "good fat" omega-3 fatty acids.*
- *Unlike meat from grain-fed animals, the meat from grass-fed animals contains conjugated linoleic acid, or CLA, a potent defense against cancer, heart disease, and diabetes.*
- *Meat from grass-fed cattle stays fresher longer than meat from feedlot cattle because of its high vitamin E content.*
- *Grass-fed and grass-finished animals produce far less salmonella, E. coli, and other harmful bacteria than grain-fed animals, and those bacteria are far less likely to contaminate their meat.*
- *Many pastured farms raise unusual or heirloom breeds unavailable elsewhere.*
- *Grass-fed meat tastes better.*
- *Eggs from grass-fed chickens, ducks, and geese are far more nutritious (higher in vitamins, minerals, and essential fatty acids) than eggs from factory farms.*

Benefits for the Farmers and Producers

- *Most farmers and ranchers are proud of their products and eager to share details of their land management, feeding methods, breeding programs, sources of new animals, processing methods, and other information that's impossible to obtain from factory farms.*
- *Farms and ranches that raise animals on pasture are often family operations. The owners know their customers and try to keep them happy by fixing problems quickly.*
- *Supporting local agriculture keeps your investment in the area instead of in foreign countries.*
- *Custom processing (if available) provides more organs and other food for dogs than are sold at USDA-controlled facilities. Some farmers save meaty bones and organs for dog owners.*

Benefits for the Environment

Pasture feeding:
- *reduces greenhouse gases produced by cattle;*
- *encourages plant biodiversity;*
- *reduces environmental pollutants, such as arsenic, from commercial poultry operators;*
- *eliminates the need for hormones and other drugs;*
- *eliminates the routine use of agricultural antibiotics, which is blamed for drug-resistant strains of E. coli and other bacteria;*
- *eliminates the use of chemical fertilizers, which create fertilizer runoff contamination that adversely affects wildlife;*
- *improves soil fertility; and*
- *improves the health of farm workers, who are at high risk of respiratory infection, chemical exposure, and other problems from factory farms.*

Fortunately, a revolution is brewing, and it's one that may remedy the ills of modern food production. Farmers and ranchers are rediscovering the benefits of pasture feeding, and because the animals they grow are significantly healthier than animals raised in confinement, their meat, bones, organs, and eggs are significantly better for people and dogs.

Managing the cost

To make food for dogs more affordable, some farms have pet specials. Staying in touch with farmers and sharing orders with friends has helped many caretakers improve their dogs' diets.

Real milk

The same comparisons that apply to factory-farmed and pasture-fed meat and eggs apply to milk. Raw colostrum from pasture-fed cows and goats, recommended by holistic veterinarians as a potent immune system tonic, and raw cow or goat whey, a cheese-making by-product that is easy to digest and rich in beneficial bacteria, are popular extras for those who can find them. So is raw butter, a traditional food that improves health by providing fat-soluble vitamins; short- and medium-chain fatty acids that stimulate the immune system and protect against disease; glyco-spingolipids, which prevent intestinal distress; and conjugated linoleic acid (CLA), which helps protect against cancer and heart disease.

Milk from pasture-fed cows contains five times more CLA and twice the omega-3 fatty acids and beta-carotene of milk from cows fed a commercial dairy diet.

To find a pasture-fed dairy or goat farm, check farmers' markets and health food stores. You may also be able to find companies that produce and sell pasture-fed animal products for pets.

Fish facts

The problems stemming from factory-farmed animals are not unique to furry and feathered species. Wild-caught fish is the finned equivalent of pasture-fed meat, but most of America's salmon, trout, halibut, mussels, oysters, and other food fish are farmed in crowded open-net cages set up in the ocean or fresh water. Fish farms often use large quantities of antibiotics and pesticides to control disease, and parasites proliferate.

Upgrade to pasture-fed ingredients in preparation for breeding or competition, to strengthen immunity, and after illness or injury.

Find good sources. Talk to farmers and ranchers. Visit farms and farmers' markets. Join a CSA (Community Supported Agriculture) program.

Buy a freezer and take advantage of volume discounts.

Reduce expenses by sharing orders.

Make friends with hunters who can share deer and other wild game.

Researchers blame farmed fish for human exposure to antibiotic-resistant bacteria, dioxin, and PCBs, as well as possible retinal damage from the ingestion of color additives.

For your fish-loving dog and for your own improved health, look for wild-caught fish and avoid farmed fish. Check with vendors about the source. Unless wild-caught Pacific salmon or farmed fish of any kind has been tested for parasites, it is probably safer cooked than raw.

Note: Dont feed any fish to your dog that isn't safe to eat yourself. For example, the fish in many freshwater lakes around the Northeast are contaminated with mercury, a result of historic fallout from incinerators. State health and fish and game departments usually publish warnings in these areas, informing the public about the dangers of eating fish from contaminated waters. If you see such signs, or are aware of local warnings, do not allow your dog to eat the fish.

CHAPTER 5

Dog Safety and Management

Portrait of a Healthy Home
Twenty ways to improve your dog's health—and yours, too!

Admit it. If you thought that conditions in your house were dangerous to your health, you would change them or move.

That standard shouldn't be any different for your dog, and yet many of us expose our beloved friends to life-threatening toxins and life-shortening conditions. Many of the dangers lurk in products we use casually, without knowledge of their effects on our dogs. Ironically, while some of these conditions are potential threats to our *own* health, we often fail to consider them until they wreak havoc with the vitality of one of our animal friends.

Many of these hazards are chemical in nature. Exposed to toxic chemicals almost everywhere they go, our pets have to bear an ever-increasing load of toxins. The lawns and yards they romp in are often treated with pesticides and fertilizers, the sidewalks and streets where we walk them are awash in poisons, and, too often, even the rugs and floors they lie on all day are cleaned with harmful chemicals. Holistic veterinarians theorize that this constant bombardment of toxins, paired with unhealthy diets and overzealous vaccination schedules, inevitably results in the rampant allergies and autoimmune dysfunctions so commonly seen in today's dogs.

We can't fix the entire environment overnight, but fortunately, we can *easily* improve the health conditions in our homes. Below are descriptions of

There are also a number of safe commercial cleaning products available today. Look for products that carry the "Green Seal of Approval."

commonly found household health hazards. Reducing your dog's, and your own, exposure to as many of them as possible can improve your health, and maybe even extend your lives together.

Here are 20 ways to improve your dog's health—and yours, too!

We'll divide our suggestions into five areas: Cleanliness, Diet, Environment, Emergencies, and Lifestyle.

Cleanliness

1. Use safe cleaning agents
Did you know that most brand-name all-purpose cleaners, bleach, floor wax or polish, glass cleaner, and

Chemical	Found In	Concerns
Sodium hypochlorite	Chlorine bleach	Lung and eye irritant. If mixed with ammonia or acid-based cleaners, including vinegar, it releases toxic chloramine gas. Short-term exposure to the gas may cause mild asthmatic symptoms or more serious respiratory problems.
Ammonia	Glass cleaners	Lung and skin irritant. See sodium hypochlorite for problems with mixing.
Phenol and cresol	Disinfectants	Corrosive. May cause diarrhea, fainting, dizziness, and kidney and liver damage.
Formaldehyde	Preservative in many household products	Probable carcinogen. Even very low levels can cause watery or burning eyes, stuffy or burning nose and throat, nausea, coughing, wheezing, rashes, and allergic reactions.
Perchloroethylene or trichloroethane solvents	Dry cleaning, spot removers, and carpet cleaners	Eye, skin, and lung irritant. If ingested can cause liver and kidney damage. Probable carcinogen and can accumulate in fatty tissues.
Hydrochloric acid or sodium acid sulfate	Toilet bowl cleaners	Can burn the skin; may cause vomiting, diarrhea, and stomach burns if swallowed. May cause blindness if splashed in eyes.

Four Hazard Levels

The "signal word" system identifies four different levels of potential dangers posed to the consumer by non-pesticide household products. The four levels are:

Danger: *Indicates a product that represents the greatest potential harm to consumers and their families.*

Warning: *Indicates a moderate hazard.*

Caution: *Indicates a mild to moderate hazard.*

(No signal word): *Indicates the product is not hazardous. (Please note: Signal words are found on labels of new household products. Products manufactured before 1987 or products not intended for household use may not contain signal words.)*

disinfectant dish soaps contain hazardous materials? Read the list of "cautions" on the backs of the labels. If the hazard begins, "Caution," or "Warning," it signals that the product is not likely to produce permanent damage as a result of exposure, if appropriate first aid is given. If the hazard begins, "Danger," it indicates that even greater precautions should be taken, since accidental exposure or ingestion could cause tissue damage. Examine the labels of all your household products to determine the level of caution you should employ when using the product—or whether to use it at all.

Many common household agents can cause respiratory problems, damage the nervous system, cause diarrhea, dizziness, kidney and liver damage, and cancer. Never mix cleaning products. Products that are safe when used alone can sometimes become dangerous when mixed with other products. A common mishap occurs when people unwittingly mix products containing bleach (sodium hypochlorite) with products containing ammonia or acids. Such mixtures will release highly dangerous gases.

Use effective, safe alternatives. You can make them at home, or buy them.

Today, there are also a number of safe commercial cleaning products available. Look for products that carry the "Green Seal of Approval." To earn a Green Seal, a product must pass rigorous tests and meet the most stringent environmental standards. Green Seal products must demonstrably reduce air and water pollution, cut the waste of energy and natural resources, slow ozone depletion and the risk of global warming, prevent toxic contamination, and protect fish and wildlife and their habitats. To get a list of Green Seal products, call (202) 872-6400 or see greenseal.org.

2. Flea control

Fleas are annoying. They can make you and your dog near-crazy with itching, transmit larvae for tapeworms, and aggravate allergies. But when we're locked in a battle for control over a rampant flea population, we tend to go overboard, enlisting the aid of any and every chemical known to science—pet sprays, collars, shampoos, powders, dips, and tablets, as well as chemical sprays applied to our rugs, floors, and even yards.

Unfortunately, many of the products on the market are quite toxic to the pets they are trying to protect. Organochlorines, found in some flea dips and shampoos, can cause exaggerated responses to touch, light, and sound; spasms and muscle tremors; and seizures. Carbamates, found in dips, collars, powders, and sprays, can cause profuse salivation, muscular twitching, slowed pulse, labored breathing, vomiting, watery eyes, and paralysis, to name but a few symptoms. Pyrethrins, derived from chrysanthemums and thus often considered "natural," are the least toxic chemicals commonly used in flea shampoos and sprays, but to be effective, they require far more frequent applications.

Read the labels of these products carefully. When a label tells you to avoid getting the product on your own skin, to wash it off quickly and thoroughly, to avoid breathing the fumes, and to dispose of the empty container in a certain manner, it's telling you that the product is really not that "safe." After all, how can it be so dangerous for you and harmless to your dog?

Vacuum frequently

A powerful vacuum is a pet owner's best friend. A model with strong suction and multiple attachments can not only help you keep the sofa, the rug, and your going-on-a-date outfits dog-hair free, but also prevent fleas from completing their life cycle in your home.

Fleas spend only a portion of their time on the dog, and their eggs, larvae, and pupae are likely to be found in any area where the dog lives. Female fleas are prolific, laying as many as 20 to 50 eggs per day for as much as three months. Development of the larvae that hatch out of the eggs takes place *off* the dog, usually on or near the dog's bedding and resting areas. Concentrating your efforts on removing the opportunities for the eggs to develop is the most effective population control strategy.

The best way to remove the eggs' opportunities to develop is to remove the eggs, and to this end, your vacuum will be your most valuable tool in the flea war. Vacuum all the areas that your pet uses frequently, at least every two to three days. Since fleas locate their hosts by tracing the vibration caused by footsteps, vacuuming the most highly trafficked hallways and paths in your house will be most rewarding. Don't forget to vacuum underneath cushions on the couches or chairs your dog sleeps on. Change vacuum bags frequently, and seal the bag's contents safely in a plastic bag before disposing.

Wash your dog's bed

Flea eggs and developing flea larvae cannot survive getting wet. We can presume that any dog who has fleas will have flea eggs in his bed (since fleas usually

If you have cats or toy dog breeds, skip the essential oils in any of our recipes until you have checked with your holistic veterinarian; these animals are particularly sensitive to essential oils. Also, the use of essential oils may interfere with the action of homeopathic medicines. If you use homeopathy, check with your homeopath before using any essential oil in your home.

Wash your dog's bowl daily, with soap and hot water. 'Nuff said!

lay their eggs *off* the dog). So, if fleas are a problem in your neck of the woods, wash his bedding as frequently as possible. It is not necessary to use bleach, or insecticidal or detergent soaps, all of which can irritate the dog's skin; plain water will kill the eggs and larvae.

If you can't wash the dog's entire bed, at least wash the floor underneath the bed as often as you can. Purchase several covers (or sheets, or towels) for the bed and rotate them in and out of the wash.

3. Wash food and water bowls daily

Washing your dog's food and water bowls with soap and hot water will not only make them look better and make the dog's food and water more attractive to him, but also will kill any harmful bacteria that may attempt to grow there. If you feed your dog raw meat, it is *imperative* that you wash his bowls well daily, even if they *look* clean from his attentive licking. Pathogenic bacteria present on raw meat can quickly reproduce to harmful levels at room temperature.

Natural Cleaning Supplies
Here's a list of natural products to have on hand.

White vinegar: *Used in many formulations to clean and disinfect.*

Baking soda: *We recommend buying the largest box available.*

Washing soda: *This product is often found near the laundry detergents in supermarkets and health food stores.*

Borax: *Great for strengthening cleaning power!*

Mild soap: *Available in flakes and liquid—not deter-* gent! *Many products today are detergents made from petroleum distillates, which are both toxic and nonrenewable. Vegetable-based soap made from coconut or olive oil is known as castile soap and may be found in health food stores and some supermarkets. It is sometimes difficult to find unscented, but if you want to use your own favorite essential oils this is critical.*

Essential oils: *These differ from fragrance or perfume oils. Essential oils, found in health food stores, some specialty shops, and on the Internet, are volatile oils of plants.*

Dog Safety and Management

Favorite Essential Oils for Natural Cleaning

Oil	Scent	Properties
Citronella (Cymbopogon nardus)	*Strong, lemony*	*Insect repellent, deodorant, energizing, stimulating, soothing, tonic*
Cypress (Cupressus sempervirens)	*Smoky, woody, balsamic, and spicy*	*Antimicrobial, astringent, energizing, stimulating*
Eucalyptus (Eucalyptus globulus)	*Powerful, fresh, camphor-smelling*	*Antiseptic, anti-inflammatory, antiviral, bactericidal, decongestant, expectorant, stimulating*
Lavender (Lavandula angustifolia)	*Sweet and floral, refreshing*	*Analgesic, antidepressant, antimicrobial, antiseptic, bactericidal, balancing, calming, soothing*
Lemon (Citrus limonum)	*Sweet, citrus, fresh*	*Anti-infectious, astringent, antiseptic, bactericide, uplifting, tonic*
Lemongrass (Cymbopogon citratus)	*Strong, lemony, herby undertones*	*Insect repellent, antiseptic, antimicrobial, bactericide, calming*
Peppermint (Mentha piperata)	*Cool, fresh, strongly minty*	*Decongestant, energizing, stimulating*
Pine (Pinus sylvestris)	*Fresh, resiny*	*Expectorant, diuretic, pulmonary antiseptic*
Rosemary (Rosmarinus officinalis)	*Fresh, penetrating, herby*	*Analgesic, antiseptic, energizing, stimulating*
Tea Tree (Melaleuca alternifolia)	*Warm, spicy, antiseptic*	*Antifungal, anti-infectious, anti-inflammatory, antimicrobial, antiseptic, decongestant, antiviral, disinfectant, energizing, stimulant*

While we're on the topic, the safest bowls are stainless steel. Some ceramic bowls may allow chemicals to leach into the dog's food and water. And plastic bowls can contain a number of carcinogenic substances.

Diet

4. Feed your dog the best food

Advocates of homemade diets have a saying: "You can pay for fresh, real food now, or you can pay the veterinarian later." Dogs have thrived on our table scraps for thousands of years; eating what we eat is good for them—as long as what we eat is healthy! If you can, feed your dog a homemade diet that includes fresh meats; fresh, raw bone (ground or whole, as you deem safe); and fresh or lightly steamed vegetables; with occasional additions of grains, dairy products, eggs, fish, and fruit.

If you can't see your way clear to feeding your dog "real" food, feed him the best-quality kibble or canned food you can afford. Supplement the commercial food

Natural Housekeeping

Carpet and floors

Our dogs spend much of their days on our carpets. Having no carpet to collect all the day-to-day gunk is probably the healthiest option; however, many homes have wall-to-wall carpeting or large, room-sized rugs. So our job is to clean our carpets in the healthiest, but also in the least destructive, manner. You can deodorize, disinfect, or clean carpets depending on your current need.

If you just need to freshen your carpet, a simple mixture of baking soda and borax (equal parts) sprinkled on the carpet and vacuumed up will do the trick. To make this even more effective, you can add several drops of your favorite essential oil to the powdered mix. Lemongrass and citronella oils are excellent choices if you are concerned about fleas. To make a safe carpet shampoo, the following recipe (from The Naturally Clean Home *by Karyn Siegel-Maier) will cover a 10-foot x 13-foot room.*

Rosemary-Lavender Carpet Shampoo
2 cups baking soda
½ cup soap flakes (you can substitute with borax)
20 drops lavender essential oil
8 drops rosemary essential oil
½ cup white vinegar
2 cups warm water

Loosen dirt by vacuuming or sweeping carpet. Combine baking soda, soap flakes, and essential oils in a large glass or stainless steel bowl, breaking up clumps. Sprinkle this mixture on the carpet. In a bucket, mix the vinegar and warm water. Dip a clean sponge mop into the bucket, squeezing out the excess liquid. Go over the carpet with the sponge mop, working in sections. Wait one hour and vacuum.

For **wood floors,** *the best cleaner is a mixture of equal parts warm water and white vinegar. Combine in a spray bottle; spritz a small section and dry-mop. To 3 cups of this mixture you can add 15 to 20 drops of an essential oil of your choice. We like peppermint since it smells great, will kill germs, and keeps mice away!*

For cleaning **tile or vinyl floors,** *mix a gallon of hot water and 2 to 3 tablespoons of a liquid castile soap. To this mix you can add either lemon (great in the kitchen), or pine essential oil. Use 10 to 20 drops of oil and feel free to mix oils.*

Dip your mop into the mixture, squeeze out the excess water, and mop in small sections. The best part of this mix is there is no rinsing involved, and the residue won't hurt your dog if she happens to lick the floor when you are done.

Clean counters

Especially important are the areas where we prepare our own and our dogs' food. To clean counters, mix for each cup of hot water, 1 tablespoon of vinegar and a scant teaspoon of borax. Add about 10 to 12 drops of essential oil. (Lavender and lemon essential oils are antibacterial, antifungal, antiviral, and antibiotic.) Remember, essential oils are potent; use sparingly.

To scour and disinfect wood chopping blocks, mix a couple of tablespoons of salt (any salt will do, but sea salt is grittier) and a like amount of fresh lemon juice and vigorously rub the mixture into the wood (it helps to wear gloves). Let this soak for 10 to 15 minutes, then rinse while scrubbing under hot water. Allow the wood to dry thoroughly.

Bathrooms

Who among us has a dog that has never taken a drink out of the toilet? Given the ingredients in most toilet bowl cleaners, you invite long-term health problems for your dog with even the occasional lapper.

Instead, make your own germproof toilet bowl cleaner by combining the following: 1 cup water, 3 tablespoons of liquid castile soap, 20 drops of tea tree oil, and 7 to 10 drops of eucalyptus oil. If you have a hard-water ring in the bowl, combine borax and vinegar with lemon essential oil, mix in a container, and pour into the bowl. Let it sit undisturbed for about 12 hours and the stains should be gone.

Dog Safety and Management

with occasional healthy treats from your table—and not the unhealthy chunks of fat cut off of your steak, nor old, smelly food from the back shelf of the refrigerator. Add some of the leftover steamed vegetables to his dinner. Make a little extra brown rice or oatmeal and mix it into his breakfast.

Don't forget to feed only healthy treats. Chunks of fresh fruit make great snacks for dogs; many enjoy crunching crisp cubed apples, or banana slices (no grapes or raisins). A raw carrot makes a great chew toy, and helps the dog keep his teeth clean. Dogs who prefer meaty treats will jump through hoops for dried salmon or beef.

5. Provide fresh, clean water

It's not enough for dogs to have a bowl full of water at their disposal at all times—they should have a *clean* bowl full of *fresh, pure* water at their constant disposal.

Many people fill the dog's bowl only when it's bone dry, and fail to wash it out until it turns green with algae. For shame! Dogs drink more when they have fresh water and for normal, healthy dogs, drinking water is a good thing. Water helps regulate all the body's systems.

At least two or three times a day, dump out the water in your dog's bowl (you don't have to waste it—you can use it for the houseplants) and refill it with fresh water. Once a day, wash the bowl out with hot, soapy water.

Environment

6. Provide non-slip surfaces

Whether they are polished wood or shiny vinyl, the smooth, glistening floors that most of us aspire to own pose certain risks to certain dogs. Dogs who are arthritic or who have suffered physical injuries can really hurt themselves by slipping on slick floors. For these dogs, use carpet or sisal-grass runners in hallways or other areas where your dog needs traction. Surround his food and water bowls with a rubber-backed rug so he can lower his head to eat or drink without his hind legs slipping out from under him.

7. Don't smoke around your dog

You already know you shouldn't smoke, for your own health. But did you know that secondhand smoke has been associated with lung and nasal cancer in smokers' dogs?

Studies conducted at Colorado State University's College of Veterinary Medicine and Biomedical Sciences showed that dogs who live with smokers are more likely to have cancer than dogs who live with non-smokers. Long-nosed dogs with nasal cancer were 2.5 times more

Keeping Your Lawn Green, Organically

Organic gardeners will eagerly tell you: Pesticides and herbicides are not needed to keep your lawn green and thick. You do have to understand your grass, however!

Basically, a beautiful lawn is a place where the desirable species of grass is winning a war against weeds. Your role is to supply your grass with the nutrients it needs to grow well, and to water and mow the lawn in a fashion that suits the grass and discourages weeds.

Fortunately, grass and weeds have fairly different needs and growing styles. As long as you are aware of these differences, and cater to the grass, you'll be rolling in green. Your local nursery will be a great source of information, and there are numerous books that can help, but in a nutshell, here are the basics:

- *It doesn't hurt grass to be mowed frequently, but it does damage weeds. However, cutting grass too short does discourage the plant. Weeds, in contrast, need their tops intact to thrive. So, adjust your mover to its highest setting—three to four inches is perfect—and mow as frequently as you like. This suits the grass just fine, but the practice will kill weeds in just a few weeks.*
- *Remove the bag attachment from your mower. Contrary to popular belief, this practice does not "choke" the grass, but helps nourish the soil, which can become more rapidly depleted without this mulching.*

- *Water your lawn as infrequently as possible, but when you do sprinkle, water it deeply. Many experts suggest placing a cup in the area where you are sprinkling and leaving the water running until there is at least an inch of water in the cup. This practice encourages your grass to send its roots deep into the soil after the water as the soil dries. Because weed roots cannot grow as deeply, they will dehydrate and die before you water again.*

   This practice seems to be the most difficult to accomplish for many amateur gardeners, who worry that the grass will die if it's not watered every other day. But unless the grass roots are encouraged to dive deep for a drink, they will remain within the top few inches of soil, where they will have to compete mightily with the roots of weeds, which thrive under a program of frequent, shallow watering.
- *Ask someone at your local nursery about soil amendments tailored to the local soil conditions; they may suggest a soil test so you can adjust the soil pH with lime (for over-acid soils) or gardener's sulphur (for over-alkaline soils) to get it just right for growing grass (which thrives at pH 6.5).*
- *Nursery staff can also recommend an appropriate organic fertilizer. Most lawns require only two "feedings" a year, although additional applications of organic liquid seaweed (available at nurseries) will thrill your already happier grass.*

likely to live in smoking households than among non-smokers. Short-nosed dogs with lung cancer were 2.4 times more likely to live with a smoker.

If you must smoke, do it outside, and away from your dog. Don't smoke in an enclosed space such as a closed room (or worse, a car) that has your dog in it.

8. Preserve air quality

The air in the average home is 2 to 20 times more polluted than the air outside. It's not unheard-of for the concentrations of dangerous air pollutants in homes to rise to 100 times the concentration outdoors! And even low concentrations of volatile chemicals can cause chronic or acute illness, cancer, and even genetic mutations in humans and their companion animals.

Dogs are particularly at risk. Many common solvents are heavier than air; they sink to the floor level, where our dogs spend most of their time. And dogs have a faster respiratory rate than we do; pound for pound, they end up breathing more "bad air" than we would in the same environment.

There are many ways to improve the air in your

home. Limit (better yet, eliminate) petroleum-based products in your home; all of these substances release health-damaging chemicals into the air. Use natural cleaning products. Open the windows in your home at least once a day, for enough time to really fill the place with fresh air. Place non-toxic houseplants throughout your home; they improve air quality by removing carbon dioxide and releasing oxygen. Don't use chemical "air fresheners" in your home; use scented flowers or dried herbs to lend a harmless perfume to your home instead.

To freshen a room's odor, sprinkle baking soda liberally on carpets. Vacuum it up after 30 minutes or so. Vanilla extract, poured into a shallow dish on a high shelf where Fido can't reach it, can make a room smell good.

9. Poisonous plants

Many common house and garden plants are highly poisonous if consumed. Few dogs eat plants, but you never know! Bored or agitated canines have done stranger things. The following plants are dangerous to dogs:

> **All plant parts:** Azaleas, buttercup, calla lily, laurels, rhododendron, tiger lily, philodendrons, poinsettia, mistletoe.
>
> **Bulbs:** crocus, daffodil, tulip.
>
> **Berries:** Christmas berry, jasmine, red sage.

The best course is to eliminate poisonous plants from your home decorating and landscaping plans.

10. Handle air pollutants carefully

If you were as familiar as toxicologists are with the health effects of indoor air pollution, you really wouldn't consider bringing home most, if not all, commercial housekeeping or yard chemicals. Say there is a potentially dangerous product—a mineral spirits paint remover, for example—that you deem necessary to use in a home improvement project. Do a little homework, and see if there is a safer alternative (there usually is).

After a romp on an expanse of public lawn, it's advisable to rinse your dog's paws (at least) and coat (especially if he likes to roll on the grass!).

If you just can't (or won't) find an alternative, at the very least, take the following precautions:

Buy just the amount you think you will need for the project. Schedule the activity so that it occurs when the weather is mild enough for you to *thoroughly* ventilate your home while the product is in use *and* for at least a couple of weeks afterward. Keep the product's container closed *every moment* it is not being used. Keep all pets (and children, pregnant women, and other vulnerable individuals) away from the area where the product is in use) for this period of time. And then dispose of the remains of the product in a safe, legal manner (following instructions on the label) as soon as possible; once unsealed, most containers are not completely vapor-proof.

11. Pick up poo

We all know that poop smells bad—yes, even *your* dog's poop. It also attracts flies and can spread worms. (The larvae of tapeworms, hookworms, and roundworms are all expelled in an infected dog's feces. Any dog, or person, for that matter, who comes into skin or mouth contact with larvae-contaminated feces can become infected with the worms.) Ideally, everyone would pick up their dog's feces daily. This would prevent worms, coprophagia (dogs who eat their poo—*eww!*), dirty looks from neighbors, and delays for emergency shoe-cleaning.

12. Chew-proof the house

Not all dogs are apt to chew on weird, random things around the house when they are bored and unsupervised, though some are. *All* puppies have this proclivity.

If your dog is a chewer—again, we know that *all* puppies are—he should not be left unsupervised in any room where there are items that could be dangerous if chewed. This includes exposed electrical cords, clothing items or shoes, electronic items (such as cameras, remote controls, cell phones), and just about any toys. When left unattended, vulnerable individuals should be safely confined to a crate or puppy pen.

13. Keep your yard "green"

Don't use pesticides in your yard. Dogs absorb insecticides, herbicides, and fungicides from the soil by walking, lying, and rolling on it. They are also exposed to many potent insecticides in the home, such as ant, roach, or fly sprays. Long-term exposure to these chemicals decreases the vitality of the animal by taxing the organ and glandular function, and increases the animal's chances of suffering from cancer, allergies, and kidney and liver problems. Signs that an animal's body is working overtime to rid itself of toxins include oily, smelly secretions on the skin and in the ears, and excessive eye "goop."

Outside, use native species of plants in your garden; they will naturally resist many local pests. Alternatively, plant disease-resistant strains of plants, flowers, trees, and vegetables, available at most nurseries. The health of these strains is less dependent on the use of chemicals. Use "friendly" enemies of pests, like ladybugs, which hungrily consume the aphids that plague roses and other plants. Ask your neighbors about their pesticide use, and let them know about your most successful organic gardening techniques.

Rinse your dog's feet after exercising her on a public lawn. Rinse any fetch toys she may have played

Keep a collar with current identification on your dogs at all times—no exceptions.

When you travel, or your dog is in anyone else's care, add a temporary ID to his collar with the caretaker's contact info.

Have an identifying microchip implanted in your dog. If, for some reason, your dog gets separated from his collar, this will increase the odds that he is identified and returns. Most animal shelters scan for microchips routinely. Find out if your local shelter does.

with on the lawn, too. Of course, call your veterinarian immediately if your dog ever shows signs of illness following exposure to grassy fields.

In Case of Emergency

14. Keep emergency numbers handy

Every phone in your house should have a list of emergency numbers next to it: emergency services, your doctor, dentist, and close family members or friends. If you own a dog, that list should also include the number for your veterinarian, holistic practitioners, all-night and weekend emergency clinic, and poison control center. You should also list numbers for a couple of your dog-loving friends, people who could enter your house and care for your dog if something happened to *you*. If you travel with your dog, make sure you also have these numbers with you. You don't want to be scrambling for any of these in a real emergency.

15. Keep a first-aid kit handy

Just as you plan and prepare your dog's daily meals and training, advance planning and preparation for the unthinkable accident may help save your dog's life during the critical time between the beginning of the emergency and access to veterinary care.

The time to plan, obviously, is *before* your dog is involved in an accident. Start gathering the contents for a first-aid kit today. A good *holistic* first-aid kit might contain Rescue Remedy (or another brand of the flower essence remedy) for shock; gauze pads; cotton; tape; Q-tips; pure water (distilled or spring water); a clean glass or plastic spray bottle; elastic bandages; adhesive tape; tweezers; scissors; hydrogen peroxide; soap (castile or other natural type); and herbal cleansing solutions (calendula and hypericum are miraculous).

16. Have an emergency plan

Natural disasters can and do strike anywhere, anytime. In the mass confusion following a fire, earthquake, flood, mudslide, snowstorm, or hurricane, our animal friends can easily get lost or separated. Another disaster can happen if any of the above calamities cuts off your food and water supply.

Store provisions for your pets along with your family's emergency supplies. Disaster preparedness experts recommend keeping at least a two-week supply of food and water for both the humans and animals in the house. Canned and dry foods should be stored (along with a can opener!) in a cool, dry place. Be sure to check the dated shelf life, occasionally buying new stocks and using the stored goods. Keep at least 10 gallons of water on hand, rotating and using the

bottles so that none are stored for more than a couple of months.

Having identification on your animal friend may be his only chance to be returned to you if he gets lost in a disaster. Even if the phone (or even the house at the address!) listed on your dog's ID tags is missing after a disaster, the information can be used by rescuers to reunite you with your beloved friend. It can also be a good idea to keep a good photo of your dog with your most important papers, the kind of papers you'd grab first if you had to run out of your house in an emergency. The photo should clearly show the dog's size and markings.

Lifestyle

17. Balance quiet time and busy time

Those of us who lead chaotic lives tend to dream of and crave days of quiet, restful sleep. People who are housebound and depressed can benefit from activity and stimulation. Balancing rest and action gives the body the opportunity to stress and then rebuild tissues, and lends the individual a healthy ability to cope with whatever life throws his or her way.

Dogs are no different. Some lead incredibly stressful, busy lives, and could use more rest—dogs who go to work with their owners, for instance, may benefit from a few hours a day of protection from noise and visitors. Dogs who are understimulated will benefit from mild physical exercise and mental challenges.

18. Exercise. Period.

Exercise is good for all dogs—within reason, and within the dog's abilities. As always, balance is key. An extremely long run or vigorous romp at the dog park on a daily basis may excessively stress the dog's joints and muscles, and deny him the opportunity to repair damaged tissues, resulting in stress fractures, arthritis, or strained muscles or ligaments. Strenuous workouts such as these should be limited to three to

Exercise is good for you and your friends, canine and human! Get as much as you can!

four days a week, even for healthy, fit dogs. Alternate hard workouts with shorter, easier exercise sessions, such as walks or short backyard play sessions.

There are far more dogs receiving too little exercise than dogs who get too much, however. Many people with old dogs, obese dogs, or dogs with physical handicaps feel that it's cruel to "make" their dogs go for walks. But the more muscle tissue and coordination the dog has, the better—and he'll lose both if he's not walking at least a little, a few times a day.

19. Socialization

Dogs and humans are social; loners are aberrations, not the rule in either species. Dogs and humans should be able to greet each other happily, communicate well, and part easily from their friends. We all want our dogs to be safe and comfortable with other people, so it's well worth the effort to properly socialize your dog to canine and human visitors to your home. Ask any friend who stops by to feed your dog a handful of treats, one at a time, to help your dog understand that strangers can be a good thing. Use a tether or baby gate to prevent an over-exuberant or overprotective dog from exhibiting unseemly behavior. Arrange occasional play dates with healthy dogs with compatible temperaments.

20. Spend quality time together

We know it sounds hokey, but human–canine relationships are not much different from human–human relationships. Most of us want dogs who like and trust us and whom we like and trust. We want to be able to take them places without them embarrassing us, and we'd like to be able to have friends come over without having to apologize for our canine partners' behavior. We want them to pay attention to us! And we want them to understand what we are trying to tell them and to comply with most of our requests without us yelling or repeating ourselves.

The health of every relationship depends on the individuals spending time together—and not just on infrequent weekends, and not just laying around watching TV! Take up a hobby together: walking, squirrel chasing, agility, flyball. Work on honing your communication skills. Teaching your dog new tricks is a great way to bond, improve his manners, entertain yourself, and impress your friends. The more time you spend playing with your dog, training your dog, or just lying around petting or massaging your dog, the better your relationship will be.

Preventing Great Escapes
How to safely confine burrowers, beavers, bounders, and bolters.

Roaming is an innate behavior for dogs. They are hunters and scavengers, and left to their own devices will wander a territory far larger than the average backyard. Escaping, however, is a learned behavior. Dogs who are given the opportunity to escape often do. Once they figure out how, they will try harder and harder, even when the fence is belatedly fortified. Dogs who become escape artists hone their skills to a fine edge. Keeping them safely confined at home where they belong can be a huge challenge. Our nation's animal shelters are full of escape artists.

The best avenue for managing a dog's wanderlust is to prevent him from wandering in the first place. The problem starts when you bring home the new puppy before you are fully prepared, promising to put up that fence before Rover grows up.

A tiny puppy won't wander far from the back stoop, even when you leave him out on his own for a bit. Before you know it, though, Rover is six months old, already has a habit of making neighborhood rounds, and you still haven't finished the fence. When Mr. Jones from down the road calls you up and threatens to shoot Rover if he chases his goats one more time, you rush to the hardware store to buy some metal fence posts and hog wire. Hastily you throw up a pen in the backyard that attaches to the back deck. "That should hold him until I get the rest of those post holes dug!" you think.

As you settle yourself back on the sofa to watch the last half of the football game, Rover is already testing the fence; he's late for his daily visit to the Smiths' garbage can! He checks out the gate latch, but it doesn't yield to his tentative pawing and gnawing. He trots around the inside of the enclosure, searching for a way out.

In the far corner he finds a three-inch gap between the wire and the ground and pokes his nose under. Getting his nose on the other side of the fence encourages him to try harder. He starts to worm his way under. The soft ground gives way beneath his claws. He digs harder. Before you can say "end zone," he's free, headed for the Smiths' omelet scraps and bacon drippings. You eventually retrieve him and fill the hole, but the damage is done. Rover is on his way to a lifetime career as a master escape artist.

A wood or wire overhang can discourage many escape artists.

Repair any problems that you observe with your fence *before* your dog notices the weakness and takes advantage of it.

Burrowers, beavers, bounders, and bolters

Whether your dog's escape efforts focus on tooth or claw or he excels in feats of aerial accomplishment depends both on genetics and learning. Dogs who are genetically programmed to dig, such as terriers, are likely to burrow under the fence, especially if a handy soft spot presents itself.

If, however, the first weak spot in the fence is a loose board, we can inadvertently train Rover and our terrier to eat their way through fences, turning them into beavers rather than burrowers. Once Rover discovers that the fence is breachable, he'll test every spot where his teeth can gain purchase, and you'll forever spend your football-watching time patching his holes.

Herding dogs such as Border Collies and sporting breeds like Labradors have a natural ability to leap tall buildings in a single bound. Given the opportunity, they'll often make jumping fences their specialty.

However, you can inadvertently teach a less athletic dog to bound over fences by starting small. Confident that a four-foot fence will contain the beagle mix you just adopted from the shelter, you leave him in the backyard and go off to work. That night, your new dog greets you in the driveway after terrorizing cottontails in the neighbors' woods all day. You raise the fence six inches, positive that this will hold him. Flush from his exploits the day before, your dog has to struggle a little harder to make it over 4-foot-6, but nothing breeds success like success. A little extra oomph, and he's out again for another rousing day of bunny-bashing.

You raise the fence to five feet this time, absolutely sure there's no way he can get over that. But again, even more confident of his jumping prowess, your dog tries a

A fence that is too tall is *far* better than one that is just tall enough.

wee bit harder, and he's up and over. There's a good chance that if you had *started* with a five-foot fence Snoopy never would have tried to jump it at all. What you've done is taught him to jump higher and higher, consistently reinforcing his belief that if he just tries hard enough he can make it.

Bolters have learned to watch for a moment of human inattention, then charge through the tiniest crack in the gate or door. While the other escape methods work best in the absence of humans, bolting requires the unintentional complicity of the visitor who doesn't know (or the family member who forgets) that Dash must be manacled and hog-tied before a door is opened to the outside world. Once again, prevention is the better part of valor. If Dash is taught from early days to wait politely at a door until invited out, he won't learn the fine art of door-darting.

Prevention

It's *always* easier to *prevent* a behavior problem from happening than it is to fix it after the fact. There's no excuse for letting a puppy learn how to be an escape artist. Prevention measures are relatively simple. Don't let your puppy learn that roaming is rewarding—keep him at home, and stop any embryonic escape attempts in their tracks by taking the following prophylactic measures:

- Provide a safe, secure enclosure. Before the new puppy comes home, make sure your fence is flush to the ground, or even buried a few inches. Check for rotten spots, and crawl behind shrubs and brush to look for holes or loose boards.
- Go overboard on fence height. Raise the fence to at least five feet for a small dog (perhaps higher for very athletic small dogs like Jack Russell Terriers) and six feet for medium to large dogs. Make sure there are no woodpiles, doghouses, deck railings, or other objects close enough to the fence to provide a launch pad.

Train your dog to sit and wait for your signal before he is released to run through any door.

- Teach your pup to wait at doors until invited through. Use "Wait!" at every door to the outside world, every time you open it, whether you are going to let him go through it or not.
- Install dog-proof latches on gates. There's no point in waiting until after he's been hit by a car to discover that Rover can learn to work the latch. In fact, a padlock will prevent accidental release from the outside by a visitor or intruder at the same time it keeps Rover from practicing his latch-opening skills.
- Minimize Rover's motivation to roam by neutering at a young age (eight weeks or not long thereafter), and providing him with ample exercise and companionship at home (see "A Stitch in Time" on page 241).
- Consider keeping Rover indoors when you're not home. Boredom and loneliness provide strong motivation to escape, and Rover has plenty of time to plan and execute the great escape when you are not there to interrupt unwanted behaviors such as digging under and chewing through fences.

The fix

What if it's too late for prevention? Maybe you adopted Rover from the shelter after his last adopter taught him to jump a six-foot fence, and then returned him because he kept escaping. Do you give up on Rover, too? Not at all. There are lots of steps you can take to fortify your defenses and keep your escape artist at home, depending on his proclivities.

- **Burrowers:** If you're going to bury the fence for a dedicated burrower, bury deep—at least six inches to a foot. If you bury it two inches, you'll just teach him to dig deeper. You might do better setting the fence in cement, or lining your fence trench with large rocks or small boulders. You definitely need a cement pad at the gate, since you can't bury the gate.
- **Beavers:** If Bucky has learned to gnaw his way through your fence, you could be in big trouble. Lining the inside of the fence with heavy-duty wire—such as chain link—may stop him. It may not, however, and he may break teeth in his attempts to eat his way out. Sheets of FRP are good for this also. Cement block walls can be effective, but may not be aesthetically pleasing. Ceramic tiles can be glued to the blocks to make them more attractive, but they're not cheap.
- **Bounders:** If you have a scaler, who hooks his nails in the chain link and climbs up and over, you can cover the inside of the fence with a flat, solid surface so his nails can't get a purchase. A material primarily used in boats, FRP (fiberglass reinforced plastic) is now regularly used in animal shelters and may withstand tooth and nail, but may be prohibitively expensive if you have a large fenced area.

For fence jumpers, hang a wide pipe or tube on the fence so that it rolls, keeping a dog from getting a grip on the top of the fence.

A Shocking Solution

Many dog owners are turning to electric shock collars to keep their dogs contained. Non-visible electronic fences are quite the rage, especially in communities where shortsighted homeowner regulations prohibit the installation of physical fences. Many dog owners are pleased with the results—no unsightly fence to impede their view of the sunset, and Rover magically stays within his delineated boundaries. Many dog owners are not so pleased. There are a myriad of things that can fail with non-visible shock fencing systems. Here are just a few:

- For most dogs, there is a stimulus strong enough to entice the dog through the fence. For some, it might be that bunny or squirrel venturing a tad too close. Once the dog is outside the fence line, he's rarely motivated to brave the shock to get back in.
- Some dogs learn that the shock stops once they cross the line. Dogs who are determined to escape can learn to grit their teeth and risk one shock to get to the other side.
- Shock collars are a punishment tool, and their use risks all the potential negative side effects of punishment. They can cause fear and/or aggression. If a dog receives a shock while a child is walking by, he may associate the shock with the child and become aggressive toward children. Or mail carriers. Or joggers. Or other dogs. Some dogs have become terrified and refuse to go into their own

yards after receiving shocks from the collar during the training process.

- Electronic equipment can fail. Batteries die, and when the dog no longer hears the warning beep he is free to come and go as he pleases. Some collars have malfunctioned and delivered repeated shocks to hapless, helpless dogs until their owners arrived home from work at the end of the day to rescue them from their torture.
- The non-visible fence does not, of course, provide the dog with any protection from intruders, so Rover is at the mercy of other dogs or humans who may enter the yard and do bad things.

We do not recommend the use of "electronic collars" (shock collars) for containment purposes. Ever.

Or, you can install a "roof" at the top of the fence that comes in at a 90-degree angle; he won't be able to reach behind his head and pull himself backward over the ledge when he gets to the top. Some people use wire mesh to create an angled-in barrier—similar to those at the top of prison fences, only without the razor wire!—that impedes jumping.

Another option that I've seen work is to top

your fences with a "roll bar" that prevents your dog from getting a purchase at the top of the fence and pulling himself over. This is easily installed by running a wire or rope through sections of fat PVC pipe and hanging them along the top of the fence.

If you have a sailer, who gets a good running start and clears the fence with the greatest of ease, plant a hedge or place some other obstacle in his takeoff zone, interrupting his stride and making it impossible for him to jump. If you put your last fence extension inward at a 45-degree angle you may also fool his eye and foil his leap.

- **Bolters:** The dog who bolts through open doors needs an airlock—a system of double gates so that if he makes it through one, he is still contained behind the next. Self-closing gate springs are a must, to prevent visitors and family members from being careless twice in a row. A good solid recall—teaching Dash to come when called—taught with positive methods, of course, is an excellent backup plan for the door darter. Family members also need to remember not to panic and chase when Dash slips out—a good game of keep-away just makes door-darting more fun for the dog.

Make sure your fence is secure before you bring that new dog home. Even if it keeps your current dogs safely confined, a canine newcomer may have new talents that test your confinement system.

Be careful any time you put your dog in a new containment area. Check the area first to ensure it is secure, and watch him after you put him in to be sure he's not testing the fence.

Consider the safest approach—always keep your dog indoors when you're not home.

Collar, Tag, and 'Chip
No, the microchipping system isn't perfect yet. . . . Get one anyway.

We've all heard at least one tragic story involving a lost dog and a disconsolate owner. We've all seen a lost dog scared witless, running down a street with that classic lost dog expression, almost blind with fear.

A lost dog's chances of finding his way back to his concerned owner are vastly improved if he's wearing a collar and identification. People may try harder to catch a stray dog who is wearing a collar and tags; they may feel he's less likely to be abandoned and more likely to be lost. A collar gives a Samaritan something to reach for. And, obviously, the identification makes it ridiculously easy for the owner to be immediately notified and summoned to reclaim his errant friend.

Sadly, there are thousands of dogs lost each year who are *not* wearing a collar and ID, and too many of them are unable to ever return to their homes. The American Humane Association estimates that only about 15 percent of lost dogs and 2 percent of lost cats ever find their way back from shelters to their original owners. Implanted microchips can improve that sad statistic.

A microchip is a tiny transponder, coded to display a unique identification number capable of being read by a handheld scanner. The transponder is embedded in a sealed glass or bioplastic tube, often described as the size of a grain of rice—long-grain rice, anyway. (The tubes are 2mm x 11mm.)

The chip does not contain a battery or any other technology that can wear out; it draws power from and responds only to a scanner held fairly close to the dog and tuned to the correct frequency. The rest of the time, it is completely inert. The chips are implanted under a dog's skin above his shoulders, with a pre-loaded, sterile syringe and a large-gauge needle. No anesthetic is required, and dogs generally react little more than to a regular vaccination injection.

The owner of the implanted dog then registers the chip with the manufacturer, linking her name and contact information, including numbers for the dog's veterinarian and an alternate contact person.

Shelters scan every dog brought to their facilities. The scanner reads the chip, a call to the chip maker's registry locates the owner's name and contact information, and within minutes, a call is placed and the owner receives the joyous news, "We have your dog."

Reality bites, sometimes

That's exactly the way the system works—sometimes. The companies that provide microchips and chipping services toss around high numbers to promote the technology; for example, one company reports more than 200,000 pets reunited with their owners so far. These numbers are cause for celebration, and definitely a reason to embrace and support the practice.

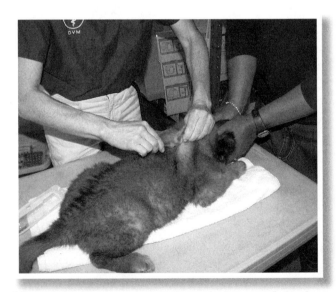

Microchip implanting services are increasingly easy to find and afford. Some shelters offer free chipping on special days; others chip every adopted dog.

Unfortunately, there are some significant problems that prevent the concept from working perfectly all the time:

- Competing microchip manufacturers have created and promoted incompatible technology—scanners that can't read every chip, and chips that can be read only by certain scanners.
- Not all shelters have scanners. (And so it follows that not all shelters have *all* scanners.)
- Not all shelters that have scanners scan every dog who gets brought in. Overworked shelter staff may be ill-equipped or disinclined to scan a dog that is defensive, or seems aggressive or dangerous.
- Scanners can sometimes fail to read or even detect the presence of a compatible chip, whether due to a technology malfunction or operator error.
- In the early days of microchipping, the implants sometimes "migrated," or moved to a place where they couldn't be detected or weren't detected because the person scanning the dog didn't expect the chip's location to be so far from the norm. (This is actually a *former* problem. Manufacturers say chips now are made with a special coating that, once in contact with body fluids and subcutaneous tissue, helps the body to form a layer of connective tissue around the chip, holding it in place.)
- Owners may fail to register their dog's microchip, or fail to update the registry with current information after they move.
- There are several competing chip registries, which can potentially delay notification of an owner.

Still worthwhile as a backup

Despite all the potential problems, the fact remains that thousands upon thousands of dogs *do* get identified and recovered, thanks to their microchip implants. There have been reports in the media of dogs and cats who were found hundreds and even thousands of miles away from their original owners. There have

The chip does not contain a battery or any other technology that can wear out; it draws power from and responds only to a scanner held fairly close to the dog and tuned to the correct frequency.

been pets who were identified and brought back to their original owners as much as a decade after being lost! These reunions, between collarless, tagless pets and their owners, would simply not be possible without microchip technology, imperfect as it is.

And, fortunately, there are a number of things that a dog owner can do to reduce the number of potential problems that could otherwise hinder the effectiveness of the microchip identification system. First, keep a collar and current ID on your dog. Then, because bizarre things happen, have your dog microchipped, in case he becomes lost and separated from his collar.

Keep a collar with current identification on your dog at all times—no exceptions.

When you travel, or your dog is in anyone else's care, add a temporary ID to his collar with the caretaker's contact info.

Have an identifying microchip implanted in your dog. If, for some reason, your dog does not have his collar on when he is lost, this will increase the odds he is identified and returned.

Register the microchip and your contact information as soon as possible. Keep your contact info current!

Before you have a microchip implanted in your dog, do some research in your community. Call all the veterinary hospitals in your area and ask if they implant microchips, and if so, which type? Then call every animal shelter in your area and ask them the same questions. Don't settle for ambiguous answers; ask to be transferred to one of the staff members who actually scans incoming pets. Find out whether they check for 125- and/or 134.2-kHz chips, and if so, how? Do they use more than one scanner? Or do they have a forward and backward scanner?

If you are extremely fortunate, the animal shelters in your community have and reliably use either a forward and backward scanner, or both types of scanners. (We suggest a letter-writing campaign to urge your shelter to obtain and use an ISO scanner that can read or at least detect all chips.) The next best scenario is the community in which only one type of chip is sold and its corresponding scanner is used reliably by all the area animal shelters.

If your local shelters do not regularly scan for microchips, or do not scan for *all* the chips that are distributed by vets, clinics, and other shelters in your area—consider having your dog tattooed in addition to or instead of microchipping. Two lines of defense are always better than one.

All in a Day's Care
Doggie daycare provides supervision, socialization, and stimulation.

The powerful Akita lunges at the Scottie, her mouth agape, teeth flashing. With a guttural growl, her jaws close around the neck of the little black dog. She pins the wiry terrier to the ground, where he struggles, belly up, in a fruitless attempt to sink his own teeth into his attacker's leg. As a handful of spectators laugh from a nearby doorway, the Scottie's struggles subside until he is motionless on the floor, the Akita pinning him to the ground with her superior weight.

What horror is this? Are we witness to the awful blood sport of underground dog fighting? Far from it. Rather, this is a perfectly happy scene from a perfectly well-managed dog daycare center. Shortly after the Akita pinned the Scottie to the floor, the little black dog leaped up unscathed, chased the big dog around the room three times, and then took *his* turn pinning *her* to the floor amidst a reciprocal chorus of happy growls and snarls. It's all in a day's play.

Once upon a time, it was commonplace for groups of dogs to wrestle and romp together. Farmers and ranchers kept at least several dogs at a time: some to herd livestock and protect the homestead, some for hunting, one or two to kill rats in the barn, and maybe an unusually fortunate small house dog. The dogs had the run of the farm, romped and ran together, and led doggie lives. In a society more casual than today's, even town dogs tended to roam freely in compatible packs, sorting out their differences with an occasional scuffle that rarely turned into anything serious.

In modern society, our dogs are more likely to stay at home, safely confined to the house or the fenced backyard, plied with vaccinations, toys, and regular meals. As a result, while many of today's dogs live longer, healthier lives than their ancestors did, they also miss out on socialization and exercise with their canine pals.

Most dogs today also lack the stimulation of a real job—the herding, hunting, ratting, carting, or guarding that they were bred to do. Left home alone all day while their families are at work and school, they are bored, lonely, restless, and unemployed. Without the opportunity to interact regularly with others of their own kind, they even forget how to speak "dog," and when they *do* meet up with other canines they are often socially inept, fearful, or aggressive. The sad result is a growing population of pets who exhibit inappropriate behaviors in the home, and who are "not good with other dogs."

Daycare to the rescue

Enter the rapidly growing phenomenon of commercial doggie daycare. Our ancestors would have laughed heartily at the notion, but an increasing number of dog owners are realizing the benefits of paying to provide their dogs with a day full of activity and supervision. Imagine the relief of owners who realize (often too late!) the difficulty of housetraining the new puppy when no one is home to take her outside regularly; now they can happily drop Puddles off at daycare in the morning, knowing that the staff can further the pup's understanding of proper potty behavior. Those who have dogs with separation anxiety can stop administering tranquilizers (and stop taking them themselves), knowing that their house is *not* being systematically reduced to toothpicks in their absence.

In addition, in a well-supervised daycare program, Timid Tess can learn how to be a dog. She won't be allowed to run with scissors, and she will learn how to play well with others. Bouncing Bob, who now spends his days at home sleeping, storing up energy for wild

Choosing Doggie Daycare:
Characteristics of Good and Bad Facilities

Things to Look For

- **Adequate staffing for supervision of canine clients:** *Minimum of one staffperson per 10 dogs, ideally with a second person on the premises in case of emergency. Staff monitors dog activity closely.*
- **Knowledgeable, caring staff:** *Staff is well-educated and skilled in dog handling and behavior management, and employees obviously like dogs.*
- **Clean facility:** *No lingering odors. Dog waste is promptly removed and appropriately disposed of. Floors are routinely cleaned and disinfected. Facility is neat and free of debris and clutter. Canine clients are required to be reasonably flea-free.*
- **Safe environment:** *Matted floors (indoors), with no direct access of dogs to outer doors. Fences (outdoors) are high enough to keep dogs contained and in good repair. Dogs are divided into size and play-style-appropriate play groups. Choke chains, if any, are removed prior to group play. Introductions of new dogs are done slowly and carefully.*
- **Enriched environment:** *Dogs have plenty of toys and equipment to play with, on, under, and through, as well as access to safe, comfortable napping spots. Staff spends time interacting with dogs. Dogs are walked outdoors routinely (for indoor facilities) to maintain and encourage good housetraining habits.*
- **Comprehensive screening process:** *Owners are questioned as to dog's history with other dogs and people, and other potential health and behavior issues. New dogs are evaluated in an intake interview prior to the intended stay, and introduced to other dogs one at a time, starting with the most congenial.*
- **Vaccination requirements:** *Center maximizes protection for all canine clients by requiring proof of current vaccinations or, alternatively, satisfactory titer levels [see page 248].*
- **Compatible philosophies:** *Confirm that the center's dog handling and training philosophies are aligned with yours, and that the staff supports them.*

Things to Avoid

- **Overcrowding:** *A general rule of thumb is 100 square feet per large dog; 50 to 60 square feet per small to medium-size dog. Overcrowding leads to aggression.*
- **Limited access:** *Center should not have policies prohibiting owners from visiting their dogs at any time, with or without warning.*
- **Unwillingness or inability to meet dogs' needs:** *Center should be willing and able to feed and medicate dogs as requested by owner.*
- **Poor customer service:** *Loving dogs is not enough; staff should also be courteous and friendly to human clients.*
- **Dogs left unattended:** *This should never happen. If a second person is not on the premises as backup at all times, arrangements must be in place for someone to arrive quickly if an emergency requires the regular daycare attendant to leave.*

greetings and demands that you pay attention to him when you get home, can romp with his pals all day and come home just as exhausted as you are after a tough day at the office. A tired dog is a well-behaved dog.

Many doggie daycare programs also offer training packages, grooming services, pickup and delivery, and will even transport Fido to his vet appointments for you. Others go above and beyond, including massage, aromatherapy, and hydrotherapy in their service packages. Some provide you with photos to take home—action shots of Fido and Friends at play. Still others hold special events, such as holiday parties and outings to nearby dog-friendly parks, for you to socialize with your dog's pals and their owners. You might even find one that operates a retail pet supply store for the convenience of one-stop shopping for your dog's food, training tools, toys, and other accessories.

Many benefits

A dozen doggie daycare operators polled recently on a daycare e-mail list were in almost unanimous agreement that the top two benefits of their services were exercise for Fido, which tires him out and promotes good manners; and the opportunity for him to socialize with other dogs—an important ongoing experience if Fido's owner wants him to be friendly with others of his kind.

They also listed numerous other benefits, including socialization with humans, relief from boredom, prevention of destructive behavior, a chance for the dog to have fun, and a lessening of owner guilt, for those who feel badly about leaving Fido home alone all day. All of these benefits help to create a strong bond between dog and owner, a relationship that is vitally important in order to ensure that the dog will be a beloved family member for the rest of his life.

Daycare operators offered words of wisdom to owners looking for a suitable facility for their dogs.

Jamie Lewis, of Zip A Dee Doo Dog Daycare, near North Hollywood, California, stressed the importance of having knowledgeable and caring staff, who can provide constant supervision and monitoring of the dogs. From responses to the poll, a ratio of one staff-person for every 10 dogs seems to be the accepted norm, ideally with a second person on the premises at all times in case of emergency.

Cleanliness and safety, which go hand-in-glove with vaccination requirements and disease control, were also at the top of the list for almost all of the operators who responded. Several emphasized the importance of confirming that the staff's dog handling and training philosophies are in alignment with yours, and making sure that the dogs actually play together for most of the day and are not simply stuffed into crates or kennels.

The right stuff

Not surprisingly, doggie daycare centers have an endless supply of anecdotes that they are willing to share—some funny, others poignant.

Kellyann Conway of Maritime Pet Kennel, Inc., in Tarpon Springs, Florida, tells of Alex, a Doberman client who had been coming to daycare religiously, once or twice a week, for the five years since they had opened. One day Alex's mom called the center to tell them that Alex had been diagnosed with a rare liver disease and, according to his doctor, probably only had a month or so left to live. Because Alex loved daycare so much, she wanted to continue bringing him for as long as possible. The Conways agreed, as long as the veterinarian agreed. Alex lived for another 15 months. Owner and vet were both convinced that the combination of exercise, fun, and friends, as well as the anticipation of going to doggie daycare, kept Alex going. His blood counts taken the day after daycare were always noticeably improved, and he even ate all of his food on daycare days.

Just like us, having something in life to look forward to and enjoy can keep our dogs happier, healthier, and better behaved. Maybe it's time to look for a doggie daycare center near you.

Picking Playmates

It pays to manage your canine pal's social life at the dog park.

Spend any amount of time watching dogs play, and you'll quickly learn how much fun two or more canine pals can have romping and wrestling. And you can't beat playtime for exercise and burning off energy. But dog play does a whole lot more than simply provide an opportunity for fun and exercise; it helps dogs learn important communication and life skills. Play and socialization can mean the difference between a dog who is friendly toward other dogs, and one who is shy, anxious, or even aggressive.

Unfortunately, not every social encounter provides the kind of positive learning experience that helps dogs develop good social skills. In some cases, playtime can actually teach dogs to behave badly around other dogs. If social time goes very wrong, it can do emotional or even physical harm to your dog. But with a little caution and a bit of dog sense, you can ensure your dog's play encounters provide the best in both fun and social learning.

Why dog play is important

Puppies and dogs learn essential canine manners and social skills when playing. Through play, they can also learn to tolerate frustration and to control their excitement. Without puppyhood play, dogs have a much greater risk of nervousness or aggression toward other dogs later in life.

Perhaps the most important behavior that puppies learn from playing with other puppies and dogs is bite inhibition—the ability to control their mouths. While bite inhibition is first established when a puppy is six or seven weeks old, ongoing play with other dogs throughout puppyhood reinforces a soft mouth. There is no better way for a dog to learn to control how

Many owners have learned the hard way that not all socializing at the dog park is fun. Unless you pay attention to your dog and his playmates, interrupt play that begins to result in aggression, and steer clear of playground "bullies," your dog can get hurt and/or traumatized—potentially ruining his future social life.

hard or softly he bites than through playing with other dogs.

Socializing with other dogs, however, should not start and end in puppyhood. Playtime during adolescence teaches dogs social skills that they will use for successful adult interactions. They begin to learn to behave as "dogs" instead of as "puppies." As young adults, they continue to refine those skills. It's not uncommon for young adult dogs to suddenly begin experimenting in their behavior with other dogs. Positive social interactions at this stage of life are very important to reinforce appropriate behavior and social interactions.

As dogs mature and grow older, continuing social interactions will help them maintain their meeting and greeting skills. In her book, *The Other End of the Leash*, trainer and behaviorist Patricia McConnell writes, "Dogs need to learn that part of what's normal and familiar in life is to meet unfamiliar people and dogs." Regular interactions with novel dogs help reinforce the idea that meeting new dogs is simply a part of everyday life.

Will they be friends?

Your role in your dog's play with other dogs is always to pay attention. Too often, people take their dogs to dog parks or play areas and ignore them while they visit with the people. Taking the opportunity to socialize with other dog people is certainly one of the perks of dog parks, but you have to pay attention to your dog, too!

When two dogs meet for the first time, there is sometimes a bit of initial tension. If both dogs are friendly and have good social skills (and they are off leash so they have the opportunity), they will generally approach each other on a bit of an arc or circular path. They may sniff and check each other out. At that time, they will either choose to disengage, or to engage in either play or conflict.

How can you tell what will happen? Watch the dogs and they will tell you through their body language. For example, ears back, a slightly lowered body stance, barely visible hackles on the shoulders, and a

A bully over-asserts his or her authority, even when—maybe *especially* when—the other dog issues no challenge whatsoever. Bully dogs are also quick to "pile on" if another dog is getting picked on.

low tail may tell you that the dog is nervous about the meeting. Depending on the reaction of the second dog, the nervousness may be calmed, or it may be intensified. Learn and watch for *your* dog's signals; his behavior will let you know whether he is comfortable in any given situation.

If dogs choose to disengage, respect their choice. Give them the opportunity for personal space. Encouraging dogs to continue to engage when they are setting good boundaries for themselves could lead to an avoidable conflict.

A "play bow" indicates playfulness, even in rough play.

If the dogs decide to play, continue observing their behavior. Watch how they play. Does your dog seem to be enjoying the interaction? Does the other dog? Are they frequently changing positions, with one dog in charge or on top first, then the other? Sometimes this is hard to see. Try to notice if they seem to be taking turns. If your dog is not enjoying the play or if the play seems one-sided, you may want to separate the dogs and take your dog to another corner of the park.

If you see that the dogs are not happily greeting, you may be able to separate them before a conflict erupts. A cheerful, "Come" or "Let's go!" can sometimes help give your dog permission to leave the situation. Please note: The timing of the "Come" will make a difference.

If you call too early, your dog may not be able to make a graceful exit (and may choose to continue with the greeting rather than be rude or put himself in harm's way). This is not a time to worry about whether your dog responds instantly to your call. Try calling again when you see a pause in the greeting ritual.

Playtime gone bad

Some squabbles and dog fights can't be avoided. But many can. An inappropriate play situation can lead to tension or a fight between dogs. It may also teach your dog to behave badly in future social situations. While it is important to give dogs the opportunity to deal with a variety of social situations, you want to make sure the "play" will not (as one dog trainer puts it) "send them to therapy."

What can you do when you see that playtime is taking a turn for the worse? Get your dog out of the situation—immediately. Watch for four situations in particular: overly aroused dogs, bully dogs, pack behavior, and predatory behavior.

Overly aroused dogs

If you see the dogs are becoming overly aroused—getting so wound up that their play style begins to look less playful and more aggressive—it is very important to have them take a break from play. It may be that the dogs just need a little break, and then they will be ready to play again. Some dogs, like some children, get more active or wound up when they are tired.

If you know your dog is tired, or you see his arousal level going up, you may need to help him disengage. If you can't have him take a break (for example, taking him to another part of the park while the other dogs continue to play), you may need to remove him from the park altogether. Letting tired dogs continue to play could result in them forgetting their basic manners, or ending up in a fight.

Bully dogs

Beware, also, of dogs exhibiting bully behavior. Some young dogs do "test out" bullying. Usually, the dog will try out the behavior on one or two dogs, get firmly told off, and consequently modify his behavior.

Occasionally you may run into a confirmed bully at the dog park or other off-leash area. This dog may be uninterested in actual play, spending most of her time between scanning the park for potential victims and bullying those victims. When she does engage in play, she will always be the dog "on top," rolling the other dogs to the ground or standing over them. She is often the first dog to rush toward any other dog–dog conflict in the park, seeking an opportunity to jump on whatever dog is on the receiving end of punishment.

If you see a dog exhibiting bullying behavior in a play area, keep your dog away! Bullies can and will create an atmosphere that can result in conflicts and even fights between dogs who would otherwise get along just fine.

If *your* dog has a tendency to bully other dogs—for example, if he continually "picks" on another dog or does not stop playing even when the other dog obviously wants to disengage—use caution in choosing playmates. Playing with other dogs that "allow" or tolerate the bullying could actually serve to reinforce your dog's bully behavior. Ideally, you'd find dogs who will play with your dog, but who won't tolerate bullying behavior. Let *them* teach your dog not to be rude!

Finding the ideal dogs to teach your dog manners may be difficult, however, and you may have to intervene instead. The type of intervention will depend on your dog's age and the severity of the behavior. It could be as simple as a brief time-out each time the bully behavior begins. Or, it could mean a more involved behavior-modification program. If your dog is behaving like a bully, consult with a behaviorist experienced in dog-to-dog interactions. Letting the behavior go unchecked may result in a dog who doesn't get taken anywhere any more.

Pack behavior

In addition, where groups of dogs congregate, watch for pack behavior. When dogs "pack up," the rules of play change. A group of friendly dogs that get along smashingly well with each other can suddenly engage in conflict when a new dog enters the scene. In addition, one dog in a playgroup can sometimes become a target for the rest. Interrupt and extract your dog if a group of dogs begins to charge, chase, or pay extra attention to any single dog. Whether your dog is part of the pack, or on the outside of it, he could learn unwanted behavior.

Predatory behavior

Predatory behavior occurs when one dog reacts to another dog as if he is a prey animal. The result can be fatal, with the predatory dog trying to kill or succeeding in killing the other dog. Predatory behavior may simply be due to a momentary error; the dog who sees a cute fluffy little dog bouncing through an open field may think for a moment that it's a bunny rabbit. In this case, the predatory dog may or may not do harm to the fluffy little dog. He may run up, discover it's a dog, and immediately back off. Or, he may be in such a prey-drive state that he doesn't register the cute fluffy creature as a dog at all, possibly hurting or killing the small dog.

What behaviorist Jean Donaldson has referred to as "predatory drift" is a different type of risk for small dogs playing with big dogs. It occurs when a bigger dog suddenly, and seemingly without warning, reacts to a smaller dog when the small dog squeals or struggles when playing or fighting (out of excitement or because of a minor injury). It's thought that an instinctive part of the big dog's brain is triggered to kill the squealing "prey."

Predatory drift could occur in an instant, even when two dogs know each other, like each other, and play together regularly, or even with two dogs who are family members. The phenomenon is an uncommon but very real risk for any small dog who lives or plays with larger dogs.

Dealing with fights

Whenever you have dogs playing with other dogs, conflicts will arise. They may argue, or actually get into a full-blown fur-flying squabble. What should you do? Should you let them "work it out"? This is a judgment call and one that should be approached with great caution—erring on the side of intervention.

For example, a young dog is being picked on by a group of adolescent dogs at a park. The young dog exhibits calming signals and unsuccessfully tries to hide under a chair to escape the snarls, nips, and body slams of three bullies. Her guardian says she thinks her young dog is overwhelmed and that perhaps it is time to leave. Another dog's owner replies, "Oh no, you shouldn't take her away. She needs to learn to work it out with the other dogs."

This is not a situation in which the dog should "work it out" on her own—she is being mistreated by a group of bullies! She needs help and protection from her person. Left to her own resources, she may be forced to either tolerate abuse, or resort to serious aggression to get the bullies to back off. Fortunately, her person has the good sense to leave, in spite of pressure from the other owners.

Not all dogs can handle the stress of socializing in a crowded park. It's easy for misunderstandings to flare up into fights.

Reading Canine Body Language:
What Are Dogs Really Saying During Play?

Understanding a dog's body language takes lots of observation and practice. While some of the ways dogs communicate through their body language is overt, much of it is very subtle—difficult to describe and sometimes hard to see in action. But with practice, you can develop a keen eye for body language that will help you read your dog, and the dogs she meets during her play adventures. Here are some things to look for:

Invitations to play

How can you tell one dog is inviting another to play? Behaviors that say, "Hey, let's play" may include:

- Play bows—when the dog's front legs are lowered and his tail and behind are in the air.
- Pawing at the air.
- Mouth open in a relaxed "grin."
- Eyes and ears relaxed.

Signs of stress and uncertainty

Dogs give two very clear signals that may indicate both excitement and stress when meeting another dog:

- Raised hackles—hair standing on end over the shoulders, back, or hindquarters.
- A wagging tail.

A wagging tail does not always mean a friendly dog, and raised hackles don't always mean an aggressive dog. Raised hackles and wagging tails can both be signs of nervousness or uncertainty.

"Calming signals"

Turid Rugaas, a dog trainer from Norway, pioneered a concept she calls "calming signals." According to Rugaas's observations, calming signals are the specific behaviors that dogs use to communicate friendly and non-threatening intentions to other dogs—and even people. When a dog uses calming signals, he can often "calm" a stressed or uncertain dog, settle an excited dog, or appease an aggressive dog. By noticing calming signals, you may be able to tell if the dogs involved in a stressful interaction are actively working toward a peaceful outcome. Some common calming signals include:

How the other dog responds to the challenge may determine whether the threat will escalate or defuse.

- Turning away of the eyes, head, or body
- Moving slowly or in a circle.
- Sitting or lying down.
- Quick licks of the nose.
- Sniffing the ground.
- Yawning.
- Acting distracted or disinterested.
- Freezing in place until the potential for conflict passes.

Threatening behavior during greetings

During initial greetings, behavior that may indicate a threat or challenge include:

- Walking straight up to another dog (rather than approaching slightly from one side).
- Charging.
- Head over the other dog's shoulder during greeting.

Dog Safety and Management

In response to the brown dog's slightly raised hackles, hard stare, and direct approach, the white dog uses "calming signals" to communicate her peaceful intentions: lying down, staying still, and averting her gaze.

Some genial dogs frequently volunteer to be the "bottom dog," throwing themselves down and inviting their play partners to wade in and wrestle. This is in contrast to a frightened dog who has been forcibly rolled over and pinned.

- *Eyes narrow or a hard stare.*
- *Ears forward or pinned back.*
- *Tail straight out or high over the back.*
- *And, of course, barking, growling, snarling, lunging, and snapping.*

Threatening behavior during play

When two dogs roughhouse, much of their play mimics "fighting." They make a lot of growling noises. Their teeth chomp at each other's necks. They tackle, roll, and wrestle. So how can you tell when rough play is not a game? Here are a few things to look for:

- *Repeated body slamming—a dog ramming another dog with his full body, shoulders, or hips—especially when only one dog is doing the slamming.*

> *When dogs are playing well together, you should see the dogs taking "turns"—first, one dog being the "aggressor," then the roles switching. For example, they may take turns chasing each other or rolling each other.*

- *Chasing, cornering, or crowding a dog.*
- *A group of dogs paying too much attention to or "picking on" one dog.*

It's difficult to know when to let dogs "work it out" and when to intervene. Here is a loose set of guidelines. Trust your own judgment and err on the side of protecting your dog!

- If a dog admonishes another dog or puppy, the correction is administered quickly, fairly, and without doing harm, and the second dog responds by backing off, letting them work it out is okay.

- Sudden, quick disagreements that are over in a matter of seconds—and where neither dog shows any indication of wanting to continue the argument—may be okay. For example, if two dog friends are playing and suddenly have a minor squabble, disengage, and start playing again, it's probably safe to let them continue to play.
- Immediately interrupt any situation that seems to be escalating by separating the dogs. Avoid any

potential risk to your dog, especially if the other dog is unfamiliar.

- If a dog seemed to enjoy fighting with other dogs, don't let him "work it out" under any circumstances, as it will reinforce the fighting behavior.

Many large and small dogs play together without incident. However, small dog owners should be aware of the risk of predatory drift, in which even a familiar packmate can suddenly regard a small dog as a prey animal and try to injure or even kill it.

Finding the perfect playmates

- Always protect your dog in social situations. Provide him with safe playmates. Don't force your dog to remain in social situations that are obviously uncomfortable. Watch out for rude dogs—dogs who invade your dog's space or intimidate your dog. Step between them or move your dog away.
- Size does matter! Many dog parks have separate areas for small dogs and big dogs, and for good reason. A tiny dog probably should not play with a huge dog, no matter how sweet or gentle the big dog is, nor how energetic and tough the smaller dog. Even the sweetest big dog can inadvertently hurt a smaller dog in play. The risk of predatory behavior and predatory drift is another good reason to avoid large dog/small dog play.
- Consider the dogs' ages; similar energy levels and play styles are often associated with age. You

shouldn't put your 12-year-old, arthritic dog in with a bunch of rowdy, body-slamming adolescents. On the other hand, a good *mix* of dogs, both older and younger, can help teach a young dog how to get along well with all sorts of dogs.

- How many dogs are present? Because dog parks are fenced, they protect dogs from cars and other hazards. But the fencing also provides a barrier that can inhibit a dog's ability to create space from the other dogs. It's important to evaluate whether there is adequate space for the number of dogs in the park.

    Even in larger or open areas, some dogs may be happy meeting and visiting with a few dogs, but too many will cause stress. A dog may be comfortable greeting 5, 10, or even 15 new dogs in one outing. But 20 or 30 dogs may put him over the top. Some large, open-space dog parks regularly host up to 30 or more dogs. This amount of stimulation may simply be too much for some dogs. Each dog has a different tolerance for meeting and greeting new dogs. Get to know your dog's comfort level.

- The most important thing: know your dog. Learn her behavior cues and stress signals. Watch for them. Observe her body language. Look at her ears, tail, hackles, and how she carries her body. Does it look like she's having fun? Does it look like

Pay close attention to your dog and the others around her at the park. Don't hesitate to steer clear of packs and bullies.

When you find dogs who get along well with your dog, ask their owners when they usually come to the park. It may be worth coordinating your visits!

Consult a behaviorist if your dog experiences a trauma and becomes fearful of other dogs, or if she begins to develop a tendency to bully others.

she's trying to end the game or keep it going? Is she getting too wound up? Don't wait until your dog is pushed too far. Pay attention to the early signals. Your dog's safety and comfort depend on it.

Know her social strengths and weaknesses. Just as with people, different dogs enjoy different games. Some dogs love nothing more than to get a whole pack of friends to chase them. Some dogs never run or wrestle with other dogs, but thoroughly enjoy cruising, sniffing, and marking around other dogs. Some dogs are flexible and can adapt to a variety of play styles.

Knowing how your dog likes to play is important when it comes time to choose playmates. If you provide her with opportunities to play with appropriate partners, she will maintain her strengths and overcome her weaknesses. Learn how to stretch and expand your dog's social skills in a way that will keep her healthy, happy, and playing with other dogs for years to come.

CHAPTER 6

Dog Health: Veterinary Matters, Including Holistic Dog Care and Alternative Health Care

Looking for Dr. Right
Selecting the best veterinarian for your dog shouldn't be left to chance.

When shopping for a veterinarian, how can you tell whether one doctor or another will be the best practitioner for your pet?

Well, it's a trick question; there isn't any way to guarantee that any particular individual is the best.

The emphasis should be on the first part of the question: shopping. Only through rigorous research can you find the best-equipped facilities, with the most receptive staff, and the most communicative and skilled veterinarians. It may be possible to luck into finding the ideal veterinary practice by picking a name out of the yellow pages, but with your dog's health (and, sometimes, his life) depending on your decision, it's best not to leave your choice to chance.

We've compiled a list of points to consider when conducting a search for a top-notch veterinary care provider for your dog. Take some time to call around and visit a couple of clinics now—you won't have time if you wait until your dog is ill.

A clean, organized practice

Generally, even the reception area will reflect the quality of the service that the professionals will provide. Does the building look well cared for, with clean windows and floors? Is the receptionist happy and helpful, and quick to greet you and your dog? Is infor-

mation about services and prices readily provided? Do the veterinary assistants seem cheerful and glad to be there? If possible, ask whether you can see more of the facility. Not only should the reception and examination rooms be clean, well lighted, and well organized, but the treatment and surgery areas and the kennel and cage room should be, too.

"People" doctors and veterinarians alike operate under similar pressure to provide snappy yet thorough service. No one likes to waste time in a doctor's office, but no one likes to feel rushed out of the office without satisfactory answers to their medical questions, either. You probably won't be able to ascertain whether or not this kind of service is available at

You *and* your dog should feel comfortable with your veterinarian as well as with her staff. The clinic itself should be clean, organized, and welcoming.

a clinic without actually utilizing their services. However, if after choosing a clinic, it seems that the practice is consistently running behind schedule, you may want to choose another. Efficiently run clinics should be able—with only occasional exceptions—to get you and your dog into an examination room close to your appointment time, and adjust their schedules to handle emergencies without disrupting the entire practice for the entire day.

Good communication skills

Veterinarians tend to be busy, but if you can arrange to meet the veterinarian for even just a couple of minutes, you should be able to determine whether he or she is someone with whom you could communicate. It's important that the veterinarian will be willing and able to explain a disease process or a treatment in terms that you can understand.

The office staff, too, should be able to talk to you knowledgeably—never condescendingly—about the details of your dog's care and treatment.

Accessible doctors and staff

You should know—before you have need—exactly when your veterinarian is and is not available. Obviously, you also need to know who you should call, or where you should go, in the hours your veterinarian is not available. (Any emergency clinic you might have to utilize to help your dog should also meet the same criteria.)

Accessibility entails more than just office hours; it also concerns whether or not you can actually reach your veterinarian or an assistant to ask questions about your dog's condition and care. If you leave a message for the veterinarian, will someone from the office return your call promptly?

If your dog has to spend a night at the clinic, ask whether someone is present all night, and whether there a number you can call to check on your dog's condition in the middle of the night if you want to. A surprising number of clinics do not employ all-night staff, a fact that should be known in advance by the owners of any dogs with separation anxiety issues. If your dog has to spend a night at the clinic, make certain you ask about night staff.

The importance of integration

Keep your options open when directing your dog's health care. Every day the already dazzling array of options for caring for your dog grows even more. There are myriad modalities in the realm of holistic care, including complementary and alternative options, as well as conventional veterinary medicine, with its low- and high-tech diagnostic and treatment procedures. Which way do you go when your dog has a health concern?

There are a number of ways to integrate holistic and conventional care for your dog. Some veterinarians practice "integrative medicine," using both holistic modalities and conventional care, in a fully equipped clinic. This situation is the easiest to manage because you are only working with one practitioner.

There are an increasing number of veterinary practices that include vets who practice conventional veterinary medicine, as well as vets who use holistic therapies. While you may work directly with two or more vets, these integrated clinics simplify sharing information between the vets. They facilitate active involvement of all parties in the care of your dog.

Unfortunately, these clinics tend to be the exception and not the rule. If you aren't lucky enough to live close to such a clinic, it's best to form your own team of veterinarians who are willing to work together. If you are already working with a veterinarian, and you have

Defining the Terms

Conventional, Orthodox, Allopathic

Modern Western medicine is also called conventional, orthodox, or allopathic (pronounced "al-lo-PATH-ic") medicine.

At its best, allopathic medicine works fast, relieves pain, clears symptoms, and saves lives using drugs, surgery, and radiation. These treatments do not necessarily address the underlying causes of illness, so they cannot reverse or cure chronic conditions such as arthritis, heart disease, diabetes, autoimmune disorders, or cancer. In addition to allowing chronic illnesses to progress and worsen, allopathic medicine's treatments can cause adverse side effects.

Iatrogenic

Pronounced "EYE-a-tro-JEN-ic," this term refers to illnesses caused by medical procedures. Iatrogenic illnesses are now a leading cause of death and discomfort in human and veterinary medicine.

Holistic, Alternative, Complementary

These terms are increasingly used interchangeably. All three use nutrition, physical manipulation, and other methods to help the body heal itself. The term "holistic" refers to treatments that affect the entire patient, everything from the physical body to lifestyle, psychological factors, family, and environment. "Alternative" refers to methods or treatments used in place of conventional, allopathic procedures, such as a medicinal herb used instead of antibiotics or a homeopathic remedy prescribed instead of an anti-inflammatory drug. "Complementary" refers to holistic or alternative treatments used in combination with conventional procedures.*

Homeopathy, Homeopath, Homeopathic

Homeopathy is a system of medicine, originating in the late 1700s, that utilizes very detailed medical and emotional histories and treats individuals with extremely diluted substances called "remedies." Homeopathic remedies are intended to trigger the body to take corrective action. To treat dogs, homeopaths should be veterinarians, or work with a veterinarian.

Traditional Medicine

This is the most confusing term of all, because most people use it when they refer to conventional, allopathic medicine. However, allopathic medicine is the newest, least traditional of the world's major medical practices. Acupuncture, massage, nutrition, and herbal medicine are literally thousands of years old and are more properly called "traditional."

In contrast, modern Western medicine is less than 100 years old, and most conventional, allopathic treatments are substantially younger. We reserve the term "traditional medicine" for acupuncture, nutrition, herbal medicine, massage, and other ancient therapies.

---

a strong relationship, open a dialogue with him or her about bringing another practitioner into the mix.

"The thing to do is find a [conventional] veterinarian who's open minded to holistic and complementary approaches—more and more are," says Allen Schoen, DVM, who practices integrative holistic animal health care in Sherman, Connecticut. Keep in mind that it is just as important that your *holistic* veterinarian is open to *conventional* diagnostic procedures and treatments if you decide to pursue them.

Experienced, gentle handlers

The people who work in veterinary clinics vary tremendously in their backgrounds, temperaments, education, practical training, and goals. Better clinics will hire more experienced and knowledgeable staff, and pay them enough to stay. This may result in somewhat higher costs for care and treatment at those clinics; it's worth the price. When it comes to sick, vulnerable animals, the difference between indifferent or aggressive

Editor Nancy Kerns's dog lived for several years with a serious heart condition. The effectiveness of a combination of herbal and conventional medicine to treat the condition was confirmed by high-tech — a Holter monitor worn by the dog for 24 hours. (Note: The recorder for the monitor was removed from its vest-pocket for this photo.)

handling and gentle, attentive, and caring handling, can literally make the difference between life and death. And even if your dog is only visiting the clinic for routine health care, you want him to feel as positive as possible about his experience there.

Ask the receptionist about the staffers at the clinic; do they have specialized training or credentials in dog training or veterinary assisting? And observe the staff carefully; do they seem calm, caring, and competent?

Specialized clinics

While there is certainly a benefit to using the same doctors often enough that they recognize and are familiar with you and your dog, there may be situations where you would benefit from using several clinics to meet your needs. For instance, you might visit a low-cost clinic for puppy vaccinations, a state-of-the art clinic with a built-in lab and the latest in anesthesiology equipment when your dog requires surgery, and a holistic practitioner when trying to boost your dog's general wellness.

Many veterinarians have additional interest, training, or expertise in certain types of medicine. Some veterinarians are board-certified in specialized care like dermatology, reproductive health, dentistry, or orthopedic surgery. What kinds of services your veterinary candidates offer will partially dictate what kind of equipment they have at their disposal and, to a certain extent, might even affect the prices of their services.

For instance, reproductive health (spaying and neutering) clinics provide a practical example of efficiency; generally, the staff and doctor are very well-versed in doing the surgeries, yielding a streamlined process and a lower overhead for better pricing.

At the other extreme are veterinarians who offer emergency care. These professionals require an array of diagnostic equipment, such as radiograph (X-ray) machines, ultrasound, magnetic resonance imaging (MRI), CAT scans, and a well-equipped laboratory. Very often, the assistants at emergency clinics are the most highly trained.

Sometimes, economics will dictate your decision, especially if your dog requires only simple, routine care. Most of us would really rather not pay the overhead costs for a full-service hospital when we are simply in search of a required rabies vaccination. Full-service clinicians bristle at the low prices charged by minimal-care walk-in clinics, but they should understand that costs may be prohibitive for some dog owners if they have to pay for an office visit and physical exam every time they cross the threshold.

Recently, more and more veterinarians have been selling their private practices to a company that reopens the practices as part of its "network" of veterinary health care providers. The chain then manages the clinic. This model enables the participating practices to maximize their efficiency (and profits), but just as with managed-care networks for humans, it may result in less personal care. If you have a dog with a complicated health history or a condition that requires extended care and diagnosis, you may want to avoid the "chain" veterinary practices. While the individual staff members and doctors may be more than competent, your dog would probably benefit from consistent attention from a doctor who is intimate with his medical history and reactions to various treatments.

Credible qualifications for alternative care

When it comes to alternative care or non-traditional complementary therapies, the practitioners' training and experience is of paramount importance. Look for doctors who are certified with the national association for that modality, for instance, the International Veterinary Acupuncture Society (IVAS) for acupuncturists, the Academy of Veterinary Homeopathy (AVH) for homeopaths, and the American Veterinary Chiropractic Association (AVCA) for chiropractors. Most holistic veterinarians are associated with the American Holistic Veterinary Medical Association (AHVMA, pronounced "Ahh-vma"). Each of these associations offers continuing education for its members.

A lack of credentials with one of these associations does not mean a practitioner is unqualified, but it may mean that he is operating in the outer reaches of his chosen field. Talking to other clients in the waiting room about their experiences with the veterinarian or asking for references is always a good idea, but it should be considered mandatory in this case.

Get Emergency Veterinary Care, STAT!

Some conditions that require immediate emergency care:

- *Shock (symptoms include pale gums or skin, weak pulse, shivering, cold paws and legs, drop in body temperature).*
- *High temperature (normal is 100.5 to 102.5).*
- *Severe wounds or profuse bleeding.*
- *Poisoning (signs may include drooling, vomiting, depression, or convulsions).*
- *Unusually depressed or frantic behavior, particularly if the episode follows injury or illness.*
- *Lack of usual appetite or failure to eliminate as usual.*
- *Any wound that is non-sensitive at the time of injury but develops sensitivity in the days following.*
- *Seizures (unless the dog is under treatment for chronic seizures, and the episode is minor).*
- *Heat exhaustion or heatstroke (signs include panting, glazed expression, bright red gums, increased heart rate, disorientation).*
- *Bloat (symptoms include distended stomach, inability to vomit, restlessness).*
- *Wheezing or difficulty breathing.*
- *Sudden frequent sneezing (could be a foxtail).*

If you're in doubt, call your local veterinarian or emergency clinic for advice.

Pleased to See You!

How to keep your dog calm and secure throughout a veterinary visit.

Let's face it: Most dogs aren't crazy about going to the vet. And why should they be? After all, vet visits are stressful at best. They often mean a new environment, slippery floors, and even more slippery exam tables. Vet offices are full of funny smells, scary sounds, strange people, and unknown animals. Plus, the poking and prodding to which they are subjected can be uncomfortable and sometimes even painful. It may be overwhelming for even the most easygoing dog.

Reasoning with your dog may help some ("Oh, honey, it's for your own good!"). But what will help even more is getting your dog accustomed to the types of experiences that he is likely to encounter on visits to the veterinarian. The following seven tips can help you help your dog learn to tolerate the occasional "well-dog" health examination. They will also help your dog be better prepared to accept necessary medical treatment in case of a serious illness or injury.

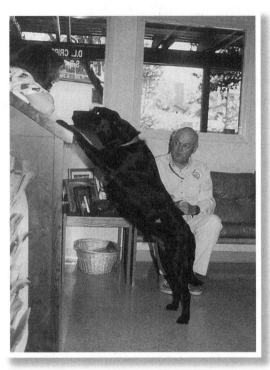

When dogs are properly introduced to the veterinary clinic and treated by the staff in a rewarding, positive manner, they can actually learn to look forward to vet visits.

Take your dog by the vet's office, just to say hello

"One of the best things you can do," says E. V. Sharp, DVM, of Creekside Veterinary Hospital in Soquel, California, "is just to stop by every once in a while. Bring your dog in, weigh him, and walk out again." New places are sometimes anxiety-producing—just because they are new. Stopping by occasionally reduces your dog's anxiety by simply transforming the vet's office from an unknown to a known environment.

Better yet, take along some great treats, preferably something that is incredibly special to your dog like pieces of steak or hot dogs. Ask the receptionist, the vet

tech, and even your veterinarian to give your dog a few treats, too. If you have a puppy, start your "social" vet visits as early as possible. But don't worry if you have an older dog or a dog that is already anxious about vet visits. Fun and happy social visits can dramatically reduce an adult dog's stress level too.

Be sure to call ahead and tell your vet what you want to do. Ask if there is a good time to stop by for a few minutes. You'll want to make sure that your social visit is convenient for the vet and the office staff. You'll also want to make sure they are not dealing with an emergency or an infectious disease at the time of your visit.

Dog Health

Take the time to touch your dog everywhere, every day!

Getting your dog accustomed to being touched all over is essential for your dog's comfort during an examination. In a routine exam, a veterinarian may look in your dog's eyes, ears, and mouth, listen to his heart and lungs, touch and probe his belly, manipulate his joints, and take his temperature. Dogs that are handled, petted, and touched all over daily will be less likely to perceive this as invasive, and more likely to regard it as affectionate (if somewhat personal!) touching.

In addition, when you regularly spend time touching your dog, you will be more likely to notice changes such as lumps, swelling, or tenderness that may indicate health problems.

Stop by, weigh in, have a few treats, and go home!

One great way to help your dog learn to tolerate being handled is to make it part of play and relaxation. When you play rowdy games such as fetch, wrestle, or tug-of-war with your dog, you can encourage the game and help your dog tolerate touch through play

pats, ruffling his fur, and gentle roughhousing. When you spend quiet time with your dog, stroke and pet him all over. Play with your dog's ears, muzzle, belly, and around his tail. Try holding your dog's paw while

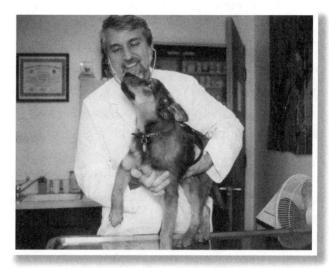

This puppy enjoys being hugged and touched all over—which makes her health exam fun for her *and* her veterinarian.

you rub his tummy. Massage his shoulders and hips. Stroke your dog's ears and gently place your finger inside the ears. Touch around his legs and in between his toes.

"It's also a good idea to pinch them every once in a while," says Dr. Sharp. Not hard, of course, but enough that a little needle pinch for vaccinations or drawing blood won't be a totally unusual experience.

Another very important part of this routine is to take note of your dog's sensitive spots. Most dogs have one or more spots where they prefer not to be touched. Some dogs don't like to have their paws touched. Others may not like their hips, ears, or tails touched.

You can help even the most reluctant dog accept the handling of sensitive areas with a little patience and some great treats. Have your dog near you in a comfortable position. Then feed your dog his favorite treats while briefly touching the sensitive spot. For example, if your dog is sensitive about having his paws handled, gently and quickly stroke your dog's paw and then give him a slice of hot dog or another great treat.

Once your dog is happy about the brief touch (because he knows the hot dog is coming!), you can leave your hand on his paw just a little bit longer before giving him the treat. Gradually work up to holding the paw, then giving gentle squeezes, and eventually touching between his toes.

Don't try to rush it or push your dog to do anything that is uncomfortable. The goal is to help your dog learn to accept or even enjoy being touched everywhere. If your dog exhibits any aggression around being touched, please consult with a behaviorist to help you work through the problem.

When your dog is happy about being touched all over, ask friends, a trainer, or other family members to touch your dog, too. The more accustomed dogs are to being handled by different people, the easier it will be for them to be handled during regular vet visits or in the case of an illness.

Remember being a kid and wanting to dress your animals up? That can actually help, too! "If your dog enjoys it, put things on him," Dr. Sharp says, laughing at the idea. Bandanas, doggie sweaters, booties, dog packs, and other items can help your dog accept things like bandages or Elizabethan collars if the need ever arises.

Play with your dog's mouth

"Probably the hardest thing we deal with regularly are dogs who are not used to having their mouths handled," says Dr. Sharp. She recommends brushing your dog's teeth regularly to help him get used to having his mouth handled. "It really pays off! It's good for the dog and the vet. It can extend times between teeth cleanings, too." With some dogs, Dr. Sharp notes, it can even mean the difference between being able to perform teeth cleanings with the dog awake and having to give the dog anesthesia.

In Dr. Sharp's opinion, it's not as important to brush the teeth really well as it is just to do it! Even brushing the outsides of the teeth can make a big difference. Always use canine toothpaste; people toothpaste isn't safe for dogs. Plus, the great flavors available in doggie toothpaste, such as chicken, beef, or malt, can make brushing all the more enjoyable for your dog.

Another good exercise is opening your dog's mouth, looking in, and then immediately popping a treat in his mouth. Your dog will learn that your opening his mouth means treats are coming.

Dogs can also learn to enjoy having their mouths' handled if you dab a little peanut butter, yogurt, or cottage cheese on your finger and then rub your finger over your dog's gums or along the roof of his mouth. Your dog will get used to having fingers in his mouth, plus he'll get a special taste treat.

Get your dog used to being leaned over, held onto, and picked up

Even dogs that are handled regularly can have a tough time when someone leans over them, holds them down, or picks them up—understandably so! But during routine vet visits and especially during an emergency, your dog may need to be lifted onto a table, the veterinarian will need to lean over your dog, and your dog may need to be held for vaccines or exams as well as for emergency procedures.

Bending over your dog from various positions in play and other activities can help him learn to accept this behavior from humans. In addition, you can help your dog tolerate being held through everyday affectionate behaviors. For example, if your dog enjoys a good belly rub, try reaching over your dog's shoulder to rub his belly.

Smaller dogs are more often used to being carried, but for some larger dogs, the only time they are physically picked up is at the vet's office. That, itself, can be a traumatic experience. You can set up specific training times to familiarize your dog with being lifted, or you can incorporate this into regular activities. When you groom your dog, for example, consider lifting him onto a low table. If you are not sure how to lift your dog properly (for your safety and his), ask your veterinarian, groomer, or trainer to show you how.

Teach your dog to sit, stand, lie down, and turn around

Basic training can really help lower your dog's stress at the veterinary clinic. Your dog will be a whole lot more relaxed if you can ask him to move his own body, rather than having to push, pull, or cajole him into position.

The basic behaviors that are essential for ease during vet exams include:

Sit and down: Because many dogs want to flop over or slink away instead of holding still, knowing sit and down can make it easier on both your dog and the vet during an exam.

Relax: Also known as "Roll on your side," this trick is great for positioning dogs when the vet needs to scrutinize just one side of your dog.

In the summer, veterinarians spend an awful lot of time extracting stickers from abscesses in between dogs' toes. This job is much easier if a dog enjoys "shaking hands."

Stand: This is another basic position that is good for specific exams. Plus, it's easier to pick your dog up from a stand if you need to lift him onto the table.

Turn: Veterinarians often want to turn your dog so that he is facing a different direction on the table. Instead of having to physically move your dog, a simple turn behavior (carefully if he is up on a table) can eliminate the need for having to physically manipulate him into position.

Touch or target: If your dog is trained to touch your hand with his nose on cue, then you can use a hand touch to help move or position your dog, or to move his head up or down. It may also be useful in helping dogs who need to be given nose drops!

Shake: Also called "Give me a paw," this exercise can help turn foot examinations into a fun activity for your dog!

Watch me: Any type of eye-contact exercise is a good tool to turn his head in a particular direction, but this is also a great exercise to keep your dog occupied while being examined.

Familiarize your dog with a muzzle and crate, just in case!

Getting your dog used to wearing a soft muzzle doesn't mean your dog is bad, or that he will necessarily bite. For some dogs, using a muzzle is a good way to ensure safety if the vet needs to examine a sensitive place. Even sweet, gentle, and well-socialized dogs can bite when they are threatened, scared, or hurt; it's an instinctive and normal reaction. Plus, a dog that is seriously ill or has suffered a painful injury may lash out without even realizing what he is doing.

Purchasing a soft muzzle (the fabric kind with an opening on the end that allows your dog to take treats while wearing it) and helping your dog learn to wear it comfortably can become a fun game—and it will ensure that your dog is prepared, just in case.

To help your dog learn to wear a muzzle, simply hold a treat on the "nose" part of the muzzle. Let your dog put his nose through and take the treat. Have your dog do this several times every day for a week or more. When your dog becomes excited when he sees the muzzle (because he knows it means treats), you can slip it on for a few seconds, feed your dog a treat or two, and then take it right back off. After a week or more at this stage, you can start leaving it on for a few seconds at a time and gradually increase the time. Keep this game fun!

Once your dog can comfortably wear the muzzle for a few minutes at a time, you can put it away and bring it out occasionally to remind your dog how much fun the muzzle is to wear. Then, if your dog ever needs to wear a muzzle during an emergency, he will be prepared.

Crate training your dog is equally important. Crates are not only wonderful aids for housetraining, they also make comfy sleeping quarters and provide safe travel compartments. Your dog's ability to settle into a crate can mean the difference between a stressed-out dog and a comfortable dog if he should ever need an overnight stay at the veterinary hospital.

"We can really tell when a dog is crate-trained," says Dr. Sharp. "The dogs who are crate-trained go in and lie down." Dogs who aren't crate-trained more often bark or cry when confined.

Liberally employ treats and toys

When you do take your dog to the vet for a regular exam or for treatment for an illness, be sure to bring along treats or toys to help reinforce your dog's good behavior. Be generous with your rewards and really let your dog know when he is doing a good job.

Use chew toys to help dogs who tend to "hide" in the waiting room; this helps many dogs feel safer and more secure. Some dogs will lie under a chair (preferably behind your feet) with a chew toy and settle in until it is their turn to see the vet. You may also want to try TTouch or other types of relaxing massage to help

> ### Getting the Most from a Visit to the Vet
>
> *Dr. E. V. Sharp, from Creekside Veterinary Hospital of Soquel, California, offers these additional helpful suggestions for your next vet visit:*
>
> - *If your dog has any sensitive spots or any issues that may affect the vet's ability to examine your dog, tell your veterinarian about it! He or she may be able to take steps to help your dog feel more secure and to ensure everyone's safety.*
> - *If you are bringing your dog to the vet because of a specific problem (like a skin or ear problem), don't erase the evidence by bathing or grooming your dog before the visit. "Bring them in as stinky and smelly as they are," says Dr. Sharp, because "we need to see it!"*
> - *If your dog is not feeling well, take very detailed notes on the symptoms. The more descriptive the better. If your dog is vomiting or has diarrhea, for example, note how often, how much, what color, and what consistency.*

your dog "de-stress" while in the waiting room. (The inventor of TTouch, Linda Tellington-Jones, was a huge fan of the human physical therapy called the Feldenkrais method, which she adapted for use with animals. She also incorporated some aspects of acupressure, massage, and training into her healing modality, which became known as TTouch (pronounced Tee-touch). This therapy is said to affect the nervous system, influencing the mind *and* the body, helping the two systems to work together more efficiently and effectively.)

Your vet may also find it useful to employ your dog's favorite toy or treat. Dr. Sharp recalls dealing with a Border Collie whose stress reaction manifested itself through aggression; she won him over by playing ball with him in the exam room! "This was a flyball dog," says Dr. Sharp, "and playing ball totally broke through his aggressive behavior."

Keep up the good work!

After your dog has become well-accustomed and trained for trips to the vet, it's a good idea to continue with your daily handling and occasionally stop by the vet clinic just to say "hello." And, if your dog has been doing great at the vet and then suddenly, after a traumatic visit, does an emotional backslide, don't worry! Just read back over these tips and re-acquaint your dog to the different elements involved in vet visits. You can help your dog recover and learn to again relax during regular vet exams.

A Stitch in Time
Neutering saves lives, and prevents a number of canine cancers.

Most people respond with a warm, fuzzy "Awwww" reaction when they see a litter of puppies. After all, nothing could possibly be cuter than a bunch of roly-poly baby dogs tumbling and tussling together on the floor. Or could it?

Anyone who works or volunteers at an animal shelter for any length of time soon finds his "Awwww" reaction tempered by the sobering knowledge that millions of unwanted dogs and puppies are euthanized in shelters around this country every year.

For those who regularly deal with the hapless victims of our throwaway society, spay/neuter is a mantra. Rarely, in the shelter worker's opinion, is there a sufficiently valid reason for not surgically rendering a dog incapable of reproducing.

The average dog owner, however, is more concerned with his own individual rights or the dog's well-being than with the state of animal welfare in general. There is a whole host of commonly offered arguments against spaying and neutering. How valid are they?

Intact male dogs are more likely to suffer prostate cancer (and testicular cancer, something a neutered male can't get). But they are also more likely to be aggressive and unruly, to wander and fight, and cause unwanted pregnancies.

Surgery isn't natural. I would rather be responsible by keeping my dog home or on a leash than take the risks of surgery and alter my dog unnaturally.

There is some truth to this argument. Surgery certainly isn't natural. Neither are collars and leashes, prepared dog foods, fences, veterinary care, or the daily killing of healthy "surplus" dogs and puppies. Dogs haven't lived truly natural lives for centuries. If we are picking and choosing which parts of "natural" we want to re-create for our canine companions, we are better off not choosing this one. If we truly wanted to be natural it follows that we would then let our female dog get pregnant and have puppies every six months, and no responsible dog owner advocates that.

It's true that every surgery carries risks, but the risks of spay/neuter surgery are minuscule compared to the dangers of overpopulation. Far more dogs die from lack of homes, from mammary tumors, prostate, testicular and ovarian cancers, and hormone-related behavior-problems, than ever die from spay/neuter surgery.

Sterilization will change my dog's personality; she or he will get fat and lazy.

This concern seems valid. We have all seen spayed or neutered dogs who were, indeed, fat and lazy. But let's think about this for a moment.

Dogs, like humans, get fat if their caloric intake is greater than the calories burned off by exercise and other physical demands. It is true that sterilized dogs often get less exercise. Male dogs who are neutered no

It's true that spayed females and neutered males tend to gain weight more easily than intact dogs, but this is far from a reversible problem. Just reduce the dog's daily rations! Spend all the money you save on fetch toys, and the "problem" is solved.

longer escape their yards and run for miles in pursuit of females in season, or nervously pace the fence in sexual frustration trying to find a way to escape.

Spayed females dogs no longer experience the immense drain on their systems caused by growing puppies in their bodies for 63 days and feeding them for another six to eight weeks. Nor do their bodies go through the stress of reproductive-related hormonal changes that result in an expenditure of nervous energy. It's true that sterilized dogs of both sexes are calmer and more content to stay home, but that doesn't mean they have to be fat and lazy. It does mean they are better companions.

It's simple: If your dog gains too much weight, cut back on food and increase exercise! Here are several tips for a simple weight-control program:

- **No free feeding.** Your dog should get meals, not all-day snacks. In a natural environment a wild dog makes a kill (along with the rest of the pack), gorges himself, and then doesn't eat again until the next kill. Dogs' systems are not designed for grazing. Besides, controlled feeding increases your dog's dependence on you, which can make your training more successful.

- **Measure the food.** Use a measuring cup and dole out a specific amount. Eyeballing it isn't accurate enough; we tend toward generous. "He looks a tad hungry today . . . what's a few extra kibbles?" If we are measuring a specific amount we can instruct all family members to stick with the feeding program. A measuring cup also gives us an accurate gauge if Rover is looking a little too prosperous and we decide we need to cut back from, say, one cup twice a day, to three-quarters of a cup twice a day.

- **Weigh your dog.** Pick her up and stand on the bathroom scales, then weigh yourself alone, and subtract. Weigh her once a week so you will notice sooner, rather than later, if she starts to put on pounds. If she is gaining, cut back the kibble and/or the treats.

- **Don't swear by the bag.** Use the feeding instructions printed on the dog food bag as a guide, not gospel. Dog food companies seem to lean toward the generous side of meal rations. Perhaps they'd like you to use more of their product?
- **Count the treats.** If you train with treats, be sure to count those treats as part of your dog's meal ration. If he is sufficiently food-motivated you can even use his kibble as training rewards.
- **Give your dog plenty of exercise.** Since he is no longer burning off calories in his frustrated attempts to find females (or she's no longer making puppies), it's your job to make sure he works out. Throw the tennis ball, a stick, or the Frisbee for him for 20 minutes a day. Take her jogging or swimming. Find a doggie play-group or a local dog park (if there are none in your area, start one!) and let her work out by romping with her canine buddies. If you are a portly couch potato, your dog will likely be one too!

I want my (male) dog to have fun; I want my (female) dog to experience the joy of motherhood.

Stop and think, men! Unneutered male dogs are far more likely to escape their yards, run free, risk getting shot or hit by cars, get picked up by animal control officers, and get in fights with other male dogs. If the lack of visible equipment is your concern, ask your veterinarian about "Neuticles," artificial implants that are now available to help owners feel better about neutering their male dogs.

Our choices are to neuter, and reap the benefits of having a calm, contented canine companion who stays home (and who no longer risks prostate or testicular cancer), or to keep our unneutered male strictly, safely, and unhappily confined to lead a life of constant sexual frustration as he senses females in season for miles around.

So, you've lined up homes for every one of your dog's puppies. Don't be so proud. Each of the homes you found COULD have provided housing for a puppy on "death row."

The female dog, too, benefits from spaying. While many females do seem to enjoy motherhood, at least at first, by the time their babies reach the age of six weeks most mom dogs are eager to escape their persistently pushy pups. There are far more life-threatening complications from gestation and birthing than there are from spay surgery. The maternal instinct can also trigger behavior problems; a significant number of dogs develop protective maternal aggression during motherhood. For some dogs this behavior goes away when the puppies are weaned and placed in new homes. Others continue to display aggressive behavior even after the puppies are long gone.

My dog is purebred and has papers.

"I can make money selling puppies. I want another one just like her. All my friends want one of her pups. I already have homes lined up for the puppies."

Certainly, if we are to continue enjoying purebred dogs, someone has to breed them. Why shouldn't that someone be you? Maybe because there is a lot more involved in responsible breeding than just putting two registered dogs of the same breed in the same room together.

For starters, AKC papers are not an assurance of quality. Papers simply mean that both of your dog's parents were registered. Ostensibly. Every month, the AKC *Gazette* publishes names of breeders who have falsified records, or at least kept records poorly enough that the organization revokes their registration privileges. Even if your papers are accurate and your dog's parents were both champions, that doesn't mean your dog is breeding material.

The responsibilities of breeding should not be taken lightly. If done properly, it is an expensive, time-consuming activity. Prospective canine parents must be checked for hip dysplasia, eye problems (such as progressive retinal atrophy), and any other genetic health problems specific to your breed.

Dogs intended for breeding should be outstanding representatives of their breed. If you plan to breed, you need to be willing to campaign your dog on the show circuit and have experts in the breed (judges and other breeders) confirm that your Labrador Retriever is one of the best around. Then you will need to do the research to find the "right" male to breed her to; one who complements her strengths and doesn't underscore her weaknesses.

Once you have gone to all the expense and trouble to be a responsible breeder, chances are your friends aren't going to want to pay the prices that you will ask for your well-bred puppies. Labs can have huge litters—as many as 12 to 15 at a time. You may not have all the homes for them that you thought you did. Many of these will be pets, not show-quality puppies. They will sell for less than the show-quality pups, and a responsible breeder will have them spayed and neutered before they are sold to ensure that they are not used for future breeding.

Don't forget to consider the additional vet bills; you want to be sure your female is in optimum health, and that the puppies get veterinary examinations before they are sold. A responsible breeder will also take back any of the puppies he has bred, at any time during the dogs' lives if the owner can no longer keep them. Not only may you be left with more puppies to place than you had planned, you may also end up with more adult dogs than you intended to own. Chances are excellent that this hobby will cost you a hefty sum of money rather than make you rich.

Finally, consider that every friend or family member who takes a puppy from you could have provided a home for a puppy at an animal shelter or rescue group. Breed rescue groups exist for virtually every recognized breed, so if your friends have their hearts set on purebred dogs they can contact breed rescue groups or go on the breed request waiting lists that are now maintained by many animal shelters. Regardless of how many homes you have lined up for your pups, you are contributing to the pet overpopulation problem.

I want my kids to experience the miracle of birth.

Understandable. But is this reason enough to let your dog breed, knowing that "surplus" dogs and puppies are killed every day? Your kids can watch videos that document the birth process. If you want to let them experience the joy (and hard work!) of raising a litter of puppies, sign up with your local shelter or rescue group as a volunteer foster home.

For many reasons, most shelters cannot feasibly raise litters of puppies in their kennels, and must often euthanize underage pups. Shelters are desperate for foster homes who can give tender-aged baby dogs a chance to grow up and return to the shelter for adoption when they are eight weeks old and able to withstand the rigors of shelter life. You can even solicit your friends to apply to adopt your foster pups once they have returned to the shelter. You get the joy of puppy raising and the satisfaction of providing a community service without contributing to pet overpopulation. It's a win-win!

I live in a "no-kill" city. We have solved the pet overpopulation problem so it's okay to breed again.

"No-kill" is a myth; it actually means "Someone kills them somewhere else." In San Francisco, often touted as the first "no-kill" city, more than 4,000 animals are still euthanized every year at San Francisco Animal Care & Control, one short block away from the "no-kill" San Francisco SPCA. While the SPCA labels these 4,000-plus animals as "unadoptable" in order to justify the deaths and claim their "no-kill city" title, it is simply a matter of semantics, public relations, and allocation of resources.

In some jurisdictions, an upper respiratory infection (the canine equivalent of the common cold) or a broken leg, both treatable, qualify a dog as unadoptable. Even if San Francisco's 4,000 animals were truly not redeemable, surrounding communities in the San Francisco Bay Area continue to euthanize unwanted animals by the tens of thousands. Don't kid yourself; we are far from solving the pet overpopulation problem.

My dog is old and my veterinarian says spay/neuter surgery is too risky.

Okay, you win. This is truly a valid excuse. At some point in a dog's life the benefits of spay/neuter are outweighed by the risks of surgery. There is no magic age when this happens; it depends on the individual dog. Follow your veterinarian's recommendation if she tells you that sterilization is not indicated due to your dog's age and/or condition.

Hot Shots: To Vaccinate or Not to Vaccinate
You should decide whether your dog needs that vaccination.

Most dog owners are responsible and understand the importance of protecting their companions from preventable disease. That's surely what motivated the dozens of people standing in a long line with their dogs and puppies at a low-cost vaccination clinic offered in a local pet supply store.

In addition to vaccinations, the veterinary business running the clinic also offers flea and tick treatments, heartworm tests and preventive medication, and identification microchip implanting, so at the head of the line, a young man in a white coat and holding a clipboard asked each client what she wanted for her pet.

No universal protocol

Many dog owners are surprised to learn that there is no single, universally accepted canine vaccination schedule. Most trust their veterinarians to give their dogs whatever vaccinations the vet recommends—and

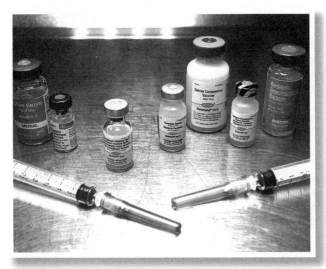

Which vaccines should your dog receive? It is *your* responsibility to determine the real risks of the diseases they are supposed to defend your dog against, and weigh the potential benefits of vaccination against the potential harm.

many vets recommend more vaccinations than most dogs require in order to be protected from contagious disease.

This can probably only rarely be accurately attributed to opportunism on the part of the vet. Most vets use the vaccination schedules they receive with the vaccinations they buy from drug companies.

Historically, this was a sound choice. For decades after the first veterinary vaccines were developed, veterinarians and government regulators alike trusted the companies that studied, developed, and manufactured the lifesaving vaccines to recommend appropriate schedules for their use. Today, though, they are realizing their trust of the vaccine makers may have been slightly overextended for a decade or two.

Obviously, vaccine makers are in the business of selling vaccines. So it follows that most of them recommend that their vaccines be administered annually—despite the fact that independent studies have shown that many vaccines convey immunity from disease for many years, if not the lifetime of the dog.

In a policy statement about vaccines, the American Veterinary Medication Association (AVMA) acknowledges, "The one-year revaccination frequency recommendation found on many vaccine labels is based on historical precedent and United States Department of Agriculture regulation, not on scientific data. Even in those cases where scientific data was submitted to qualify the label claim, the data generated does not resolve the question about average or maximum duration of immunity."

For a long time, the few experts who realized dogs may receive far more vaccines than they need were not particularly worried. But in the late 1980s, as medical science learned exponentially more about the immune system, proof began to turn up that repeated vacci-

Dog Health

nations could have deleterious effects on companion animals.

Today we know that adverse events may be associated with the disease antigen, the adjuvant (an agent added to increase or aid the effect of the antigen), carrier substance, preservative, or a combination of any of these. The AVMA vaccination policy statement says "Possible adverse events include failure to immunize, anaphylaxis, immunosuppression, autoimmune disorders, transient infections, and/or long-term infected carrier states."

To their credit, when vaccines can be directly linked to specific, reproducible injuries or illnesses, the vaccine makers (and regulators) leap to study the problem, as in the case of vaccination site–associated feline sarcoma. Unfortunately, the problems experienced by dogs that many practitioners and researchers suspect may be linked to over-vaccination are all over the map. Some suspect excessive vaccines are linked to the increased incidences of many diseases, including cancer, epilepsy, severe allergies, thyroiditis,

Don't vaccinate elderly dogs. If your dog has been vaccinated many times in his younger years, he is probably as well immunized against disease as he will ever be. Plus, his exposure to disease decreases as he ages and travels and exercises less.

Opposed to All Vaccines?

You may have heard about owners or breeders who avoid having their dogs vaccinated altogether, or some who use a very minimal vaccination protocol, out of concern for the unknown effects that vaccines may have on their dogs' immune systems and long-term health.

Be aware that this strategy should never be casual. People who take this step consciously and responsibly take other actions to ensure their dogs are protected from disease. For example, they may vaccinate one puppy in a litter, in hopes that the virus he sheds will actually infect his littermates and build their immunity. Then they use titer tests [see page 248] to verify whether the strategy worked.

You should also be aware that skipping a rabies vaccine could have legal consequences. Every state requires dogs and cats to be vaccinated against rabies; some states require the vaccination annually; in

others, the requirement is every three years. And to protect public health, if your dog bites someone and does not have proof of a current rabies vaccine, at a minimum, he will be quarantined. Check with your local animal control officers to learn more.

If you decline to have your dog vaccinated, especially against the core diseases, it is incumbent on you to take alternative steps to protect your dog. Make sure you know all about the diseases your veterinarian recommends vaccinating against so you can actively avoid exposing your dog to high-risk environments, are alert to the signs of disease, and are ready to take fast action to treat a dog who exhibits early signs of an illness. Make sure you establish a relationship with a veterinarian who is comfortable with and will support your protocol; if your dog does end up contracting a core disease, you will need veterinary care, conventional and complementary, to pull your dog through.

autoimmune hemolytic anemia, Addison's disease, and even behavioral problems such as aggression.

Get information

Fortunately, educated owners can do a number of things to make sure that their dogs are adequately protected against disease, without over-vaccinating.

There are canine vaccines for more than two dozen diseases, with many vaccines available in combination with others. Very few dogs are at risk for all or even most of the diseases. So the first step is to learn about the diseases against which the vaccines are designed to defend your dog.

Before agreeing to any vaccination, ask your vet about the disease it prevents. What is its incidence? How is it transmitted? Is it more prevalent in some cli-mates or parts of the country than others? Is the disease treatable, and if so, how many dogs recover? Then you can extrapolate the answers to your dog and locale.

If you learn that the disease kills many dogs who contract it, and the virus is everywhere, well, you'll probably authorize that vaccine, right? But if you lived in a city apartment with a Papillon who never visits a park, a vaccination for a tick-borne disease like Lyme is really not needed.

Today, most veterinarians discuss vaccines in terms of "core" versus "non-core" products. Core vaccines are those that can protect your dog from the diseases that are widely distributed in your part of the country, virulent, and highly infectious. Think of them as the vaccines with the highest benefit-to-risk ratio. Non-core vaccines are those that are intended for a minority of dogs in special circumstances. They may target diseases that are of limited risk in your area, or

Titer Tests: A Terrific Tool

The term "titer" refers to the strength or concentration of a substance in a solution. When testing vaccine titers in dogs, a veterinarian takes a blood sample from a dog and has the blood tested for the presence and strength of the dog's immunological response to a viral disease. If the blood contains satisfactory levels of vaccine titers, the dog is considered sufficiently immune to the disease, or possessing good "immunologic memory," and not in need of further vaccination against the disease at that time.

Titer tests do not distinguish between the immunity generated by vaccination and that generated by natural exposure to disease agents. A dog may have developed immunity to a viral disease by receiving a vaccine against the disease, by being exposed to the disease in the natural environment and conquering it (sometimes without having demonstrated any symptoms of exposure to the disease), or by a combination of the two.

Therefore, titer tests really measure both the "priming of the pump" that comes from vaccines, and
the immunity resulting from natural exposure to disease during a dog's lifetime. Only an indoor dog who has been totally sequestered from the natural environment is likely to have developed all of his immunity from vaccinations.

By "titering" annually, a dog owner can assess whether her dog's immune response has fallen below adequate levels. In that event, owners can administer appropriate core vaccines, or non-core vaccines that are of special value to a dog at special risk for a certain disease.

Experts suggest ordering vaccine titer tests only for parvovirus and distemper; it's not necessary to test titer levels for every disease. Measuring the titers for those two core vaccines can offer the dog owner a reliable picture of the dog's immunological status as well as the competence of the dog's immune system. If he has developed adequate antibody levels to those two vaccines, the odds are very good that he has developed adequate antibody levels to any vaccines he has been given.

those that present only a low-level threat to your dog's health.

"Core" vaccines

These are the vaccines for diseases that most experts agree puppies and dogs should be protected against—diseases that are highly contagious and potentially fatal.

Ronald D. Schultz, PhD, is department chairperson and a professor at the School of Veterinary Medicine, University of Wisconsin in Madison. He's also one of the country's leading experts on veterinary vaccines, having performed research for or with literally every veterinary vaccine company in the United States We'll use Dr. Schultz's list of "core" vaccines for dogs:

Canine parvovirus type 2 (CPV-2)

Canine distemper virus (CDV)

Canine adenovirus type 2 (CAV-2)

Rabies virus (RV)

For what people commonly refer to as "puppy shots," many veterinarians use a combination vaccine that contains antigens for distemper, hepatitis, leptospirosis, parainfluenza, and parvo (referred to by its initials, DHLPP). If you are concerned about over-vaccination, ask your veterinarian if she can vaccinate your puppy against just parvo, distemper, and adenovirus (the rabies vaccine is usually given separately later, after the puppy is 16 weeks old). A vet can purchase and use individual vaccines, but she may have to buy them in bulk, and won't be happy about it if you are the only one in her practice who wants them.

Most experts agree that puppies should be vaccinated against distemper, parvo, and adenovirus, not before 6 weeks, and at least once after the age of 12 weeks; the rabies vaccine is given after 16 weeks. About two weeks after the last vaccination with distemper, parvo, and adenovirus, ask for a vaccine titer test to confirm your puppy has been successfully immunized.

A Few Final Vaccination Tips:

- *Use vaccine titer tests to determine whether your dog is adequately immunized against the core diseases.*
- *Don't rely on low-cost clinics for your dog's vaccinations. These clinics exist to sell vaccines, not to provide full care or detailed advice. They cannot provide the full hands-on exam that your dog should receive at least once a year, and may not take the time to determine whether a vaccination is contraindicated for your dog.*

  Instead, establish a relationship with a veterinarian who will take the time to examine your dog, ask about his health history, answer questions about the benefits and risks of various vaccines, and recommend an individualized vaccination protocol for your dog that takes your dog's health, his lifestyle, and his environment into account.
- *Do take your dog to your veterinarian at least once a year. A thorough annual (or better yet, semiannual) health examination and annual titer test is the best way to find problems early, before they are difficult and costly to treat. Your veterinarian can also help you develop a sound preventive health program to keep your dog vital to the very end of a long, happy life.*
- *Vaccinations are contraindicated for dogs who are not healthy. Do not vaccinate dogs who suffer from chronic or acute health problems, are running a high temperature, or have a history of vaccine reactions. This sounds simple, but many times people go to the vet for an injury, say, an abscess or to remove an embedded foxtail, and the vet notices the dog is "overdue" for vaccinations. The dog is currently battling a local infection! Do not have him vaccinated at that time.*
- *Don't vaccinate elderly dogs. If your dog has been vaccinated many times in his younger years, he is probably as well immunized against disease as he will ever be. Plus, his exposure to disease decreases as he ages and travels and exercises less.*

"Non-core" vaccines

Then there are the non-core vaccines. Some experts (including Dr. Schultz) refer to all the other vaccines that are available as non-core, suggesting that these be given only to dogs that need them, and only as often as needed. For these vaccines, the ratio of benefits to drawbacks is less weighted toward the benefits—at least for most dogs.

A good example is leptospirosis. The duration of the immunity typically conveyed by the lepto vaccine is generally less than one year, so to convey optimal protection from this disease, it must be given at least twice a year, every year. Also, the vaccine used must contain all four strains of the disease that are currently available to vaccine makers, because the strains do not provide cross-protection. Lepto poses a very minimal risk in many regions of the United States. And where it is more common, there have been recent reports of new strains emerging, for which there are no vaccines yet.

All of this suggests that administering the vaccine would benefit only those dogs living in an area with a current, high rate of infection—and only if they are properly vaccinated at frequent intervals with all the available strains.

Other vaccination tips

When they learn that over-vaccination may be harmful to their dogs, many people ask, "Why would my veterinarian suggest doing something that could hurt my dog?" The fact is, information about the potential risks of over-vaccination is fairly new. Veterinary colleges, the AVMA, and the American Animal Hospital Association (AAHA) have changed their suggested vaccination schedules only in the past few years.

Heartworm: Don't Take It Lightly

Conventional preventatives are still the best way to protect your dog.

Conventional heartworm preventatives are the best form of protection currently available. Fortunately for those of us who worry about the side effects of using the conventional drug preventatives, there are numerous ways you can minimize their use and still protect your dog.

People have learned of the benefits of a natural diet and limited vaccinations, and have seen the health improvements in their dogs from these changes. Now, many want to know if they can discontinue administering heartworm preventatives to their dogs, or whether those can be replaced by natural options.

Heartworm preventatives can cause serious side effects in some dogs, including depression, lethargy, vomiting, anorexia, diarrhea, dilation of the pupils, loss of balance, staggering, convulsions, and hypersalivation. Some dogs are especially prone to side effects from ivermectin, the main ingredient in one of the most widely used heartworm preventatives. Also, some of the preventatives are combined with drugs aimed at killing other pests such as fleas, mites, roundworms, and hookworms.

On the other hand, heartworm can be a devastating disease. Dogs with moderate or severe infestations display a chronic cough and can't engage in much activity, as worms choke their hearts and major blood vessels, reducing their blood (and thus oxygen) supply. The disease often leaves its victims incapacitated, incapable of doing much more than a slow walk without gasping for air, and it kills many dogs. Even the treatment for heartworm disease can be deadly, regardless of which method is used, so it is important to understand the risks that you take if you choose not to give your dog heartworm preventative.

In fact, most (certainly not all) holistic veterinarians consider the use of pharmaceutical preventatives to be less harmful than a heartworm infection.

"Alternative" preventatives?

Some holistic practitioners recommend various herbal or homeopathic preparations for heartworm prevention, and anecdotal evidence from some dog owners can be found on many discussion lists devoted to natural dog care. However, consumers should be aware that none of these alternatives have been studied for safety or efficacy, nor are there any studies indicating that they are effective at protecting against heartworm infection. In addition, some herbal dewormers, such as wormwood and black walnut, are potentially toxic when used at dosage levels needed to control intestinal parasites.

Conventional heartworm preventatives are the best form of protection currently available. Fortunately for those of us who worry about the side effects of using the conventional drug preventatives, there are numerous ways you can minimize their use and still protect your dog.

Facts About Heartworm Disease

What it is

Heartworm disease is caused by an infestation of a parasite, Dirofilaria immitis, commonly called heartworm, with an elaborate life cycle. It starts in an infected animal; more than 30 species, including dogs and wild animals such as coyotes, foxes, and ferrets act as "reservoir" species. Adult worms, residing in the host animal's heart, lungs, and associated blood vessels, mate and the females release their young (called microfilariae). These circulate in the host animal's blood for up to two years. They develop into their next stage of life, L1 (for first larval stage), only if ingested by a mosquito during a mosquito's blood meal.

It takes the L1 larvae 8 to 28 days, depending on environmental temperatures, to develop into their third stage (L3), when they migrate from the mosquito's stomach to its mouth. The L3 larvae enter their next host through the mosquito's next bite.

As many as 10 to 12 L3 larvae can be transmitted to a dog in a single mosquito bite. The L3 larvae molt and migrate through the dog's tissues in search of major veins, which they infiltrate and use as a path to reach the heart. It takes them about 90 to 100 days to develop into L5, the form that breaches the circulatory system. Only ivermectin affects them (and not all of

them) once they have reached the L5 form or beyond. However, all the drugs affect the L3 and L4 forms, which is why it's important to administer a preventative drug at least every 45 days during heartworm "season." (Note: DEC must be given every day during heartworm season.)

If no preventatives are used, the larvae continue to develop to sexual maturity. If both sexes are present, they can mate and produce microfilariae about six to seven months after the infected mosquito bite that put them in the dog. Adult heartworms can live three to five years, with males attaining a length of 17 cm (about 6¾ inches) and females a whopping 27 cm (more than 10½ inches).

Symptoms of infection

Mild disease: *Cough.*
Moderate disease: *Cough, exercise intolerance, abnormal lung sounds.*
Severe disease: *Cough, exercise intolerance, difficulty breathing, abnormal lung sounds, enlargement of the liver, temporary loss of consciousness due to poor blood flow to the brain, fluid accumulation in the abdominal cavity, abnormal heart sounds, death.*

Conventional preventatives

The two most common (and generally considered safe) heartworm preventative ingredients used today are ivermectin (used in Heartgard by Merial, and other products) and milbemycin oxime (used in Interceptor by Novartis).

There is also an older, daily heartworm preventative available, diethylcarbamazine or DEC. For many years, this drug was available from Pfizer as Filaribits. Though Filaribits has been discontinued, you can still find generic versions of DEC.

DEC is very safe in terms of side effects, but can be life-threatening if given to a heartworm-infected dog with circulating microfilariae, due to the risk of a rapid die-off of the microfilariae and resulting anaphylactic reaction. Also, missing just one or two days of medication can allow your dog to become infected. If you use DEC, it is essential that you test for heartworms before starting this drug, and every six months while using it. (Avoid Filaribits Plus, which has oxybendazole added to control intestinal parasites and has been known to cause liver damage.)

There are other heartworm products that include drugs for other purposes. Heartgard Plus adds pyrantel to control intestinal parasites, including roundworms and hookworms. Adult dogs rarely have problems with roundworms, but if your yard has been infested with hookworms, this product might be good to use until the hookworms have been eliminated.

Sentinel is a combination of the products Interceptor and Program (lufenuron). Lufenuron is a medication that acts to prevent fleas from reproducing; it's not a pesticide and does not kill fleas or keep them from biting your dog. This may be helpful for a short time if you have a flea infestation, and employ several nontoxic methods to get the flea problem under control, such as diatomaceous earth to treat the house and nematodes to treat the yard.

Selamectin, a more recent entry to the market, is a topical product that is also indicated for fleas, one kind of tick, ear mites, and the mites that cause sarcoptic mange. While this may be great if your dog has mange, fleas, ticks, and ear mites, it's best to use drugs with a minimal and targeted action over ones with broad-spectrum activity.

The injectable product moxidectin (ProHeart 6 by Fort Dodge) has been withdrawn from the U.S. market due to numerous reports of adverse effects, including death. Stay clear of injectable heartworm preventatives, as there is no way to remove them from your dog's system if there is a bad reaction, and the time-release drug will continue to affect your dog for months.

Temperature and timing

So, how can you reduce your dog's exposure to conventional heartworm preventative drugs, without decreasing his protection from the nasty parasite?

First, it is not necessary to give heartworm preventatives year-round in most parts of the country. Heartworm development in the mosquito is dependent upon environmental temperatures. Heartworm larvae cannot develop to the stage needed to infect dogs until temperatures have been over 57° Fahrenheit (14° Celsius), day and night, for at least one to two weeks. The amount of time it takes will vary depending on how warm it is; the warmer the temperatures, the faster the heartworm larvae develop.

If temperatures drop below that point at any time during the cycle, development may be prevented, but don't rely on this. Temperatures can vary according to where the mosquito lives, and may be warmer under the eaves of houses or in other protected areas than the general ambient temperature.

Heartworm preventatives work by killing heartworm larvae that have already infected the dog, but before they can mature into adult worms that cause damage. When you give your dog heartworm preventative, you are killing any larvae that have infected your dog within the last one to two months. Any larvae that have been in your dog longer than 60 days are more likely to survive the treatment and go on to mature into adult worms.

Also, your dog may become infected the day after you give heartworm preventative; the drugs do not provide any future protection at all.

If your goal is to provide full protection for your dog with minimal drug administration, you'll have to

1: Adult worms in an infected animal mate and produce microfilariae.

2: Microfilariae are consumed in blood by mosquito; larvae develop in mosquito.

3: Infected mosquito bites dog; transmits larvae through bite.

4: Larvae migrate through dog's tissues to circulatory system and to the heart.

5: Larvae reach adulthood and take up residence in dog's heart, lungs, and associated blood vessels. They mate and produce microfilariae, starting cycle all over again. Adult worms may live for three to five years.

monitor the temperatures in your area. Mosquitoes may be capable of transmitting heartworm larvae to your dog around two weeks after your local temperature has stayed above 57°F day and night.

Give the season's first dose of preventative four to six weeks after daytime and nighttime temperatures first exceed 57°F to destroy any larvae that infected your dog during that time. Continue to give the preventative every four to six weeks, with the last dose given after temperatures drop below that level on a regular basis.

For some parts of the country, this can mean giving preventatives only between July and October, while in others, where temperatures remain mild all year, they may have to be given year-round.

If you do not give your dog heartworm preventatives (because the area you live in is very low risk or because the temperatures are not right for heartworms to develop), and then take your dog to an area where heartworm is a problem, you must treat him with heartworm preventative upon your return to protect him.

Heartworm Testing

Heartworm testing is recommended before administration of any drug. It's best to know ahead of time whether there are microfilariae present, so you can be ready to treat the dog for an anaphylactic reaction caused by the microfilariae's rapid die-off, and to choose the safest preventative to use if the dog is infected. Ivermectin (Heartgard) is safer in this regard than milbemycin oxime (Interceptor), which has a much stronger effect against the microfilariae.

The most common current method of heartworm testing is called antigen testing. This type of test can identify only adult female heartworms, and therefore will not show a positive result until about five to seven months after the dog has been infected, the time needed for the larvae to develop into adult worms in

> ## Ivermectin Toxicity
>
> *Ivermectin has a bad reputation among some dog owners, but not all dog owners need to worry unduly about the drug's toxicity. Ivermectin toxicity is genetic, and there is now a test available to determine whether a dog is sensitive to ivermectin and other drugs. (Dogs with ivermectin toxicity may also be sensitive to loperamide [Imodium], cyclosporin [Atopica], acepromazine, digoxin, butorphanol [Torbutrol/Torbugesic], and several chemotherapy drugs.)*
>
> *Breeds known to be affected include Collies, Australian Shepherds, Shelties, Border Collies, Old English Sheepdogs, English Shepherds, McNabs, Long Haired Whippets, and Silken Windhounds. To learn more about this test, see the following Web site on multidrug sensitivities: www.vetmed.wsu.edu/depts-VCPL.*

the body. For this reason, it is no use doing a heartworm test on any dog younger than five months. Heartworm tests are very sensitive, but they are not 100 percent reliable. They are highly specific, with very few false positives, but they are not always able to detect very low heartworm burdens, or infections with only male heartworms.

It is generally recommended to do a heartworm test on any dog over the age of six months before initially starting preventatives. If you give preventatives only part of the year, you may want to do a heartworm test before restarting the medication in the spring or summer, especially if there is any question about the timing of starting and stopping the drugs the previous year.

If you give preventatives year-round, it is still recommended to test for heartworm infection every two to three years, for added security, particularly if you use minimal dosage amounts or increased time between doses. Note that your dog needs a yearly veterinary exam in order to get a prescription for preventatives, even if your dog does not need to be tested for heartworm.

Keeping Those Pearly Whites Clean
Tartar-encrusted teeth are not just unattractive; they are absolutely dangerous to a dog's health.

Cleanliness is healthiness

Just as with humans, tartar or calculus forms on a dog's teeth when plaque—a combination of salivary proteins and bacteria—accumulates on the teeth and is not brushed or mechanically scraped away by vigorous chewing. And just as with humans, some dogs seem more prone to tartar accumulation than others. Some of this may be due to an inherited trait; it's also thought that the chemistry in some dogs' saliva seems to promote tartar formation.

Raw Foods = Great Teeth

A properly formulated and prepared "bones and raw food" diet can contribute to canine oral health.

Dogs raised from puppyhood on a raw diet benefit the most, but individuals may improve with exposure to the healthy food whenever they happen to get it.

However it happens to accumulate, the mineralized concretion acts as a trap for even more plaque deposits. Soon, the gums become inflamed by the plaque, and bacterial infections may develop. The dog will have bad breath and unsightly red gums. He may experience pain when he's eating his food, playing with toys, or during recreational chewing. Chronic mouth pain can cause behavioral changes, including crankiness and sudden onset of "bad moods." But even more serious dangers are lurking unseen.

When plaque deposits begin to form in proximity to and then, gradually, under the dog's gums, the immunoinflammatory response begins to cause destruction of the structures that hold the dog's

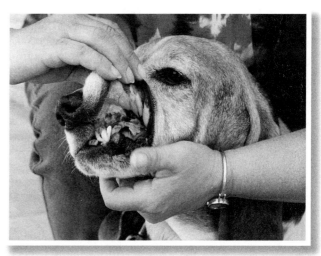

The accretion of tartar on this dog's front teeth is fairly minor, but all the teeth behind the canines are invisible under a thick layer of dental calculus. Given this dog's gentle nature, anyone with a little training could scrape away most of the tartar. But only a veterinarian can provide the antibiotics needed to prevent a systemic infection that the teeth-cleaning procedure could cause.

teeth in place: the cementum (the calcified tissue that covers the root surfaces), periodontal ligament (connective tissue that helps anchor the teeth), and alveolar bone (the bone that surrounds the roots of the teeth). As these structures are damaged in the inflammatory response "crossfire," the teeth can become loose and even fall out.

A more serious danger is the bacterial infection and resultant inflammation in the gums, which can send bacteria through the dog's bloodstream, where it can wreak havoc with the heart, lungs, kidneys, and liver. Dogs with chronic health problems that affect these organs and dogs with immune-mediated disease are at special risk of experiencing complications due to periodontal disease. For this reason alone, owners of these dogs should be the most proactive in keeping their dogs' teeth clean.

Appropriate fears

People whose dogs are in poor health, however, are often the most reluctant to schedule a tooth cleaning. Most frequently, they cite the effects of anesthesia on their dogs' already compromised health as their biggest concern. In many cases, though, there are more serious things they should be concerned about, because the fact is that the vast majority of dogs, even old ones, come through the anesthetic experience without peril, as long as the veterinarian provides appropriate supportive care.

Anesthesia-free cleaning

Most of us have seen signs or advertisements for "anesthesia-free tooth cleaning" for dogs and cats. To most people, this sounds like a good idea, especially if you have a very old dog, a dog with a heart condition, or any other dog you'd hesitate to put through general anesthesia.

The procedure can be a terrific service for some dogs, but only if rendered under the direct supervision of a veterinarian, if not by a veterinarian. Unfortunately, some vets don't offer the service—often because they don't believe it's necessary. This pretty much guarantees that some pet owners will seek out non-veterinary technicians who perform the procedure—illegally—in grooming shops or pet supply stores.

We suggest that dog owners who are concerned about the risks of anesthesia ask their own trusted veterinarians to provide dental cleanings without anesthesia—and to seek out another veterinarian who does provide the service if their own veterinarians do not or will not.

Far more perilous than properly administered anesthesia are the risks posed by dental "technicians" who are not well trained or are inexperienced, and who are working without the benefit of veterinary support or supervision.

Undoubtedly, some of the people who provide "anesthesia-free tooth cleaning" services outside of veterinarians' offices are well-educated and experienced. Some may be former (human) dental hygienists or licensed veterinary health care technicians. Some do a terrific job.

But the fact is, no matter how talented or experienced or well-educated they are, if they are not working with a vet who will perform a complete physical

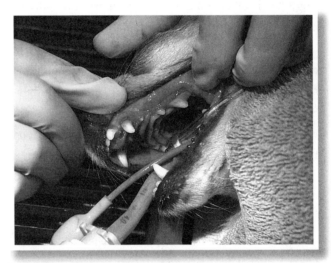

The veterinarian or technician must spend long moments on each tooth—the cute ones in the front *and* the difficult-to-reach ones in the back. The surfaces on the inside of the dogs' teeth (closest to the tongue) must also be cleaned. This is tough to accomplish with even the most compliant dog.

examination of the dog before the procedure and provide care afterward (if needed), they are performing veterinary medicine without a license. And because their services are illegal, it's not possible for a consumer to confirm their credentials or even have legal recourse if they injure or harm a client's dog.

The best candidates for anesthesia-free service

Fortunately, some veterinarians now offer anesthesia-free dental cleanings in their clinics, in recognition of the fact that some dogs may be adversely affected by

Taking Tooth Cleaning into Your Own Hands

Toothbrushes

Any soft-bristled toothbrush may be used; it doesn't have to be a special brush for dogs, although several manufacturers have innovative brushes that can make the task marginally easier.

Nylabone, for instance, makes a handy two-sided brush that allows you to scrub both sides of a tooth at the same time. The bristles of Crazy Dog's "Easy Grip PetAdent" are arranged in a semicircle, for the same purpose. The PetAdent's bristles are black, reportedly because they are easier to see against white teeth. Several manufacturers also make rubber or plastic "fingertip" brushes that you slip on like finger of a glove; they have bristles affixed to the tip. Four Paws Products makes a long-handled brush with a large head at one end and a small head at the other—great for long-nosed dogs and big dogs. These are all useful, but not necessary.

Tartar accumulates at a faster rate on the back molars, close to the salivary glands. To reach this area, you'll need to approach your dog from the front, and may need a helper to prevent the dog from backing away.

The value of toothpaste

Toothpaste is not necessary to get the dog's teeth clean, though it can make the project easier. Don't use the stuff from your family's medicine cabinet, however. Special meat- or peanut butter–flavored toothpastes for dogs have two advantages: they are far more attractive to dogs than "people" toothpastes, and they contain substances that are better suited to killing the bacteria found in dogs' mouths.

Toothpastes can work two ways: mechanically and chemically. Pastes contain inert abrasive materials such as calcium or silicate, which take a significant mechanical role in helping scrub plaque and other matter from the teeth and gums. But even those dentifrices without abrasives can play a mechanical role, by lubricating the bristles of a toothbrush for better action.

---

anesthesia, and yet would benefit from dental care. The best candidates include dogs with tartar-encrusted teeth who exhibit any of the following:

- Poor kidney and/or liver function (detected with a blood test).
- Congenital heart defects (including murmurs), impaired heart function (such as congestive heart failure), or arrhythmia
- A recent injury or infection of any kind (even skin infections, including "hot spots," are good cause to delay scheduling any procedure that requires anesthesia).

- A history of seizures (some preanesthetic sedatives can lower the seizure threshold).

If your dog has one of the conditions listed here, or another health problem that concerns your veterinarian, he may be a good candidate for anesthesia-free tooth cleaning. But you should understand that the procedure is not a walk in the park; it can be hard on the dog, and the cleaning is necessarily less thorough than one conducted with the dog asleep.

"It's so much easier to do a good job on a dog who is asleep," says Jenny Taylor, DVM, founder and

Examine your dog's teeth at least once a month, and arrange a veterinarian's examination at least once a year.

Accustom your dog to having her mouth opened and touched. Reward her for allowing you to inspect every tooth: in the front, side, and back. Gradually increase the amount of time you want her to stay still.

If tartar has already formed and hardened on your dog's teeth, schedule a professional cleaning as soon as possible to prevent gum inflammation and infection. Daily brushing afterward may be enough to prevent the need for future cleanings.

If your dog develops tartar buildup rapidly, the best thing you can do is to brush his teeth daily. Providing chews and an improved diet may help, but daily brushing is proven to be most effective.

co-owner of Creature Comfort Holistic Veterinary Center in Oakland, California. "You get a vastly more thorough examination and a much better cleaning when the dog is unconscious."

To do a good cleaning, the veterinarian or technician will need to spend long moments on each tooth—the cute ones in the front and the difficult-to-reach ones in the back. The outer surfaces (closest to the lips) are the easiest to reach and are always the most tartar-encrusted, but even the surfaces on the inside of the dogs' teeth (closest to the tongue) should be examined and cleaned. This is tough to accomplish with even the most compliant dog.

Also, working without anesthesia may require the vet or technician to work without the benefit of the fastest and most effective tool in the tooth-cleaning arsenal: the ultrasonic scaler. Few dogs will sit still in the face of its noise and vibration, so the vet frequently can use only hand-held scalers. It can be difficult to manipulate the sharp tools with the required force to remove stubborn calculus without causing inadvertent injury to the dog's gums, tongue, or lips, especially if he's wiggling.

Finally, there is the dog's experience to consider. A few happy-go-lucky dogs will comply with any procedure dreamed up by humans, as long as they get kisses and treats. But for some dogs, it's torture. "People need to understand that working in the mouth can be a traumatic experience for some dogs," warns Dr. Taylor. "We do a lot of things to keep the dog as comfortable as possible, but the procedure can cause some discomfort. Some dogs can tolerate a little pain and not hold it against anyone. But others can get upset no matter how tactful we are."

For all of these reasons, even veterinarians who perform anesthesia-free tooth cleaning for certain dogs may promote an anesthetized procedure to the owners of dogs who are not at any special risk of complications from anesthesia. "Sometimes an anesthetized procedure is the kindest, safest thing for the dog," says Dr. Taylor. "You have to consider each dog's case individually and weigh all the factors: health, age, condition of the teeth, and temperament."

Don't delay

In the best of all possible worlds, dog owners would provide appropriate home care to prevent their dogs from developing tartar buildup and gingivitis. (Some dogs go through their entire lives with sparkling white teeth, with absolutely no effort on their lucky owners' parts; we're not talking about them!) For dogs who develop tartar buildup very quickly, daily brushing can go a long way to reduce (although probably not eliminate) the need for professional cleanings.

For people who have concerns about professional tooth cleaning with anesthesia, prevention should be key. Maintaining your young, healthy dog's mouth is largely a matter of daily discipline.

What Promotes Bloat?
Every dog owner should know the symptoms of this fast-killing disorder.

Imagine seeing your dog exhibit some strange symptoms and rushing him to the vet within minutes, only to have the vet proclaim his case to be hopeless and recommend euthanasia. For too many dog owners, that's the story of bloat, an acute medical condition characterized by a rapid accumulation of gas in the stomach.

In fact, that was exactly the case with Remo, a Great Dane owned by Sharon Hansen of Tucson, Arizona. "He was at the vet's in under seven minutes," says Hansen, describing how quickly she was able to respond to Remo's symptoms. He had just arisen from an unremarkable, hour-long nap, so Hansen was stunned to see Remo displaying some of the classic symptoms of bloat, including restlessness, distended belly, and unproductive vomiting.

Despite Hansen's quick action, Remo's situation rapidly became critical. Radiographs showed that his stomach had twisted 180 degrees. Remo was in great pain and the vet felt the damage was irreversible. Hansen made the difficult decision to have Remo euthanized at that time.

Bloat, or more technically, gastric dilatation and volvulus (GDV), is a top killer of dogs, especially of deep-chested giant and large breeds, such as Great Danes and Standard Poodles.

Large- and giant-breed dogs, especially those with deep chests, are at greatest risk of bloat, but dogs of any size can be stricken. Nervous dogs and underweight individuals are also more likely to bloat than calm or overweight dogs.

Gas accumulation alone is known as bloat, or dilatation. The accumulation of gas sometimes causes the stomach to rotate or twist on its axis; this is referred to as torsion or volvulus. Bloat can occur on its own, or as a precursor to torsion.

Both conditions can be life-threatening, although it often takes longer for a straightforward gastric dilatation without volvulus to become critical. "Bloats without torsion can last for minutes to hours, even days in low-level chronic situations, without it becoming life-threatening. But with torsion, the dog can progress to shock rapidly, even within minutes," explains Alicia Faggella DVM, DACVECC, a board-certified specialist in veterinary emergency and critical care.

"A dog can go into shock from bloat because the stomach expands, putting pressure on several large arteries and veins. Blood does not get through the body as quickly as it should," continues Dr. Faggella. In addition, the blood supply to the stomach gets cut off, which can cause tissue to die while toxic products build up.

While some less acute cases of bloat may resolve themselves, it often takes an experienced veterinarian to know just how serious the problem may be, and whether surgical intervention is required to save the dog's life. In addition to repositioning the stomach, it may also be "tacked" to the abdominal wall in a procedure called gastropexy. While dogs who have had gastropexy may experience gastric dilatation again, it is impossible for the stomach to rotate, as in volvulus or torsion.

Causes of bloat

Theories about what causes GDV abound, including issues related to anatomy, environment, and care. Research from Purdue University, particularly over the past 10 years, has shown that there are certain factors and practices that appear to increase the risk of GDV, some of which fly in the face of conventional wisdom.

The most widely recognized and accepted risk factor is anatomical—larger, deep-chested dogs are more vulnerable. When viewed from the side, these dogs have chest cavities that are significantly longer from spine to sternum, when compared to the width of the chest cavity viewed from the front.

This body shape may increase the risk of bloat because of a change in the relationship between the esophagus and the stomach. "In dogs with deeper abdomens, the stretching of the gastric ligaments over time may allow the stomach to descend relative to the esophagus, thus increasing the gastroesophageal angle, and this may promote bloat," says says Lawrence Glickman, VMD, and lead researcher on a number of studies related to GDV at Purdue University in West Lafayette, Indiana.

But it isn't just large- and giant-breed dogs that can bloat; smaller breeds do as well. "I've seen Dachshunds, Yorkies, and other small terrier breeds with bloat," says Dr. Faggella. She emphasizes that all dog guardians should be familiar with the signs of bloat, and be ready to rush their dogs to the vet if any of the symptoms are present.

Likelihood of an incident of bloat seems to increase with age. Purdue reports that there is a 20 percent increase in risk for each year increase in age. This may be related to increased weakness over time in the ligaments holding the stomach in place, Dr. Glickman explains.

Another key risk factor is having a close relative that has experienced GDV. According to one of the Purdue studies that focused on non-dietary risk factors for GDV, there is a 63 percent increase in risk associated with having a first-degree relative (sibling, parent, or offspring) who experienced bloat.

Symptoms of Bloat

Unproductive vomiting
Apparent distress
Distended abdomen, which may or may not
  be visible
Restlessness
Excessive salivation; drooling
Panting
The dog's stomach feels taut to the touch,
  like a drum
Pacing
Repeated turning to look at flank or abdomen
Owner feels like something just isn't right!

Personality and stress also seem to play a role. Dr. Glickman's research found that risk of GDV was increased by 257 percent in fearful dogs versus non-fearful dogs. Dogs described as having a happy personality bloated less frequently than other dogs. "These findings seem to be consistent from study to study," adds Dr. Glickman.

Dogs who eat rapidly and are given just one large meal per day have an increased susceptibility to GDV compared to other dogs. The Purdue research found that "for both large- and giant-breed dogs, the risk of GDV was highest for dogs fed a larger volume of food once daily."

The ingredients of a dog's diet also appear to factor into susceptibility to bloat. A Purdue study examined the diets of more than 300 dogs, 106 of whom had bloated. This study found that dogs fed a dry food that included a fat source in the first four ingredients were 170 percent more likely to bloat than dogs who were fed food without fat in the first four ingredients. In addition, the risk of GDV increased 320 percent in dogs fed dry foods that contained citric acid and were moistened before feeding. On the other hand, a rendered meat meal that included bone among the first four ingredients lowered risk by 53 percent.

Another study by Purdue found that adding "table foods in the diet of large- and giant-breed dogs was associated with a 59 percent decreased risk of GDV, while inclusion of canned foods was associated with a 28 percent decreased risk." The relationship between feeding a home-prepared diet, either cooked or raw, hasn't been formally researched.

Anecdotally, however, many holistic vets believe that a home-prepared diet significantly reduces the risk of bloat. "I haven't seen bloat in more than five years," says Monique Maniet, DVM, of Veterinary Holistic Care in Bethesda, Maryland. She estimates that 75 to 80 percent of her clients feed a raw or home-cooked diet to their dogs.

Dr. Faggella also noticed a difference in the occurrence of bloat while in Australia, helping a university

---

Breeds at Greatest Risk

In a Purdue University study of records from 12 veterinary hospitals, researchers found that pure-bred dogs were 2.5 times more likely to develop GDV than mixed breed dogs. This, and subsequent research, found the following breeds to be at a higher risk for developing GDV:

Airedale Terrier	*Irish Setter**
*Akita**	*Irish Wolfhound**
Basset Hound	*Newfoundland**
*Bloodhound**	*Old English*
Borzoi	*Sheepdog*
Boxer	*Rottweiler**
*Collie**	*Saint Bernard**
*Gordon Setter**	*Standard Poodle**
*Great Dane**	*Weimaraner**

* Breed included in at least one of the Purdue studies.

---

set up a veterinary critical care program. "I didn't see bloat as commonly there [as compared to the United States]," she says. They feed differently there, with fewer prepared diets and more raw meat and bones, which may contribute to the lower incidence of GDV, she adds.

Preventive action

Because the theories and research on what causes bloat aren't always in agreement, the ways to prevent GDV can conflict as well. One thing that everyone can agree on, though, is that feeding smaller meals several times a day is the best option for reducing the risk.

One of the top recommendations to reduce the occurrence of GDV from the Purdue researchers is to not breed a dog that has a first-degree relative that has bloated. Results of their study suggest that "the incidence of GDV could be reduced by approximately 60 percent, and there may be 14 percent fewer cases in the population, if such advice were followed."

In addition, Glickman says they recommend prophylactic gastropexy for dogs "at a very high risk, such as Great Danes. Also, we do not recommend that dogs have this surgery unless they have been neutered or will be neutered at the same time."

The concern about performing a gastropexy on an unneutered dog is that it "might mask expression of a disease with a genetic component in a dog that might be bred."

While gastropexy hasn't been evaluated in its ability to prevent GDV from happening the first time, research has shown that just 5 percent of dogs whose stomachs are tacked as a result of an episode of GDV will experience a repeat occurrence, whereas up to 80 percent of dogs whose stomachs are simply repositioned experience a reoccurrence.

Controversial gas reliever

After Remo's death, Sharon Hansen learned that some large-breed dog owners swear by an anti-gas product called Phazyme for emergency use when bloat is suspected. Phazyme is the brand name of gel caps containing simethicone, an over-the-counter anti-gas remedy for people. GlaxoSmith-Kline, maker of Phazyme, describes it as a de-foaming agent that reduces the surface tension of gas bubbles, allowing the gas to be eliminated more easily by the body.

Less than a year and a half later, Hansen had an opportunity to try the product when her new rescue dog, Bella, a Dane/Mastiff mix, bloated. "Bella came looking for me one afternoon, panting and obviously in distress," explains Hansen, who immediately recognized the signs of bloat.

Hansen was prepared with caplets of Phazyme on hand. "I was giving her the caplets as we headed out to the car," says Hansen. Almost immediately, Bella began to pass gas on the short ride to the vet. "She started passing gas from both ends," Hansen says. By the time they arrived at the vet, Bella was acting much more comfortable, and seemed significantly less distressed.

At the vet's office, gastric dilatation was confirmed, and luckily, there was no evidence of torsion. Hansen credits the Phazyme for reducing the seriousness of Bella's episode. This is a generally accepted practice among guardians of bloat-prone dogs, but not all experts agree with it.

Dr. Faggella cautions against giving anything by mouth, as it could cause vomiting, which could lead to aspiration. "If you suspect bloat, simply bring your dog to the vet immediately. The earlier we catch it, the better," she says.

Dr. Nancy Curran, DVM, a holistic vet in Portland, Oregon, agrees that trying to administer anything orally could lead to greater problems. However, she suggests that Rescue Remedy, a combination of flower essences that is absorbed through the mucous membranes of the mouth, may help ease the shock and trauma. "Rescue Remedy helps defuse the situation for everyone involved. It won't cure anything, but it can be helpful on the way to the vet," she says, recommending that the guardian take some as well as dosing the dog.

The holistic approach to prevention

"We may be able to recognize an imbalance from a Chinese medical perspective," says Dr. Curran. She's found that dogs prone to bloat typically have a liver/stomach disharmony. Depending on the dog's situation, she may prescribe a Chinese herbal formula, use acupuncture, and/or suggest dietary changes and supplements to correct the underlying imbalance, thereby possibly preventing an episode in the first place.

Dr. Maniet also looks to balance a dog's system early on as the best form of prevention. Each of her patients is evaluated individually and treated accordingly, most often with Chinese herbs or homeopathic remedies.

Both holistic vets also recommend the use of digestive enzymes and probiotics, particularly for breeds susceptible to bloat, or for dogs with existing digestive issues. "Probiotics and digestive enzymes can reduce gas, so I'd expect that they will also help reduce bloat," explains Dr. Maniet.

Another avenue to consider is helping your fearful or easily stressed dog cope better in stressful situations. While no formal research has been conducted to confirm that this in fact would reduce the risk of bloat, given the statistics that indicate how much more at risk of GDV fearful dogs are, it certainly couldn't hurt. Things to consider include positive training, desensitization, the Tellington TTouch method, calming herbs, aromatherapy, or flower essences.

While there is an abundance of information on how to prevent and treat bloat, much of it is conflicting. The best you can do is to familiarize yourself with the symptoms of GDV and know your emergency care options. While it may be difficult to prevent completely, one thing is clear. The quicker a bloating dog gets professional treatment the better.

The Price of Prescriptions

The truth and consequences of purchasing veterinary prescription drugs.

Deborah, one of the members of the local dog-training club, regularly fills her prescription for Synthyroid at a large chain pharmacy in town. She will take this drug for life due to her underactive thyroid gland. Deborah regularly checks pricing for the drug at several pharmacies to ensure she continues to pay competitive rates.

Susan, also a club member, regularly purchases Soloxine, a lifetime prescription medication also indicated for an underactive thyroid condition. Both prescriptions have the same basic active ingredient: Levothyroxine. Susan, however, administers the prescription she buys to her dog, Jo.

Like many guardians of companion dogs, Susan is faced with new options about deciding where to economically and safely purchase prescription medicines for her dog.

Traditionally dispensed solely from the veterinarian's office, prescription drugs for companion dogs represent a ripe peach—ready for picking by retail chain pharmacies and emerging Internet-based pharmacies that have sniffed out a promising new niche in the lucrative pharmaceutical market. These drug

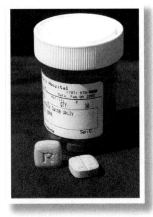

While some canine drugs are formulated only for dogs, others are identical to medications taken by humans, and may be purchased for less money at a pharmacy (with a vet's prescription).

retailers have discovered the more than 35 million dog owners in the United States who anticipate the same access to sophisticated medicines for their dogs as they have come to expect for themselves.

As quickly as animal pharmaceutical companies rush to the Food and Drug Administration's Center for Veterinary Medicine (CVM) with applications requesting approval for new drugs or new drug uses for animals, the pharmaceutical retailers are rushing to the consumer with discount price offers. But just how attractive are these discount drug deals, and how will this increased competition for the guardian's dollar in the companion-animal drug market affect the veterinarians' practices?

New competition

Until very recently, the sale of veterinary pharmaceuticals was a profitable part of the average veterinary practice, accounting for about 20 to 30 percent of the total average practice income. Most veterinarians follow the recommendations of practice consultants and drug manufacturers to mark up pharmaceuticals about 100 percent over their cost of the drugs. This subsidizes other veterinary services, such as affordable spay and neuter programs and upgrades in medical equipment. It also helps to hold fees at moderate levels for hospitalization, radiographs, and professional services like examination and diagnosis, thereby enabling these procedures to be available to a greater number of animals.

In other words, many of the services provided by the veterinarian's office are not priced to the consumer in direct relationship to the veterinarian's cost

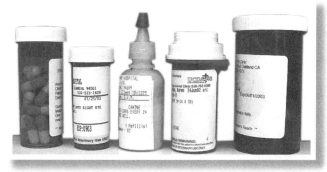

No matter where you buy your dog's medications, their use must be monitored by your veterinarian. If your dog requires multiple prescriptions, the doctor should also check for possible drug interactions.

of providing the service. And today one of the most lucrative segments of the veterinary market—long-term prescription drugs—is under siege by other drug retailers and Internet pharmacies.

Some veterinarians, feeling the pinch as more and more clients request written prescriptions that they can fill elsewhere (rather than purchasing their dogs' medications from the veterinarian), have instituted a charge for writing prescriptions.

However, other veterinarians say they understand why some clients, especially those whose dogs require long-term or especially expensive drug therapy, need to economize where possible, given their significant and ongoing investment in their animals' care.

Different prescription needs

Generally speaking, there are a handful of situations involving prescription veterinary medications. Some lend themselves to bargain hunting; others do not.

In the first scenario, a dog has an acute illness of some kind, requiring the immediate administration of a short-term medication. Say, he's got conjunctivitis, and needs an antibiotic ointment, or a urinary tract infection, and needs antibiotic therapy for a week. Most of us, in situations such as these, would gladly

pay the veterinarian for the relatively inexpensive medications, and take them home with the dog.

Emergency medical situations are another example of a time when most of us would rather pay our veterinarians for immediate access to any medications required—at almost any price—to save our dogs.

But there are other situations when doing some bargain hunting makes sense. One is the case where someone has a dog with a serious medical condition that calls for expensive, long-term drug therapy. People whose dogs receive prescription medication for long-term health problems such as heart conditions, thyroid problems, seizure disorders, Cushing's disease, and even serious behavior problems may spend as much as hundreds of dollars a month on their dogs' drugs. Saving half of that money by buying the drugs for less from an outlet other than the veterinarian may well be imperative for preventing what some veterinarians call "economic euthanasia," when an owner feels forced to put a dog to sleep because she can't afford the medicine needed to keep him well.

Keep in mind that insuring your dog with a veterinary health insurance plan or joining a membership discount organization may eliminate the need to shop for discounted prices.

Pricing a prescription

The most important piece of information to take away is that prescription drug prices vary dramatically among retailers. It takes a bit of work to gather all the relevant information from the possible sources of prescription medications for your dog, but it's well worth the effort.

- First, check for human brand-name equivalents and generics. Ask your veterinarian if she can prescribe a human drug with the same ingredients as the veterinary drug. Sometimes, the equivalent human drug costs less than the veterinary drug, even though there may be absolutely no difference between them. The practice of giving drugs that have been approved for humans to animals is known as prescribing "off-label," and is restricted by the FDA to animals not used in the production of food for human consumption.

An example of this is Etogesic, manufactured for animals by Fort Dodge Animal Health, and Lodine, the human equivalent manufactured by Wyeth-Ayerst Pharmaceuticals. Both drugs are nonsteroidal anti-inflammatories commonly prescribed for pain. Both utilize the same active ingredient: Etodolac. Price both prescriptions for a full accounting of available costs for the drug.

- Next, call every pharmacy in your area and ask how much they charge for that prescription. Make sure to ask for the price of the veterinary drug, its human equivalent (if it has one), and its generic form. Make sure you confirm the dose and the amount with the pharmacist.

- If the drug comes in tablets, ask about "pill splitting." Often, drugs cost less, compared milligram to milligram, in higher-dose tablets than lower-dose tablets. For example, say your dog is supposed to take 80 mg of a drug per day; 40 mg in the morning and 40 mg at night. It may be less expensive to buy 80 mg tablets and cut them in two, feeding him half a tablet twice a day, than to buy 40 mg tablets. (This won't work with capsules, and works best with tablets that are scored in the middle. Tiny tablets may be too difficult to cut accurately.)

Trying alternative pharmacies

You may be able to realize further savings by taking your veterinarian's prescription to an Internet or catalog pharmacy. These outlets can sometimes offer deeper discounts than "brick and mortar" businesses, since they have less overhead. However, keep the following in mind when shopping at mail-order pharmacies:

- For an accurate price analysis, add shipping and handling costs to the price quoted for the medicine. These factors may erase any savings that you thought you would realize by purchasing from a catalog or Internet pharmacy.

- It's easier for unscrupulous pharmacies to get away with illegal practices when they don't maintain local retail outlets. There have been numerous complaints that Internet pharmacies, especially, dispense "knock-off" and foreign drugs, or drugs not approved by the FDA for use in animals. Ask for a written guarantee that the pharmacy offers only drugs approved by the Food and Drug Administration (FDA), does not use bulk drug chemicals manufactured for overseas production to concoct imitations of approved drugs, and does not sell foreign-made versions of U.S. products. Some U.S. drug companies will not accept responsibility for their products purchased in the U.S. over the Internet if the products were manufactured to non-U.S. specifications.

- Your veterinarian must be kept "in the loop." Several Internet pharmacies have engaged "staff" veterinarians to write prescriptions for consumers who order drugs online. In all but a few states it is illegal to dispense prescription drugs without the benefit of a traditional doctor–patient relationship. This law ensures that a medical professional monitors the condition of any patient taking the prescription medication, including making a proper diagnosis, checking for drug interactions, and managing the possible side effects of the drug.

The administration of some drugs to a dog may require follow-up blood tests, urine tests, or other actions to monitor the impact of the drug on the dog's various body systems. Also, a veterinarian should check dogs taking multiple prescription medications for the possible harmful effects of drug interactions. No matter where you buy your dog's medications, their use must be monitored by your veterinarian.

- Mail-order pharmacies may not be fast enough. Some prescriptions, such as antimicrobials prescribed to treat infections, should be administered to the animal immediately. Adding time for shopping, ordering, and shipping drugs may endanger the dog's health.

Work with your vet

If you contemplate buying medicines from retailers, catalogs, or Internet sources, run the prices by your veterinarian before making your purchase. Some veterinarians feel that if their good clients find a much lower price for prescription medications outside their practice, they will do everything they can to at least meet the price.

Dangers of Antibiotic Misuse
Threats include drug-resistant "super bugs" and loss of natural protectors.

Back in the early days of antibiotic discovery, while they were being touted by some enthusiasts as absolutely miraculous, silver-bullet germ killers, the very people who were instrumental in their development were warning us about their potentially harmful aspects. These early scientists, including Louis Pasteur, Alexander Fleming, and Rene J. Dubos, all understood that there were shortcomings to the antibiotics as medicine, and they warned us of dire consequences if we did not understand the naturally adaptive mechanism of evolution that the "bugs" would use against us and our antibiotics.

The dire predictions of the early scientists were well-founded. The basic "job" of a species of bacteria, as with any species, is to survive and reproduce. Whenever a colony of bacteria is confronted with a potentially lethal mechanism (in this case, synthetic antibiotics), one of its natural survival mechanisms is to evolve ways to protect itself from the invader.

Bacteria, with their extremely rapid reproduction rate, are uniquely adapted to use evolution as a survival mechanism. No synthetic antibiotic yet produced has been able to kill 100 percent of the pathogenic bacteria it is meant to kill (without also killing the patient). Given the fact that just one surviving bacterium can produce an entirely new, antibiotic-resistant generation within days, it only takes an extremely small percentage of survivors to regenerate a new subspecies of resistant bacteria.

But bacteria are even "smarter" than this, and they have "learned" how to develop even more insidious methods of avoiding the killing powers of antibiotics. Bacteria contain plasmids—mini-chromosomes that can carry genetic information about methods of avoid-

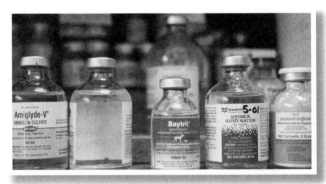

Antibiotics are one of the most useful and powerful tools that veterinarians have at their disposal for treating our dogs. However, the decision to use the drugs should not be made lightly. Indiscriminate use and overuse of antibiotics can help create deadly drug-resistant bacterial strains.

ing antibiotics from one generation to another in what we think of as the normal evolutionary manner.

With bacteria, however, the scenario goes beyond simple evolution. A bacteria's plasmids can transfer antibiotic resistance information from one species to another (say, from streptococcus to staphylococcus), and the plasmid can transfer resistance information about more than one antibiotic at a time. So, if one streptococcal strain survives an insult from several different antibiotics (say, penicillin, ampicillin, lincomycin, tetracycline, and cephalexin) and thereby "learns" how to resist each of these antibiotics, this streptococcal strain can transfer this multiple antibiotic resistance "know-how" to its offspring and to other, entirely different species of bacteria.

There's more. Recently, scientists have discovered that many bacteria have the ability to somehow predict the mechanism of destruction the next antibiotic we produce will use—and they are not only able to form resistance to antibiotic pressures they have never been exposed to, but also can transfer this ability to other species of bacteria.

It's no wonder that experts in the field of antibiotics have been worried, from the time when the drugs were developed to now.

To be sure, it is true that many of the resistant strains of bacteria likely have been created by inappropriate use of the antibiotics. Whenever a patient does not use the full antibiotic dosage or does not continue the dosage throughout the full time-frame recommended by the manufacturer, more bacteria will be left alive to evolve ways to avoid the antibiotic pressure. However, even given perfect compliance with antibiotic dosage amounts and length of time, there will always be some bugs that aren't killed, and some of these bugs will ultimately learn how to resist the antibiotics being prescribed to kill them.

There are at least four areas of concern when we use antibiotics:

1. Resistant strains of bacteria that will make future treatments for this patient difficult, if not impossible;
2. Resistant strains in the environment that may create super strains of bacteria that could affect entire communities;
3. Destruction of the normal flora that live on us all and that are actually beneficial; and,
4. Adverse side effects.

Resistant strains in the environment

In 1942 the total amount of antibiotic available in the entire world amounted to about 32 liters of penicillin. Today some 20 million pounds of antibiotics are used annually in this country alone. As we've seen, every time an antibiotic is used, it creates an environment where bacteria are "encouraged" to evolve protective mechanisms, and the result is that our environment has become literally saturated with resistant strains of bacteria.

Don't Create Resistant Bacteria

There are several general things you can do to help avoid the creation of resistant bacteria in your household:

- *Synthetic antibiotics can be life savers—life savers that can have dire consequences if used inappropriately. Reserve their use for those rare occasions when they are absolutely necessary to save a life.*
- *Not all symptoms are bad. Fever, for example, is one method the healthy dog uses to overcome bacterial infections. Resist using antibiotics for every little ailment that comes along life's pathway.*
- *If you absolutely must use antibiotics, use them at the recommended dosage and for the entire period of time recommended by the manufacturer.*
- *Avoid the routine use of antibiotic-laden household cleansers that can only perpetuate the creation of resistant bugs. Let your dogs (and your family!) develop their own immunity to the naturally occurring bacteria in the environment by interacting naturally with them. Bathe your dogs only when absolutely necessary*

Much of the total amount of antibiotics produced in this country (some estimates indicate more than 80 percent of total production) is fed to food animals at sub-therapeutic levels—levels that promote animal growth (and allow for cheaper meat for the consumer), but that allow for a faster production of resistant bacterial strains. It is a simple matter for these resistant strains to be passed to farmers and people living nearby. Of course, this transfer of resistance can go the other way too—from people to animals.

The concern doesn't end with food animal production. Consider that perhaps 100 to 150 million dogs, cats, and other pets are ingesting antibiotics each year—each of these with the potential to cause

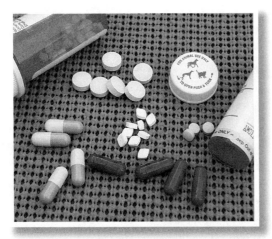

It's becoming more common for veterinarians to need to try more than one synthetic antibiotic to successfully treat some bacterial infections in their patients.

resistant strains of bacteria. Horticulturists and farmers use antibiotics to wage war on plant bacteria, and even our waterways are contaminated with antibiotics. Then there's the recent movement to hyper-hygiene, an attempt to remove any and all "bugs" from the household environment by coating every surface with "protective" antibiotics.

Every year we are literally dumping millions of tons of antibiotics into our living environment—each ounce of antibiotic with the potential to create yet another antibiotic-resistant strain of bacteria.

Furthermore, scientists have shown that multi-resistant bacteria spread to others as a contaminant (meat contaminated with very small amounts of multi-resistant salmonella, for example) has a much better chance of causing severe infection (in our example case, life-threatening diarrhea) in those people who are currently on antibiotics. In other words, ingestion of antibiotics is an important contributing factor in the increased likelihood of getting severe disease when exposed to resistant bacteria, whatever the source of the bacteria.

There may be an even deeper problem for us pet lovers. As the problem of antibiotic-resistant bacteria grows, in order to reserve at least some antibiotic effectiveness for severe cases in people, there will likely be more hue and cry that we quit using them entirely for "lesser" species such as dogs and cats. Already, considerable effort has been made toward banning the agricultural antibiotic use in food animals to promote growth, and that effort is certain to extend to our pets eventually.

There are a myriad of reasons—for our health, for the health of the environment, and for the future health of our pets—that we should be concerned about the overuse of antibiotics.

Destruction of normal flora

About 100 thousand billion bacteria live on the skin and in the gut of a normal, healthy human being. This amount is about 10 times more than all the tissue cells that make up an average 150-pound person. Almost none of these bacteria ever cause harm, and many of them are not just beneficial, they are absolutely necessary to maintain a healthy inner and outer environment. For example, a healthy gut actually requires that certain bacterial species be present in adequate numbers, and many of the bacteria normally found on the skin help provide a healthy protective activity against outside invaders.

Only a very small percentage of bacteria ever become pathogenic (causing harm), and the body has many natural mechanisms to keep these pathogens from gaining a foothold. What's more, it almost always takes some change in the normal body's homeostatic mechanisms to allow these species to revert to unhealthy ones.

If you use an antibiotic that is effective enough to kill most of the pathogenic bacteria, you have not only instigated the process of creating resistant bugs, but also set off the reaction that can kill many of the beneficial bugs in and on the body. The most common symptom you'll see from the kill-off of the beneficial bacterial species is diarrhea, the result of destroying the normally protective flora of the gut. However, many medical scientists now speculate that a loss of the normal flora of the body may ultimately lead to chronic conditions such as immune-mediated diseases and cancers.

Support your dog's defenses

In addition to reduced and more thoughtful use of antibiotics, there are several natural methods we can use to maintain our dogs' health and to treat any disease that may arise:

- Probiotics (which literally means "for life," as compared to antibiotics, which means "against life") help your dog maintain a healthy bacterial flora. These beneficial, "good-guy" bacteria are found in the gut in enormous numbers, with smaller numbers occurring in other locations on the body—such as the vagina, mouth, and skin. Probiotic bacteria include several species of *Bifidobacterium* and *Lactobacillus*.

  Probiotics have a number of healthful functions including enhancing digestive functions; maintaining control over potentially hostile yeasts and pathogenic bacteria; helping to maintain normal levels of certain hormones; helping to decrease cholesterol; and acting as anti-tumor agents. Perhaps their most vital activity, though, is their ability to destroy pathogenic bacteria by producing natural antibiotic products.

  Probiotics are easily killed by synthetic antibiotics, and returning them to their natural habitat is essential for the long-term health of any animal that is or has been on antibiotic therapy.

  The ideal way to recharge the gut with healthy bugs is to supplement with a probiotic product that contains one or more of the abovementioned species. A dollop of unsweetened natural yogurt on top of your dog's daily meal will go a long way toward helping him maintain intestinal health. If you are dealing with a specific disease, though,

you may need to check with your holistic vet for the appropriate probiotics to use.

- Immune-enhancing and antioxidant supplements can sometimes be used in place of (or to prevent the need for) antibiotics. As the body defends itself against bacteria and the polluting toxins from the environment, cells form oxidative products or free radicals that are toxic to inner tissues. Antioxidants counter these toxic by-products and in turn enhance the ability of the immune system to function properly. Several nutrients, including vitamins A, C, and E, selenium, and zinc, act as antioxidants.

  Herbal antioxidants include almost all the spice herbs, such as basil (*Ocimum basilicum*), oregano (*Origanum vulgare*), thyme (*Thymus vulgaris*), and cayenne (*Capsicum annuum*), along with many others. Herbals that have a direct effect on the immune system include astragalus (*Astragalus membranaceous*), echinacea (*Echinacea spp.*), calendula (*Calendula officinalis*), and thuja (*Thuja occidentalis*).

  You can provide these as a supplement to the diet on a daily or weekly basis, and the beautiful aspect of herbs is that they can often simply be added to the diet as a tasty sprinkle atop your dog's food. Do a taste test to see which herbs he

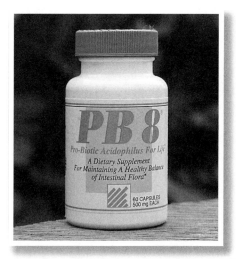

Dog owners should give their dogs probiotics during and after all use of synthetic antibiotics.

likes the best; it's these herbs that are likely to be the ones he needs the most. Herbs and nutritional supplements can also be given at therapeutic levels whenever an infection arises. Check with your holistic vet for dosages.

- Few people are aware that many herbs offer antibiotic action without concomitant risk of resistance. Within many herbs lies an almost complete medicine chest of substances that are active against a wide variety of microorganisms. There are two keys here: 1) a typical herb contains dozens of bioactive ingredients, and 2) these bioactive ingredients have activity against many different microorganisms, including the viruses against which synthetic antibiotics are totally ineffective.

  Some of the common herbs with active antibiotic activity include: aloe (*Aloe vera*), calendula (*Calendula officinalis*), echinacea (*Echinacea spp.*), garlic (*Allium sativum*), goldenseal (*Hydrastis canadensis*), lavender (*Lavandula officinalis*), licorice (*Glycyrrhiza glabra*), oregano (*Origanum vulgare*), peppermint (*Mentha piperita*), sage (*Salvia officinalis*), and thyme (*Thymus vulgaris*).

- Many of the alternative medicines, including homeopathy, acupuncture, and chiropractic, work by restoring whole mind/body/spirit balance, and it is this restoration that allows the physical body to create an inner environment inhospitable to pathogenic bacteria.

  Homeopathy is said to act by enhancing the patient's "vital force." Acupuncture is supposed to balance whole-body "chi." By aligning the spine, chiropractic treatment enhances the body's "innate" ability to return to homeostasis. While none of these methods is specific for "fighting" germs, perhaps this is their real saving grace as medicines; while helping the patient return to normal health, none of these methods destroys beneficial bacteria, nor do any of them force the bacteria to develop resistance.

Use Corticosteroids with Caution

Depending on the situation, these drugs can save lives, or threaten them.

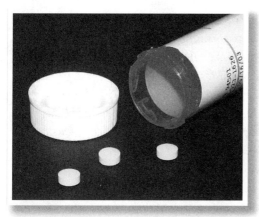

Corticosteroid drugs are less frequently overused than they once were, but the "quick fix" they provide in cases of allergy tempts many to abuse their use.

Corticosteroids are perhaps the most enigmatic of all the drugs in the Western medicine man's arsenal. It has been said by many practitioners that they are the most used and most abused of all our medicines. Corticosteroids are a necessary component of a healthy physiology and they can be life saving . . . or they can cause multiple adverse side effects that can be devastating to a dog's health and well-being. Since this class of biochemicals affects nearly all cells of the body, their beneficial effects can be widespread—and their adverse effects may be totally debilitating and long-lasting.

What they are

Naturally occurring corticosteroids are a class of steroid hormones that are produced in the cortex (thus the "cortico" prefix) of the adrenal gland. The adrenal medulla (inner part) manufactures epinephrine and norepinephrine, the hormones responsible for the "fight or flight" reaction, among other functions. Corticosteroids are made from the same steroidal chemical base that also produces the male and female sex hormones and the androgenic steroids made famous by athletes who want to enhance their muscle mass. However, the corticosteroids are slightly different from the androgenic and sex hormones in their chemical structure, and they are very different in the ways they affect the body.

Corticosteroids are further divided into two major classes of compounds: mineralocorticoids and glucocorticoids.

Mineralocorticoids are a vital component of the body's hormonal balancing system, even though they make up only a small portion of the overall mix of the corticosteroids in the body. Mineralocorticoids function in the kidneys (in the distal tubules) where they stimulate the exchange of sodium and potassium—increasing renal excretion of potassium and increasing resorption of sodium, which in turn helps maintain

Inflammatory and Allergic Conditions Often Treated with Glucocorticoids

Acute hypersensitivity (bites and stings)
Allergic bronchitis
Atopy (skin condition)
Chronic bronchitis
Degenerative joint disease
Encephalitis
Eosinophilic granuloma complex
Eosinophilic gastrointestinal (GI) disease
Flea allergy dermatitis
Heartworm pneumonitis
Intervertebral disk disease
Parasite hypersensitivity reaction
Urticaria (itchiness)
Uveitis

the body's water balance by increasing resorption of water.

The principle steroid with mineralocorticoid activity is aldosterone. Cortisol, the major "natural" glucocorticoid in dogs (and other non-rodent species), has weak mineralocorticoid activity. But in the natural state, cortisol's mineralocorticoid activity is of some importance because, in the healthy animal, there is so much more cortisol secreted than aldosterone.

The name glucocorticoid derives from early observations that these hormones were involved in glucose metabolism. The vast majority of glucocorticoid activity in most mammals is from cortisol, also known as hydrocortisone.

Synthetic glucocorticoids are used extensively in veterinary therapy.

Activities of glucocorticoids

Glucocorticoids (especially cortisol, the predominant natural glucocorticoid) stimulate several processes that collectively serve to increase and maintain natural conversion of glucose. These effects include:

- Stimulation of gluconeogenesis, the synthesis of glucose from other sources such as amino acids (protein building blocks) and lipids (fats). Glucocorticoids stimulate the enzymes that enhance this process, especially in the liver.
- Mobilization of amino acids from tissues, generating a substrate for gluconeogenesis.
- Inhibition of glucose uptake in muscle and fatty tissue, thus conserving glucose.
- Stimulation of fat breakdown, releasing fatty acids, which provides energy to various tissues and adds more substrate for gluconeogenesis.

Glucocorticoids have potent anti-inflammatory and immunosuppressive properties. Excessive glucocorticoid levels resulting from administration as a drug or hyperadrenocorticism (Cushing's disease) have

Potential Adverse Effects of Glucocorticoids

Abortion
Alopecia—loss of hair
Calcinosis cutis—calcium deposits in the skin
Delayed wound healing
Diabetes mellitus
Gastrointestinal ulceration
Growth suppression
Hyperlipidemia—excess fat in the blood
Iatrogenic hyperadrenocorticism—Cushing's disease
Immunosuppression—secondary infection, infections that worsen
Insomnia, agitation, behavioral changes
Insulin resistance
Ligament and tendon rupture
Muscle atrophy
Osteoporosis
Panting
Polyphagia—excess hunger
Polyuria (excess urination) or polydipsea (excess thirst)
Proteinuria—excess loss of protein in the urine
Psychosis or behavioral changes
Seizure threshold lowered
Skin thinning

effects on many systems. Just a few of the examples include inhibition of bone formation, suppression of calcium absorption, and delayed wound healing.

Insufficient production of cortisol is called Addison's disease (or hypoadrenocorticism). This disease may be caused by autoimmune destruction of the adrenal cortex or as the result of infectious disease and is often accompanied by an aldosterone deficiency. Aldosterone deficiency can be acutely life-threatening, causing severe electrolyte imbalance and loss of normal cardiac function. Other signs of Addison's disease include weakness and lethargy, diarrhea, and cardiovascular disease.

Control of cortisol secretion

Cortisol and other glucocorticoids are secreted in response to adrenocorticotropic hormone (ACTH) from the anterior pituitary gland. The secretion of ACTH is in turn under the control of the brain's hypothalamic peptide, corticotrophin-releasing hormone (CRH), creating a classic hypothalamic-pituitary-adrenal axis of control over the ultimate secretion of the glucocorticoids. It is important to recognize that, in the natural state, the brain (hypothalamus) is the primary controlling organ, and whenever the animal is stressed, there will be increased production of cortisol.

Any form of glucocorticoid (whether drug-induced or endogenous—from stress, for example) exerts a negative feedback on this axis and shuts down further secretion of the glucocorticoids. The negative feedback mechanism is medically important because after shutdown, the axis may take several days to gear up again to a normally functioning level.

Effects on inflammation and immune function

From the medical perspective and certainly from the holistic perspective, the most important thing to realize about the very potent anti-inflammatory and

Corticosteroid therapy often increases a dog's thirst—and urgent need to urinate.

Severe alopecia can be caused by corticosteroids.

immunosuppressive properties of the glucocorticoids is that there is absolutely no way to separate these two properties.

Whenever the glucocorticoids are administered (or produced naturally), the result will be a combination of anti-inflammatory and immunosuppressive activities. Thus, using glucocorticoids is always a balancing act; the multiple actions of glucocorticoids simultaneously allow for beneficial and adverse effects.

Natural options

There are many natural alternatives to the glucocorticoids, substances that have anti-inflammatory activity and/or that enhance a balance of the immune system's function.

- **Herbs:** Many herbal remedies are anti-inflammatory, enhance the immune system, prevent pain, and are specifically directed toward a body system, balancing it in response to inflammation or pain.

   Of special interest here is meadowsweet, the original source of aspirin (the old botanical name for meadowsweet, spirea, is how aspirin got its name). The term salicylate (the "active" ingredient in aspirin) comes from the Latin name for willow, *Salix*. The herbs that contain salicylate include meadowsweet, wintergreen, the bark of aspen and cottonwood, birch, black cohosh, and willow.

In addition, there are several herbs—examples include licorice, wild yam, yucca, sarsaparilla, and fenugreek—that contain steroidal saponins that have a chemical structure very similar to cortisone. These steroidal saponins have direct anti-inflammatory, cortisone-like effects, and in addition, some of them inhibit an enzyme in the liver that breaks down natural cortisone, thus making it available longer.

Herbal steroids typically do not create an atrophic effect on the adrenals, and in fact are often used to aid in the weaning process from therapeutic glucocorticoid levels.

- **Acupuncture:** Acupuncture has been shown to be beneficial to the immune system and for prevention of inflammation. In addition, acupuncture alleviates the pain of arthritis and may promote healing.

- **Homeopathy:** Homeopathy works by enhancing the vital force, an unmeasurable component of the healthy body that has been likened to the immune system.

- **Stress:** The contribution of a low-stress lifestyle to health is also unmeasurable, but undoubtedly valuable. Remember that the body constantly produces glucocorticoids, and whenever there is an excess production, there is the potential for disease. Excess glucocorticoids are produced with excess stress; think about the "Active Dog, Tiny Apartment Syndrome," a dog left home alone for extended periods (away from the healthy "pack" and forced to abnormally control elimination patterns), constant noise pollution, lack of exercise and open air walks—all these are potential stressors.

CHAPTER 7

Complementary Care: Holistic Care, Acupuncture, Chiropractic, Herbal Remedies, Aromatherapy, Homeopathy, Massage, and More

The Holistic Paradigm
Holistic healthcare isn't just improving the diet or using herbs.

The value of natural diets and supplements cannot be fully realized until the human caregiver is willing to adopt a holistic lifestyle. Likewise, no course of natural canine therapy can be entirely effective unless all elements of wellness are first considered.

The word "natural" on a product label may lead some people to think that the product must be safer and deeper in its therapeutic or nutritional values, but the truth is that all this word really suggests is *the possibility* of greater purity and superior quality. Even cream-of-the-crop products that really *are* made with all-natural ingredients cannot guarantee any greater levels of efficacy over conventional alternatives *unless they are used as part of a holistic agenda that factors all elements of physical, emotional, and environmental health into the wellness equation.*

Caring for someone *holistically* is not an easy job—especially when that someone is not human. And although it's great to include our dogs as members of our families, it is important to remember that they are really not like us at all. Sure, we can give them human names, dress them in silly clothes, give them fancy haircuts, and feed them foods that are packaged to appeal to human sight and smell—but we must always remember that their health is highly dependent on how well we are able to respect and honor the "ways

of dogs." The family dog, after all, is still an animal by nature.

Diet as an example

Dogs need foods that are fit for them, not necessarily for us. It is common practice for pet food manufacturers to draw consumers to their products by the way their products are packaged, how the product looks,

One important aspect of holistic dog-keeping is choosing a dog that is naturally suited to your environment. Keeping heavy-coated Northern breeds such as Huskies or Malamutes in a hot and/or humid climate puts the dogs at a health disadvantage.

Reduce the number of chemicals in your home. Use safe, natural cleaning products, low-toxic water-based paints, and natural fibers.

Avoid pesticide use in favor of integrated pest management.

Reduce the causes of stress in your dogs' lives— overactivity, excessive noise, social isolation.

Find a holistic veterinarian before you need one!

As always, feed the best-quality diet you can afford. Include fresh, wholesome "human" food whenever possible.

smells, and even tastes to humans (believe it or not, some companies even use human taste testers).

But this does not diminish the reality of what dogs need: muscle and organ meats, connective tissues, raw bones, and even an occasional snack of pre-digested vegetable matter (dogs sometimes eat grass and other things twice, to improve digestion). Which brings us to raw food—many people will not feed it to their dogs simply because they (humans) find it too repulsive. The dog may not think it's repulsive, and he doesn't care about the shape or color of his kibble, either.

Consider negative influences

Thinking holistically also means going places within the human mind where we really don't like to go—places where we are forced to consider the consequences of our actions and reassess the impacts of our bad habits. In this uncomfortable place we are forced by our love to consider aspects of our own behavior that may contribute to the misery of our dogs. Loud music, angry arguments, cars with exhaust leaks, loud vehicles, new carpets and linoleum (toxic gassing), fresh paint, wood smoke, fireworks, or even a box of dark chocolates left out on the coffee table may contribute to our dogs' stress and increased risk of illness.

Then there are issues of unnecessary and/or over-vaccination, prophylactic use of antibiotics, tail docking, and ear cropping—things we would *never* do to our human children, but often will not think twice about when it comes to our beloved pooches.

Indeed, moving toward adopting a completely holistic lifestyle can be difficult—but it's what true love and true healing are all about, isn't it?

Ancient Art, Modern Science

Fortunately for dogs, veterinary acupuncture is becoming mainstream.

It is generally accepted that the practice of veterinary acupuncture had its beginnings in ancient China. According to legend, veterinary acupuncture was discovered when lame horses were used for battle and became sound after being pierced by arrows at distinct points.

Regardless of the accuracy of the folklore, there is evidence that veterinarians practiced acupuncture around 2000 to 3000 BC. The early use of the technique on animals was probably prompted by the economic importance of horses, camels, elephants, cows, pigs, and chickens as sources of transportation and food. Now, veterinary acupuncture is used worldwide to treat all types of animals including many exotics.

Eastern tradition

Acupuncture gets its name from the Latin words *acus*, which means needle, and *pungare*, which means to pierce. Most of us can conjure up images of an acupuncture session, but few understand the reasoning behind needling—perhaps because there are several schools of thought that purport to explain the effectiveness of the practice.

According to practitioners of traditional Chinese medicine, there are channels of energy, called meridians, that run in regular patterns through the body and over its surface. The energy, called *Qi* or *Chi*, flows in these meridians just like water flows in a stream. If something blocks the flow of energy, it backs up, much as water would back up if a dam were placed across a stream. Disease results from disturbances or imbalances in the energy.

Placing needles at specific points, called acupuncture points or acupoints, unblocks the obstructions in the meridians and reestablishes the free flow of energy.

The theory is that by restoring energy circulation through the meridians, acupuncture treatments allow the body's internal organs to correct imbalances in digestion, absorption, and energy production. This is thought to encourage the body to use its own healing powers to correct imbalances and disharmony that manifest as chronic or acute disease or lameness.

Acupuncture, therefore, is a means of balancing the energy in the body and allowing the body to heal. Because acupuncture helps maintain the body's balance, it is also a powerful tool for preventing disease.

The Western perspective

While it is clear that acupuncture has a long history of effective treatment of many injuries and diseases, scientists using traditional diagnostic tools have been unable, until recently, to explain how the therapy works. In the last 25 years, however, Western scientists

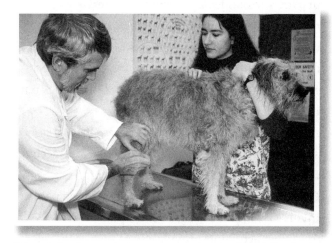

This veterinarian regularly uses acupuncture on the small animals in his practice. "It's an amazing adjunct to conventional veterinary medicine, and sometimes, all the animal needs," he says.

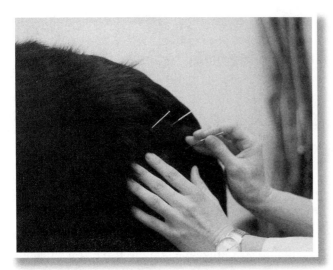

Acupuncture needles are very fine, and rounded at the tip. Unlike pointed, painful hypodermic needles, acupuncture needles do not cause more than a tiny momentary prick; some dogs seem not to notice them at all.

have made enormous strides toward understanding the curative mechanisms and the physiological basis of acupuncture.

For example, scientists have learned that the epidermis at acupuncture points is usually thinner than that of surrounding areas. Below the surface of the skin, each acupuncture point has a unique structure composed of a thin connective-tissue column surrounded by thicker connective tissue. The column or acupuncture point contains a lymph vessel, arteriole, and vein that are surrounded by a network of nerve fibers.

When an acupuncture needle pierces the skin and underlying muscle, it stimulates some of the nerve fibers, which carry messages to the brain to release endorphins, morphine-like compounds that block pain pathways in the brain.

Endorphins are often referred to as "the feel-good" substances that are released naturally and account for feelings of euphoria such as the "runner's high." Only those acupoints associated with treating pain are involved with the release of endorphins.

Other acupoints provide effects such as the release of cortisol, a natural steroid. Research is ongoing to

determine how stimulation of these acupoints affects the body.

Acupuncture and moxibustion

Acupuncture therapy involves the insertion of very thin needles into precise anatomical locations or acupuncture points on the body to balance the body's energy and produce a healing effect.

Acupuncture needles are solid, flexible, stainless steel needles with a smooth shaft that is rounded at the tip. At most, there may be a momentary sensation of pain as the needle is inserted. No pain should occur after the needle is in place. This is unlike hypodermic needles, which are pointed and have sharp cutting edges surrounding the hollow barrel and may be painful when inserted.

The goal of acupuncture therapy is to encourage the body to promote natural healing and to improve function.

Needling isn't the only way to stimulate acupoints. As a matter of fact, the Chinese word for acupuncture is *zhenjiu*. It comes from *zhen*, which means needle, and *jiu*, which means moxibustion. In Chinese medicine, acupuncture and moxibustion are considered part of one therapy.

Moxibustion is a method of heating or stimulating acupuncture points by burning an herb over them. *Moxa*, from the Japanese *moe kusa* or burning herb, refers to the herb mugwort (*Artemisia vulgaris*) which is related to the chrysanthemum family. The mature leaves of the plant, which have a wooly underside, are harvested, cured by drying in the sun, and ground into a fine powder or "wool" that is shaped into cones.

Commercially available *moxa* sticks are 6 to 12 inches long and about a half-inch in diameter. The end is ignited and then blown out so that it burns much like the red tip of a cigar. This hot end is held about an inch to an inch and a half above an acupoint while being moved up and down or in a circular pattern for 3 to 15 minutes to stimulate the acupoint.

Veterinary acupuncturists can include this technique when warranted by the animal's condition.

Conditions commonly treated with acupuncture

While acupuncture is not appropriate for all medical problems, it is used effectively to treat a number of disorders. Acupuncture is primarily used to treat functional problems such as paralysis, pain, and non-infectious inflammations including allergies. This encompasses a host of common canine complaints such as arthritis, spinal disc problems, many musculoskeletal problems, lick granuloma, asthma, gastrointestinal problems, and certain reproductive disorders.

Acupuncture is one of the safest animal therapies when administered by a trained veterinarian. Rarely do side effects occur. You should know, however, that some animals may be sleepy or lethargic for 24 hours following a treatment, while the condition of others may seem to worsen for up to 48 hours after therapy. These symptoms are indications that physiological changes are occurring and are usually followed by a noticeable improvement in the animal's condition. The types of changes that you might see in your pet should be explained by the veterinarian at the time of treatment.

Choosing an acupuncturist

Whether your pet is the victim of an accident or develops symptoms for no apparent reason, it is essential that you see a veterinarian to have the health of the whole dog evaluated. Signs that you interpret as minor may be indicative of a more serious condition that requires professional diagnosis by a veterinarian. A thorough physical examination and competent diagnosis of your pet's general health and specific problem are key to successful treatment and recovery.

Therefore, it is imperative that you choose a licensed veterinarian who has had formal training in the field of veterinary acupuncture.

Lay practitioners cannot provide the option of laboratory tests, and certainly not a veterinary diagnosis of the animal's condition. Cancers and other serious illnesses can be missed, allowing them to progress to untreatable states.

Most states consider acupuncture a surgical procedure and therefore require that a practitioner be a licensed veterinarian to perform acupuncture treatments on animals. You can check the International Veterinary Acupuncturist Directory to find acupuncture societies and qualified veterinarian acupuncture practitioners in your state.

Cost-effective treatments

As you might imagine, the cost of acupuncture for an animal varies with the type of problem requiring treatment. Acupuncture for a simple problem (including a thorough initial examination) generally costs about $100, with additional visits costing anywhere from $35 to $80, depending on your location (areas with few practitioners and high demand often result in higher fees).

Acupuncture is not a silver bullet that can mend all ills, but experienced veterinary acupuncturists say it's common to see as many as 85 percent of their patients respond favorably. Consider this powerful and safe tool the next time you have an injured or ailing pet.

Animal "Crackers"

Chiropractic offers numerous benefits, but exposes dogs to a few dangers, too. Here's how to get the most out of a chiropractic consultation.

Chiropractic is one of the most effective, dramatic, and embattled health care modalities currently available to dog owners. The many amazed dog owners whose limping, stiff, sore dogs had to be lifted in and out of the car on the way to the chiropractor's office, and who were surprised to see their dogs leap unaided into the car to return home after a chiropractic adjustment, can attest to the therapy's effectiveness and drama. But, in trying to relate the story of their dog's miraculous recovery at the hands of a chiropractor, many people learn how controversial the therapy is, especially to the uninitiated. "You took your dog to a *what?!*" they are likely to be asked.

People often hold the misconception that chiropractic is performed only on a person's or animal's spine. Actually, the modality can be performed on any joint. Above, chiropractor Michael Gleason adjusts a dog's shoulder.

While the earliest record of soft-tissue manipulation dates back to 2700 BC, modern chiropractic stems from the latter part of the nineteenth century, here in the United States. The word *chiropractic* comes from the Greek words *cheir*, which means hand, and *praxis*, which means practice; taken altogether, this means "done by hand." Exactly what is done by hand varies from one school of chiropractic to the next, but essentially, veterinary chiropractic practitioners seek to affect the nervous system by manipulating the animal's joints, especially (but not limited to) the joints of the spinal column.

Early chiropractors focused on moving joints in small increments to position the bones in an alignment thought to remove or prevent nerve "impingement." Regarding the system of nerves in the spinal column and elsewhere as similar to an electrical system, practitioners sought to align the joints in such a way as to prevent electrical "shorts."

Later practitioners have largely rejected this model as overly simplistic. Today, most describe the goal of chiropractic in a broad sense, as building the body's health by improving nerve function. Some of what its most ardent fans see as chiropractic's most powerful gifts—enhanced range of motion, restored joint function in aging or injured animals, and increased vitality and energy—are viewed by modern chiropractors as charming but secondary effects of improved general health.

Most of the controversy surrounding chiropractic stems from the lack of a unified and solely scientific explanation for the modality. As with many of the alternative and complementary health care modalities, chiropractic shines in anecdote; the sheer number of

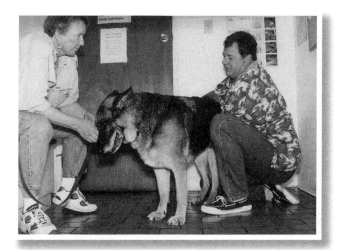

According to Dr. Gleason, arthritis can often be prevented if a dog is treated with chiropractic throughout its lifetime, starting in its youth. Arthritic, old dogs such as this one can benefit from chiropractic, and the degenerative process may be slowed, but, says Dr. Gleason, "the damage has been done."

dogs whose health improved with chiropractic care is convincing enough for many people. Laboratory studies that could either support or disprove the benefits of chiropractic don't exist.

Candidates for chiropractic

Obviously, people whose dogs' health improved with chiropractic defend the unconventional therapy. Which dogs are the most likely to benefit? Dogs with lameness, or an abnormality in their gaits; sporting dogs to optimize their athletic effectiveness; older dogs; and arthritic dogs.

Contraindications for chiropractic?

Dr. Michael Gleason, an instructor who has taught at the American Veterinary Chiropractic Association (AVCA), asserts that chiropractic can help most dogs become healthier, but does caution his veterinary and chiropractor students about a few conditions under which chiropractic care may be detrimental. "Know-ing when *not* to adjust is just as important, if not more important, as knowing *how* to adjust," Dr. Gleason says. "Generally, the contraindications for chiropractic include fracture, tumors, acute inflammation, and acute infection. The interesting thing is, that doesn't mean the patient won't experience a benefit from chiropractic; it means you don't adjust the site of the fracture, for example. An experienced practitioner can modify his or her techniques and work around the conditions. But if you are going to adjust a dog where contraindicated, you really have to know what you are doing," he says.

Qualified practitioners

Then there is the matter of untalented and unsafe practitioners. A talented person can use chiropractic to work miracles on dogs with all kinds of ailments. But a poorly trained individual—or even a well-educated but unskilled individual—can wreak havoc on a dog's body and psyche.

Most states permit only two classes of professionals to perform chiropractic on animals: veterinarians who have received "adequate training" in chiropractic, and chiropractors who have received "adequate training" in animal anatomy and physiology. Officially, there is currently only one educational program that seems to qualify as providing this training: the AVCA, which offers a 150-hour postgraduate course in animal chiropractic. The AVCA admits only doctors of veterinary medicine (DVMs) and doctors of chiropractic (DCs) to this program.

Be aware that there are a number of weekend and other short courses available to chiropractors, veterinarians, and even laypeople in the use of chiropractic for animals. Most professionals believe that any training less than the AVCA's 150-hour course would be insufficient to provide adequate training.

Beyond training, things to look for in a practitioner include compassion for and rapport with the animal.

Another is gentleness. Competent chiropractors should never need mallets or ropes to accomplish their adjustments.

What to expect

First, if the practitioner is a veterinarian, he or she will perform a general health examination in addition to a chiropractic evaluation. (If the person is a chiropractor, he should require a referral from your veterinarian, to ensure the dog does not have any health conditions that could contraindicate chiropractic.) The practitioner should ask questions about your goal for chiropractic treatment: are you seeking treatment to improve a specific condition, or to improve the general health of your dog?

The chiropractor may make small, gentle adjustments to joints on your dog's legs, shoulders, neck, and back. When the adjustments are made, your dog should not show any signs of pain or alarm (beyond, perhaps, a quick glance at the practitioner following a particularly big adjustment). A few dogs, especially those suffering from chronic pain or those who are always extraordinarily guarded about their bodies, may react more. If your dog protests the treatment, talk to the practitioner and ask whether he or she could use less forceful techniques. If he is unreceptive, or if the treatments do not benefit the dog, try another practitioner.

The practitioner should also tell you what to expect following the adjustment, and approximately how many more treatments he recommends.

Smell This, You'll Feel Better

Yes, these products smell good. But the emphasis is on "therapy."

Welcome to canine aromatherapy. Dozens of health problems have resolved with the help of aromatherapy, from allergies to anxiety, bad breath to burns. It's a fascinating branch of holistic medicine.

Essential oils, the foundation of aromatherapy, are the volatile substances of aromatic plants. They are collected, usually by steam distillation, from leaves, blossoms, fruit, stems, roots, or seeds. The water that accompanies an essential oil during distillation is called a hydrosol or flower water. Hydrosols contain trace amounts of essential oil and are themselves therapeutic. Other production methods include solvent extraction (a solvent removes essential oil from plant material and is then itself removed), expression (pressing citrus fruit), enfleurage (essential oils are absorbed by fat for use in creams), and gas extraction (room-temperature carbon dioxide or low-temperature tetra-fluoroethane gas extracts the essential oil and is then removed). Each method has something to recommend it for a specific plant or type of plant.

However they are collected, essential oils are highly concentrated. To produce one pound of essential oil requires 50 pounds of eucalyptus, 150 pounds of lavender, 400 pounds of sage, or 2,000 pounds of rose petals. No wonder they're expensive!

It's not the fragrance that imparts the medicinal or active properties of aromatic essential oils but the chemicals they contain. Plants are complex chemical factories, and a single plant may contain several types of chemicals. In addition, each chemical category may have several different effects.

Aromatherapy is a modern healing art, and the therapeutic quality of essential oils is still being discovered. In other words, aromatherapy is a complex subject that deserves careful study and expert guidance.

There are essential oils with antibacterial, antiviral, and/or antiseptic effects. Some have a calming influence; others are stimulating. There are essential oils that improve circulation, act as a diuretic, repel fleas and ticks, improve digestion, reduce inflammation, relieve congestion, elevate one's mood, stimulate hair growth, prevent motion sickness, enhance immunity, improve focus and concentration, speed wound healing, improve endocrine function, or facilitate detoxification—and, because the chemistry of plants is so complex, they may do several of these things at once.

Ten years ago, few people in the United States knew what aromatherapy was, much less its canine applications. Today, hundreds of pet products contain essential oils or have "aromatherapy" on their labels. However, many people only associate aromatherapy with strongly scented candles or perfumed air sprays.

"That's recreational aromatherapy," says Kristen Leigh Bell, author of *Holistic Aromatherapy for Animals*. "What Americans are just beginning to learn is that aromatherapy is actually a branch of medicine. In fact, in France, where the healing effects of essential oils were first documented, only licensed medical doctors can practice aromatherapy."

These top-quality canine aromatherapy products are pure and truly therapeutic.

Innovations in the field

Essential oils can be sprayed into the air, applied to a pet's bedding or clothing, or diluted and applied to the fur or skin. Because aromatherapy is such a complex subject, having experts design products for us is a time-saving convenience. Some large corporations make aromatherapy products for dogs, but the most interesting developments are coming from small manufacturers.

Getting started

You may be ready to buy some essential oils and try your own custom blending for maximum effects. What essential oil should you start with? Everyone's favorite

Ask your holistic veterinarian or groomer about aromatherapy products that may benefit your dog. Some vets use them in their holistic practices.

Buy only those aromatherapy products that list all their ingredients, and that contain only natural essential oils.

Consider grooming products that contain essential oils that offer therapeutic effects.

is lavender, *Lavandula angustifolia*, a powerful disinfectant, deodorizer, and skin regenerator. It helps stop itching and has psychological benefits; it's both calming and uplifting. Lavender is one of the few essential

A Word About Quality

For best results, dog owners must be sure the essential oils they buy are of "therapeutic quality." Be forewarned, however, that there is much confusion in the marketplace as to how that term is defined. Fortunately, at the high end, there is also much agreement as to what is the best and what isn't. Professional aromatherapists agree that over 95 percent of the world's production of essential oils, including most brands sold in department stores and health food stores, are inappropriate for canine (or human) aromatherapy.

Most essential oils are chemically standardized for the pharmaceutical and perfume industries, with certain components removed and others added. Even if they are correctly labeled, 100 percent natural, and 100 percent pure, nearly all essential oils are produced from commercially grown plants, complete with traces of pesticides and chemical fertilizers, and they are quickly distilled in very large batches under high heat and pressure for maximum yield. The results are very different from oils distilled in small batches at low pressure for longer periods.

It is essential that you buy from makers who get their essential oils directly from manufacturers (distillers) or from distributors who travel to the source. They test the oils with gas chromatography or similar sophisticated equipment to ensure the oils are correctly labeled and not adulterated with synthetic oils, pesticide residues, or anything else.

The best oils are made with plants that are organically raised or responsibly wildcrafted; distilled at low temperature and pressure; treated like vintage wines and never blended with other essential oils; labeled by botanical species according to the date, time, and place of harvest and distillation; and tested for purity and accuracy of chemotype.

Any product that contains synthetic essential oils should not be used for therapeutic purposes. Pure essential oils are very expensive, so some distributors adulterate them with synthetic oils, inexpensive natural oils with a similar fragrance, inexpensive vegetable oils, or solvents. Obviously, these adulterants and synthetic oils—sometimes called perfume or fragrance oils—do not offer the complex chemicals contained in natural essential oils.

While some dogs shy away from a mist bottle at first, once they enjoy the benefits of therapeutic aromatherapy, they usually stand still and happily soak up the spritzing.

A Recipe for "Calm Dog Mist"

To make it yourself, place one teaspoon vegetable glycerin, one tablespoon grain alcohol or vodka, one teaspoon sulfated castor oil, and 10 drops grapefruit-seed extract in an 8-ounce cobalt blue, green, or opaque spritzer bottle. Add three drops valerian, two drops vetiver, four drops petitgrain, three drops sweet marjoram, and two drops sweet orange essential oil. Add seven ounces spring or distilled water (fill to top).

If desired, add several drops of flower essences such as Rescue Remedy or gemstone essences such as rose quartz. Shake well before using. Calm Dog Mist can be spritzed into your hands and massaged into the dog's neck and chest, sprayed on bedding, or misted into the air.

3. Place a drop on your dog's collar, scarf, or bedding.

4. Place two drops in your hand, rub your palms together, and gently run your hands through your dog's coat.

5. Add 15 to 20 drops to 8 ounces (one cup) of unscented natural shampoo, or add a drop to shampoo as you bathe your dog.

6. Add two to five drops to a gallon of final rinse water and shake well before applying (avoid eye area).

7. Place a single drop on any insect or spider bite or sting to neutralize its venom (avoid eye area; dilute before applying near mucous membranes).

8. Add 12 to 15 drops to one tablespoon jojoba, hazelnut, or sweet almond oil for a calming massage blend.

9. Place a drop on a dog biscuit for fresher breath.

10. Add 15 to 20 drops to a half-cup of unrefined sea salt, mix well, and store in a tightly closed jar. To make a skin-soothing spray or rinse for cuts or abrasions, dilute one tablespoon of the salt in a half-cup of warm water.

11. Mix one teaspoon vegetable glycerine (available in health food stores) with one teaspoon vodka. Add 15 drops lavender essential oil, and add two ounces (four tablespoons) distilled or spring water to make a soothing first-aid wipe, ear cleaner, or

Ask your holistic veterinarian or groomer about aromatherapy products that may benefit your dog. Some vets use them in their holistic practices.

Buy only those aromatherapy products that list all their ingredients, and that contain only natural essential oils.

Consider grooming products that contain essential oils that offer therapeutic effects.

oils that can safely be used "neat" or undiluted, though dilution is recommended for most pet applications.

Here are a dozen things to do with a therapeutic-quality lavender essential oil:

1. Diffuse it in the room with an electric nebulizing diffuser (available from aromatherapy supply companies).

2. Add 10 to 20 drops to a small spray bottle of water and spritz it around the room. Be careful to avoid wood or plastic surfaces and your dog's eyes.

Top 20 Essential Oils for Use with Pets

The following essential oils are recommended by canine aromatherapist Kristen Leigh Bell:

Carrot seed (Daucus carota): *Skin care, first aid, healing, scarring, skin conditions. Super gentle.*

Cedarwood, Atlas (Cedrus atlantica): *Improves circulation, helps deter fleas. Skin care.*

Chamomile, German (Matricaria recutita): *Also called blue chamomile. Skin-soothing anti-inflammatory. Burns, allergic reactions, skin irritations.*

Chamomile, Roman (Anthemis nobilis): *Calming and antispasmodic. Wound care, teething pain.*

Clary sage (Salvia sclarea): *Different from common garden sage. Gentle, sedating, calming.*

Eucalyptus radiata (Eucalyptus radiata): *The gentlest, best tolerated, most versatile eucalyptus (there are many). Anti-inflammatory, antiviral, expectorant. Diffuse as room air cleaner, deodorizer, flea repellent.*

Geranium (Pelargonium graveolens): *Tonic, antifungal. For skin ailments, yeast overgrowth, fungal ear infections. Repels ticks.*

Ginger (Zingiber officinale): *Fresh, warm, spicy (don't settle for ginger that smells stale, musty, or rank). Motion sickness, indigestion (see peppermint); useful in massage oils for sprains, strains, dysplasia, arthritis.*

Helichrysum (Helichrysum italicum): *Horrible smelling, incredibly effective essential oil (some people and dogs do like it). Also called immortelle or everlasting. Heals skin conditions, cuts, abrasions, wounds, injuries. Relieves pain.*

Lavender (Lavandula angustifolia): *Used in pet aromatherapy products more than any other essential oil. Gentle, antibacterial, antipruritic (anti-itch), stimulates rapid healing, acts as a central nervous system sedative, very relaxing, deodorizing.*

Mandarin, green (Citrus reticulata): *The sweetest essential oil, very relaxing. For fear, anxiety, stress. Avoid red mandarin, which is not the same, and use only organic green mandarin. This is not a distilled oil but is pressed from the rind of the fruit.*

Marjoram, sweet (Origanum marjorana): *Pleasing, smooth herbal fragrance, calming, antispasmodic effects, strongly antibacterial. A recommended replacement for tea tree oil in blends for pets. Bac-terial skin infections, wound care. Repels insects. Reduces undesirable behaviors of intact males.*

Myrrh (Commiphora myrrha): *Deep, warm, earthy fragrance. Anti-inflammatory, antiviral. Puppy teething pain, irritated skin. Boosts immune system. Opoponax myrrh (Commiphora erythraea) has similar properties and repels ticks.*

Orange, sweet (Citrus sinensis): *Popular, uplifting, pleasant. Calms, deodorizes, repels fleas, treats skin conditions. Use organic sweet orange oil to avoid pesticide residues. Pressed, not distilled.*

Peppermint (Mentha piperita): *Digestive aid; stimulates circulation for injuries, sprains, strains, arthritis, dysplasia. Insect repellent. Relieves pain and itching. To prevent nausea and motion sickness, mix one tablespoon vegetable oil, seven drops ginger, and eight drops peppermint; give three drops orally.*

Ravensare aromatica (Cinnamonum camphora): *Gentle antiviral, antibacterial.*

Rose (Rosa damascena): *Expensive, wonderful, makes any shampoo, spray, or grooming product luxurious. Stabilizes central nervous system. Calming. Add one to two drops to blends for itchy, irritated, or dry skin.*

Thyme linalol (Thyme vulgaris, chemotype linalol): *Common garden thyme has six known chemotypes, or chemical profiles. Thyme linalol is the most gentle and useful. Relaxing, antibacterial, antifungal without the harsh skin irritation associated with common thyme. Balancing tonic.*

Thyme thujanol (Thyme vulgaris, chemotype thujanol): *Like thyme linalol plus immune system stimulant, liver detoxifier, antiviral. Kurt Schnaubelt, PhD, founder of the Pacific Institute of Aromatherapy, recommends applying thyme thujanol immediately after a tick or tick bite is discovered in order to help prevent Lyme disease. For immune-boosting blends or when a powerful antibacterial is needed without caustic, skin-irritating effects.*

Valerian (Valeriana officinalis): *Relaxing, helpful for separation anxiety or fear of loud noises, storms, fireworks, new situations.*

wound rinse. Saturate a cotton pad, mist from a spray bottle, or apply directly to cuts or scrapes.

12. To remove fleas while conditioning your dog's coat, wrap several layers of gauze or cheesecloth around a slicker or wire brush, leaving an inch or more of bristles uncovered. Soak the brush in a bowl of warm water to which you have added 10 to 12 drops of lavender essential oil, and brush the dog. Rinse and repeat frequently, removing hair, fleas, and eggs.

Blending secrets

Selection in hand, you can blend a massage oil, coat spray, or other product that your dog will readily accept.

Essential oils can be diluted in vegetable carrier oils, preferably organic and cold-pressed, such as apricot kernel, coconut, hazelnut, jojoba, olive, sesame, sweet almond, or sunflower oil. The general rule for canine use is to mix one teaspoon carrier oil with three to five drops essential oil, or one tablespoon (½ ounce) carrier oil with 10 to 15 drops essential oil. Use standard measuring spoons, not tableware, to measure carrier oils; use an eyedropper or a bottle's built-in dispenser to measure drops. There are about 20 drops in 1 milliliter (ml), 15 drops in ¼ teaspoon, and 60 drops in a teaspoon of most essential oils.

Essential oils can be mixed with water, but they will not dissolve. One way to dissolve essential oils in

---

Homemade Tick Repellent

You can make an all-purpose insect repellent for pets (and people!). Blend 20 drops of rose geranium, palmarosa, or opopanax myrrh essential oil (or any combination) with three drops citronella essential oil (which repels mosquitoes) and enough vodka, neem tincture, or bay rum aftershave to dissolve the essential oils. Start with two tablespoons alcohol or tincture and add more as needed to make the oils dissolve completely. Do not use isopropyl (rubbing) alcohol. When there is no longer a thin film of oil on the surface, add one cup water, herbal tea, or aloe vera juice or gel. Apply frequently, avoiding the eyes. There are also a number of commercially produced herbal preparations that some owners swear keep ticks off their dogs.

---

water is to add them to a small amount of grain alcohol, vodka, sulfated castor oil (also called Turkey red castor oil), vegetable glycerin, or any combination of these ingredients. Then add water, herb tea, aloe vera juice, hydrosol, or other liquid.

Because essential oils don't dissolve in water, they can't be rinsed away. If a drop of essential oil ever lands where it shouldn't, such as in your eye—or worse, your dog's eye—use a generous amount of carrier oil to remove it. Always keep vegetable oil and paper towels or soft cloths on hand for this type of emergency.

Canines in a Mist

Hydrosols are the newest and most gentle canine aromatherapy.

Most essential oils used in aromatherapy are obtained by steam distillation, at the end of which a small amount of essential oil is extracted from a large amount of water. But that isn't just any water, for the liquid that condenses after steam drives volatile material from blossoms, stems, leaves, fruit, roots, or seeds is itself an aromatic substance with significant healing properties.

That liquid is called a hydrosol, hydrolat, hydrolate, flower water, floral water, or distillate water. Regardless of name, hydrosols are aromatherapy's hot topic—and for pet lovers, they're ideal. They combine the therapeutic benefits of essential oils, which they contain in minute amounts, with the safety of herbal teas. Make that *very strong* herbal teas, for hydrosols are 20 to 30 times more concentrated than any steeped or simmered tea.

Hydrosols have become buzzword ingredients in cosmetics and skin care products, in which they are valued for their pleasant fragrances, hydrophilic (water-loving) acids, and mild but effective anti-inflammatory, astringent, and antiseptic properties.

The most familiar hydrosols are rose water, orange blossom water, and lavender water. But these culinary and hand lotion ingredients are usually made from water and perfume oils, not by steam distillation. The difference is significant, for true hydrosols contain water-soluble components that never appear in essential oils. As a result, hydrosols are gentle, powerful, versatile, therapeutic, and unique.

May be difficult to find

The first step toward improving your dog's health with hydrosols is finding them. Until recently, few essential oil distributors sold hydrosols, and even now they're unusual. That's because hydrosols take up more space, cost more to ship, require more careful storage, and have a far shorter shelf life than essential oils. In addition, all of the quality concerns that apply to essential oils apply to hydrosols. For best results, buy from recommended suppliers and treat hydrosols with care.

Store hydrosols in the refrigerator or, if that's not possible, in a cool, dark location. Some suppliers ship hydrosols in spray bottles, which prevents air from entering the bottle whenever you use it. Bottles that are frequently opened are easily contaminated.

Hydrosols are best replaced after their expiration dates. Use "expired" hydrosols that are still fresh in bath water or your dog's shampoo, as air fresheners, as a dog bedding freshener, or in floor, dish, or laundry wash or rinse water. If you have plants that like acid

Hydrosols can be misted directly onto a dog or serve as a wonderful complement to massage. Spray some onto your palms and massage it into your dog's coat. Ahh!

soils, water them with expired hydrosols. Spoiled hydrosols should go down the drain or into the garden or compost pile.

Most common canine uses

To give a hydrosol in food or water, start with ½ to 1 tablespoon per day for a dog weighing 50 to 70 pounds. For toy dogs, give 1 to 1½ teaspoons per day, preferably diluted. For large and giant breeds, give up to 2 or 3 tablespoons per day. Adjust the following recommendations (based on 50 to 70 pounds) for your dog's size.

For digestive problems, divide a daily dose of ½ to 1 tablespoon of coriander, peppermint, yarrow, fennel, carrot seed, oregano, basil, or rosemary hydrosol between water and food for three weeks.

For diarrhea, feed ½ tablespoon undiluted cinnamon bark hydrosol every 30 minutes for four doses, then hourly for four doses. "This usually does the trick," explains Suzanne Catty, author of *Hydrosols: The Next Aromatherapy*. "The cinnamon not only calms the stomach and digestive tract but also helps kill any bacterial cause of the diarrhea."

For urinary tract problems, you can give your dog ½ tablespoon juniper berry, yarrow, cypress, sandalwood, or goldenrod hydrosol three times daily plus 1 tablespoon hydrosol in the water dish daily for three weeks. In case of infection, try winter savory, oregano, scarlet bee balm, or thyme (chemotype thymol).

For respiratory problems, give 1 tablespoon hydrosol twice or three times daily, and rub 2 tablespoons undiluted hydrosol on the chest and abdomen twice daily for three weeks. Try eucalyptus (*Eucalyptus globulus*), inula, rosemary (any chemotype), thyme (any chemotype), oregano, or winter savory, or a blend of two or more. Catty recommends supplementing this treatment with the use of essential oils, such as a blend of equal parts ravensara, *Eucalyptus radiata*, and palmarosa, with a drop or two of patchouli or vetiver. This blend can be dabbed onto the dog's bedding or diffused into the air with a nebulizer, available from aromatherapy supply catalogs.

For additional recommendations for pet use, see *Hydrosols: The Next Aromatherapy*, by Suzanne Catty.

Creative applications

One of the easiest things to do with hydrosols is add them to your dog's shampoo. Try diluting a natural shampoo or liquid soap (one that doesn't contain synthetic chemicals) with an equal quantity of hydrosol. Do the same with your dog's conditioner, and add a splash of hydrosol to the final rinse water. The hydrosols of flea-repelling essential oils, such as cedar or rosemary, can help keep your dog flea-free. Where ticks are a problem, use any hydrosol that has a rose fragrance, such as rose geranium, palmarosa, or true rose—although true rose is so expensive and luxurious, you'll want to save it for spritzing on your own face.

Flower Power

These gentle remedies can help ease mental and emotional problems.

Innumerable modern research studies have shown that a person's immune strength and resistance can be improved through a positive mental outlook, and that people who are happy heal more quickly than emotionally depressed people. Stated simply: emotional states can affect the physical body.

Most veterinary health care professionals would probably agree that the principle is true for animals, too. For example, most healthy dogs are usually happy dogs—or is it the other way around? And have you noticed how, just as with people, very often an anxious or angry dog also tends to be prone to more injuries and illness than a content and cheerful dog?

We have proof of this today, but it was a radical proposition when English physician Dr. Edward Bach (pronounced "Batch") posed a similar theory in the late 1920s. Bach started his medical career as a bacteriologist, but found fame as the founder of "flower essence therapy," a healing modality based on the principle that addressing psycho/emotional imbalances can lead to improved health and function. Negative emotions, Bach conjectured, suppress healing, so he looked for elements that could positively affect people's emotions and moods. His theory was that once a person felt better, he or she would begin to get better. Bach wrote, "our fears, our cares, our anxieties and such . . . open the path to the invasion of illness. Remove the disharmony, the fear, the terror, or the indecision, and we regain harmony between soul and mind, and the body is once more perfect in all its parts."

Familiar with the use and preparation of herbs through his study of homeopathy, Bach experimented with substances made from flowers, which he regarded as the most vibrationally powerful stage of plant growth, and ultimately developed 38 formulations of "flower essences," each aimed at a specific emotional condition.

Curing or preventing disease may have been Bach's ultimate goal, but the flower essences soon came to be valued by Bach's adherents for their primary ability: positively affecting moods.

Bach's goal was healing humans, but it didn't take

Depressed or chronically anxious dogs often regain an interest in life after receiving flower essence remedies.

The inventor of flower essence therapy, Dr. Edward Bach, developed 38 essences from plants found in his native England, including flowers, bushes, and trees.

Complementary Care

Bach's 38 Original Flower Essence Remedies

(Organized in Bach's original seven major groups.)

Fear

Aspen: *Fears and worries of unknown origin.*

Cherry plum: *Fear of the mind giving way.*

Mimulus: *Fear of known things.*

Red chestnut: *Overconcern for the welfare of others.*

Rock rose: *Terror and fright.*

Uncertainty

Cerato: *Constantly seeks advice and confirmation from others.*

Gentian: *Discouragement, despondency.*

Gorse: *Hopelessness, despair.*

Hornbeam: *Procrastination, weariness at the thought of doing something.*

Scleranthus: *Inability to choose between alternatives.*

Wild oat: *Uncertainty over one's direction in life.*

Insufficient Interest in Present Circumstances

Chestnut bud: *Failure to learn from past mistakes.*

Clematis: *Dreaming of the future without working in the present.*

Honeysuckle: *Living in the past.*

Olive: *Exhaustion following mental or physical effort.*

White chestnut: *Unwanted thoughts and mental arguments.*

Wild rose: *Drifting, resignation, apathy.*

Loneliness

Heather: *Self-centeredness, self-absorption.*

Impatiens: *Impatience.*

Mustard: *Gloom for no reason.*

Water violet: *Pride and aloofness.*

Oversensitivity to Influences and Ideas

Agrimony: *Mental torment behind a brave face.*

Centaury: *Weak-willed and subservient.*

Holly: *Hatred, envy, jealousy.*

Walnut: *Protection from change and unwanted influences.*

Despondency or Despair

Crabapple: *A cleansing remedy, also for self-hatred.*

Elm: *Overwhelmed by responsibility.*

Larch: *Lack of confidence.*

Oak: *The plodder who keeps going past exhaustion.*

Pine: *Guilt.*

Star of Bethlehem: *Shock.*

Sweet chestnut: *Extreme mental anguish, where all else has failed.*

Willow: *Self-pity, resentment.*

Overcare for the Welfare of Others

Beech: *Intolerance.*

Chicory: *Selfishly possessive.*

Rock water: *Self-repression, self-denial.*

Vervain: *Overenthusiasm.*

Vine: *Dominance and inflexibility.*

Emergency Use

Rescue Remedy: *For anxiety, agitation, upset, terror, shock. (A combination of five flower essences: impatiens, star of Bethlehem, cherry plum, rock rose, and clematis.)*

---

long for veterinarians who agreed with his theories to try Bach's formulations on their animal patients. Indeed, for animals, the essences' ability to improve mental and emotional states has proved to be perhaps even more valuable than for humans.

Today, a growing number of veterinarians and complementary animal health care providers use flower essences on their animal patients. And because the remedies are safe, gentle, and available at most health food stores, many animal owners are trying the flower essences on their own, with remarkable results.

Veterinarian-tested

Without a doubt, the best-known and most widely used flower essence remedy is a combination of flower essences that Dr. Bach named "Rescue Remedy." The remedy, a mixture of five different flower essences (cherry plum, clematis, impatiens, rock rose, and star of Bethlehem), is indicated for anxiety, agitation, upset, terror, and shock. Many people give the remedy to their dogs to ease show-ring or field trial jitters, for calming dogs who get anxious in the car, or for trips to the veterinarian's office.

A growing number of veterinarians also use the five-flower combination on their patients. The blend is not only useful for treating the panic that many animals experience when they visit the veterinarian, but also for treating the conditions that necessitated the animal's visit!

How to dose your dog

Flower essences generally come in tiny bottles of less than one ounce. The already diluted contents are referred to as a "mother tincture," which is usually (but not necessarily) diluted further before administration. The undiluted mother tincture can be administered directly to a dog (two drops at a time), but due to the high alcohol content, many animals object to its taste and smell.

Further dilution does not affect the action of the essence, and it saves money!

Most health food stores that carry flower essences will also sell small (about 30 ml) dropper bottles and/or mister bottles to use for mixing and administering a "working stock." Pour three parts water (well, filtered, or bottled water if possible; neither chemically treated

tap water nor distilled water are recommended) to one part alcohol (vodka, brandy, or Purol) into the bottle. Most experts suggest adding two drops of each mother tincture to be used (up to a maximum of seven essences, with Rescue Remedy counting as one essence) to the water/alcohol mixture. Then, put the top on and shake the bottle vigorously. Administer four drops of this working stock to the dog four times a day for chronic symptoms, or every 10 minutes or so in emergency or critical situations. (The potency of the essences is best increased by more frequent dosing from the working solution bottle, rather than giving a mixture with a higher percentage of mother tincture.)

Commonly, the working stock is administered with an eyedropper and squirted into the dog's mouth. Some people prefer to drop the mixture onto a treat and feed it to the dog. The mixture can also be sponged onto the dog's face, softly massaged into his skin, and rubbed behind his ears. Sometimes a dog who is panicked or aggressive will calm down after being gently misted (through a cage door, for instance) with a mixture formulated for his condition.

None of the essences' manufacturers claim that the products will heal specific conditions on a *physical* level. The essences should not replace medical treatment, and should your dog manifest any symptoms of illness before, during, or after treatment, consult your veterinarian as usual. All of the makers say that the essences may be administered by themselves or in conjunction with medical or other treatment; they won't conflict with medication, including any homeopathic remedies.

That fact that you don't have to (and shouldn't) change anything about a dog's other treatments when you administer the remedies makes it easier for many skeptical dog owners to give the remedies a try; since they cannot hurt a dog in any way, an owner has "nothing to lose" by giving them a try. And that's often precisely when the flowers seem to work their subtle, wonderful miracles.

Herbal Wisdom
The five "golden rules" of safe and effective herb use for dogs.

Unlike conventional drug therapies and surgical interventions, effective herb use does not focus on suppression or removal of disease symptoms. Instead, the herbalist begins his work from a more holistic perspective, one that starts with identification and correction of underlying issues and external influences that cause or contribute to illness.

The golden rules

1. A good diet always comes first.

Your dog's body requires good, fully digestible, nutritionally complete food in order to function as nature designed it. When used at their greatest potential, herbs are used to call upon healing energies and resources that are already in place—meaning that if a dog is on a diet of bargain-basement Brand X kibble, the herbs you feed have few tools to work from.

Simply put, herbs work in *concert* with the quality of food that goes into the body. They cannot replace a good diet, nor can they supplement a poor one. Without quality nutrition, herbs are holistically useless in therapeutic applications; don't waste your time and

Using these common kitchen spices to treat your dog's minor maladies may help educate you to turn to the herbs when you need a little help, too! Keep in mind that the freshest herbs offer the best results.

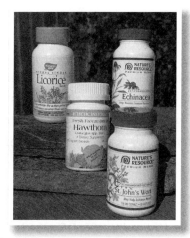

Herbs should not be used to suppress a symptom. For optimum results, herbs should be one part of a treatment plan that improves the dog's total health.

money on them if you pay $10 for a 40-pound bag of dog food.

2. Herbs generally do not serve well as direct replacements for conventional drugs.

Although herbs can sometimes be used as alternatives to conventional drugs, it is important to remember that their greatest potential rests within the holistic context in which they are applied. When herbs are used from the same allopathic perspective as one would use a drug, their greatest healing gifts are not employed.

For example, licorice root (*Glycyrrhiza glabra*, a potential alternative to anti-inflammatory drugs) can sometimes be used as a somewhat weak replacement for corticosteroid drugs. However, using licorice in this capacity without first considering the actual *causes* of a dog's ailments is really no different from using an over-the-counter anti-inflammatory drug.

If you wish to use herbs effectively, start with diet, *not* by focusing on suppression of symptoms.

3. More is not necessarily better.

Although herbs tend to be more forgiving than most drugs in terms of safety and potential side effects, this does not mean they can be used without care and common sense. Some herbs are very powerful medicines, and if misused can lead to serious health problems.

Read books, talk to experts, go to seminars and classes to learn about herbs. Find out where your comfort boundaries exist with their use *before* you use them. If you have any doubts about which herb to use, how much, and how long, consult a holistic veterinarian who is familiar with the use of herbs in your type of dog.

4. Until you are familiar with herbs and how to properly select, prepare, combine, and portion them for use in your companion, it is best to use reputable herbal products that are formulated specifically for dogs.

By doing this you not only will save time and money, but also will draw from years of experience and expertise. There are dozens of quality herb products in the marketplace that have been formulated by people who are experts in the use of herbs for animals. These products are not only formulated for optimum efficacy, but are fine-tuned to the nuances of the canine body. Use them.

5. If you wish to pursue an alternative solution for a serious health problem, don't waste time trying to figure out a self-administered solution. Consult a holistic veterinarian immediately.

On the surface, the expense of a holistic veterinarian and a natural diet may seem unreasonable. But really, providing your companion with quality nutrition and holistic care is not as expensive as you think—especially when you learn that much of what your dog needs may already be in your refrigerator and spice cabinet.

Hundreds of holistic veterinarians are in practice throughout North America and can be accessed through the American Holistic Veterinary Medical Association, which maintains a state-by-state database of all of its members. Many of these very special vets can help you get started on a path to canine wellness on the telephone, and when you factor in the money you will save by reducing veterinary costs, you will soon realize the value of health maintenance versus disease intervention.

Just remember: It all starts with how willing you are to look at the bigger picture of your dog's health.

Herbs that heal

Calendula and hypericum are two of an (injured) dog's best friends.

You come in from a jaunt in the woods with your trusty Labrador and notice, as you rinse the mud from

The goal: A happy dog who is free from itching, infection, or imbalances.

Calendula is perfect for healing wounds, like the one above this dog's ear, that the dog keeps scratching open.

his legs and feet with a hose, that he somehow got a cut on his upper leg. You *could* spray it with an alcohol-based disinfectant, or swab it with an antibiotic cream, in an effort to kill the bacteria that might infect the wound.

But, according to holistic healers, these modern wonder drugs may constitute a chemical overkill, going far past their intended purpose (killing harmful foreign bacteria) and killing the resident *beneficial* bacteria that live on the dog's skin. And what sense is there in dragging out the heavy artillery when just a light protective force is needed? Especially when there are natural, effective, inexpensive, and synergistic alternatives: calendula and hypericum, herbs that have been used for centuries for wound care.

Calendula officinalis (also known as the marigold plant, but usually called calendula) and hypericum (also known as Saint John's wort) are very safe, yet incredibly effective at cleaning the site of an injury and encouraging the body to heal. Homeopathic and herbal preparations of calendula and hypericum have proved invaluable in modern-day holistic dog care. In fact, it's difficult to find an herbal wound preparation that does not contain some form of one or both of these potent plants.

Calendula can do it

Calendula is one of the most effective remedies known to mankind for the treatment of wounds. Although it has no antibiotic properties (it does not have the ability to kill or slow the growth of living organisms), calendula seems to help prevent infection by somehow triggering the release of the body's own antibiotic substances.

Calendula also helps stop bleeding and promotes tissue granulation so that cuts and burns can heal properly. It even helps prevent proud flesh (an overgrowth of granulation tissue, an angry red color, laden with tiny blood vessels that bleed easily). Because of these properties, any wound from a minor scrape to a deep, serious gash can benefit from the use of this medicinal herb.

When to Call a Veterinarian

See page 235 in chapter 6 for conditions that require immediate veterinary help. Keep the following in mind as well:

With any illness or injury your dog experiences, ask yourself, "Do I feel completely comfortable treating this condition myself?" If you cannot answer YES with total confidence, call your veterinarian for assistance. The most important thing is not to overestimate your abilities.

Cleansing solutions made from calendula tincture can also be very useful. Whereas products like Betadine clean and disinfect wounds, they do not encourage healing. A solution made from calendula tincture cleans the wound, helps stop bleeding, stimulates the body to fight infection, and triggers the body's own internal wound-healing processes such as granulation. Calendula also demonstrates a potent antifungal action and may be used externally to combat such infections.

To start the healing process, promptly rinse the wound with distilled (if possible) or tap water and

Oil-based forms are best for dry, chapped skin and cracking wounds. These oil-based creams and salves may contain low concentrations of herbs. The label of sprays generally state the percentage of herbal extract the product contains. Tinctures tend to be strong, and must be diluted in water for topical application to cleanse wounds.

helpful for blows to the extremities like the toes and tail, where there are intricate clusters of nerves. It is also effective for spinal injuries where there is threat of damage to the spinal cord. Because of its ability to repair nerve damage, it helps to relieve pain from any type of blow such as a bruise from a kick or a painful cut. It also helps the body resolve abscesses and infections. In addition, it can be effective in preventing tetanus.

Hypericum works beautifully in wound care when applied topically along with calendula. Use the combination formula described below to flush wounds and promote tissue and nerve healing. For a wound that needs regular cleaning and dressing, use the solution every time you treat the injury.

Sound solutions

To make a calendula/hypericum solution you will need to purchase a "mother tincture" of each remedy. A mother tincture is made from a mixture of the original herb and alcohol or glycerin. Unlike the homeopathic form, which is drastically diluted, a mother tincture is a *concentrated* form of the active element of the herb.

To prepare the solution, you need a jug of distilled water and a jar or bottle. Using very clean utensils, measure out the ingredients into the container in the following ratio: one part calendula tincture, one part

then flush the site with calendula or a calendula/hypericum solution.

The topical calendula products can be used liberally and frequently. Apply them once a day for minor or mostly healed injuries, or three to five times a day for more serious conditions. Continue using them until the cut, abrasion, or burn has healed completely.

Help from hypericum

Hypericum perforatum, usually called hypericum, is used for injuries to nerve endings. It is especially

hypericum tincture, and eight parts water. Do not contaminate the tinctures by touching them with your hands or unclean utensils. Once you have added the tinctures to the distilled water, close the container and shake gently to blend.

There are several ways to apply this solution. You can pour it onto sterile cotton balls, which you use to clean the wound. You can also pour the liquid into a syringe and use it to flush the wound. This application is ideal for initial treatment of an open wound or daily flushing of a puncture wound. You can also pour the solution into a small spray bottle and mist it onto the skin.

Store the solution in a cool, dark place. Because the mixture has a limited shelf life (about one week), only make what you will need for the particular condition you are treating. If the solution becomes cloudy or fuzzy, dispose of it.

Performance-enhancing herbs

Dogs who compete in any contest can benefit from herbal supplements. In every obedience match, tracking test, field trial, agility event, show ring, athletic competition, and puppy kindergarten class, owners and handlers are eager to find whatever strategies, products, and equipment will give their dogs an advantage. One *healthy* shortcut to the winner's circle comes from Mother Nature, for with the help of medicinal herbs, dogs can concentrate despite distractions, relax under stress, keep their joints limber, improve their coats, increase their stamina, and possibly even improve their sense of smell.

Best of all, you don't have to be an expert to use herbs safely and effectively. While some preparations are not appropriate for use with pets, most herbs are safe even in the hands of novice users. Their side effects, if any, are minor, and their use is supported by centuries of experience around the world.

For best results, follow all instructions presented below. Consult a holistic veterinarian or herbalist before giving medicinal herbs to a dog taking prescription drugs.

Herbs for learning

Whenever you want your dog to pay attention, two groups of herbs will help. Valerian (*Valeriana officinalis*) and chamomile (*Matricaria chamomilla* or *Anthemis nobilis*) are nervines, herbs that nourish the nerves, and either one can help prevent your dog from being distracted, hyperactive, or overstimulated.

Memory tonics such as gotu kola (*Centella asiatica*), ginkgo (*Ginkgo biloba*), and rosemary (*Rosmarinus officinalis*) enhance blood circulation and help stimulate clear thinking. Thirty minutes to an hour before class begins, give your dog a blend of nervine and memory tonic herbs, such as a tea brewed from equal parts of valerian and gotu kola, a tincture made of equal parts chamomile and rosemary, or capsules containing ginkgo and valerian.

While most people describe valerian as smelling like old socks, most dogs enjoy it and many cats actively crave it. This fragile herb's volatile essential

Herbs that nourish the nervous system (such as valerian), and others that increase memory (such as rosemary) are especially helpful for dogs undergoing obedience training or competition.

Certain herbs used to increase memory, such as ginkgo, are thought to improve a dog's sense of smell, too. This can be beneficial for dogs who engage in tracking or police work.

oils are best preserved in alcohol tinctures. If brewed as a tea, valerian should be infused (steeped) rather than simmered, which is unusual for a tea brewed from roots, and dried valerian should be stored in a sealed glass jar, not absorbent paper.

Herbs for scent work

Memory-tonic herbs improve circulation throughout the brain and body, and some herbalists speculate that they may improve a dog's sense of smell. Ginkgo, gotu kola, and rosemary are even more effective when combined with small amounts of stimulant herbs such as cayenne pepper (*Capsicum frutescens*) or ginger (*Zingiber officinale*), which can be given in capsules.

To experiment, give the herbs 30 minutes to an hour before the activity and repeat two hours later if needed. Valerian and/or chamomile can be used at the same time to improve concentration and focus.

Unfamiliar herbs may distract your dog's nose, so don't wait until the day of an event to introduce them; start weeks ahead so that his sensory system can adjust as you experiment.

Herbs for stress

A growing number of boarding kennel operators, humane society shelter workers, handlers of traveling dogs, and veterinarians know what a difference calming nervines can make for any animal who is anxious or confused. Valerian, skullcap (*Scutellaria lateriflora*), passionflower (*Passiflora incarnata*), hops (*Humulus lupulus*), oatstraw (*Avena sativa*), and chamomile help dogs adapt and relax. Although these herbs are considered sleeping aids, none of them will sedate an active, alert dog the way pharmaceutical tranquilizers do. Instead, they allow a resting dog to relax and sleep by relieving nervous anxiety, and they help a wide-awake dog remain calm.

In addition, adaptogen herbs help dogs cope with stress. Adaptogens gradually correct imbalances, such as by raising or lowering blood pressure, reducing or increasing pulse rate, or correcting blood sugar levels, and when taken on a daily basis for weeks or months, they have been shown to help stabilize a dog's responses to stress.

Dogs who habitually become anxious and shaky in certain situations, like trips to the groomers or at shows, can benefit from calming herbs such as hops or chamomile.

Complementary Care

The most famous adaptogen herb is ginseng (*Panax ginseng* or *P. quinquefolius*), but other adaptogens gaining popularity among dog owners are fo-ti (*Polygonum multiflorum*), schizandra (*Schizandra chenensin*), ashwagandha (*Withania somnifera*), and astragalus (*Astragalus membranaceous*). Like tonic herbs, adaptogens work gradually and require months of use before their benefits are apparent.

An additional benefit of adaptogens is that they help increase stamina and endurance. This effect can be helpful for dogs that run or jog with their owners over long distances, as well as hunting, tracking, or sled dogs.

Herbs for the skin and coat

One of the best herbs for topical application is aloe vera juice or gel, which can be rubbed into the skin to soothe irritation, relieve itching, and speed healing. Chamomile tea is an excellent final rinse for all but white-coated dogs (it can temporarily darken white fur), and stinging nettle (*Urtica dioica*) tea is recommended for dark coats; both are natural hair conditioners. Work the rinse deeply into the coat and let it dry.

Topical application offers temporary relief, but the real solution to skin and coat problems comes from inside. In addition to improving the diet, consider giving "alterative" (often called blood-cleansing) herbs such as burdock root (*Arctium lappa*), dandelion leaf (*Taraxacum officinale*), dandelion root, red clover (*Trifolium pratense*), stinging nettle, and yellow dock root (*Rumex crispus*). Gradually, over a period of weeks and months, these herbs restore normal body function and act as general tonics for improved health and appearance.

In addition, bitter herbs such as dandelion leaf, wormwood (*Artemisia absinthium*), feverfew (*Tanacetum partenium*), or commercial preparations such as Swedish Bitters stimulate the gastrointestinal tract, improve digestion, and indirectly improve coat condition.

Dosages for Dogs

The herbs recommended here are considered safe to administer to dogs for several days or two to three weeks at a time, and some are recommended for longer use. Most are from the food or tonic categories of medicinal herbs, which are the least toxic and best tolerated.

Because concentration and quality vary among fresh herbs, as well as teas, tinctures, and capsules, and because the pets who take them vary in size, weight, and physical condition, it is impossible to specify a single dosage for best results. Use the chart here to determine a conservative starting point for dosing your dog. If you don't notice improvement after using an herb as directed, your dog may need more or you may need a better-quality product. Look for herbs and tinctures that have a distinctive taste, fragrance, and color. Herbal products should be stored away from heat, light, and humidity.

Suggested doses of herbs for adult dogs by weight (given 2 or 3 times per day)

Dog's Weight	Tincture	Capsule	Tea
5 to 10 lbs	1 to 2 drops	½ cap	1 teaspoon
10 to 20 lbs	3 to 4 drops	1 cap	2 teaspoons
20 to 30 lbs	5 to 6 drops	1 cap	1 tablespoon
30 to 50 lbs	6 to 10 drops	2 caps	4 teaspoons
50 to 70 lbs	10 to 14 drops	2 caps	5 teaspoons
70 to 90 lbs	14 to 18 drops	3 caps	2 tablespoons
90 to 110 lbs	18 to 22 drops	4 caps	3 tablespoons

To use a bitter herb, add small amounts to your dog's first bite of food or simply place a pinch of the herb or a drop of tincture in her mouth. She won't like it, but in response to the bitter taste her digestive organs will secrete bile and other fluids. If you accustom your dog to receiving bitters with each meal, she will usually come to accept them eagerly as she associates their taste with food.

Last, adding aloe vera juice or gel to food helps improve digestion and relieve skin and coat problems. Give up to 1 teaspoon per 10 pounds of body weight

Herbs can be administered to dogs in a variety of forms, including teas and decoctions, liquid extracts called "tinctures," or in capsules. Each form has inherent advantages and disadvantages, so you might have to experiment with your dog to find a form that he or she will readily accept.

daily or half that amount if the product is concentrated. To use fresh aloe vera, peel the leaf, remove the inner gel, and rinse it with water to remove any trace of the rind, which can have a laxative effect.

Herbs for limber joints

Conventional medicine considers arthritis irreversible and incurable; its only treatment is with symptom-suppressing drugs that temporarily alleviate pain, thus increasing mobility. However, holistic veterinarians are finding that a well-balanced all-raw diet can actually reverse the arthritic process, keep bones strong, maintain flexibility, and help prevent injury.

Arthritic dogs fed commercial food may be helped by nutritional supplements such as glucos-amine sulfate, chondroitin sulfate, or blends of herbs, but they usually begin limping as soon as the supplement is discontinued, something that wouldn't happen if these supplements actually cured the condition. Boswellia (*Boswellia spp.*), devil's claw root (*Harpagophytum procumbens*), yucca (*Yucca spp.*), white willow bark (*Salix alba*), and feverfew offer relief from symptoms, but they should be considered only part of the arthritis protocol. All of these herbs are appropriate for dogs recovering from injuries.

External applications of arnica (*Arnica montana*) tincture speed the healing of muscle sprains and bruises by increasing capillary blood circulation. Arnica tincture is an important first-aid remedy; if used within a few minutes of injury, it prevents pain, swelling and bruising. Apply generously on unbroken skin and repeat as needed.

Homeopathy: Tiny Doses, Huge Effects
A radically different (and controversial) system of medicine.

In the late 1700s, a German physician named Samuel Hahnemann discovered that *China*, a precursor for the quinine that was being used to treat malaria, actually *caused* symptoms of malaria when administered to a healthy person. Hahnemann made this discovery while translating a medical text on various drugs. He suspected that the source of *China*'s curative power had been misunderstood and he decided to give himself small doses of the substance to test his theory.

Hahnemann discovered that small doses of *China* produced in his healthy body malaria-like symptoms that abated after two or three hours. In thus observing that a drug will *cause* in a healthy person the same symptoms it *cures* in a sick one, Hahnemann gained the key insight that drugs cure diseases to which they bear marked similarities. Hahnemann called this new principle *Similia similibus curentur*—"Let likes be cured with likes," or, more simply, "Like cures like." Homeopathic physicians refer to this as the Law of Similars.

Hahnemann eventually tested this principle with about 100 different substances. The tests, called provings, consistently bore out the truth of his theory. Today there are 1,350 recognized homeopathic medicines or remedies, as they are commonly called.

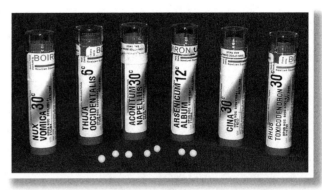

There are more than 1,000 recognized homeopathic remedies, and most are made in a variety of strengths or "potencies," though all the potencies are highly diluted. The homeopathic pellets are easy to administer; they can be slipped in the dog's mouth, or dissolved in a small amount of pure water and administered with an eyedropper.

But instead of trying to thwart the expression of disease the body is experiencing, homeopathy seeks to assist the body in working out the illness. "Homeopathy's beauty," writes Dr. Richard Pitcairn, one of the earliest proponents of veterinary homeopathy in this country, "is that the treatment provided goes with rather than against the body's own efforts to regain health."

Symptoms are not the disease

If Western medicine succeeds in eliminating the symptoms, the patient is said to be cured. Homeopathy, by contrast, says that symptoms simply *represent* the disease, or, more precisely, the body's effort to rid itself of the disease. Eliminating the symptoms alone will not eliminate the disease.

Since homeopathy views each individual as unique, a veterinary homeopath will look for what sets your dog apart from others with similar symptoms.

How it works

The term homeopathy, which means "similar suffering," points to the key difference between this system of healing and allopathy ("opposite suffering")—what we think of as conventional Western medicine. Allopathy seeks to eliminate health problems by overpowering and negating them. Thus, infections are treated with antibiotics, allergies with antihistamines, and so forth.

The physician will then know how to treat your dog, not just to alleviate his symptoms, but to restore the health of the whole animal.

Homeopathy draws a clear distinction between acute and chronic disease. Acute disease, says veterinary homeopath and educator Christina Chambreau, DVM, is disease "that ends in either death or recovery." Acute diseases can range from an upset stomach

When searching for the remedy for a dog with a chronically inflamed, weepy eye, for example, the veterinary homeopath will also consider the dog's ravenous appetite and obesity, crankiness with other dogs, tendency to seek out warm sunny areas, and so on. The dog's entire health history and personality traits help direct the practitioner to the remedy that best suits his total "symptom picture."

caused by a raid on the garbage to parvovirus. Chronic disease, Chambreau says, is "any disease that the vital force is not able to eliminate by itself." Skin problems are classic cases of chronic disease. Minor acute illnesses can often be treated at home. Chronic problems always require the assistance of a trained homeopath.

Another central tenet of homeopathy is that disease moves, from less vital to more vital organs. Untreated or suppressed skin problems, for instance,

can reliably be expected to migrate inward, to the liver, for example, or the kidneys, or eventually the brain. Homeopaths believe conventional veterinary medicine actually endangers the health of our animals through its many treatments that suppress signs of illness; the classic example is the administration of immunosuppressive corticosteroids that make an itchy, allergic dog stop scratching himself. The corticosteroids don't actually get rid of the allergy, just the dog's response.

What does all this mean for you and your dog? First, that for non-life-threatening, acute illnesses—bumps and bruises and the like—homeopathy offers a safe, effective means of treatment at home. Second, for chronic illnesses, homeopathy can often cure the problem and will not drive it into the body. Third, according to homeopaths, chronic, nagging problems like skin disorders may well be suggestive of deep-seated illness that needs to be addressed.

Homeopathy and "vital force"

Sounds great so far, right? But here's where we start to lose people. Because unlike conventional drugs, homeopathic remedies work at the level of *energy*, not matter. Hahnemann discovered that substances given in unaltered form were often too harsh, so he experimented with diluting and agitating them. He found that the more the substances were diluted and agitated, the more powerful they became.

This apparent paradox goes to the heart of homeopathy. Homeopaths believe each individual has an enlivening, animating force, called the vital force. Illnesses signify a disruption—a "dis-ease"—in this vital force. The theory goes that homeopathy helps the vital force reestablish itself. "It works in the same direction as the vital force and not against it," writes human homeopath George Vithoulkas.

"The goal of homeopathic treatment is to touch disease at its deepest level, that of the vital force, thereby [causing] change in the fundamental health of the sick individual," explains homeopathic veterinarian Don Hamilton in his recent book, *Homeopathic Care for Cats and Dogs: Small Doses for Small Animals*.

Homeopathic remedies are produced by a method of dilution and succussion called potentization. The process begins by taking one part of the material substance—which can be anything from tree bark to snake venom to metal; practically anything on earth—and diluting it in alcohol.

Your dog's first visit

A homeopathic veterinarian will ask unusual questions, and lots of them. Remember, he or she is looking for what makes your dog's condition *unique*. The more information you can provide, the better.

What is your dog's personality? Is he sensitive to noises or changes in the weather? Are his symptoms different at different times of the day or year? Is one side of his body worse than the other? With his physical complaints, what makes them better or worse? Does he seek heat or cold to relieve his pain? Does he feel better when still or when moving around? Does he prefer to be comforted or to be left alone? All of these signs will be taken into account by the practitioner when choosing a remedy.

If your dog has a stomach complaint, you'll need to describe it in detail. Not just that he has diarrhea, but what is the color and consistency? Is it accompanied with gas? If he's been vomiting, when? What does it look like? How much does he drink—a little or a lot? If he gets cut (for instance, when you clip his nails), is there much bleeding? You'll need to describe any skin problems he's had, including tumors, warts, odors, even dandruff. Your veterinarian will also want to know, if your dog has been treated conventionally for this problem, what his symptoms were like *before* that treatment began.

When your veterinarian has finished asking questions, she'll synthesize the information and look in a large set of books (or, possibly, a computer program) called a homeopathic repertory to see which of the hundreds of remedies best fits your dog. The repertory, which is simply an exhaustive listing of symptoms ("rubrics") by category, will name many remedies that may fit the general picture of your dog's illness.

Each of the remedies has its own description. These are found in the homeopathic *Materia Medica* (Latin for "materials of medicine"). This multi-volume work is a listing of all the homeopathic remedies and detailed descriptions of the symptoms they have induced in provings on healthy individuals. This tells the homeopath what symptoms they will cure in a sick one.

Search for the simillimum

All of your dog's symptoms don't have to fit the remedy that's chosen, but most of them should. This is where the veterinary homeopath will attempt to match your dog's symptoms and condition (the "symptom picture") to those of a particular remedy (the "remedy picture"). The remedy that perfectly matches your dog's symptoms is called the simillimum.

Watching your dog heal

Just as disease proceeds along certain paths, so does cure. It has long been observed that homeopathic cures proceed in several predictable ways: first, from the inside out (internal problems heal before external ones do); second, from top to bottom, with the head healing first; and third, from most important to least important organs. Finally, symptoms tend to be cured in the reverse order from which they appeared (newer symptoms go away before older ones do). A corollary is that symptoms that have been suppressed in the past will often reappear during the process of cure.

Don't administer any medicines or undertake any other treatment—even other holistic treatments like herbs or acupuncture—without *first* consulting your homeopathic veterinarian. Since homeopathy works by nudging the vital force in the right direction and then seeing how it responds, it is crucial not to introduce anything that would interfere with the picture.

The healing crisis

Two things may happen during treatment that could throw you off guard. The first is a healing crisis or aggravation—a temporary worsening of symptoms. Healing crises often take place during treatment of chronic conditions, but paradoxically, the animal may actually appear to feel better *generally* even though his symptoms seem worse. If your dog gets worse during the course of treatment, call your veterinarian.

Another possibility is the appearance or reappearance of outer illnesses such as skin problems. A dog with kidney or liver disease may have an outbreak of skin rash as the internal disease heals—especially if the internal disease was created by conventional treatment of a skin problem that pushed the illness inside. This means that Hering's Law of Cure is in motion, and is a very good sign, though it may not seem like it at the time!

What can you treat at home?

In the hands of a skilled practitioner, homeopathy can bring amazing cures of deep-seated illness. But it can also be used by the layperson to treat minor acute problems.

What kinds of ailments can you tackle at home? "You can always treat injuries," says veterinary homeopath and author Richard Pitcairn, DVM. The best candidates for at-home treatment include bite and puncture wounds, insect bites and bee stings, minor burns, and digestive upsets. Homeopathic remedies can also be extremely helpful if your dog has an emergency (shock or collapse, for instance) *if given while you are on your way to seek veterinary help.*

A good rule of thumb, says Don Hamilton, DVM, author of *Homeopathic Care for Cats and Dogs: Small Doses for Small Animals*, is that you can safely treat a problem of "short duration, where the animal is generally relatively bright and alert."

Articles on homeopathy often recommend stocking up on a few major remedies, and suggest one remedy for each ailment. This approach is simple and convenient, but it ignores the reality of how homeopathy works. *Homeopathy treats individuals, not symptoms.* So for an upset stomach caused by food or garbage poisoning, Hamilton's book lists five separate remedies; for bites and stings, he lists seven. He then tells you how to decide which one is right for *your* dog.

A risk-free system?

If you're going to treat your dog at home, you need to understand that this system of healing is very powerful. The common belief that homeopathy is absolutely safe is absolutely untrue, homeopaths warn.

According to Dr. Pitcairn, the highest risk comes when a patient receives a remedy that's very close to the correct one but is still off base—and novices are more likely to miss the mark altogether. "If you have some knowledge and you use medicines that are similar to the case, especially if they're used inappropriately, like repeating them, you can cause serious reactions, even life-threatening ones," Pitcairn says.

More commonly, the home practitioner ends up complicating his dog's condition by treating it unsuccessfully before deciding professional help is required. This muddied-waters predicament is familiar to homeopathic veterinarians and points up the need to restrict your at-home prescribing to the simplest, most straightforward complaints.

Homeopaths speak regretfully of the fact that homeopathic treatment is often a last-ditch, desperate attempt to save an animal who is deathly ill and has already been subjected to virtually every other treatment available. The case is then difficult to sort out—and the animal's vital force has been weakened. Worst, Pitcairn says, are "cases that have been through the hands of what are called eclectic practitioners . . . where they've used homeopathy, acupuncture, herbs, Prednisone, antibiotics, all together in the same animal." Homeopathy can still sometimes help such an animal, but the task is far more difficult and success less likely.

Even when homeopathy cannot cure an animal, it can still help by ameliorating his overall well-being during the time he does have left."

Lay Your Hands on Dogs

Touching your dog has surprising health benefits for both of you.

When touching your dog, whether in a casual caress or in a therapeutic massage session, look for signs that she's comfortable, such as closed or closing eyes and relaxed ears.

Those of us who like dogs can't help but touch them. We are irresistibly drawn to adore them with our hands, to pet them, stroke them, rub their ears, and get lost in the ecstasy of dog beneath our fingertips. Dogs pull not only our hearts but also our hands into a companionship of touch, a relationship we hope is mutually satisfying.

Caressing a dog can be a direct line to nirvana, calming nerves, lifting mood, relieving suffering, a spiritual experience that soothes the soul. Touching a dog feels so good because our body responds with a release of the neurochemicals of pleasure that have positive physiological effects as well.

During the past couple of decades, science has proven what we canine lovers have always known: petting a dog is good for you. Studies have shown it lowers blood pressure, decreases cholesterol levels, and reduces the risk of heart disease. Alzheimer's and AIDS patients, autistic children, and nursing home residents often improve when they have contact with a dog. Pain, grief, stress, depression—the list of studied situations in which petting a dog has proven beneficial to humans is lengthy.

One study found that as a result of touch, a dog's coronary artery blood flow increased to the same level as during intense exercise. The heart rate of dogs increased when a person joined them in a room, but would drop dramatically within one or two seconds of being stroked.

In another study, whenever dogs were exposed to a stressful stimulus such as pain or fear, their heart rate and blood pressure decreased significantly if they were petted.

Other animal studies have indicated that touching also increases immune response, slows changes associated with aging, reduces harmful cholesterol levels, enhances development of the brain and nervous system, and promotes physical development.

Touch and caress your dog every day. It can help maintain your emotional connection—and even lower your blood pressure.

Explore the use of massage, acupressure, and TTouch to help your dog relax, increase his immunity and circulation, and improve his mobility.

Watch for and respect signs that your dog does not enjoy touch, or certain types of petting.

Neurotransmitters associated with positive touch also affect behavior and emotion. Observed animals who were routinely touched were found to be more resistant to stress. In addition, their separation anxiety was diminished, they displayed less fear, and their learning capabilities were enhanced.

Types of touch

The *way* in which we touch our dogs is important.

Grooming or even just running our hands over our dogs' bodies to scan for physical problems can qualify as beneficial touch.

Massage is another purposeful touch. Besides feeling good to dogs, says Maryjean Ballner, author of *Dog Massage: A Whiskers to Tail Guide to Your Dog's Ultimate Petting Experience*, "Massage increases blood flow at the massage area, speeds arrival of fresh nutrients, expedites removal of waste products, and loosens tight muscles.

"With practice, anyone can use massage to relax or reassure a dog. In a quiet, comfortable place, lead into massage with soft petting. Let your dog guide the technique. Feedback that you're giving a good massage may include "power" tail wagging, doggie grins, drooling, leaning or sprawling against you, and flopping belly up. Massage can elicit a "glorious, incredible response," says Ballner.

Communicate through touch

The use of touch can be effective in training, too. "When I train my dogs, I use touch to guide them into position," says Kathy Diamond Davis, who trains therapy dogs.

Touch can also be the means for expressing complex emotion.

"Touch is one of the most critical ways of connecting with all other living beings," says Dr. Allen

Hands Off!

"Rough or unpleasant contact is a source of stress and is potentially harmful to animal health and well-being," says Franklin D. McMillan, DVM.

Studies show that various animals exposed to rough handling and harsh noise have many types of health problems and are more prone to chronic illness, stress disorders, behavioral issues, and even early death.

If rough handling, or physical abuse, repeatedly occur during the critical period of socialization (prior to 16 weeks of age), the dog may develop a permanent aversion to touch. However, with gradual, positive reconditioning most dogs will eventually learn to love being petted.

"There's probably a history of abuse, neglect, or lack of socialization as a puppy when a dog doesn't like to be touched," says Allen M. Schoen. "For example, when a Greyhound is adopted from a track, they have no idea what love is, but watch how they adapt. They bond like Velcro when they start getting touched."

Signs that a dog may not want to be touched

- *Dog demonstrates stress-related body language: tenses/freezes at touch, attempts to move away from touch, pupils dilate, increased respiration (panting), increased heart rate.*
- *Dog demonstrates appeasing/avoidance body language: avoids eye contact, licks, yawns, ducks head, flattens ears, lowers body toward ground, rolls on back, urinates.*
- *Dog demonstrates agonistic/confrontational body language—piloerection (hackles raised), hard stare, gives "whale eye," lunges, growls, snaps, bites.*

If a dog who has always liked being touched suddenly displays any of these signs, a veterinary examination is warranted as this may indicate an injury or illness that is causing pain.

M. Schoen, DVM, author of *A Kindred Spirit: How the Remarkable Bond Between Humans and Animals Can Change the Way We Live*. "Touch is a powerful connection that can have a negative or positive impact. It's our responsibility to relate to our dogs from the most positive perspective possible."

Ballner writes that touch transcends every other way of communicating with our animals. Touch is not egocentric, but altruistic. When we pet our dogs, it should be from a place of integrity and with the message of unconditional love.

How to Select a Canine Massage Provider

Once you've decided to incorporate massage into your dog's health care program, how do you go about finding a qualified canine massage provider? Many people assume that canine massage providers are licensed and certified just like human massage therapists, but this is not yet the case. There is no organization or board that certifies or licenses canine massage providers. Someone can call herself "certified" when she has just taken a weekend course in canine massage and received a certificate for it. Or she may have taken a correspondence course but not received any hands-on training.

Many people call themselves "canine massage therapists." The correct legal term is "canine massage provider." In most states, a person cannot call himself a "therapist" or "practitioner" or say he does "therapy" on animals unless he is a veterinarian. Otherwise, he can be charged with practicing veterinary medicine without a license.

A professional canine massage provider should have a sound education in canine health topics such as anatomy, physiology, orthopedic pathology, structure and movement, first aid, breed characteristics, behavior, and nutrition, and can help you look at and discuss the "big picture" of your dog's health. With this background, he can also work well with vets and other animal health professionals, and discuss your dog's health issues with your veterinarian. He should have new clients fill out a comprehensive health intake form about their dogs, and maintain written records of each session detailing his work.

Massage is not a "cure-all" for all conditions, and it is contraindicated in some situations. For example, dogs with kidney or liver problems may have difficulty processing the toxins released by massage. Massage on an injured tendon could prolong the injury by spreading apart the healing fibers that are trying to pull together. A competent, educated professional will not hurt your dog through ignorance of this critical information.

Some providers offer additional holistic modalities that can enhance massage. Reiki energy balancing increases the effectiveness of massage and helps the dog relax. It can also be done in place of massage if a dog has a condition that may be worsened by massage, or is too scared to be massaged. Flower remedies can help address a dog's emotional issues and enhance the effectiveness of energy balancing techniques.

Trust your dog

Most importantly, observe closely to see how your dog responds to the massage session. Can you plainly see that she enjoys it? If she looks uncomfortable or resistant, stop the session and discuss this with the provider. Massage should not hurt.

Do you feel comfortable with how the massage provider handles your dog? He should recognize and be sensitive to even subtle signals of your dog's discomfort, and adjust his technique if she responds poorly.

Do you see improvement in her well-being after several sessions? She may experience a temporary increase in soreness immediately after a session, but in the long run, she should exhibit improved mobility and reduced pain.

Walking in Water

Underwater treadmills are the latest rehabilitation tool for injured dogs.

Hydrotherapy and aquatic exercise are the hottest new tools in canine physical rehabilitation. And that's not just a jump in a lake. Today's cutting-edge therapists work with veterinarians' referrals and use sophisticated underwater treadmills and other specialized equipment to provide rehabilitation for a variety of medical conditions. And they are frequently able to achieve better results in less time than through the recovery regimens prescribed by more conventional veterinary practitioners.

The *latest* therapy tool also uses a warm pool, but adds an underwater treadmill. The therapist can effectively reduce the amount of body weight the dog must carry as he walks on the treadmill simply by increasing the depth of the water. As the dog progresses, the water height can be reduced to create more load on his limbs.

For example, in an underwater treadmill apparatus with the water level at shoulder height, the dog's rear paws support less than a third of his weight, compared to the usual two-thirds on land. As he gains strength, he'll work in a shallower pool, against a current, or with the treadmill tilted at varying degrees of incline.

Part of the plan

The underwater treadmill should be used as part of an overall treatment plan rather than its sole focus. For example, a typical surgical rehabilitation schedule at one rehab facility we've visited would begin one to two weeks post-operatively and include passive range-of-motion exercises to be performed by the owner three times a day, daily walking from 5 to 10 minutes at a time, and crating to limit movement. A month to six weeks later, the dog would begin two to three ses-

This young Golden's injury prevents her from putting weight on all four legs, but with her weight partially supported by water, she is able to use her weak leg in a full stride. This work will strengthen her muscles and associated soft tissues.

sions a week at the clinic, where he'd undergo hands-on tissue work, hydrotherapy, and movement therapy, while continuing at-home work with the owner.

These rehabilitation centers are also a perfect location for complementary practitioners to offer adjunct services. A client may receive acupuncture from a veterinarian, or massage and myofascial release work from credentialed providers.

Using several therapeutic techniques, such as soft-tissue massage, joint mobilization, and acupuncture, often results in a better outcome than using just one.

Those best qualified to work with dogs on the underwater treadmill include physical therapists who have expanded their practices to include dogs, and veterinarians or veterinary technicians who have formal training in animal rehabilitation.

Currently, there's no such title as an "animal physical therapist," although some specialized training programs exist. The term "physical therapist" (PT) is reserved for professionals who work with humans.

While some dogs respond very well, hydrotherapy shouldn't be viewed as the magic bullet, Patterson warns. As evidence, her center has only one underwater treadmill but is chock full of other therapeutic equipment, including balance boards, oversized exercise balls, and even a mini-trampoline.

Still, underwater treadmill work is a promising therapy that could become a new standard of care. And while results so far are strictly anecdotal—no rigorous studies of outcomes have been done—word of mouth has been encouraging. John Sherman, DVM, a veterinarian affiliated with North Carolina State's School of Veterinary Medicine, believes the treadmills will be available in every major metropolitan area someday. "This is an up-and-coming veterinary specialty," he says.

CHAPTER 8

Cancer

Canine Cancer Crisis
Know thine enemy—so you can take fast action if it strikes your dog.

Cancer has to be the most feared diagnosis in all of medicine, one that sends patients and their families on a bewildering journey through statistics, treatment options, and life-or-death decisions that have to be made right now. Cancer has become so widespread that the care and treatment of its human patients is one of the world's largest industries. Now cancer affects a significant percentage of veterinary patients as well.

Most medical dictionaries define cancer as a disease resulting from an abnormal and uncontrolled division of cells that invade and destroy surrounding tissue. In most cases, this cell division creates malignant growths called tumors. Cancer cells often migrate via the blood or lymph, resulting in the development of additional tumors throughout the body.

Oseosarcoma (bone cancer) most frequently occurs in canine leg bones. Amputation of the affected limb can eliminate the pain of bone cancer, but radiation and/or chemotherapy are usually needed to prolong the dog's life.

Cancer has no known cause, but its risk factors include genetics, diet, hormone imbalances, exposure to radiation, viruses, vaccinations, and environmental toxins such as lawn chemicals, flea and tick dips, asbestos, and tobacco smoke.

In the 1960s, about 4 out of every 1,000 dogs were diagnosed with cancer in the United States each year. At that time, the most common canine cancers involved the breast in females, the testes in males, and connective tissue, skin, lymph nodes, mouth, throat, and bones in both genders.

In 1997, a Morris Animal Foundation survey found that cancer was the leading cause of non-accidental death in America's dogs. Today nearly half of dogs over age 10 die of cancer.

The similarities between canine and human cancers are striking, but there are differences. For example, dogs have 35 times as much skin cancer as humans, 4 times as many breast tumors, 8 times as much bone cancer, and twice the incidence of leukemia. Humans have 7 times as much lung cancer as dogs and 13 times as much cancer of the stomach and intestines.

Cancer's symptoms

The early warning signs of cancer in dogs are similar to human warning signs publicized by the American Cancer Society. These include any abnormal swelling (especially a swelling that continues to grow), sores that don't heal, weight loss, bleeding or discharge from any body opening, a reluctance to move or exercise, a loss of stamina, or difficulty breathing, urinating, or defecating.

Any sort of lameness in an older dog, especially large breeds, should be investigated as a potential cancer case. Even minor or subtle symptoms, such as sleeping more than usual, refusing to play, or having less interest in social interaction, can be warning signs.

Types of cancers

There isn't room to describe every cancer that affects dogs, but the following alphabetical list describes some common diagnoses. Becoming familiar with the descriptions below will help you make sense of these and other canine cancers.

Bladder cancer

Bladder and ureteral cancers are most common in older dogs. While some studies have shown a higher risk in females and other studies found no gender differences, there may be a higher risk in neutered dogs of both sexes.

Bladder tumors have been associated with the use of flea and tick dips, flea and tick shampoos, or exposure to aromatic hydrocarbons such as paraaminobiphenyl, paranitroliphenyl, and betanapthylamine. The authors of one study suggest that it is not the active ingredients in flea and tick products that cause bladder cancer but rather "inert" or "carrier" ingredients such as benzene, toluene, xylene, and petroleum distillates, all of which are known carcinogens and which often make up 95 percent of the total product. They are used as solvents for the active ingredients.

A Purdue University study published in 2004 found that Scottish Terriers exposed to lawn chemicals have an increased incidence of bladder cancer. Scottish Terriers were chosen for the study because they develop bladder cancer 20 times more often than other breeds, but dogs of any breed can develop the disease.

Other bladder cancer risk factors include obesity and living in a marshy area.

Hemangiosarcoma

Originating in the endothelium (the lining of the spleen and blood vessels), hemangiosarcoma forms highly malignant tumors that develop throughout the body, especially in the spleen, liver, and heart.

German Shepherd Dogs, Golden Retrievers, Boxers, and English Setters are at higher than average risk, and the disease is most common in middle-aged or older dogs of medium to large size. In many cases, symptoms are noticed only after the disease has progressed to an advanced stage.

Initial symptoms include bleeding (especially nosebleeds), weakness, pale mucous membranes in the mouth and eyes, panting, and abdominal swelling. Death often occurs quickly, within one to four months of diagnosis. Many dogs with this disease die suddenly without manifesting clinical symptoms.

Spayed females are four times more likely to develop vascular tumors (cardiac hemangiosarcomas) than intact females; neutered males are also at higher risk of hemangiosarcoma than intact males.

Histiocytosis

The most common cancer found in Bernese Mountain Dogs, histiocytosis is rare in other breeds, although it can occur in Rottweilers, Golden Retrievers, and Flat-Coated Retrievers. Its symptoms include depression, fatigue, lethargy, loss of appetite, and weight loss. Malignant histiocytosis progresses rapidly and has usually metastasized by the time symptoms develop. Most patients die within two to four months of diagnosis.

Systemic histiocytosis creates skin abnormalities on the face and legs.

Most patients are middle-aged or older. Histiocytosis that spreads to the lungs can interfere with breathing, and anemia is another common symptom.

Histiocytomas are benign tumors that usually appear on the heads of dogs under three years of age. They are not considered a health risk.

Leukemia

Leukemia, or chronic lymphocytic leukemia (CLL), usually affects older dogs and involves the rapid reproduction of mature lymphocytes throughout the body, including the bone marrow. Because elevated circulating lymphocyte counts are easily identified in complete blood panel tests, CLL is often discovered when the blood is tested for other reasons.

Chronic lymphocytic leukemia tends to progress slowly and is often not treated until the circulating lymphocyte count increases to very high levels or the dog becomes lethargic, CLL's main symptom.

The condition can progress to a lymphoblastic crisis, also called lymphoblastic leukemia, which is a more aggressive form of the disease, comparable to advanced stage lymphosarcoma. With conventional treatment, most dogs with lymphoblastic leukemia survive for about a year.

Lung cancer

While unusual in dogs, lung cancer does occur, and the number of cases diagnosed each year appears to be increasing. However, this may be the result of improved diagnostic techniques rather than an increasing number of cases.

According to some research, short-nosed breeds exposed to secondhand smoke have twice as much risk of lung cancer as long-nosed breeds. (Conversely, long-nosed breeds living with smokers have an increased risk of *nasal* cancer.) Exposure to asbestos can increase the risk of cancer of the lining of the lungs (mesothelioma), and dogs with this type of cancer are likely to live with owners whose work or hobbies expose them to asbestos.

Lymphosarcoma (lymphoma)

The third most common cancer in dogs, lympho-sarcoma (also known as lymphoma) affects lymphocytes (a type of white blood cell) and tissue of the lymph nodes, spleen, liver, gastrointestinal tract, and bone marrow.

Although lymphosarcoma strikes dogs of all ages, most patients are over age five, with males and females at equal risk. Boxers, German Shepherd Dogs, Doberman Pinschers, Golden Retrievers, Scotties, West Highland White Terriers, and Pointers may be most vulnerable to this disease.

There are five classifications of lymphosarcoma, depending on the tumor's primary location.

The most common type involves external lymph nodes. It is also the most likely to be overlooked because many dogs have only mild symptoms such as fatigue or decreased appetite. More obvious symptoms include weight loss, vomiting, diarrhea, excessive thirst or urination, weakness, or difficulty breathing. In some cases, the only signs are enlarged lymph nodes under the neck, behind the knees, or in front of the shoulders.

The other classifications are gastrointestinal (symptoms include vomiting, diarrhea, weight loss, and loss of appetite), mediastinal (affecting the chest, creating breathing problems and excessive thirst and urination), cutaneous (affecting the skin, which can be dry, flaky, scaly, irritated, and itchy), and bone marrow (producing anemia, infections, and bleeding).

Because lymphosarcoma spreads quickly, its diagnosis involves biopsies, aspiration of affected tissue, blood tests, urinalysis, and a search for tumors throughout the body using X-rays, sonograms, or other methods.

Mammary cancer

The most common cancer in female dogs is breast or mammary cancer. According to some studies, mammary tumors are more common in purebred dogs than in mixed-breed dogs of the same age, and they are far more common in dogs that are intact or were not spayed until after age two and a half years. Spaying offers maximum protection to dogs spayed before their first heat cycle and almost as much protection to those spayed before their second season. Obesity is a risk factor for mammary cancer, and the breasts most likely to be affected are those farthest from the head.

Approximately half of dogs with mammary gland tumors have more than one. These tumors tend to develop between the ages of 6 and 10 years.

Mammary tumors vary by size, texture, and condition. They may contain fluid or be ulcerated or inflamed. None of these symptoms reveals whether a tumor is malignant, and in dogs that have not been spayed, about half the tumors tested are benign.

Lymph node involvement increases the risk of cancer spreading to the lungs or other organs.

Survival rates are higher for dogs with small rather than large tumors and for dogs whose tumors have not metastasized.

Osteosarcoma

Highly aggressive and fast growing, osteosarcoma affects more than 8,000 American dogs every year and causes an estimated 85 percent of all canine bone tumors.

The illness has been diagnosed in six-month-old puppies, but it is most common in older Great Danes, Golden Retrievers, German Shepherd Dogs, Great Pyrenees, Saint Bernards, Newfoundlands, Bernese Mountain Dogs, Irish Wolfhounds, Rottweilers, Labrador Retrievers, Doberman Pinschers, Weimaraners, Boxers, and other large-breed dogs. It is almost 500

> Become familiar with canine cancers and their symptoms.
>
> Document changes in your dog's appearance and behavior.
>
> Check for lumps and other symptoms while petting or massaging your dog.
>
> Report unusual symptoms to your veterinarian.

times more likely to affect dogs weighing over 80 pounds than those weighing less than 23 pounds, and males are at greater risk than females.

Any stress on weight-bearing legs is a risk factor, including previous fractures and infections. Bone tumors are most likely to affect the legs but can also occur in the skull, ribs, vertebrae, or pelvis.

Osteosarcoma is twice as common in spayed females and neutered males as in their intact counterparts.

After producing tumors that weaken bones, osteosarcoma spreads throughout the body. Its main symptoms—lameness, intermittent pain, leg swelling, and fractures at the tumor site—may be mistaken for arthritis or other chronic conditions until the disease is advanced. As pain increases, behavioral symptoms such as irritability, aggression, and a reluctance to exercise become more obvious.

Without treatment, most dogs with osteosarcoma die within two months of diagnosis, and only 20 percent survive for two years. Limb amputation is commonly performed to provide pain relief, but it does not usually cure the disease or prevent its metastasis. The most common cause of death is the spread of cancer to the lungs.

Prostate cancer

In humans, prostate cancer is a common but slow-growing cancer that affects older men. In dogs (the only other species to have significant amounts of prostate cancer) the disease is fast-growing, aggressive, and likely to spread to lymph nodes, lungs, and bones. In one study, one out of every 150 male dogs age eight and older was found to have prostate cancer. In most cases, prostate cancer is diagnosed in its advanced stages.

Skin cancer

The skin is the most prevalent tumor location in dogs, comprising an estimated 58 percent of all canine cancers. Most skin cancer tumors contain mast cells, squamous cells, or melanin-pigmented cells. These tumors are usually soft or solid raised, nodular masses. If malignant (many are benign), treatment depends on their stage or grade.

Mast cell tumors, also called mastocytomas or mast cell sarcomas, are the most frequently diagnosed cancers in dogs. They are most common in middle-aged Boxers, Pugs, Rhodesian Ridgebacks, Boston Terriers, Schnauzers, Beagles, Labrador Retrievers, Dachshunds, Fox Terriers, English Bulldogs, Staffordshire Terriers, and mixed-breed dogs.

Squamous cell carcinomas are common in lightly pigmented dogs such as Beagles, Dalmatians, Whippets, and white English Bull Terriers. Nail bed squamous cell carcinomas tend to occur in black-coated large-breed dogs.

Melanomas are usually solitary black tumors. Melanomas of the mouth and nail bed are usually malignant.

Testicular cancer

Human males tend to develop only one type of testicular cancer (seminomas) while intact dogs can develop any of three different types (Sertoli cell tumors, seminomas, and interstitial cell tumors).

A Dictionary of Cancer

Aspirate: When used as a verb (and pronounced "as-per-ate"), it means to remove cells from a tumor with a syringe and needle. When used as a noun (and pronounced "as-per-it"), it refers to the cells removed in this manner.

Benign: The best news. A benign tumor does not invade and destroy tissue where it originates, and it does not spread to distant sites in the body. The term applies to any disorder or condition that does not produce harmful effects.

Biopsy: The surgical removal of tissue and its examination under a microscope.

Carcinoma: Any cancer that develops in the tissue lining external and internal organs of the body (epithelium). Carcinomas can occur in any tissue that contains epithelial cells. Related term: carcinomatous.

Cytology: The examination of cells collected by aspirating a tumor.

Fibrosarcoma: A malignant tumor of connective tissue. Fibrosarcomas, which can develop in soft tissue or bone, may affect any organ but are most common in the legs. This type of tumor is also called a malignant fibrous histiocytoma.

Grading: Low-grade tumors spread slowly, if at all; intermediate tumors spread at a moderate rate; and high-grade tumors are the most aggressive, fast-spreading, and difficult to treat.

Lymphocytes: White blood cells that occur in the lymph nodes, spleen, thymus gland, intestinal wall, and bone marrow.

Malignant: Life-threatening, producing harmful tumors whose cells invade and destroy tissue where they originate and spread to other sites in the body. Left untreated, malignant tumors cause progressive deterioration and death.

Mast cells: Large cells in respiratory and connective tissue that contain substances released when allergic reactions occur.

Metastasis: The spread of a tumor from its site of origin to distant parts of the body. Metastasize, this term's verb form, describes the spread.

Neoplasia: Literally "new growth," this term applies to any growing tumor, malignant or benign.

Prognosis: Expected outcome, prediction of an illness's progression.

Protocol: The treatment plan for a disease or condition, including surgery, radiation, chemotherapy, or other treatments.

Sepsis: An overwhelming systemic infection resulting from the inability of bone marrow to produce normal blood cells. It is often the cause of death in cancer patients.

Squamous cells: Cells that make up most of the skin's outer layer.

Staging: The evaluation of a tumor's magnitude and growth rate.

Canine risk factors include undescended testicles, which remain in the body cavity instead of migrating to the scrotum, as well as inguinal hernias. Neutering prevents the development of testicular cancer. Breeds associated with testicular tumors include Samoyeds, Cocker Spaniels, Beagles, and English Bulldogs.

Links between cancer and environmental toxins have long been suspected, and during the Vietnam War, working dogs exposed to parasitic infections, chemicals used to treat those infections, and agricultural chemicals such as herbicides developed increased levels of testicular cancer.

Conventional Cancer Care

Many well-known and new treatments are helping canine cancer patients.

Your nagging feeling was right—there really is something wrong with your dog. And it's not just a pulled muscle or a torn toenail. It's cancer.

As you struggle to wrap your mind around that diagnosis, the veterinarian describes your options: surgery, radiation, or chemotherapy, alone or in combination. Or your dog might be eligible to participate in a clinical trial testing a new drug, or you may want to consult an oncology specialist or consider a promising new state-of-the-art treatment. There are no guarantees that any of these treatments will work, and if the prognosis is especially grim, you may want to say goodbye now. Please decide within 24 hours. This is a medical emergency.

No wonder a Morris Animal Foundation survey found that the number one fear of American pet owners is cancer.

You struggle to comprehend median survival times, treatment plans, treatment side effects, quality of life issues, and the demands that different protocols will make on your schedule—not to mention your checkbook.

Meanwhile, your faithful companion stares at you with trusting eyes.

"A cancer diagnosis is an incredibly emotional experience," says Gerald Post, DVM, ACVIM, who has specialized in pet cancer care for 15 years. "There's so much to consider, and there is a huge element of uncertainty. Even when you use the most accurate statistics for a particular group of animals with a particular type of cancer that is treated in a specific way, there is no way to know how your particular dog, who's in the treatment room right now, will respond. When it comes to dogs and cancer, there are still many unknowns."

So how can one make informed decisions?

"You have to consider all the factors," he says.

"At our clinic, we start with the diagnosis and then discuss what the cancer's biological behavior is, what tests are needed, and what can be done. To answer this last question, we look at conventional therapies that are already widely used and experimental therapies that are ongoing. We include what our experience has taught us about probable outcomes, what the owners want, and how the dog is feeling. All of this information helps narrow the choices so that the owner can consider the most promising options."

Survival rates

When it comes to cancer, some types are better than others—"better" meaning that they have a higher survival rate and are easier to treat than other cancers.

"The ideal patient in any oncology practice is one that doesn't have cancer," says Dr. Post. "That's the best situation of all. But among cancer patients, I'd be happy if all of mine were otherwise healthy middle-aged dogs, each with a small (less than 3-centimeter) mast cell tumor on his or her body. These dogs can handle surgery very well, and they are likely to make a full and complete recovery."

At the opposite end of the spectrum are patients with worst-prognosis cancers. "Whenever a young dog comes in with acute leukemia, or a middle-aged Golden Retriever has just been diagnosed with a ruptured splenic hemangiosarcoma, you can't help but feel heartsick. These are difficult, difficult cases."

Dr. Post says that osteosarcoma used to be in that category, "but we're making progress there. It's still a horrible disease, and sometimes we do have to amputate a leg, but with chemotherapy, we can increase survival time to a year or sometimes longer. A year is a fairly long time in veterinary oncology, and those 12 months are very precious to the dog's human family."

In human medicine, cancer patients are considered cured if they go for five years without the disease recurring. While veterinary medicine doesn't formally define the term, Dr. Post considers any dog who goes for more than two years without a malignancy to be cured.

Conventional treatments

Surgery

Surgery remains the most widely used and most effective treatment for cancers that cause solid tumors. It can be used by itself to remove a tumor, or it can be used in combination with chemotherapy, radiation therapy, or other treatments to enhance their effectiveness.

In many cases, tumors are removed along with a margin of tissue surrounding the tumor. Radical surgery, such as amputation, has a longer recovery time and more potential complications than minor surgery. However, improvements in anesthesia and innovations such as laser surgery, in which a laser beam replaces scalpels for maximum precision, are making all surgeries safer and more effective.

Radiation

Radiation therapy damages and then kills rapidly dividing cancer cells. In veterinary oncology, high-energy units similar to X-ray machines deliver radiation as a primary therapy or to clear surgical margins of cancer cells.

Radiation is usually recommended in the treatment of mast cell tumors, soft-tissue sarcomas, squamous cell carcinomas, oral melanomas, brain tumors, nasal tumors, and tumors that have not spread to other parts of the body.

Radiation is delivered in small doses and given several times, often daily, over a period lasting three to four weeks. Small doses decrease this therapy's most common side effect, which is damage to normal tissue. According to oncologists, this damage, which can be uncomfortable for the patient, is not usually life-threatening and usually disappears after the conclusion of treatment.

A few veterinary clinics implant radioactive beads in difficult-to-treat tumors in a radiation treatment called brachytherapy. Another new technique is tomotherapy, which rotates the beam source around the patient, targeting the tumor from different angles. And some clinics replace radiation with photodynamic or drug-laser therapy, in which an injected drug is activated by laser light.

Chemotherapy

Chemotherapy is the use of drugs that damage and kill cancer cells when administered intravenously or orally in frequent doses alone or in combination with surgery and/or radiation therapy. Chemotherapy is usually recommended for cancers that have spread or metastasized to other parts of the body and for tumors that cannot be surgically removed.

When Comet, a seven-year-old Golden Retriever, was diagnosed with lymphoma, his treatments (which included a splenectomy and chemotherapy) made him so ill that his vets stopped treatment. An experimental bone-marrow stem-cell donation from a related dog stopped the cancer in its tracks, and 18 months later, he's still fine.

Chemotherapy drugs have different mechanisms, such as damaging a cell's DNA (genetic material) or interfering with cell growth and division. Their side effects vary, though most experts say that dogs have fewer adverse reactions to these drugs than human patients do.

Nausea, vomiting, and diarrhea are the most common reactions, but in dogs, they tend to be of shorter duration and of a milder nature than the side effects experienced by humans taking chemotherapy. Some chemotherapy drugs can cause kidney damage or bone marrow suppression. Bone marrow produces red and white blood cells. Low white blood levels can make the dog more susceptible to infection. Anemia, a low red blood cell count, is less common in dogs undergoing chemotherapy.

Chemotherapy seldom causes hair loss in dogs, but some breeds (Poodles, terriers, Bearded Collies, Old English Sheepdogs, and others) seem to be more prone to this side effect. If experienced, canine hair loss is most apparent on the face and tail, especially in terriers and Poodles.

For some canine patients, chemotherapy is an ongoing, permanent protocol; they receive it for as long as they live. For others, treatments are eventually discontinued for as long as the cancer stays in remission.

The problem with cancer is that no matter which of these treatment plans you adopt, it can—and usually does—come back. Worse, when it returns, it usually spreads or metastasizes, moving from the original site to other parts of the body.

Surgery, radiation, and chemotherapy are not only used to treat cancer in hopes of achieving a cure, but also used alone or in combination to relieve pain or discomfort, slow tumor growth, or otherwise improve the patient's quality of life. Palliative treatments are those that reduce the symptoms of a disease without addressing the disease itself. In humans as well as canines, surgery, radiation, and chemotherapy are often palliative rather than curative.

New treatments

Experimental, high-tech therapies touted as breakthroughs in human cancer care are being adapted for use with dogs. One is the stem-cell transplant.

In January 2004, Seattle residents Darrell and Nina Hallett learned that their Golden Retriever, Comet, had lymphoma. They took him to Bellingham Veterinary & Critical Care in Bellingham, Washington, where his spleen was removed and he was put on chemotherapy. Comet did not respond well and within a few weeks was so ill that his treatments were stopped.

Comet's veterinarians, Edmund Sullivan, DVM, and Theresa Westfall, DVM, conferred with scientists at the Fred Hutchinson Cancer Research Center in Seattle. Dr. Sullivan and Dr. Westfall were aware that hundreds of experimental bone-marrow and stem-cell transplants had been conducted on dogs at the Fred Hutchinson Center as researchers perfected techniques now used in human cancer treatment.

In addition, there were reports of the treatments being used with great success outside the center. Several years ago, a stem-cell transplant was successfully performed at the University of Massachusetts on a dog with lymphoma; in the 1980s, a Virginia veterinarian did bone-marrow transplants (which include stem cells) on a dozen dogs, three of whom survived for at least three years.

With help from Comet's breeder, 40 of his relatives in five U.S. states and four countries were tested, and three were found to be perfect matches. The largest, a dog in Florida, was chosen because larger dogs yield more stem cells.

The June 2004 transplant was conducted at the Hutchinson Center, where a special machine separated stem cells from the donor's blood. Comet was given total body radiation to suppress his immune system and encourage acceptance of the donor stem cells. His donor's stem cells were then delivered intravenously.

Dr. Sullivan brought Comet from the center to his

Bellingham clinic for two weeks of protective isolation, and his owners had a glass window installed so Comet could see the rest of the clinic. Two weeks after that, the stem cells began to reject their host, causing sores on Comet's muzzle. After an anti-rejection drug cleared that condition, Comet had no further problems.

Today, two years after Comet's initial diagnosis and 18 months after his stem-cell transplant, he is thriving. Dr. Sullivan looks forward to performing stem-cell transplants as appropriate patients and donors appear.

Navy is still alive, well, and cancer-free today, five and a half years after her experimental cancer treatment. (Photo courtesy of Dr. Marion Haber)

Another Golden Retriever, an 18-month-old female pup named Navy, made medical history when her owner, Marion Haber, treated Navy's cancer with anti-angiogenic therapy, a medical strategy that is still new to humans. Haber had worked as a research fellow at the Angiogenesis Foundation, a nonprofit organization in Massachusetts that promotes research on angiogenesis and its control.

"Angiogenesis" is the growth of new blood vessels that tumors (and other tissues) create to supply the oxygen and nutrients that will allow them to grow and spread. Anti-angiogenic therapy starves tumors and prevents their growth by cutting off this blood supply with drugs.

The study of angiogenesis has produced a new diagnostic tool as well, for if a blood test reveals elevated angiogenic growth factors, the cause is likely to be a tumor.

In September 2000, Haber, then a student at the Tufts University School of Veterinary Medicine in Boston (she is now a veterinarian), discovered a tumor in Navy's chest while practicing examinations on the dog. A surgeon removed the tumor, extra tissue, and five ribs, which were replaced with three prosthetics.

A few weeks later, a tumor appeared on Navy's leg. Knowing her pup's situation was desperate, Haber rejected amputation and radiation therapy and turned instead to angiogenesis.

Navy's treatment, now known as the "Navy protocol," combined three drugs already approved by the U.S. Food and Drug Administration—Celebrex, tamoxifen (sold as Nolvadex), and doxycycline—with a goal of inhibiting blood vessel cell proliferation and invasion. Navy received her first multi-targeted drug cocktail on Christmas Day 2000. By early March 2001, her veterinary oncologist could find no trace of cancer, and Navy experienced no adverse side effects. As angiogenesis pioneer Judah Folkman told reporters at the time, "That's a remarkable achievement."

While Navy's recovery was dramatic, it may not have been representative. When anti-angiogenic drug trials for human cancer patients were conducted in the 1990s, everyone wanted the new "miracle drugs," and their popularity (in clinical trials at least) soared. News reports inflated the public's expectations, leading to disappointment. Instead of being touted as a cure, anti-angiogenic drugs are now described as a treatment option that helps stabilize cancer as a chronic manageable disease.

According to the Angiogenesis Foundation, anti-angiogenic drugs show promise in the treatment of canine brain, lung, mammary gland, mast cell, oral, bone, prostate, soft tissue, and lymph system cancers. The foundation works with veterinarians and zoo managers to treat dogs and other animals. Anti-angiogenic drugs are used alone or in combination with conventional chemotherapy or radiation therapy. While other dogs have received the Navy protocol, Navy remains its most dramatic success story.

Clinical trials

Just as human cancer patients participate in clinical trials that test new protocols, so do dogs with cancer.

Dr. Post is chairman and founder of the Animal Cancer Foundation, a resource for veterinary oncologists. "I'm encouraged by the continuing progress being made in conventional therapies," he says, "but I'm always on the lookout for novel therapies that are being developed by biotechnology firms. If you're a mouse or a rat and you get cancer, we can cure you, but if you're a person, it's a different story. The model in which tumors are induced in laboratory rats and mice just doesn't apply to human health.

"Dogs and people develop cancer spontaneously, they share the same environmental risk factors, and they are more closely related to each other than to rats and mice. It makes sense to use their tumors to test novel therapies that can help our animals and at the same time reveal something about how experimental therapies are likely to work in people."

According to the National Cancer Institute's Center for Cancer Research (CCR) Comparative Oncology Program (COP), another organization that promotes clinical trials that test experimental therapies in dogs with cancer, the types of canine cancer that could produce results for humans include osteosarcoma, breast and prostate cancer, melanoma, non-Hodgkin's lymphoma, head and neck carcinoma, and soft-tissue sarcoma.

Clinical trials recruit and enroll carefully defined patients, such as "dogs with suspected or confirmed transitional cell carcinoma of the bladder with measurable disease" or "dogs with suspected or confirmed appendicular osteosarcoma with no prior treatment with radiation therapy, systemic chemotherapy, or bisphosphonates, no complicating disease(s) that would limit survival, no pathologic fracture of affected limb or advanced metastatic disease, and informed client consent."

The trials are usually paid for by pharmaceutical companies or other sponsors and conducted at veterinary teaching hospitals or research centers.

Cancer's high cost

Any illness can be expensive, but cancer has to be the most costly disease that affects our dogs. Some owners have maxed out their credit cards, borrowed from friends and family, and taken second mortgages just to pay the vet bills.

> Become familiar with cancers that tend to occur in your dog's breed and immediate family.
>
> Consider ahead of time what you might do if your dog is diagnosed with cancer.
>
> Look into pet health insurance, or put money aside for your dog's medical care.

According to the American Veterinary Medical Association, Americans spent $7 billion on veterinary care in 1991 and an estimated $19 billion in 2001. Increasingly sophisticated equipment is one reason for the increasing cost. Some veterinary clinics have their own linear accelerators, which reduce radiation therapy side effects by pinpointing tumor sites precisely, along with spiral computed tomography (CT) scanners for diagnostic imaging, magnetic resonance imaging (MRI) devices, and other technologies formerly available only to human patients.

Canine cancer treatments range from a few hundred dollars for the simplest procedures to $20,000 or more for cases that involve long-term therapy and multiple protocols. In most clinics, chemotherapy costs, which vary according to the patient's size, range from $500 and up for palliative care to more than $5,000 for three to six months of treatment.

Because most clinical trials are funded by their sponsors, the owners of participating dogs are charged only a minimal fee, such as an initial evaluation. But not everyone is eligible or wants to participate in a fully funded clinical trial, and that leaves most owners who choose to pursue conventional care facing painful financial decisions.

Comet's stem-cell transplant cost his owners $45,000. Spending the money on Comet, they told the *Seattle Times* last year, was "infinitely better" than using it for the kitchen remodel they had planned.

Navy's treatment cost her owner $2,000, part of which was paid for by donations from fellow classmates at Tufts.

Fund-raising efforts are one way to pay the vet bills if you're on a budget. Another is pet health insurance, which was once considered a novelty but is catching on. According to an American Animal Hospital Association survey, 1 percent of pet owners now carry pet health insurance, with the average premium costing slightly less than $150 per year.

Like their counterparts in human medicine, though, pet policies vary. Some companies provide

The photo shown here is particularly appropriate as an illustration for any mention of the genetic inheritance of canine cancer. All five of these dogs are related to Shady, the dog who is fourth from the left; from left to right, they are Shady's niece, cousin, daughter, and sister. The dogs all belonged to New York dog trainer Nancy Strouss, and were *great* dogs, with titles galore and phenomenal dispositions. They were athletic, friendly, intelligent, everything you could ask for in a Golden Retriever. And each died of cancer. (Photo courtesy of Nancy Strouss)

only accident coverage, while others offer options such as minimum coverage, vaccination, and routine care coverage, or more expensive coverage that covers office visits, surgeries, hospitalization, prescriptions, diagnostic tests, X-rays, lab fees, teeth cleanings, and checkups.

Cancer "riders," if available, can extend the animal's treatment for that illness. Most policies—again, like their human counterparts—are more likely to cover conventional treatments than holistic or alternative ones.

Insurance companies usually exclude previously existing conditions, and some exclude congenital problems and hereditary defects. Some plans require policyholders to use only veterinarians in their system. Most plans have a maximum age limit for new patients, some charge more for certain breeds, and at least one company adds a surcharge for coverage in New York City.

A growing number of veterinary clinics offer their own wellness packages, which include discounted prices for routine care, or they may be linked to a specific insurance company or plan.

In general, pet insurance policy buyers should

Laurie Kaplan wrote a book about her experiences with helping her Siberian Husky, Bullet, fight lymphoma. *Help Your Dog Fight Cancer: An Overview of Home Care Options* is a useful text for anyone whose dog has any type of cancer. (Photo courtesy of Laurie Kaplan)

expect to deal with co-payments, deductibles, reimbursement benefit schedules, documentation, forms that have to be signed by the veterinarian, forms that bounce back, fine print, payout limits that may not be clearly explained, and other frustrations. Compare policies, talk to people who already have coverage, and ask your vet's office to help you weigh your dog's health risks. If you decide to buy health insurance, be sure the company is licensed in your state.

Quality of life

A treatment may extend a dog's life, but if that life is defined by loss of mobility, anxiety, depression, pain, and suffering, is the treatment worth pursuing? At what point do quantity of life and quality of life fall irrevocably out of balance?

To help vets and pet owners answer these questions, the Animal Medical Center in New York City developed a "performance scale" that assesses quality of life. It considers alertness/mental status, appetite, weight/body condition, activity/exercise tolerance, and elimination. As one would expect, dogs who score close to normal in all five categories tolerate treatments well and do better overall than low-scoring dogs.

Some veterinary oncologists ask owners to define, before treatment begins, their hopes, goals, and expectations as a way to begin the discussion about what will work, what won't, and whether the client's expectations are realistic. This is an excellent exercise—one you can begin today.

If your dog had cancer, what side effects would be worth working through and which would not? As you learn more about cancer treatments, you will undoubtedly see some that you might consider and some that you definitely wouldn't. But the more you understand about this illness and its treatment, the more prepared you will be to make decisions on your companion's behalf.

Don't Despair; Just Care

Holistic care and home support are effective for treating canine cancer.

Cancer always sounds like a death sentence, no matter how the diagnosis is delivered. When patients are cured, they're the exception rather than the rule—especially when they are very young or very old or when their cancers are well established.

"It's true that some cancers have a high survival rate," says Carol Falck, VMD, a holistic veterinarian in Pompano Beach, Florida, "but cancer is never good news, even if it's easy to treat or detected early. Cancer is a chronic disease, an aberration of the immune system. Whenever and however it appears, it indicates that the body has been out of balance for a long time."

Unlike conventional veterinary medicine, which identifies dozens of specific cancers and treats each as a unique illness, holistic medicine takes a "whole body" approach.

"Holistic medicine does not specifically treat cancer," says Dr. Falck. "Instead, it helps patients eliminate factors that allowed their cancers to develop in the first place. In holistic medicine, there are no specific protocols for different cancer diagnoses the way there are in conventional medicine. Rather, cancer is considered an imbalance that should be corrected so that the body can repair itself."

Because cancer is such a frightening disease, it's easy to panic and feel overwhelmed as you try to make sense of diagnoses and treatment options. "But you don't have to decide everything that same day," says Dr. Falck. "You have time to consult a holistic veterinarian or get a second opinion. And you don't have to decide on a 100 percent conventional protocol or a 100 percent natural protocol. Integrative or complementary medicine combines the best of both worlds. In addition, there's a lot you can do at home with holistic therapies to help your dog heal."

Complementary medicine

Although the terms alternative, natural, complementary, integrative, and holistic are often used interchangeably, they have slightly different meanings.

"Alternative" is a catch-all phrase that describes any treatment that has not been endorsed by conventional medicine. "Natural" therapies are based on centuries-old botanical, nutritional, and physical treatments, most of which are gentle as well as effective, though they work more slowly than conventional treatments. "Complementary" and "integrative" describe the combination of natural and conventional therapies. "Holistic" applies to any treatment plan that considers all of the factors in a patient's life, not just his lab test results.

Consult a holistic veterinarian about natural cancer therapies and integrative/complementary treatments.

Improve the quality of your dog's diet, and add supplements or foods that improve digestion and assimilation.

Explore at-home support therapies to improve your dog's quality of life.

Avoid pesticides and products that interfere with immune function.

Focus on positive thoughts and use holistic therapies to help your dog do the same.

In contrast, conventional or orthodox medicine trains its practitioners to identify specific diseases and treat them by attacking their symptoms. This approach is also called "allopathic," which literally means "symptom-suppressing." The downside of conventional medicine is that it seldom addresses an illness's underlying causes, so it does not correct or eliminate the illness at its source. Treated illnesses often continue to progress, even while their symptoms subside temporarily. This is why recurring cancers are so common and so serious. Another problem with conventional medicine is that its treatments can cause side effects more painful and incapacitating than the illness itself.

"In addition," says Dr. Falck, "conventional medicine usually ignores the emotional aspects of disease. I think holistic medicine does an excellent job of incorporating physical and emotional aspects into a treatment plan."

Specific treatments that fall under the holistic/alternative umbrella include diet, nutritional supplements, homeopathy, herbal medicine, aromatherapy, flower essences, chiropractic, acupuncture, acupressure, massage, and several others. In complementary or integrative cancer care, these treatments are used to improve the results of conventional therapy and to counteract its adverse side effects.

For example, acupuncture and medicinal herbs help alleviate the nausea caused by chemotherapy, while nutritional supplements help restore lost hair. Aromatherapy and herbs speed the healing of surgical wounds and help prevent skin damage caused by radiation treatments. Herbs, aromatherapy, and flower remedies alleviate stress and help bring emotions into balance. And an improved diet supports all cancer therapies.

What Are the Alternatives?

Non-conventional cancer treatments appeal to many dog owners.

The high-tech world of modern medicine has so many weapons that its "war on cancer" arsenal promises something for everyone. But all along, there have been patients, physicians, veterinarians, and animal caregivers who refuse chemotherapy, radiation treatments, surgery, prescription drugs, and other oncology protocols.

What do they use instead? Everything from an improved diet to homeopathy, medicinal herbs, vitamins, nutritional supplements, and energy therapies. The aim of all of these treatments, which are used singly or in combination, is to engage the healing properties of Mother Nature while avoiding debilitating side effects.

Rather than describe every alternative cancer treatment—an impossible task that, alone, would fill a book—we'll describe several frequently used alternative therapies. These protocols tend to be simple and affordable, especially compared with conventional medical therapies. In some cases, they completely cured a dog's cancer. In others, they significantly improved the patient's quality of life, resulting in companionship and an active lifestyle for months or years beyond the original prognosis. Unfortunately, there are no guarantees, for no treatment *always* cures cancer or extends the patients' life. Sometimes, nothing works.

If you decide to use one or more of these protocols, please do so with the help of a knowledgeable holistic veterinarian—or a sympathetic conventional vet—who can monitor your dog's condition, document his or her progress, and provide support throughout the dog's treatment.

This can be especially important when the patient goes through rapid detoxification or a so-called "healing crisis"—when the dog gets dramatically worse before getting better—something any natural therapy might trigger. "Information, encouragement, and assistance from someone who understands what's going on can be a blessing, especially if the symptoms are unexpected or dramatic," says trainer Nancy Strouss, of Nyack, New York, who has lost six Golden Retrievers and one black Lab to cancer.

Nutrition

Diet is so important in the treatment of cancer that all holistic veterinarians encourage their clients to improve the quality of their dogs' food. Organizations like the Weston A. Price Foundation and your local farmer's market or co-op can help you locate organic, pasture-fed ingredients, including raw or cultured dairy products.

Unlike products from factory farms, the meat and milk of pasture-fed animals contain conjugated

Engaging the services of a trained, professional canine massage provider can have profound positive impacts on your dog's health. Some providers utilize additional healing modalities, such as acupressure, TTouch, or "energy balancing" techniques.

All ingredients in an anticancer diet should be fresh, highly bioavailable, easily digested, and highly palatable, with a good taste and smell.

cheese, ground flaxseed, garlic, and broccoli. Misty's cancer disappeared, and she enjoyed an active, athletic lifestyle with no recurrence of the disease. "We lost her in May 2005 to old age," Stauffer reports, "shortly before her fourteenth birthday."

Because flaxseed oil is highly perishable and quickly goes rancid at room temperature, this ingredient requires constant refrigeration. Coconut researcher Bruce Fife, ND, suggests replacing the flaxseed oil in this protocol with coconut oil. "Coconut oil is far more stable than flaxseed oil," he explains, "and it has significant anti-tumor properties."

Carbohydrates feed cancer cells, so feed canine cancer patients a grain-free, low-carb or no-carb diet.

linoleic acid, or CLA, which inhibits the development of tumors. Upgrading to pasture-fed ingredients can actually help your dog fight cancer.

Carbohydrates feed cancer cells, while fats do not. This may explain why some dogs with cancer have responded well to a diet recommended for human patients by the late Johanna Budwig, PhD. A German pharmacologist, chemist, and physicist, Dr. Budwig is best known for her research on fats and oils and for her use of flaxseed oil and sulphur-rich quark cheese (a cultured dairy product similar to cottage cheese) to treat cancer. She advocated the use of nutrition, sunlight (a natural source of vitamin D), and stress management as a stand-alone alternative cancer treatment.

Five years ago, Misty, a German Shepherd Dog belonging to Craig Stauffer in Sunnyvale, California, developed mammary cancer. Following the biopsy of two tumors, Misty was given six months to live. "The recommended treatment was the removal of all mammary tissue followed by chemotherapy," says Stauffer.

Instead, Stauffer researched alternatives and learned of Dr. Budwig's treatment. He began supplementing Misty's dog food with flaxseed oil, cottage

Antioxidant supplements

Antioxidants are naturally occurring substances that protect cells from damage caused by oxygen molecules known as free radicals, which are believed to encourage the development of tumors. Antioxidants include beta-carotene (found in carrots, cantaloupe, and other orange-colored foods), vitamin E (found in nuts, wheat germ, and some vegetables), vitamin A (found in liver, egg yolks, and cod liver oil), vitamin C (found in citrus fruit, hot peppers, and leafy vegetables), and the mineral selenium (found in grains).

Human clinical trials suggest that synthetic vitamin E may contribute to, rather than prevent, certain illnesses, something that advocates of whole-food nutrition have long maintained.

Some herbs and nutritional supplements used in the treatment of cancer are (or are claimed to be) powerful antioxidants. Antioxidant supplements may be helpful in combination with most natural cancer treatments, but they can interfere with others. Be sure to study a protocol carefully before adding antioxidants, and for best results use food-source rather than synthetic products.

Other supplements

Melatonin, a hormone produced in the brain's pineal gland in response to darkness, helps us sleep and has potent antioxidant properties. It is a popular treatment for canine thunder phobia and separation anxiety, and because it has been shown to help humans recover from breast and prostate cancer, it's being given to some dogs with these conditions.

Several years ago, shark cartilage seemed to be the most promising alternative treatment for cancer, but uneven results, quality problems, insufficient research, and concern about the ecological effects of shark hunting reduced its popularity. Bovine cartilage shares similar properties, and some holistic veterinarians prescribe cartilage supplements for cancer.

> Reduce the carbohydrates your dog eats. Carbs cause a net energy loss to the cancer patient, but are readily utilized by cancer cells.
>
> Use fish oil supplements (high in omega-3 fatty acids) to reduce or eliminate some of cancer's metabolic alterations.
>
> Feed the most appetizing food you can find. Anorexia and weight loss will speed your dog's death.

When New Jersey resident Gayle Roberson's 11-year-old Toy Poodle developed an almost non-stop gagging cough and a heart murmur, an X-ray revealed a major mass in his chest. None of the medications his veterinarian prescribed produced results, so Roberson experimented with bovine cartilage. "By the end of the first bottle, he was coughing less," she says. "After the second, he was so much better that I had his chest X-rayed again. The mass had almost completely disappeared and his heart murmur was downgraded from a 5 to a 1. This was sensational, and he lived to be 17!"

Beta glucan (more correctly called Beta-1,3/1,6-Glucan) is a simple sugar derived from the cell wall of *Saccharomyces ceresvsiae*, common baker's yeast. Researchers have been testing its immune-boosting properties since the 1940s.

Ted Keller, a registered pharmacist in Colorado, says he has seen dramatic results with beta glucan in human *and* animal cancer patients. "The best example I can give is a dog diagnosed with T-cell lymphoma and given six months to live. Thanks to beta glucan, the dog was still alive two years later, to the amazement of her veterinarians. . . . The earlier the diagnosis, the better the beta glucan works. For melanoma, beta glucan works wonders as long as it hasn't metastasized to the brain."

Herbal treatments

Search online for herbal cancer treatments and you'll find thousands. A few are backed by serious research, some are hyped by multilevel-marketing companies, most are described with exaggerated claims, many have been used for centuries in traditional medicine, and some have saved dogs' lives. Distinguishing one from the other requires careful study or the help of an herbalist.

Several reputable companies make herbal tonics, teas, extracts, and other products that help dogs fight cancer. Some contain medicinal mushrooms (such as maitake or reishi), aloe vera, cat's claw, or Chinese herbs, all of which are highly regarded as natural cancer treatments. *All You Ever Wanted to Know about Herbs for Pets*, a terrific book by Mary Wulff-Tilford and Gregory Tilford, is helpful for anyone interested in treating pets botanically.

The Tilfords' favorite anticancer herb is red clover, which, they say, inhibits the activities of carcinogenic compounds, helps improve blood structure, and strengthens lymphatic functions that are crucial in cleansing cell tissues throughout the body.

Red clover also contains plant sterol constituents that may inhibit the production of blood vessels that feed newly formed tumors. *Herbs for Pets* includes instructions for making a tonic support formula for cancer patients by combining red clover, the Chinese immune-boosting herb astragalus, dandelion root (which gently stimulates the liver, improves digestion, and assists with the removal of waste), and garlic (which has its own anticancer, anti-tumor properties).

The herbal formula Essiac is another tonic tea that enhances immune function and helps the body heal itself.

The yellow spice turmeric is becoming known as a cancer fighter, even by conventional medical practitioners. Turmeric's key ingredient is curcumin, a phytopolyphenol pigment with anti-inflammatory, antioxidant properties. Curcumin helps starve tumors by disrupting their blood supply, and it stimulates the immune system, enhances cardiovascular function, and improves digestion. Some cases have been reported in which turmeric or curcumin caused tumors on a dog's head or body to turn black and disappear.

Australian herbalist Robert McDowell works with canine cancer patients around the world. McDowell's standard approach to all cancers involves maritime pine bark extract, an immune system tonic, in combination with a specific support formula directed at the patient's particular cancer. "Maritime pine is a special antioxidant nearly 25 times more powerful than vitamin C," says McDowell.

Chinese herbs

Chinese herbal medicine is a primary component of traditional Chinese medicine (TCM). In conventional Western medicine, drugs are chosen for their ability to exert specific physiological actions; in TCM, the practitioner chooses treatments, including herbs, based on the manifestations of disease and energetic imbalances he detects in each individual's body. In other words, a TCM practitioner may prescribe different herbs (and other treatments, including acupuncture) to different individuals with the same disease. Most of the herbs (and mineral or animal-based ingredients of predominantly herbal medicines) used by TCM practitioners have been used to treat people for thousands of years.

When Audrey Blake's nine-year-old Golden Retriever, Dylan, was diagnosed with hemangiosarcoma in November 2002, Blake knew she didn't want Dylan to undergo conventional therapy.

Dylan lived comfortably with cancer for three years. (Photo courtesy of Audrey Blake)

"Surgery wasn't an option because his liver was involved, and I didn't want to put him through chemotherapy," says the Riverhead, New York, resident. "Another factor was that two of my friends had just lost their Goldens to hemangiosarcoma. Both dogs died a few weeks after surgery. The odds weren't good, so I decided that even if all we had was three months together, I wanted those months to be as comfortable as possible for him."

Fortunately for Dylan, his veterinarian was Dr. Jiu Jia Wen, who majored in acupuncture and traditional Chinese herbal medicine at Beijing Agricultural University in China. Dr. Wen prepared a blend of 20 Chinese herbs that Blake added to Dylan's food. The herbs were easy to administer and affordable, she says. By their next checkup, the tumor had stopped growing, and by the following month, it was shrinking.

"I was ecstatic," says Blake. "Dylan was active,

playful, and happy." After about a year, the tumor began to grow again and a second herbal blend was added to his food. Eventually, the cancer won out, and Dylan died shortly before his twelfth birthday.

"I still miss him," says Blake, "but I have no regrets. I would use this same protocol again, and I recommend it to others. Older dogs and hemangiosarcoma are never a good combination, but the Chinese herbs worked incredibly well."

Artemisinin

Artemisinin is an extract derived from the Chinese herb *Artemesia annua*, also known as sweet Annie or annual wormwood. A traditional cure for malaria, the plant is now a treatment for cancer. Like the parasite that causes malaria, cancer cells hoard iron in order to replicate their DNA. When artemisinin comes in contact with iron, it becomes a toxic chemical, releasing free radicals that destroy affected parasites or cancer cells.

For a while, it seemed artemisinin might have been the magic bullet that would quickly cure cancer in humans and pets. In 2003, a research study was under way at the Washington Cancer Institute Department of Orthopedic Oncology at Georgetown University Medical Center, vets who used the herb were reporting promising results, and an "artemisinin and cancer" online forum attracted hundreds of members.

Now the dust is settling. The research study was canceled for lack of funding, and not every dog who took artemisinin improved. In addition, some veterinarians worried about adverse side effects.

Despite these disappointments and concerns, artemisinin remains a popular alternative. Henry Lai, PhD, Narendra P. Singh, MD, and other researchers at the University of Washington, Seattle, have published artemisinin studies in peer-reviewed medical journals. Because of their solid theoretical and experimental results, even conventionally trained veterinarians take artemisinin seriously.

"I can think of at least three reasons why some dogs have not been completely cured of cancer by artemisinin," Dr. Lai told us. "First, artemisinin treatment is usually started too late, when dogs are at an advanced stage of cancer. Second, I don't think artemisinin is completely effective unless we can prolong its half-life of action and increase its selectivity. We are working on solutions for that problem, but they will be expensive. The third reason is that a lot of owners feed high doses of antioxidants such as vitamins C and E to their dogs, and antioxidants counteract the action of artemisinin."

Artemisinin works as an oxidant, explains Dr. Lai; therefore its action is opposite to that of antioxidants. "It is known that antioxidants decrease the effect of artemisinin on malarial parasites, and we have experimental data showing that this is also true for cancer cells. It seems that people in developing countries respond better to artemisinin than people in the United States, possibly because they don't take a lot of antioxidant supplements."

Giving antioxidants to dogs several hours after artemisinin is one possible solution. "But some antioxidants, such as vitamin E, stay in the body for a long time," says Dr. Lai, "so they would continue to counteract artemisinin. Stopping antioxidants during the initial phase of artemisinin treatment might produce better results."

Even if cancer returns and causes the patient's death, dogs on artemisinin often outlive their original prognosis. Kathy Rowley's Greyhound, Tera, was diagnosed with a bone tumor in her lower left hind leg. "That was on a Tuesday," Rowley recalls. "The following Saturday we started her on artemisinin. The next day she seemed to feel better, and on Monday she was bouncing off the walls and acting totally normal. We couldn't believe it.

"Two weeks later our vet examined her leg and was shocked that she had no pain. He suggested we do X-rays in three months, even though we knew the odds of her still being alive in three months were slim. But she kept getting better, and after three months, the tumor had shrunk dramatically. The vet said he would not have believed it if he hadn't seen it with his own eyes."

Tera's tumor didn't disappear, but it didn't begin to grow again until the following spring. "We increased her dose of artemisinin," says Rowley, "but for some reason it just stopped working. When pain began to incapacitate her, we knew it was time. Tera died in July 2004, shortly before her tenth birthday. The artemisinin might not have cured her, but the extra 14 months that we shared with our lively, happy dog were nothing short of a miracle."

Tera's bone cancer was held at bay for 14 months. (Photo courtesy of Kathy Rowley)

Cancer salves

Escharotic salves, often called black salves, were so popular in the early twentieth century that entire hospitals were devoted to their use. The name comes from the eschar (thick dried scab) that develops after the salve destroys tissue to which it is applied. Most such salves contain bloodroot (*Sanguinaria canadensis*) and zinc chloride, a preservative said to enhance the effectiveness of the salve.

Holistic health guru Andrew Weil, MD, revived interest in cancer salves when he wrote about using one on his six-year-old Rhodesian Ridgeback, Coca, who developed a growth on her right side near the shoulder. Dr. Weil describes the experience in his book, *Spontaneous Healing*, concluding, "The end result was a

perfectly circular, slightly depressed area of skin, with no trace of tumor. The bloodroot had removed it more neatly than one could have done with a scalpel. Later, hair grew over the spot, concealing it completely. I could not have asked for a better outcome, especially as the dog had shown no signs of discomfort."

In humans, treatment with escharotics can be painful and scarring. While dogs tend to have higher pain thresholds than humans, this is still not a treatment to approach casually. Keeping the affected area bandaged and attending to its healing can be a challenge.

Patricia Weissleader, who lives near Palm Springs, California, has treated several of her rescued dogs with black salve. "In every case," she says, "the salve removed the tumors and the dogs were healthy."

Weissleader now runs an online group devoted to black salves. "The salve will always remove visible tumors," she says, "and we're always learning about ways to speed the healing of the area after that."

Homeopathy

Few approaches to healing are as controversial as homeopathy, in which extremely dilute substances are matched with symptoms on an individual basis and given, usually one at a time and often only once, to stimulate a healing response. Because it is so different from what they are used to, most mainstream physicians, veterinarians, and researchers consider homeopathy irrational, ineffective, or dangerous.

As cancer researcher Ralph Moss, PhD, says, "The argument that any positive results reported for homeopathy have to be due to the placebo effect seems arrogant. Homeopathy is no weirder than the basic postulates of quantum mechanics, which were vehemently resisted by the older generation of scientists, only to become the foundation of today's particle physics." He notes that 3,000 peer-reviewed articles deal with homeopathy, including 140 clinical trials and 100 articles on randomized controlled trials.

What's in an Anticancer Diet?

While the experts don't all advocate the same approach to nutrition and cancer, they do agree on one thing: don't try this on your own. It's essential that your vet works with you on formulating a diet that meets your dog's specific needs, especially if your pet is undergoing any sort of additional treatment such as chemotherapy. Even supplementation is discouraged without the input of a professional.

But if your practitioner suggests you try an altered diet by preparing homemade meals, here are some of the things he might recommend.

- **All ingredients should be fresh, highly bioavailable, easily digested, and highly palatable, with a good taste and smell.** Many cancer patients lose their appetites, either due to their treatments or illness; these dogs must be tempted to eat, a lot.

- **Organic foods.** Conventional veterinarians may beg to differ, but holistic practitioners of all kinds are quite comfortable with the numerous studies that link common chemical pesticides and fertilizers to cancer, as well as reproductive and neurological damage. Dr. Anne Reed, a holistic veterinarian in Oakland, California, recommends that her clients utilize organic meat as part of their anticancer diets. "Giving a dog as clean a diet as possible can only help," she says. "I feel like the last thing the canine cancer patient's body needs is to deal with the pesticides, antibiotics, and extra bacteria that tend to be in nonorganic meat. You don't want their bodies to have to focus on clearing out toxins as well as fighting the cancer."

- **Fresh, organic meats, either raw or cooked.** Fresh, clean, high-quality meat is both appetizing and highly bioavailable.

- **Fish oil supplements.** Rich in omega-3 (n-3) fatty acids, which have been linked to tumor inhibition and strengthening the immune system, fish oil may be more readily absorbed by the dog's body than a close cousin, flaxseed oil.

- **Vitamin C.** Known and used for its antioxidant properties, this vitamin can easily be given in pill form. Antioxidants neutralize free radicals as the natural byproduct of normal cell processes. In addition, antioxidants must be supplemented whenever omega-3 supplements are given.

- **Fresh vegetables.** Cruciferous veggies like broccoli and dark-green, leafy vegetables like spinach are healthy for any dog, but especially for cancer patients. According to the National Institutes of Health and the American Institute for Cancer Research, diets high in cruciferous vegetables—such as broccoli, cauliflower, cabbage, watercress,

---

New York veterinarian Stacey Hershman, DVM, a classically trained homeopath, uses homeopathy as a support therapy rather than a stand-alone cancer treatment. "I just haven't seen spectacular results, especially in advanced or complicated cases," she says. "I love homeopathy and I use it every day, but for cancer patients I use it in combination with other holistic treatments, addressing symptoms as they develop. I think it's excellent for that."

While there are many home-study guides for treating animals with homeopathy, cancer is a complicated subject. For best results, consult an experienced veterinary homeopath.

Cryosurgery

When surgery is the best option, an alternative procedure called cryosurgery can sometimes be used to destroy cancer tissue by freezing.

In October 2004, Labrador Retriever breeder Ed Katz of Elka Park, New York, discovered that his three-month-old puppy, Doc, had an aggressive mast cell

and bok choy, among others—have been associated with lower risk for lung, stomach, and colorectal cancers in humans. According to the American Cancer Society, broccoli, in particular, is the source of many phytochemicals that are thought to stimulate the production of anticancer enzymes.

In addition, the fiber that vegetables provide is essential to maintain normal bowel health, which, in turn, is key to overall health. Pureeing the vegetables and mixing them into food may improve acceptance for some dogs, while others will be content to crunch them raw or lightly steamed.

- **Digestive enzymes.** Holistic practitioners often recommend these to help support the dog's digestive abilities, especially during the transition to a new diet.
- **Garlic.** Small amounts, such as a clove a day, may be recommended. According to the National Cancer Institute, studies provide compelling evidence that garlic and its organic allyl sulfur components are effective inhibitors of the cancer process.
- **Safflower oil.** According to Lisa Barber, DVM, assistant professor at Tufts University School of Veterinary Medicine, there is some anecdotal evidence that this oil can help achieve remission in patients with a difficult form of lymphoma, epitheliotropic cutaneous T-cell lymphoma.
- **Limited carbohydrates.**

Veterinarians have a variety of pharmaceutical appetite stimulants that may be helpful for keeping an inappetent dog eating. The goal is to prevent anorexia and weight loss at all costs. If a canine cancer patient stops eating, the veterinarian should consider "enteral" feeding—using either a nasogastric tube (which goes through the dog's nose and throat and into his stomach) or a gastrostomy tube (which is surgically placed in the dog's stomach and emerges from the dog's side). Such measures, while dramatic for the owner, can be of enormous value to the patient and are generally of short duration.

tumor on his paw pad. The cancer had already spread to his lymph nodes and his spleen was enlarged. Doc's veterinary oncologists recommended amputation, 25 radiation treatments, and intensive chemotherapy.

Instead, Katz took Doc to Marty Goldstein, DVM, in South Salem, New York, who performed a 23-minute cryosurgery procedure and sent the puppy home with artemisinin and nutritional supplements. Doc healed quickly and today, says Dr. Goldstein, you can't tell which paw was affected.

According to Katz, Doc is the most athletic, happy, intelligent, bouncy, resilient Lab imaginable. He celebrated his first birthday last summer, continues to take his artemisinin and supplements, and has been cancer-free, with "perfect" blood tests, for more than a year.

Cryosurgery is not always successful, warns trainer Nancy Strouss, whose nine-year-old Golden Retriever, Valley, underwent the procedure to treat a mast cell tumor on her toe. "The cryosurgery was painful," says Strouss, "and the cancer came right back. When her toe was amputated, it came back again, and soon it metastasized through her body."

Enzyme therapy

No discussion of holistic cancer treatments would be complete without mentioning enzyme therapy. Enzymes are most familiar as digestive aids that break down fats, proteins, and other foods, but when they are used to treat cancer they are taken *between* meals on an *empty* stomach.

Bromelain, a protein-digesting enzyme found in pineapple, has cancer-fighting as well as anti-inflammatory properties. Familiar enzyme products for dogs include Prozyme, a plant-based powder that is sprinkled on food to improve digestion, and Wobenzym. Both products contain bromelain; Wobenzym contains pancreatic enzymes as well.

Systemic oral enzyme therapy is usually well tolerated by dogs of all ages. However, Wobenzym and other products containing bromelain can thin the blood.

Cancell/Protocel

One of the more controversial alternative treatments for cancer is a product called Cancell, also called Protocel, Cantrol, Entelev, and Cantron. It was created in the 1930s by a Dow Chemical biochemist who claimed that the product balanced the vibrational frequency of cancer cells, returning them to a healthy state.

Protocel's ingredients are copper, sodium, potassium, and a proprietary blend of tetrahydroxyquinone, rhodizonic acid, inositol, croconic acid, catechol, triquinoyl, and leuconic acid. According to its manufacturers, Protocel is a powerful antioxidant that helps cleanse the cells, thus supporting immune function.

"Cancell has been the subject of a long-running guerilla war between its enthusiasts on the one hand and the FDA on the other," says Dr. Moss. "Every time it is suppressed under one name, it pops up under another."

Animal studies conducted by the National Can-

Cancer

cer Institute (NCI) decades ago concluded that Cancell lacked substantial anticancer activity and that no further research was warranted. In 1989, the FDA was granted a permanent injunction against Cancell's manufacturers, prohibiting them from distributing an unapproved drug. However, many have argued that the NCI falsified its reports of the tests it conducted, and some of the evidence against Cancell does appear to be biased.

Bioresonance therapy

For Gigi Gaulin, DVM, of Santa Fe, New Mexico, the leading edge of alternative veterinary medicine is a technology developed in Germany 30 years ago and used in 65 countries around the world. "Bioresonance therapy" utilizes a patented device that measures the patient's "electromagnetic oscillations" through electrodes placed on the body. The frequencies it measures are then returned to the patient as a form of healing energy, with "bad" frequencies inverted and "good" frequencies enhanced.

Dr. Gaulin is one of nine veterinarians in the United States who are using Bicom Resonance Therapy equipment. Where cancer is concerned, she says, the treatment proceeds in stages, clearing underlying conditions. "Cancer isn't an entity all of itself. It's part of a process; eliminating cancer is a process, too. You start by removing energetic blocks, opening up the lymphatic system, and supporting the organs that help the body correct imbalances."

Treatment sessions last anywhere from 20 to 90 minutes, and are commonly used on a weekly basis. Dr. Gaulin reports that most patients experience improvements in energy, attitude, appetite, specific symptoms, and overall condition. As they become stronger, she says, their quality of life increases and cancer growth slows. "The changes and improvements that result can be truly astounding," she says.

Find a really good veterinarian *now*—before your dog is ill—and develop a good working relationship with her. If your dog is diagnosed with cancer, you will need her support and willingness to try alternative therapies.

Look for alternatives that work well for your dog's specific cancer.

Choose a therapy that will be comfortable—and possible—for you and your dog.

Is Cancer Prevention Possible?

If so, experts are certain the key will lie in a healthy immune system.

What could be better than curing your dog's cancer? That's easy! How about avoiding the illness in the first place?

No one has done any clinical trials or statistical studies that *prove* you can prevent cancer in at-risk dogs. "But common sense and clinical experience make a strong case for avoiding anything that exposes an animal to known carcinogens or weakens the immune system," says Stacey Hershman, DVM, a holistic house-call veterinarian in Rockland County, New York.

Just like their human companions, dogs live longer, healthier lives when they eat the right foods, get enough exercise, breathe clean air, drink clean water, and stay away from harmful substances. They may also be helped by immune-boosting herbs, supplements, special foods, and a few things you might not have thought of. Here's a review of recommendations from holistic veterinarians and other experts.

Good genes

An important first step in selecting a puppy or adult dog is learning everything you can about the immediate family—parents, grandparents, siblings, aunts, uncles, and cousins. Some breeds are notoriously prone to cancer, and some lines within those breeds reinforce the trend. Look for good genes and good health when selecting puppies or adopting adult dogs.

Of course, rescued dogs seldom come with this documentation, and even the best-bred dog can develop cancer. But starting with good raw material can reduce the risk—and if you know that your dog may be prone to certain types of cancer, do what you can, starting today, to make that diagnosis less likely.

Spaying/neutering

The statistics are convincing: female dogs have a significantly lower risk of developing mammary tumors if they are spayed before coming into season for the first or second time, and testicular cancer is obviously not a problem in neutered males.

But while early spaying reduces the risk of mammary cancer, it quadruples the risk of developing cardiac hemangiosarcomas (vascular tumors) compared to intact females. In addition, a study of 3,218 dogs neutered before one year of age showed that both males and females had a significantly increased chance of developing osteosarcoma (bone tumors) compared to intact males and females.

Understanding your dog's inherited risks can help you make informed decisions about whether and when to schedule surgery.

Vaccinations

For Dr. Hershman and most holistic veterinarians, routine vaccinations top the list of things to avoid. "Vaccines really disrupt the immune system," she says, "especially combination vaccines that are given annually." Like many holistic veterinarians, she recommends a single-dose parvovirus vaccination at age 10 to 12 weeks, followed by a single-dose distemper vaccination four weeks later and a rabies vaccination after age six months.

"I check the effectiveness of these shots with blood titer tests," she says. "If immunity is strong, there's no need to revaccinate. If it's weak, I repeat whatever the puppy needs for protection."

Label directions warn veterinarians not to vaccinate a sick animal; Dr. Hershman includes injured or stressed animals in that caution. "Vaccinating a dog who's being spayed, neutered, or treated for an injury is totally irresponsible," she says. "You want the animal to be healthy, with a strong vital force, not in a weakened, vulnerable state, when you introduce substances designed to challenge the immune system."

Responding to decades of research by immunologists, veterinary textbooks and colleges no longer recommend annual vaccinations for dogs, but most veterinary clinics continue to prescribe them. "They routinely prescribe antibiotics, steroids, and other symptom-suppressing drugs, too," says Dr. Hershman, "and those take a toll on the immune system. Whenever you can use nutrition, homeopathy, acupuncture, medicinal herbs, or other natural therapies instead of symptom-suppressing drugs, you strengthen the dog's immunity. A strong immune system is the best defense against cancer."

The right diet

Advocates of home-prepared diets for dogs have long claimed that their animals are healthier than they would be on commercial pet food. Beth Taylor and Steve Brown, authors of *See Spot Live Longer*, agree. They blame dry and canned dog foods for a host of problems because they usually contain inferior-quality proteins, fats, and carbohydrates, a variety of toxins, highly processed grains, chemical preservatives, allergens, and other questionable ingredients.

Many veterinarians blame grain-based pet foods for diabetes, digestive problems, and other canine disorders. After all, the canine digestive tract evolved on a diet of prey animals, consisting mostly of meat and bones, not wheat and corn.

Every few years, aflatoxin, which grows on corn, rice, and other grains, contaminates pet foods and kills dogs. In addition to causing liver damage, aflatoxin is a potent carcinogen, so even "safe" levels that don't cause obvious disease outbreaks can contribute, over time, to cancer.

Another carcinogen found in grain-based foods is acrylamide, once believed to exist only in industrial waste. However, acrylamide has recently been found almost everywhere in the human diet. This tasteless, invisible by-product is formed when high-carbohydrate foods are fried or baked at high temperatures. French fries and potato chips contain the highest concentrations, but acrylamide occurs in breads and breakfast cereals as well.

The U.S. Environmental Protection Agency (EPA) considers acrylamide so dangerous that it set the "safe level" for human consumption at almost zero, with the maximum safe level in drinking water set at 0.5 parts per billion. A small serving of French fries contains over 400 parts per billion. No one has tested pet foods, but any processed foods that contain carbohydrates, especially those extruded at high temperature like grain-based kibble or canned under high heat and pressure, pose a risk.

"Considering how ubiquitous these carcinogens are," says San Francisco–area dog health researcher Mary Straus, "and considering that cancer cells thrive on carbohydrates, avoiding grains altogether may be one way to help lower the risk of cancer."

In addition to reducing levels of carbohydrates and carcinogens, feeding a home-prepared diet of pasture-fed, organically produced ingredients ensures that your dog will not ingest pesticide and drug residues. Food prepared at home from conventionally farmed ingredients may not be free of pesticide residues, but it is unlikely to contain chemical preservatives, artificial colors or flavors, or the by-products of high-heat processing.

In his book, *Work Wonders: Feed Your Dog Raw Meaty Bones*, Australian veterinarian Tom Lonsdale observes, "We need more information about the cancer epidemic in domestic dogs. However, basic nutritional and medical principles tell us that diet is the likely main factor. Without waiting for extra information, and because cancer often takes years to develop, it's best to start puppies on a cancer-prevention diet early. From the whelping box to the grave, let 'Prevention, not treatment' be our motto."

Dietary supplements

Antioxidant supplements, which help protect the body from damage by free radicals, have many health benefits, including cancer protection. Best-selling antioxidant supplements include vitamins A, C, and E, beta carotene, lycopene, and the mineral selenium. Bear in mind that some alternative cancer treatments, such as artemisinin, are not compatible with antioxidants.

Food-source antioxidants, vitamins, and other nutrients derived from whole foods are recommended by many holistic veterinarians because they are recognized as food by the body and are more easily assimilated than synthetic vitamins grown in a laboratory. The words "whole food" or "food source" indicate natural rather than synthetic ingredients.

One of the simplest cancer-resisting supplements you can add to your dog's food, according to Bruce Fife, ND, is coconut oil. Dr. Fife, the author of several books about coconut's health benefits, recommends feeding dogs 1 teaspoon of coconut oil per 10 pounds of body weight per day in divided doses. That's 1 tablespoon (3 teaspoons) for a 30-pound dog and 2 tablespoons for a 60-pound dog.

"The medium-chain fatty acids in coconut oil help treat or prevent all kinds of illnesses," he says, "and they have significant anti-tumor properties. Giving your dog coconut oil every day is inexpensive health insurance."

Dried shredded coconut (the unsweetened kind) is an excellent source of fiber, another factor in cancer prevention. Try adding a teaspoon to a tablespoon of shredded coconut to your dog's home-prepared food. If feeding dry food, add a little water or soak the shredded coconut first.

Vegetables are controversial ingredients because they're hard for dogs to digest. But a simple lactofermentation process not only improves the digestibility and assimilation of vegetables, it increases their vitamin content and makes them a valuable source of beneficial bacteria. In fact, the treated vegetables are both a prebiotic (food that feeds beneficial bacteria) and probiotic (food that contains beneficial bacteria). In Europe, lactofermented vegetables are the key ingredient in a popular cancer treatment.

See page 188 for recipes for lactofermented vegetables.

Lactofermented vegetables are a key part of at least one popular cancer treatment protocol.

Environmental factors

Take two individuals from the same litter of puppies of a breed or family that has a high cancer risk. Place one with a family of heavy smokers who live next to a busy highway, use lawn chemicals, drink fluoridated tap water, and have high-current power lines in the backyard. Place the other pup on a pristine organic farm. Feed both the same diet and let several years go by. You don't have to be an oncologist to know which dog is more likely to develop cancer.

Secondhand smoke is a serious problem for pets, especially those who spend hours every day at the feet of their smoking companions. "I tell all my clients who smoke that they're putting their dogs' health at risk," says Dr. Hershman. "I saw it happen in my own family, and it breaks my heart. Secondhand smoke is as dangerous to dogs as it is to infants."

Busy highways, driveways, parking lots, and areas where trucks and cars idle are dangerous for dogs because of gas and diesel exhaust. A dog's nose is much closer to the ground—and exhaust pipes—than the human nose, so dogs are more likely to inhale damaging particles.

Lawn treatments and agricultural chemicals are known to cause cancer in animals. Dogs pick up pesticides, herbicides, and other chemicals through their feet and, when they sniff the ground, through their noses. Keep your dog off the grass in chemically treated neighborhoods, and explore organic alternatives for your own lawn and garden.

Even household chemicals pose a threat to our canine companions. According to the U.S. Consumer Product Safety Commission, more than 150 chemicals found in the average home are linked to birth defects, cancer, and psychological abnormalities. If labels carry a "keep away from children and pets" warning, or if product labels suggest they should be used only in well-ventilated areas, look for alternatives.

Fluoride has gotten such good press over the decades that most Americans think it's essential for healthy teeth. It's even added to some canine toothpastes. But in many countries, fluoride is considered a hazardous industrial waste, and its use in water supplies is prohibited. In September 2005, 11 unions representing more than 7,000 scientists and researchers at the EPA called for a national moratorium on the fluoridation of America's drinking water, citing cancer risks.

A December 2005 analysis of more than 22 million tap-water quality tests, most of which were required under the federal Safe Drinking Water Act, found that water suppliers across the United States detected 260 contaminants in public tap water. Of the 141 unregulated contaminants detected in water supplies between 1998 and 2003, 52 are linked to cancer, 41 to reproductive toxicity, 36 to developmental toxicity, and 16 to immune system damage. Water contaminated with 83 agricultural pollutants, including pesticides and fertilizer ingredients, flows through the taps of over 200 million Americans in 41 states.

Installing a water filter or using uncontaminated, unfluoridated bottled water sounds like a very good idea! So does avoiding fluoridated toothpaste.

Regarding sources of electromagnetic radiation, a study published in 1995 in the *American Journal of Epidemiology* compared dogs treated at a veterinary teaching hospital for histologically confirmed lymphoma. Electric wire codes and magnetic fields were measured at the homes of 93 diagnosed cases and 137 controls, and a correlation was found between magnetic fields emitted by power lines and electrical appliances and the incidence of lymphoma. Dogs living in homes with very high current codes had the highest

Use topical pesticides only as often as absolutely necessary—for dogs who regularly hike in tick-infested woods or brush, for example. Don't apply monthly; use only as needed to protect your dog.

Is Cancer Prevention Possible?

risk, while dogs living in homes with buried or underground power lines had a lower risk.

Immunologist and veterinarian Richard Pitcairn, DVM, PhD, author of *Dr. Pitcairn's Complete Guide to Natural Health for Dogs & Cats*, considers all sources of radiation (including repeated diagnostic X-rays) dangerous because their effects are cumulative in the body. He recommends that dogs not be allowed to rest near a color TV set. Fortunately, the new flat-screen TVs and computer monitors emit much lower levels of electromagnetic radiation than older cathode ray tube models. In general, the fewer electrical appliances in close proximity to pets, the better.

Topical pesticides

Anyone who lives where fleas, ticks, or mosquitoes are a problem knows what a challenge they can be. Unfortunately, topical and systemic pest-control products contribute to a host of health problems, including increased cancer risks.

A well-balanced raw diet can help a dog repel parasites, but sometimes the attack is overwhelming.

"I definitely prefer natural alternatives to pesticide sprays or products like Frontline, which make the entire dog toxic to biting parasites," says Dr. Hershman. "But alternatives don't always work. One of my patients is a raw-fed search-and-rescue dog who often picked up more than 200 ticks on training weekends. He's a German Shepherd Dog, so finding and removing them all was a time-consuming, stressful challenge. After his owner tried every natural repellent we could find, none of which solved the problem, he now applies K9 Advantix, a systemic pesticide that repels fleas, ticks, and mosquitoes, on a reduced dosage schedule only when needed.

"When it comes to cancer prevention," she says, "the less often you use conventional pesticides, the better. A good diet and natural repellents are always worth trying first."

Cancer preventives

Several holistic cancer treatments can be used to help healthy dogs remain cancer-free. The thinking here is that cancer cells develop all the time, even in healthy bodies, but they don't create problems until conditions encourage their growth. Preventive treatments disrupt cancer cells before they take up residence in vulnerable parts of the body.

Henry Lai, PhD, the University of Washington researcher who first tested artemisinin (an extract of *Artemesia annua*, or annual wormwood) on dogs with cancer, takes artemisinin as a preventive himself and has tested it on laboratory animals.

"It is hard to recommend a protocol for cancer prevention," he says, "but, based on studies on rats, a good dose could probably be somewhere between 8 milligrams of artemisinin per kilogram of body weight per day at the high end and 10 mg/kg once per week at the low end. I take 100 mg per day for 10 days each month. Even though this approach hasn't been tested yet on humans or canines, I think it makes sense."

Following Dr. Lai's example, a dog weighing 60 to 75 pounds could take 50 mg artemisinin for 10 days each month, and the amount could be increased or decreased as needed for larger and smaller dogs.

The antioxidant Protocel can be used in a similar way.

According to Illinois veterinarian Dan King, DVM, "This should be effective because Protocel works on early cancer cells as an antimetastatic. That is, it deals with individual cells and prevents them from spreading and growing. Because it works slowly, I would use Protocel on a preventive maintenance schedule of ¼ teaspoon twice per day for a dog weighing 50 to 75 pounds for three months on and six months off. Small dogs could take ⅛ teaspoon twice per day for the same length of time."

Medicinal herbs

Ask a dozen experts about their favorite herbs for cancer prevention and you'll generate a list too long to publish here. But a few herbal products are so effective that they are recommended by almost everyone.

"Many mushrooms have anti-tumor and immune-stimulating activity," says Carol Falck, VMD, of Pompano Beach, Florida. "They have been used medicinally for thousands of years in China and Japan, and they work very well for dogs."

Dr. Falck often uses Myco-Immune by Thorne Research, which is a liquid extract of seven medicinal mushrooms, including cordyceps, reishi, shiitake, maitake, and turkey tail. "This combination stimulates the immune system in several ways, helping it resist the growth of cancer."

She also recommends a green tea extract (G.T.-Ex by Thorne Research) because green tea enhances cellular immune function, increases natural killer cell activity, and may inhibit some cancer cell lines.

Another favorite supplement for dogs at risk of cancer is curcumin, says Dr. Falck. "Curcumin is the yellow pigment in turmeric, the spice that gives curry its distinctive color. Both turmeric and curcumin have been shown to inhibit tumor growth. I also like astragalus, an herb with strong immune-stimulating properties. I use several Chinese herbal formulas containing astragalus, depending on the patient, including Astragalus for Animals by Buck Mountain Botanicals."

Garlic is well known and often used for its cancer-inhibiting properties. Small amounts of fresh minced garlic or aged garlic extract can be added to any dog's dinner. Garlic is an ingredient in Herbal Compounds tablets created by Juliette de Bairacli Levy, whose Natural Rearing philosophy pioneered home-prepared diets and alternative medicine for animals.

"This formula is very antiseptic," says Natural Rearing advocate Marina Zacharias, who imports the product from England. "It definitely helps the immune system."

For patients at high risk, Zacharias likes a Chinese formula called Bioprin for its antiviral, antibacterial, antifungal, and anti-tumor properties. "I also use a probiotic called Florenz and, over the animals' life span, a form of liver support given to match their needs, such as homeopathic Liver Terrain."

Zacharias says she has seen good results from prevention efforts taken to protect individual dogs in high-risk families. "Of course, there is no empirical evidence to say that these measures prevented cancer, but when we see a good-quality, healthy life, it's evidence that the efforts are warranted. We all have to die from something, but when we see cancer in a naturally raised dog, it's usually when the dog is older, at the end of its natural life span."

Closely related to herbal medicine is aromatherapy. San Diego holistic veterinarian Stephen Blake recommends massaging the paw pads of at-risk dogs once or twice per day with a drop of blended frankincense, sandalwood, and Douglas-fir essential oils. For best results, use organic or wildcrafted oils from reputable distributors. "These essential oils are great for detoxification and for supporting the immune system," he says.

Exercise

Although few of us appreciate the important role it plays, the lymph system is a key factor in cancer prevention. Lymph is a clear fluid, similar to blood but lacking red blood cells. It contains the immune system's lymphocytes (T-cells and B-cells) and circulates through channels that carry waste to the lymph nodes, filtering bacteria and other toxins.

The more lymph circulation is impaired, the less efficiently the body removes toxins and the more favorable conditions are for the growth of cancer. Lymph circulation improves with active exercise and deep, diaphragmatic breathing. Gentle to vigorous brushing that moves from the feet to the heart is a simple addition to daily grooming that also stimulates lymph circulation.

"Exercise is so important," says Dr. Falck. "Exercise stimulates the immune system and releases endorphins, and an added benefit of consistent exercise is increasing gastrointestinal motility, which helps normalize stools and eliminate toxins from the body. It also facilitates weight management, which is important because obesity is a risk factor for some types of cancer."

Malillumination

You probably haven't thought about light as a cancer preventive, but it may well be. Not just any light, though. Unfiltered natural light, Mother Nature's full-spectrum light, activates the hypothalamus and keeps the entire endocrine system balanced.

When photobiologist and time-lapse photography pioneer John Ott began to photograph living plants, he discovered that depriving them of unfiltered natural light interfered with their normal growth and reproduction.

He soon learned that the health of fish, birds, reptiles, and other animals (including humans) is adversely affected by insufficient light and by the wrong kind of light, especially fluorescent light. Ott coined the term "malillumination" to describe the phenomenon, which is now known to suppress immune function and contribute to skin damage, cancer, and other problems.

Light enters the eyes not only to facilitate vision but also to activate the hypothalamus. This region of the brain, in turn, controls the nervous and endocrine systems, which regulate functions throughout the body.

Exposure to natural light, preferably for several hours daily, is necessary for your dog's health. A shady screened porch, the shelter of a tree, or even an open window or doorway can give the dog's body what it needs. Some plastics allow the transmission of full-spectrum natural light, but glass windows, windshields, and sunglasses (which we hope your dog doesn't wear) do not.

Emotional well-being

For many health care experts, emotional well-being is as important to cancer prevention as diet and exercise.

"I believe strongly that emotions are linked to general health via the immune system," says Dr. Falck. "We can support our pets emotionally by encouraging social interaction with people and other animals, by providing a safe and loving environment with balanced opportunities for play and rest, and by minimizing stress."

Dr. Blake strongly stresses the importance of positive thinking.

"Never talk to an animal as though he or she is a tumor instead of a spiritual being," he says. "Negative thoughts generate negative energy, which feeds the disease and weakens the patient's vital force. No matter how serious the risk of cancer, it's important to picture your dog as well and happy, not sick, and to engage him or her in meaningful conversation and meaningful activities every day."

> Study your dog's breed and line for cancer risk factors.
>
> Avoid unnecessary vaccinations and symptom-suppressing drugs.
>
> Work with a holistic vet to find alternatives that work.
>
> Improve your dog's immune system with diet and supplements.
>
> Protect your dog from environmental toxins, lawn chemicals, secondhand smoke, and pesticides.

Chapter 9

Having Fun with Your Dog

Tricks for Clicks
Regard all training as "trick training" for more fun and success!

Did you ever watch someone showing off his dog's tricks? Sit up. Roll over. Jump through a hoop. Catch the ball. Balance a treat on Buddy's nose. Shake paw. High five. Wave. And take a bow!

Did you happen to notice that it looked like human and canine were both having tremendous fun? No choke chains, no prong collars, no electric shock boxes. But lots of treats, toys, and lots of praise, smiles, and high-wagging tails.

Yet if you were to see that same dog and owner combination in a traditional compulsion-based training class you might well see frowns, a stern, commanding tone of voice, intimidating human body language, heavy metal around the dog's neck, and a lot of appeasing body language signals from the dog—ears back, tail down, head lowered, averted glances, yawning, and nose licking. Why the difference?

We tend to think of basic behaviors such as sit, lie down, come, and stay, as *serious* obedience. They are *important*, and Buddy *has* to do them in order to be a well-behaved dog. Tricks, on the other hand, are frivolous. It doesn't really matter if Buddy rolls over when we ask him to. After all, it's just for fun . . . .

It's all tricks!

Teaching Buddy to sit when we ask him to is just as much a "trick" as teaching him to crawl on his belly across the living room rug. They are both simply

Approached in the right way, teaching your dog to come, sit, or heel should be no more difficult or frustrating than teaching him to give you a "high five" or any other trick. (Photo by Paul Miller)

behaviors that Buddy is physically capable of doing, that we teach him to offer us in response to a verbal cue or hand signal. If we can change our attitude and remember to have fun teaching the basics as well as the tricks, we can have a dog who performs the serious behaviors with just as much enthusiasm as he does when he rolls over or catches a treat off the end of his nose.

Chances are good that if you enroll in a positive training class, your instructor will incorporate tricks into each week's lessons in order to keep the training process fun for everybody. You don't have to wait for a training class to have more fun with Buddy—you can start anytime. All you need is your dog, a hefty supply of treats, a clicker, a few props, a quiet place to train without distractions, and a commitment to having fun.

While you are teaching your dog tricks, take note of how much fun it is. Then remember to have just as much fun when you are teaching him those other, "serious" tricks like sit, down, stay, and come.

Tools of the trade: An inexpensive clicker and a ready supply of delicious treats—something the dog is motivated to work for. (Photo by Paul Miller)

"Charging" the clicker

Although it helps if your dog already knows basic good manners, it's not necessary for him to be fully obedience-trained in order to teach him tricks. If Buddy has not already been introduced to the clicker, we need to begin there. See page 47 in chapter 2 for instructions on charging the clicker, also known as "conditioning the reward marker."

Shake paw

There are several different ways to teach your dog to "Shake paw." Some dogs are naturally "pawsy." With these you can simply "capture" the behavior. *Click!* and treat when Buddy lifts his paw. Keep repeating the *click!* and rewarding for a paw lift. When you see him deliberately offering a paw in order to win the reward, add the verbal cue "Shake!", then *click!* and treat. Hold out your own hand, palm up, as the hand signal for "Shake." When you have repeated the verbal cue often enough that you think he has made the association, try asking for the behavior with just the word, without moving your hand. Give him a couple of seconds, and if he doesn't offer his paw, offer your own hand to elicit the shake. If you keep repeating this sequence, Buddy will quickly learn to offer his paw for just the verbal cue.

If your dog is not a natural shaker, you can "shape" the behavior by repeatedly clicking and rewarding any tiny lift of a paw off the ground. When Buddy is regularly lifting the paw slightly, start clicking only the more noticeable lifts. Gradually raise the criteria until he lifts the paw high enough for it to be considered a "Shake." Then add the verbal cue as described above.

You may want to "lure" the paw lift. Some dogs will paw at your hand if you hold a treat in front of them in your closed fist; then you can *click!* and treat. Others need still more help. Try holding a treat just over your dog's head, then move it off to one side.

Many dogs will lift a paw as they lean to follow the movement of the treat. *Cick!* and reward. And repeat.

If "capturing," "shaping," and "luring" don't work, try "molding." Touch the back of Buddy's leg. If he lifts it, *click!* and treat. If a touch doesn't work, you can actually lift the paw, *click!* and reward. Just be aware that molding may teach Buddy to wait for you to touch him before he will shake. The other methods encourage him to think for himself and offer the behavior voluntarily, which is what we really want.

Once Buddy knows "Shake!" you can progress to "High five" or "Wave" by clicking and rewarding simple variations on the theme. For example, for a "High five," offer your hand for a "Shake" but move it at the last minute into a high five sign—palm toward Buddy, fingers pointed skyward.

Spin and twirl

This is a fun and easy trick than can be incorporated into your heeling for a flashy dance step. You can try shaping Buddy's spin if you want (*click!* and reward for a head turn, then gradually for greater and greater head and body turns, until he turns all the way around), but it's usually easier and faster to lure it. Use one word, "Spin" for a counter-clockwise circle, and another word, "Twirl" for example, to mean clockwise. You can make them mean whatever direction you want or you can use entirely different words; just be consistent.

Have Buddy stand in front of you. If he wants to sit, back up while you ask him to spin. Let him see the treat in your right hand. Lure him in a circle to your right (his left) by moving the treat, at his nose level, in an arc toward his tail, then continue the circle with the treat until he is facing you again. When he has completed the circle, *click!* and give him the treat. Repeat. When he is doing the circle easily, start saying "Spin," first *while* he is turning, then just before. Gradually minimize the hand motion and eventually eliminate the lure, until he will spin on just the verbal cue, or

with a tiny motion of your hand or finger. For "Twirl," do the same thing, only start with the treat in your left hand and go the opposite direction.

If Buddy is reluctant to do a complete circle at first, shape it. *Click!* and reward for partial turns, gradually increasing the arc until he will do a full circle.

By withholding the *click!* and treat until a dog tries a new variation on an old trick, one can "shape" a new trick. (Photo by Paul Miller)

Roll over

This one is a little more complicated. If your dog is already trained to "Down" on cue, ask him to lie down. (Remember to *click!* and reward him for that!) If he doesn't already know how to "Down," wait until he lies down on his own, or lure him into a down by holding a treat in front of his nose when he is sitting, and then moving it slowly toward the floor. Keep clicking and rewarding him as he follows the treat toward the floor until he is all the way down.

Once your dog can lie down easily, encourage him to roll onto one side by moving the treat in an arc from his nose to a point just above his shoulder. Some dogs will do this easily on the first try, while others need a little more encouragement through shaping—clicking and rewarding when the dog makes small moves in the right direction until he finally rolls onto one side.

When he will roll onto one side for you smoothly, just keep going! Continue the arc of the treat lure so that he follows it with his nose and rolls his body all the way over. Where Buddy's nose goes, the rest of him must follow! Once your dog is doing one roll easily, try two in a row. Then more, until you can get him to do a whole series of roll-overs.

Many dogs are one-sided, meaning they'll roll easily in one direction but not the other. If your dog is having trouble with this trick, try rolling the opposite way. Then, once he has the easy direction figured out, make him ambi-pawstrous and shape the roll the other way as well.

Say your prayers

This is a fun trick that rates high on the cuteness scale. Have Buddy sit in front of a chair or stool that comes to about his mid-chest level. Lure him into lifting one or two front feet off the ground by raising the treat over his head, and then encourage him to rest his feet on the chair seat. You may need to *click!* and reward for very short paw rests at first, until he leaves his paws on the chair for longer and longer periods of time.

When he is sitting confidently with his paws resting on the chair for extended periods, lure his nose with a treat so he is looking down between his paws at the floor. *Click!* and treat. Once you know he will look between his legs without taking his paws off the chair, start using your verbal cue, "Say your prayers," or "Meditate!" or whatever word or phrase you want to use. Gradually fade your use of obvious cues until he will run over to a chair, prop up his feet, and "say his prayers" with just a verbal cue or hand signal.

Crawl

Buddy already knows "Down" from your "Roll over" trick, so the crawl is easy to teach. It works best if you do it on carpet or grass—lots of dogs won't crawl on a hard or rough surface. Ask Buddy to lie down facing you, and hold a treat in front of his nose. Keeping the treat just an inch or two above the ground, back up a step and *very slowly* move the treat toward you. As Buddy strains to follow the treat he should drag himself forward a tiny bit. *Click!* and reward. Keep repeating the sequence until he creeps farther and farther forward.

If the dog jumps up to follow the treat you may have moved it too far, or too fast. Slow down, and remember to *click!* and reward tiny bits of the crawl so Buddy can figure out how to do the right thing. The most common mistake most people make when training their dogs is trying to go too fast—asking for too much too soon. Ask for small behaviors so Buddy can win. As long as he keeps winning he will be more willing to keep trying.

Once Buddy is confidently crawling longer distances you can fade the lure and minimize the hand motion, and put the behavior on a verbal cue or a barely noticeable hand signal, as you did with the previous tricks.

Take a bow

You can end your routine with a flourish when you and Buddy take a bow together. Have Buddy standing in front of you or at your side. Put a treat in front of his nose, and move it toward his chest and down toward the floor. Here's the tricky part. If you have taught him to lie down by moving a treat toward the ground, he may try to lie down here. Watch him closely. When he has a slight bend in his elbows, *click!* and raise the treat so he stands up again, then reward. If you are slow, he will probably lie down; don't *click!* the down. The quicker he lies down for you, the quicker you will need to be at clicking for his elbow bend and raising the treat up before he goes down. Gradually encourage Buddy to dip lower and lower until he can bow with

Having Fun with Your Dog

You can end your routine with a flourish when you and your dog take a bow together. Gradually encourage him to dip lower and lower until he can bow with his elbows touching the ground and his rear end high in the air.

his elbows touching the ground and his rear end high in the air.

When you are sure you can get a half-bow or better without having Buddy go all the way into a down, you can start using the verbal cue. Use something other than the word "Bow," since "Bow" sounds a lot like "Down" and you are already risking confusion because of the similarity of the luring motion. Be creative with your word choices.

Taking the show on the road

Now you have a repertoire of six tricks with which to dazzle your friends and neighbors. You can add an almost infinite number of new tricks simply by picturing the behavior in your mind that you want Buddy to perform, and then figuring out how to use your treats to lure, shape, capture, or mold the behavior so you can *click!* and reward it. Remember to break the behavior down into small pieces so Buddy can win at each step along the way to the final desired behavior.

Try it; you might like it! And once you are convinced that "It's all tricks" you can toss those choke chains in the garbage and you and Buddy can get on with the serious business of having fun training together.

Agility Ability

In this exciting sport, dogs run, jump, and climb—and it's all off leash!

If you're into dogs, you've probably heard about agility. Maybe you've even seen it in action or tried it with your dog. Agility is one of the fastest-growing dog sports in the world, and with good reason—it's fun!

The ultimate team sport

Agility is fun for a whole bunch of reasons. It's fast. It's always different. The dogs love it. The handler is constantly challenged. But perhaps the most wonderful part about agility is the way the dog and handler work together as a team. It is the ultimate team sport—and like any team sport, the relationship of the team members is key.

From the beginning, agility seemed to be a hit with dogs and people. Agility began as a demonstration event at the Crufts Dog Show in England in 1978. The obvious enjoyment of the dogs and the enthusiasm of the crowd at the first agility demonstration could have predicted the future popularity and growth of the sport. Today, agility is practiced throughout the world. In North America alone, you can find more than 10 organizations that sanction agility trials.

The goal in agility is for the handler and dog to run an obstacle course, with the handler directing the dog through and the dog navigating the obstacles. The course generally consists of between 14 and 20 obstacles that are designed to test a dog's balance, speed, jumping, and climbing ability as well as the communication between the dog and handler. The obstacles commonly include:

- **Jumps:** A variety of jumps are used in agility including single jumps, double jumps, triple jumps, winged and non-winged jumps, panel

Agility is a leash-free sport that can be enjoyed by any healthy dog, regardless of breed, age, or size—and as long as his or her handler can keep up!

jumps, broad jumps, and tire or hoop jumps. The height of the jumps varies depending on the size of the dog.

- **Tunnels:** Flexible tunnels, 15 to 20 feet long, are used, as well as a collapsed tunnel made with a barrel opening and a fabric sleeve through which the dog pushes.
- **A-frame:** One of the "contact" obstacles (an obstacle that the dog must touch in a yellow-painted zone to ensure a safe performance on the obstacle), the A-frame is a large climbing structure over which the dog runs.
- **Teeter-totter:** Also called the seesaw, the dog tips the board as he runs across. The teeter-totter is another contact obstacle and the dog needs to touch the yellow zones for safety.
- **Dog walk:** This contact obstacle is a type of balance beam that is three to four feet in the air. The dog runs up a ramp, across the beam, and down the descending ramp.

- **Weave poles:** Up to 12 weave poles are found on a standard agility course. Weave poles are often considered the most difficult obstacles to teach a dog.
- **Table or pause box:** The dog gets on the table and stays in either a down or sit position for five seconds. This is a control exercise and requires a dog to stop in the midst of running through the course.

In a competition, the course must be run within a certain amount of time and the team can be judged "faults" for mistake, such as taking the wrong obstacle or knocking down a jump bar. The courses are always different, making communication between the handler and dog as critical as the dog's ability to navigate the obstacles.

Not just for superdogs

Big dogs, little dogs, fast dogs, slow dogs, mixed breeds, and pure breeds—all types of dogs can do agility. In fact, agility is one of the few dog sports providing as many opportunities for mixed breed dogs as for pure breeds. With the exception of AKC Agility, every dog agility organization in the United States welcomes mixed breeds in competition. Dogs as small as a Papillon and as large as a Great Dane can and do enjoy agility. Of course, not every dog (or person) is cut out for competition and only a select few will win national championships. But almost all dogs can enjoy some version of the sport.

Agility is an obvious choice for high-energy and athletic dogs. It gives dogs that are often seen as "hyper" a place to put their drive and energy. It is also a good way to help timid or shy dogs build confidence. It's a great way for both people and dogs to get some exercise.

In general, dogs who play agility should be physi-cally able to do the sport safely—they should have sound hips and elbows, have good vision, and be in good physical shape. But even dogs and handlers with some physical limitations can enjoy the just-for-fun experience of agility. For example, jump heights can be lowered for a dog that is not physically able to jump full height. A dog shouldn't do agility if it will make a condition worse, cause pain, or be unsafe in any way. It's a good idea to have your veterinarian conduct a basic health examination before beginning agility.

Competition or fun?

As with all sports, agility encompasses elements of competition. Agility can be played at the Olympic level, the city league level, or strictly for fun in the backyard or park.

In agility trials, teams compete in two ways. First, the dog and handler run against the time on the clock, with the goal of completing the course under the time limit and with no faults (called a clean run). In addition, the team is also competing against the other dog and handler teams within their class and height for placement—generally first, second, and third place dogs are recognized and awarded ribbons.

In addition to the standard agility course, dozens of games can be played in agility. Games range from those commonly found at trials, like Jumpers (which tests the dog's speed and the person's handling skills), Gamblers (which offers challenges in distance handling), and Snooker (which incorporates elements of both strategy and control), to those designed for fun or to help build specific skills.

Agility practice, even without competition as a goal, is a wonderful way to build everyday skills. Agility strengthens basic training such as the down, stay, and recall. It is a fun way to work on off-leash behaviors and develop off-leash reliability. It can help dogs become more confident in the world, and it can

Getting Started with Backyard Fun

Interested in giving agility a try, but don't have a training center near you? Here are a few things you can try at home. Remember to make these exercises as easy as possible until your dog gets the idea, offering lots of rewards along the way. Never force a dog to do any agility exercise. One of the most important aspects of agility is the dog's enthusiasm and willingness to play the game; forcing a dog to participate may spoil his natural inclination for fun. In addition, make sure your dog is physically able to comfortably do the exercises you are asking of him.

Most adult dogs can safely try out the exercises below, but if you have any doubts, check with your veterinarian first. For serious agility training, your dog should be at least a year old and in excellent condition. Excellent condition for agility means a dog who has good hips and elbows, and is a good weight (for agility, this means scrawny—you will want to be able to easily feel your dog's ribs when he is in a standing position). In addition, a dog who trains for agility should run off leash for at least 20 minutes four or five times a week. Walks alone are not enough to keep a dog in shape for agility.

Practice handling

Because agility means working with your dog on both sides of you and making lots of twists and turns while running together, it's helpful to practice "handling skills" with your dog. You will want to do these "on the flat" without any agility obstacles in the picture. First, try running in a straight line with your dog off leash on your left side. Then try it with him on your right side. If he's a bit confused, you can put a treat in your hand to help him follow you, giving him the treat when you stop. Use the palm of your hand to guide your dog as you move.

Once your dog can run in a straight line, try turning to the left, then to the right. Help your dog understand where you are turning by using your foot, shoulder, and hand closest to your dog to motion to where you want him to go. Practice turning and moving in the opposite direction, too. Try having your dog

Begin teaching your dog to jump by having him stay on one side of the jump. You move to the opposite side and then invite your dog over. You can use a treat or a toy to encourage him the first couple of times.

turn toward you, and then have your dog move away from you.

Jumping into action

You can put together a makeshift jump by placing a broomstick on top of two cinder blocks, or you can build or buy practice jumps made out of PVC pipe. When you begin teaching your dog to jump, use a very low jump—below your dog's elbows. As he begins to get the idea, you can gradually raise the jump to between his elbow and shoulder. Unless your dog is in very good shape and conditioned to jump, do not raise the jump above his shoulder height.

Begin teaching your dog to jump by having him stay on one side of the jump. Move to the opposite side and then invite your dog over. You can use a treat or a toy to encourage him the first couple of times. When your dog comes over the jump, click! and treat. Once your dog is happily coming over the jump to you, start sending your dog away from you, over the jump, to a target. The target can be a touch object like a small plastic lid. Or, have your dog wait, toss a toy over the jump, and then send him over to get the toy. When he goes over the jump to the target or toy, lavish *him with praise. Next, try walking, then running with your dog as he goes over the jump.*

Fun with a play tunnel

You can purchase a small tunnel for kids at a toy store or use a long box (like those that hold hot water heaters) with the ends cut off as a play tunnel for a smaller dog. For larger dogs, you can put together a makeshift tunnel with chairs and a bed sheet. As with jumping, begin by encouraging your dog to come to you through the tunnel. You may need to get down on the ground and stick your head in the tunnel, reaching through with a treat to get your dog to go through the first

A 12-inch-wide board, 8 to 12 feet long, balanced on two cinder blocks is a fun way to start the dog walk. Encourage your dog to walk across the board. Walk with your dog if necessary. Be sure to *click!* and treat when your dog is on the board, not when he steps off.

few times. When your dog comes through the tunnel to you, click! *and treat. As with jumping, after your dog can come to you, practice sending him to a target, and then practice running next to your dog as he goes through the tunnel.*

Walk the plank

A 12-inch-wide board, 8 to 12 feet long, balanced on two cinder blocks, is a fun way to start the dog walk. Encourage your dog to walk across the board. Walk with your dog if necessary. Be sure to click! *and treat when your dog is on the board, not when he steps off. Then spend some time helping your dog understand where his back feet are (so he won't slip off when moving quickly), by having your dog do tricks like sitting, lying down, or changing direction on the board. Encourage your dog by clicking and treating for keeping all four feet on the board. Once he gets the idea of walking across the board and knows where his back feet are, try running in both directions and with you on each side.*

Putting it together

Once your dog can jump, run through the tunnel, and run across the board, you can try putting it all together in a mini course. At first, put your obstacles in a straight line, 10 to 15 feet apart. Try running back and forth with your dog. You can encourage your dog by clicking and treating each obstacle at first. Once you have mastered running together with the obstacles in a straight line, try it with the obstacles in a circle.

Remember to keep it fun and give your dog lots of rewards. Try treats, ball play, or a great game of tug. Experiment and see what motivates your dog the most.

help people learn to better train and communicate with their dogs. (If you can teach a dog to run through a set of weave poles—which is anything but a natural behavior for a dog—you can probably teach him just about anything!) Quite simply, agility practice can improve relationships between dogs and people.

Purely positive fun

The sport of agility has, perhaps inadvertently, become a huge promoter of positive training methods. You can probably imagine that it would be difficult to drag a reluctant dog over an A-frame or force a dog to run at top speed through a set of weave poles. Agility training generally incorporates positive-oriented training techniques, including clicker training, lure and reward, and classical conditioning. Dogs are motivated and rewarded with food, praise, and toys. Although some agility instructors do use punitive methods, most do not.

Getting started

Because agility is still relatively new, many of the people who are currently involved started out self-taught—building equipment, reading books, watching videos, attending seminars, and learning by trial and error. With the growing popularity of the sport, however, agility-training facilities are popping up everywhere. If you'd like to try agility, you could begin on your own, but your best bet is to find a trainer in your area to help you get started. When you are looking for a trainer, look for someone who:

- Focuses on safety and the well-being of the dogs above all else.
- Uses motivational methods. Forcing a dog onto equipment can ruin the fun for both of you.
- Can help you understand both how to teach your dog to use the equipment *and* help you learn to direct your dog through the course. Agility is a 50/50 team sport. You each need to learn your part.

If you do not plan to compete, your instructor does not need a competition background. But if you do want to compete, look for a teacher who has competition experience to mentor you through the process. If you or your dog have any special needs or limitations, ask the instructor if she is willing to work with you around those areas.

Because agility training is a long-term training process, it becomes especially important to find an instructor with whom you enjoy working.

It's addictive

Anyone who has tried agility can tell you that it's addictive. You just may end up with jumps in your backyard, weave poles in your living room, and a whole new set of vocabulary words. You may end up practicing front crosses and reverse flow pivots as you vacuum. You may start muttering terms like "clean runs" and "yards per second" in your sleep. Like any person exhibiting signs of addiction, your friends and family may wonder if you've lost your mind—or just given it to the dog.

Furiously Fast Fun

Flyball racing may be the best possible game for high-energy dogs.

Picture this: Two racing lanes, each with a row of four jumps leading up to mechanized boxes that throw tennis balls. Now imagine two teams, each with four ball-crazed dogs. The dogs are wound so tight that they can barely contain themselves. Their excited barking reaches a deafening pitch.

Suddenly, a light flashes green and the dogs are off. The first two dogs on each team race down their rows of jumps and, with seemingly effortless motion, each dog banks off the box, hitting a pedal that shoots out the ball. If you blink, you'll miss the ball catch as the dogs race each other back over the jumps. As the first two dogs cross the finish line, the next dogs on each team take off, passing at full speed. In less than 20 seconds, all four dogs on both teams have run the course, with the winning team crossing the finish only a split second ahead.

Flyball racing is fast and furious. Most of all, it's a great time for both dogs and people!

It's for the dogs!

Flyball is an obvious choice for ball-crazed dogs, but even if your dog is not into retrieving, he can be taught to hit the pedal, grab the ball, and race back to you.

But what if you have a dog who is *too* ball crazy? Flyball training is also a good opportunity to work with dogs with ball "issues." For example, you can teach dogs who like to play keep-away with retrieve objects to reliably bring the ball back. And for dogs that are out-of-control retrievers, flyball is a good avenue to channel their drive, while helping them learn self-control.

Plus there's the exercise factor. We've all heard the saying that, "A tired dog is a good dog." Flyball works dogs hard, which may be part of why it appeals to both high-energy dogs and their human roommates.

Any size or shape

Flyball racing is open to any breed and any size dog. While speed-demon dogs like Border Collies and Jack Russell Terriers are obvious contenders for flyball, they are not the only dogs that will enjoy and excel at the sport. According to the North American Flyball Association (NAFA, the organization that oversees tournaments in North America), there are more than 170 different breeds (including mixed breeds) registered to race in flyball tournaments. In fact, NAFA's top-pointed dog for 2001 was a mixed breed.

Long-legged dogs definitely offer a speed advantage, but smaller dogs, such as small mixed breeds or terriers, fulfill very important roles on a team. Since the smallest dog on the team determines the height of the jumps for the entire team, many teams include one small speedster to augment their speedy strategy. Don't worry, a small dog doesn't have to force a standard-size tennis ball into his tiny mouth—in flyball, smaller balls can be used if those are more comfortable for the dog.

Any dog that is physically able to run, jump, and bank off the box is a good candidate for flyball. In addition, because dogs run in close proximity to other dogs—while in a highly aroused state—they must not display aggression toward other dogs.

Speed and more speed

A flyball course is 51 feet long with four jumps, spaced at 10-foot intervals. The first jump is placed 6 feet after the start/finish line, and the flyball box is placed 15 feet after the fourth jump. The jump height is set at 4 inches lower than the smallest dog, with the minimum height being 8 inches and the maximum being 16 inches.

Each dog must run in relay fashion down the jumps, trigger the release of the ball, catch the ball, and then run back over the four jumps. The next dog is released to run the course, but can't cross the start/finish line until the previous dog has returned and crossed the line. If a dog loses the ball or misses a jump, he must run again after the rest of the team has completed their turn. The first team to have all four dogs finish without errors wins.

Flyball is obviously about speed—and competitions are won and lost with fractions of seconds. But that doesn't mean your dog (or your team) has to be the fastest of the fast to enjoy competition. In NAFA sanctioned tournaments, teams are divided into divisions so that they compete against other teams of equal abilities. That way every team has a chance at winning an individual race.

Flyball fundamentals

Flyball racing seems straightforward—dogs run down the course, get the ball, and run back. But flyball racing is actually a series of more than 25 different behaviors put together. For a dog to run a course with speed *and* accuracy, each of the elements or behaviors needs to be carefully taught.

Some of the behaviors dogs need to learn include snatching the ball in the air, turning quickly, and returning to you. They need to understand single-bounce jumping so they can run with maximum speed. They need to be able to push the pedal on the box, and then to catch the ball as it shoots out. They need to master turning off the box (called a swimmer's turn) and be able to pass other dogs at full speed. When the dogs have these and other behaviors down, they need to learn to put it all together into a run.

Take a Hike!
Do your homework before you go and you'll enjoy happy trails.

If you spend your time in the company of dogs, you're probably used to walking—long walks, short walks, walks for potty stops, walks for exercise, walks to relieve boredom, and walks for walking's sake. So, what's the difference between walking and hiking? In practical application, not much. But in attitude, everything!

Think of hiking as an adventure, getting wild, and leaving the mainstay of human existence—even if only for a few hours. And sharing the hiking experience with a dog offers rewards beyond explanation.

Getting ready for your romp

If you've never hiked with your dog, but are thinking of trying it, you are in for a lot of fun. You may want to start out with a casual adventure—close to home and not too long. If your dog is nervous in the woods, make the experience fun (bring along lots of great treats or your dog's favorite toy), so you can assure that he'll soon overcome his nervousness and be as excited about hiking as you are.

Even for those dogs who obviously love the great outdoors, be sure to choose an adventure that suits both of your abilities. Think about the kind of physical condition you are in, and how adapted you are to the altitude, the outside temperature, and the terrain. For example, a dog (or person, for that matter) who lives and hikes regularly along the coast may have a tough time when hiking in higher altitudes. Likewise, a dog from a cool region may have some trouble in the heat of a summer desert. Muscles that are well suited for level or gently climbing trails may tire much faster on a steep climb. Don't try to go too far or climb too high if you or your dog is not up to the challenge.

Finding the ultimate spot

Finding a great place to hike with dogs can sometimes be a challenge, especially if you live in an urban or other populated area. Many places that offer great hiking are off limits to our dogs. Some areas will allow dogs, but only on certain trails or at specific times of the year. But places to hike with dogs are out there—you just have to look!

Probably the best way to find fun hiking spots is to talk with other people who like to hike. Ask your friends, or the folks who work at the local outdoor equipment store or feed store. You can also search through hiking guidebooks—there are dozens in most libraries and bookstores. Some say whether dogs are allowed in the area, and sometimes they even include leash restrictions.

You can also check online resources. A quick search for "Hiking in Santa Cruz," for example, came up with a few great sites, complete with directions to the trailheads and maps of the area. Once you've got a place in mind, double-check the dog rules. It's disappointing to get to a trailhead only to discover that an area that was once open to dogs is not anymore.

Here are a few additional tips for your search. National *Forests* can be a gold mine for hikers with dogs—dogs are allowed on most trails, and are often permitted off leash. National *Parks,* on the other hand, are usually less dog-friendly and rarely allow dogs on trails. Other places to check are local wilderness areas, county parks, and state parks. Rules and regulations vary dramatically from place to place and park to park, so call ahead to find out the specifics about dog regulations.

Hiking light: just the basics

When you're heading out for a hike—whether it be a quick romp through your local woods or an all-day adventure—remember this rule of thumb about what to bring: If you need it, your dog will likely need it too. For even the shortest of hikes, you will probably need to bring a few basic items:

- **A leash.** Of course. Even if the area is open to off-leash dogs and your dog is reliably responsive to your voice control, you may need a leash under certain circumstances (like if you run into a skunk on the trail and don't want your friendly dog to investigate).
- **Identification.** Your dog should always wear identification, with your contact numbers and, if you have traveled far from home, the best number to reach you locally.
- **Plastic bags** for scooping poop. If you'll be a distance from a trash can, take an extra, heavy-duty Ziploc bag for double-bagging so you can stash the goods in a pack.
- **Water** for you and your dog. A hiking dog may need to drink two to three times as much as he does when hanging out at home. Give your dog drinks of water frequently when hiking. Use caution not to wait until your dog is so thirsty that he'll want to drink too much, too fast.
- **Snacks and training treats.** If you get hungry when you hike, your dog is probably hungry, too.

It's not a good idea to let your dog drink straight from streams, rivers, or lakes, as many harbor waterborne pathogens such as Giardia. If it's not safe for you to drink, it's probably not safe for your dog.

Give your dog hiking snacks as rewards for sticking close and coming when called.

- **First-aid kit.** You may not need to bring a first-aid kit for a short walk in a local park or close to home, but for longer hikes and wilderness adventures, a first-aid kit for you and your dog is a must.

In addition, you may want to have a few items stashed in your car, for those "just in case" moments. If your dog enjoys romping through puddles and creeks, or is likely to roll in that delightfully smelly something, grooming supplies can make the ride home a little more pleasant for the human half of the team. Bring a couple of dog towels, a jug of water, and a comb and brush.

Other gear and gizmos

While the "basics" above will be enough for many adventures, you may want to consider a few additional items:

- **Dog booties.** Your dog's feet may need protection if you're hiking over rough surfaces, hot sand, or wet snow.

  Dog booties come in a variety of sizes, styles, and materials, and it's important to pick a type that will be both easy to put on and appropriate for the elements. Nylon or neoprene booties that fasten with Velcro are easy to get on and off your dog. Look for booties with heavy-duty soles, such as those made with Cordura. Leather booties lace up and are a bit of a task to get onto a dog's paws, but may hold up well in seriously rough conditions (like traveling over shale or volcanic rock). Polarfleece may be a good choice in cold and snow.
- **Dog packs.** Many dogs love carrying packs. Most dogs who weigh more than 30 pounds can safely carry a pack. Hip dysplasia, back problems, and other health issues can make packing unsafe for

some dogs, so if your dog has any health problems, it's a good idea to check in with your veterinarian before fitting your dog with a pack.

Dog packs come in different sizes and styles, from daypacks to heavy-duty mountaineering packs. If you'd like your dog to pack his own stuff, you'll want to train him to wear the pack before you head out on the trail

- **Collapsing water bowls and handy-dandy bottles.** Collapsing water bowls fold or twist and can be stashed in a pack. And the water bottles with built-in bowls for dogs to drink from? Very cool. In a pinch, however, you can use an extra plastic bag; simply roll down the sides for an "instant" bowl.

Generally, the more frequently dogs have the opportunity to walk with you off-leash, the calmer and better-behaved they become. Make sure your pockets are full of tasty treats, so you can reward your dog for her reliable recalls and leaving wildlife alone.

- **Protection from the elements.** Being too hot or too cold can be dangerous for people *and* dogs. Be sure that you are both prepared for the expected conditions—and if you're going more than a few miles, make sure *you* are prepared for the unexpected, too. For example, if your dog needs a sweater or coat for cold days at home, take one along on your hike if the conditions warrant it. If you're taking a long hike or backpacking in extreme conditions, check into a lined parka with a waterproof shell for your dog; she'll appreciate it.

In addition, be sure your pooch doesn't overheat on your adventure. Keep her cool by wetting her down.

Lions and tigers and bears

"Better safe than sorry" is a code all hikers should follow. Certain wild creatures can pose a real danger to you and your dog. It's not just the big animals (like mountain lions and bears) that can be trouble, either. Some of the biggest risks come from the smallest beings.

Ticks, spiders, and other things that crawl can certainly be trouble for dogs. In many states, for example, ticks carry Lyme disease. In other areas, they may carry Rocky Mountain spotted fever. If you're hiking where ticks live, check your dog frequently and remove any that you find. Some places are home to black widow or brown recluse spiders, both of which can be dangerous to dogs. Most snakes, scorpions, and toads are not harmful to dogs (your dog will generally pose more of a risk to them!), but there are a few exceptions. Rattlesnakes, copperheads, cottonmouths, and coral snakes, and even porcupines, for example, can all be dangerous to dogs.

And in case you haven't considered it, just imagine the car ride home if your dog decides to investigate a skunk.

Wild dogs, mountain lions, and bears are all serious concerns. If you are traveling in an area where these animals live, it is imperative that your dog is with you and on leash at all times.

Small furry creatures, like gophers, squirrels, and mice, will generally be in more danger from dogs than the other way around, as will deer and elk. *Don't allow or enable your dog to chase animals*—for his safety and theirs. A simple chase, even if your dog is not likely to catch or hurt them, can tire an animal, making it an easier target for another predator. A dog chasing any animal can easily become lost—many people have

Leave Only Paw Prints

Hiking with dogs has become an endangered activity in some areas. More and more places are restricting access for dogs. The reasons may be obvious. Wilderness areas are shrinking, the population of people and dogs is ever-growing, and the places where the two meet have become more congested. Those of us who love the great outdoors are rightly concerned about the well-being of our wilderness areas, and about the future of hiking with dogs. So what can you do?

Respect wildlife and help your dog do the same. *If your dog enjoys a good chase, keep him on leash! What might seem like a harmless chase could put undue stress on wild birds and animals.*

Try to have as little impact on the area as possible. *Pack your trash. Scoop your dog's poop and carry it out. Try not to disrupt plants and other natural features. Use special care not to pollute water sources, too.*

Act as an ambassador for all dog people. *Always follow posted guidelines and rules for dogs. It's hard to believe, but not everyone likes dogs! It could be terrifying for some people to have your dog bark and run up to them on the trail—or just plain rude to allow* your wet, dirty dog to crash some other hiker's picnic lunch. Help others see that those of us who hike with our dogs really care about others and the wilderness. We want to see it remain available and untouched for all to enjoy—dogs included!*

Respect the wilderness as a precious and fragile treasure. "Take only memories, leave only paw prints."

Having super-alert trail companions like terriers along on hikes will help you detect and see wild animals before they melt out of sight. Such vigilant dogs should also be leashed at all times, lest they rocket after an animal and disappear with it.

permanently lost their dogs in this very way. And a dog who becomes accustomed to chasing every animal he sees is likely to cause a serious accident someday, when he encounters someone on a horse.

Along with taking care around animals, you'll want to be aware of other natural features that may pose a hazard to you or your dog. For example, fast-moving or very cold water can also be dangerous. And some dogs are oblivious to the risk of cliff edges; keep them close to you.

If the area where you hike features poison oak, ivy, or sumac, take special care to protect yourself. Dogs seldom suffer the itchy, painful rash associated with these three plants. A more realistic fear is that your dog will play in the poisonous plant, and the oils will get on you when you pet him.

The rash that humans get from these infamous plants is caused by a chemical called urushiol, which is present in the plant's leaves, bare branches, and even its roots. Under hot, humid conditions, the poisonous oil becomes harmless in about a week. However, under dry conditions, the oil can retain its harmful effect for as long as six weeks.

If you are particularly sensitive to the rash, keep your dog away from these plants, even if it means keeping him on leash for the entire hike. If he does romp through the plants, try not to touch him until you've bathed him, which you should do as soon as possible. Use a soap (like Fels Naptha laundry bar) or a commercial solution formulated to cut the oil, and wear rubber gloves and protective clothing.

Wonderful experiences await

Don't be scared off by all of these words of caution and hints at possible dangers. Still, it's good to know what might be there, so that you can take the simple precautions needed to protect yourself and your dog. If you're new to hiking or traveling to a new area, how do you find out what animal, plant, and other natural dangers might be found along the trail? Many trail-

Bring plenty of poop bags with you on hikes; long journeys tend to cause dogs to eliminate more frequently than on their daily walks.

Carry enough water for yourself and your dog. It's not a good idea to let your dog drink straight from streams, rivers, or lakes, as many harbor waterborne pathogens such as *Giardia*.

heads have signboards that will update you on animal sightings and any special dangers.

If the area you are visiting has a ranger station, you may be able to call ahead and ask. You can also quiz people who have visited the area and look in the guidebooks. If these options aren't available, simply be aware of your surroundings and use common sense.

Hiking is one of the most wonderful experiences you can share with a dog. Traveling down a trail together lets you share the adventure and fun. Plus, when hiking with a dog, you will get to see the wilderness through different eyes—your dog's. Pay attention when her ears go up, or when she lifts her nose to the wind. Her canine curiosity may lead you places you would never go on your own.

Doggie Camp

Relax, learn—or do both!—with your dog in a gorgeous resort setting.

Camping means different things to different people, but to dogs, camping means fun!

Like most things with the word "camp" in them, dog camps generally take place in the country and involve sleeping away from home. The camps come in two main types: intensive training-oriented seminars and "fun camps," where dog-oriented socializing and entertainment are the order of the day.

Camp Gone to the Dogs, the oldest and most famous "fun camp," has offered week-long vacations for people and their dogs at Vermont school campuses and country inns since 1990. "When we feature sports like agility and obedience," says camp founder and director Honey Loring, "the emphasis is never on competition. Our goal is to have fun."

In training-oriented camps, the focus is on in-depth education in canine sports and occupations, including competition obedience, Schutzhund, agility, Flyball, tracking, field training (hunting), search and rescue, water sports, sheep herding, mushing, backpacking, clicker training, disc dog (Frisbee), and more.

Watersports camps are a blast in summer. (Photo courtesy of Camp Gone to the Dogs, Putney, Vermont.)

Insider Tips from Veteran Campers

- *Policies vary from camp to camp, but sports and fun camps depend on campers to bring well-socialized dogs. Anyone with an extremely shy, fearful, or occasionally aggressive dog should consult with camp directors before registering. Dogs should not bark excessively.*

- *Some camps require certain titles, training, or experience as prerequisites. Read contracts and waivers carefully before signing.*

- *Bring appropriate equipment and food for your dog. Campers are expected to clean up after their dogs immediately and thoroughly. In most camps, dogs must be leashed unless specifically allowed off leash. Dogs left in rooms must be crated and must stay quiet. In most camps, state health regulations do not permit dogs in dining rooms, and some states prohibit smoking in all rooms.*

- *In most cases, campers must be 18 or over, although some camps allow children age 13 to 17 if accompanied by an adult, and 4-H dog camps are specifically for children.*

- *Most camps allow campers to bring two dogs, with an additional fee for the second dog. Some camps have special classes and play groups for puppies.*

- *Females should not be in season. Vaccination requirements vary, but most camps require proof of rabies vaccination.*

- *The more rustic or specialized the camp, the more campers are expected to be physically active.*

- *Things you may want to bring: flashlight, alarm clock, lawn chair, camera, fan, tape recorder, sheet for placing under kennel, and cell phone (but keep it turned off during classes). Required at some camps: sleeping bag or sheets and blanket, pillow, and towels (for you and your dog!).*

Whether your concept of a vacation with your dog is relaxing or intense, and your idea of "camping" is electricity-free or just free of cable TV, there is a camp for you.

Some camps accommodate more than 250 participants and auditors (observers). That's big! And some are so small, they limit attendance to 6 or 10. What size best suits you and your dog?

Is the camp a day camp or sleep-over camp? Day camps provide classes, lunch, and in some cases evening events, but campers are otherwise on their own. Sleep-over camps offer a total package with more camaraderie but less privacy. Accommodations range from tents to dorm rooms, cabins, motels, and RV hookups.

Going Camping with Canines
Preparation is key to enjoying your dog's overnight outdoor adventures.

Camping really is one of the few vacations that allows even the most boisterous of our four-legged friends to easily join us on the adventure. Plus, it's a wonderfully inexpensive way to see the world—no hotel bills and no kennel or dog-sitting expenses.

The perfect place

Finding a great place that offers the experience you are looking for *and* allows dogs can sometimes be a trick. Many places have dog restrictions that limit access. One of the best ways to find a good spot in your area is to ask other people who camp with dogs. Ask your friends, the people who work at your local outdoor store or animal supply store, the folks who work in your vet's office, or your dog trainer. You might be surprised at how many people know the perfect spot to camp with dogs.

In addition, check out camping guidebooks (try your local library!) or look on the Internet for information about camping in a specific area or park. Many guide sources will tell you if dogs are allowed, but if they do not, you can call the camping area and ask.

As a rule of thumb, National Forests and Bureau of Land Management (BLM) lands most often allow dogs.

Costume contests are enjoyed by all campers—and provide a good training opportunity! (Photo courtesy of Camp Gone to the Dogs, Putney, Vermont)

State parks, local parks, and private campgrounds vary from location to location. National Parks will often allow dogs in the actual campground, but usually ban dogs from any trails surrounding the campground.

Once you find a place in a guidebook or hear about a great spot through a friend, investigate a little further

WDJ's editor and her son took their Chihuahua on a backpacking trip in the Sierra mountains. The tiny dog was a trooper until the rocky trail took its toll on his feet. On their next trip, they'll pack Mokie's booties, so they don't have to pack Mokie.

before you go. Rules and regulations about dogs are always changing. A place that accepted dogs last year might not this year. Call ahead and ask if dogs are allowed and if there is an additional fee for the dog. In addition, ask if there are any restrictions for dogs on the surrounding trails or beaches. It could be very disappointing if the only place you and your dog can hang out together is at the tent site.

Ready, set, go

Getting your dog ready for a camping trip can be as simple as throwing his bed and food in the back of the truck, or as extensive as spending weeks or months conditioning. It all depends on your dog's experience and what type of trip you plan.

For dogs who haven't been camping before, getting them used to the tent or camper ahead of time is a great idea—or you may find your first night anything but restful! Try setting the tent up in your living room

or backyard for a few days and let your dog sniff and explore. If your dog is well socialized and adjusts easily to new situations, this may be all it takes. If your dog is a bit timid, you may want to specifically train your dog to sleep in the tent.

One of the most common issues for dogs who are new to camping is the issue of nighttime noises. Some dogs will cower, growl, or bark at every rustle, bump, and bang—and not without reason. Camp noises are often the noises of wild animals. Many of our city dogs have not heard the chatter of a skunk or the rustle of a family of raccoons. So how can you help your dog settle in so that you both get a good night's sleep?

First, have your dog sleep near you. Having a leash on your dog (and holding the leash while you sleep) is a good way to get a new dog used to the idea that you are still in charge, and he is still safe. Put your dog's bed right next to you, near your head. Sometimes that's all that is needed.

Second, make sure all of your dog's basic needs are met. Make sure he has had lots of exercise, isn't too hungry or thirsty, has gone to the bathroom, and is warm enough. A tired, well-fed, and comfortable dog is more likely to sleep soundly.

Third, try a socialization program specifically designed to help your dog get accustomed to being in the wild and the night noises that go with it. Start by taking regular walks in the woods or other wilderness areas. Visit different places so that your dog becomes comfortable anywhere, not just in one location. Once he is happy about his wild walks and relaxed about daytime noises, extend your outings to include picnics or other "hanging out" time. Start taking walks at dusk, when the animals and noises are at their height.

Fourth—and this is for the dog who really cannot settle!—plan on turning your first few nights camping into training sessions. Have great treats available. Try simply giving your dog a treat each time you hear a noise. Have your dog learn his "spot" in the tent. Offer the kind of reassurance that works best for your dog. For some dogs that may mean calm words; for others, a no-nonsense cue such as "go to bed" helps them feel safe. Teaching your dog to tolerate nighttime noises may seem like a lot of work, but it will be worth it when you can share years of camping fun with your dog friend.

You may also want to do a little daytime training to help him learn the camping ropes. Give your dog a place in camp to hang out. Show him his place and make it a pleasant experience by giving him a chew or stuffed Kong.

If you are in a crowded campground, help your dog understand that other campers passing by are friendly. Greet people with an upbeat tone and give your dog treats for remaining calm and quiet. You may even want to enlist the help of friendly campers, asking them to give your dog a few treats, too. Be sure to help your dog feel safe in his new environment by letting him know what is expected from the start. When your dog knows that you will be in charge in this new and exciting place, he will be much more likely to settle in.

From bones to beds

When you camp, what you bring is all you have, so advance planning is needed to make certain you and your dog are comfortable. Your dog's needs fall into a few categories:

- **Shelter and sleeping gear:** A good shelter and a comfortable bed are essential ingredients for every camping adventure. We highly recommend that you have your dog sleep with you in your tent or RV, rather than leaving him alone outside or even in your car. He will be more comfortable, protected from the elements, safe from predators, and less likely to be riled by night sounds if he sleeps near you. If you are car camping or backpacking, you and your dog will need a good tent.

  A caveat: Dog claws are hard on tent floors. Some of the best, lightest backpacking tents are most vulnerable to dog claws. You can extend the life of your tent by teaching your dog not to scratch at the floor, and by covering the floor with other gear so he walks and sleeps primarily on the bedding. Towel off a dog's paws before he enters the tent. And, if your dog might race out of the tent, be sure to snap your dog's leash on *before* you open your tent door to exit, especially in the middle of the night! There is nothing worse than having your dog charge off after an animal in the darkness, when other campers are around and you don't want to yell!

Dogs learn quickly how warm and comfortable tents and cushy sleeping bags are — especially compared to the hard, cold ground in the wilderness. Mokie loves hanging out in the tent, emerging occasionally at a gallop to chase birds and chipmunks out of camp.

Whether you are sleeping in a tent near your car or traveling by RV, bringing along your dog's regular bed or sleeping crate can add to his comfort level, which can mean a good night's sleep for you both. On backpacking trips, you can bring a lightweight dog bed or have your dog share your sleeping bag. Your jacket or parka can also double as a dog bed if you don't mind dog hair.

- **Protection from the elements:** Your dog will, of course, need his basic fur coat for protection. Will he need additional camp clothing? For cold weather or heavy rain, consider bringing a sweater or coat for your dog. For warmth and comfort, those made from fleece are a good choice; for wet weather, a parka made of Gore-Tex or treated nylon can offer good protection.

- **Food, treats, and water:** The basic rule of thumb for feeding dogs while camping is to give them the same food that they generally eat at home, and usually in the same quantity. The exception is if you are planning (and getting your dog into shape for) a strenuous excursion. Your dog may need extra energy for backpacking, sledding, or ski-joring. Don't forget to include your dog's favorite training treats in with your supplies. Even if your dog is a camping veteran, you could encounter a new or unusual experience that would benefit from a few training sessions.

  Camping generally involves lots of activity, so your dog may need to drink more water than usual. If the area to which you are heading doesn't have a drinking water source, carry or purify enough water for your dog, too. If you can prevent it, don't let your dog drink straight from rivers, streams, or other natural water sources; dogs are as susceptible as humans to waterborne diseases such as giardiasis.

- **Grooming supplies:** Ticks, fleas, burrs, mud, and other natural things will find your dog when camping, no doubt about it. If you are car camping, bring along a brush, flea comb, towel, and a dry or wet shampoo. In addition to your regular flea or tick protection, consider adding some type of protection from biting insects such as mosquitoes and biting flies. If you are backpacking, you may choose to travel light and take a minimum of grooming supplies. But definitely leave a towel, shampoo, and extra water for grooming at your vehicle—just in case you need to clean off your dog before a long drive home.

- **Leashes and other restraints:** You will need to have a regular leash and a flat collar for your dog. Even if you are going to an area where your dog is allowed off leash, he may need to be restrained part of the time; you never know when you might meet up with a porcupine or skunk on the trail. You may also want to bring an exercise pen or crate to keep your dog confined while in camp.

- **Miscellaneous:** A food and water bowl, dog pack and booties, toys and balls, your clicker and treat pouch, sunscreen and insect repellent (for dogs), and health certificate or proof of vaccinations are all good ideas. Don't forget to bring along plastic bags or a pooper-scooper. Even if you are traveling into the wilderness, it's best to clean up after your pooch. (Note: If you are burying your waste, it's usually okay to bury your dog's, too. Don't leave it exposed to contaminate the environment.) In addition, be sure to bring along a first-aid kit with supplies for your dog, as well as for you.

  Any time you travel, make sure your dog wears identification that includes a number that can be reached when you are away from home (like a cell phone or a relative's phone number).

Fun and Games
Build your relationship, solidify your dog's obedience, and have a blast!

Training is about relationships. While basic good manners and other more complex lessons are undeniably an important part of training, the most successful dog/owner teams are those who have cultivated their relationships with each other while they learn the ins and outs of "Sit," Down," "Stay," and all the other things a dog needs to know. In other words, the best teams are those who remember to have fun together along the way.

By the way: Just about everything presented here regarding dogs also applies to puppies—it *especially* applies to pups! That's because puppies are irrepressible fun machines. They romp, they play, they chase, they chew, they wrestle—in fact for a good part of your first 6 to 12 months with your new pup you will probably spend a lot of time trying to convince him to have a little less fun!

Be careful that you don't go overboard. If you insist that he be *too* serious, he'll *forget* how to play, and you'll end up with a lump of overweight canine who doesn't even want to accompany you on your walks around the block. Instead, engage your pup—and later, your dog—in structured games that direct his play energy into appropriate channels, reinforce his play behaviors, reward his sense of humor, and keep the relationship flames burning bright.

Fun games for Fido go far beyond fetching a tennis ball or a Frisbee. We're going to assume you know the old stand-bys, and introduce you to some that you may not have thought of. There are games you and Fido can play together, games the whole family can play, and games you and Fido can play with your friends and their dogs. Some of the best games also have practical applications, but don't let the practical aspects override the play. Have fun!

Games for you and Fido

Find It!

Ever wonder how those drug dogs do what they do? You can teach your dog to find stuff and wow your friends with his prowess. Dogs' noses are a bazillion times more sensitive than ours, so this is easy for Fido, once he understands what you want.

Bloodhounds aren't the only canines with good noses; any dog can be trained to search for items or people using his sense of smell. And training your dog to find your kids is a potentially lifesaving skill.

- **Step 1:** Have Fido wait and watch while you "hide" a strong-smelling treat in plain view, 5 to 10 feet away from him. Return to his side, tell him to "Find it!", and encourage him to go get the treat. Repeat this a few times until he seems to have the idea. Most dogs catch onto this pretty quickly.
- **Step 2:** Have Fido wait and watch you hide the treat in a less obvious place, such as behind a chair leg, under the edge of a cushion, or next to a toy. Return to his side, tell him to "Find it!",

and encourage him to go get the treat. When he can do this, hide several treats while he watches, and keep encouraging him to "Find it!" until he has found them all. Repeat this until he is doing it easily. If he has trouble, *don't* show him where the treats are—you will teach him to wait for you to point them out, rather than use his nose to find them himself! Move in the general direction of the hidden treat, but don't show it to him.

- **Step 3:** Have Fido wait where he can't see you. Hide several treats in the same places you hid them before. Bring him into the room and tell him to "Find it!" Keep encouraging him until he has found them all. If he has trouble, move in the general direction of the treat, but don't show it to him.

- **Step 4:** Try "Find it!" with other things—a ball, or a favorite chew toy. Show your dog the ball, have him wait and watch while you hide it in an easy place, then tell him "Find the ball!" Once he gets the idea, hide it without him watching, and tell him to "Find the ball!"

Practical applications: Are you forever forgetting where you left your car keys or the remote control? Let Fido find them for you. Teach him to find your kids, other family members, and friends!

If you have a dog who exhibits mild separation anxiety when you leave, you can hide several treats and a stuffed Kong or two. Ask her to "Find it!" just before you leave, and she will be too busy looking for hidden goodies to worry about you leaving.

Caution: Don't hide treats in places that will encourage your dog to dig into carpets or cushions or chew furniture to get to them.

Jumping Jacks

Some dogs love to jump. You may not choose to jump over jumps with your dog (although you might be surprised to discover how much fun it is), but you can create jumps from broomsticks, scraps of wood, boxes, and other household items. You can buy materials and build simple jumps if you are handy, or splurge and buy a set of agility or flyball jumps to play with—as long as you promise not to get all serious just because you paid real money for them!

- **Step 1:** Set up one low jump. If your dog is very cautious, just lay the bar on the floor and encourage your dog to step over it by luring him with a treat. As he gets braver, toss treats on one side of the low jump, then the other, until he is jumping it easily. Use lots of verbal praise as well, to keep it cheerful, exciting, and fun.

- **Step 2:** When he is jumping the low jump smoothly, add a verbal cue such as "Jump!," "Hup!," or "Over!" Start using the cue just before you toss the treat.

- **Step 3:** To fade the use of the treat, make a motion with your hand as if you were tossing the treat, then give the verbal cue. After your dog jumps, *then* toss the treat. Eventually move to random reinforcement, in which he gets a treat sometimes, but not every time he jumps. Remember to use verbal praise—your excitement will keep him enthusiastic about jumping.

- **Step 4:** Gradually raise the jump to a height that is suitable for your dog. Vary the location and type of jumps, so your dog is very jump-versatile. You can hang towels or jackets over jump bars to change the look, put flower pots or children's toys under them—be creative.

Practical applications: Hopping over small obstacles when you are hiking in the woods; and hey, Lassie jumped over fences when she ran home to tell everyone that Timmy was in the well!

Hide and Seek

This is easy and great fun, especially if you start with a young puppy who is still very dependent on you.

- **Step 1:** Take your dog for a walk in an area with some trees and other objects you can hide behind. When he is busy sniffing or bird watching, hide behind a tree. Be quiet and still, but peek out so you can watch him.
- **Step 2:** When your dog notices that you are gone, he should start searching for you. Let him search and find you, then make a big fuss over him with lots of yummy treats, tug with a tug toy, chase a ball, or whatever other reward is very meaningful to him. If he can't find you or doesn't look for you, help him—but just a little—by calling his name softly or making some other small sound that will get him started in the right direction.

Practical applications: This game teaches your dog to keep his eye on you—he never knows when you might disappear! It also teaches him to look for and find you if you happen to get separated accidentally.

Group games

Most of the following games can be played with the whole family, or are games you and Fido can play with your friends and their dogs. If your family has just one dog, pass him from one person to the next. Or get a group of your friends together with their dogs! Some

The "Sit Around the World" game is a great opportunity for your dog to practice prompt responses to "Come!" and offer a polite, uncued sit—especially in the face of distractions from other dogs and strangers.

Caution: Some dogs panic if they can't find you, especially dogs prone to separation anxiety. Remember to watch your dog, and help him if he is looking anxious, before full-fledged panic sets in. Also, some dogs could care less about where you are. If you think your dog might just run off into the woods when you play this game, keep him on a long line when you hide so you can prevent him from leaving.

of these games are great party activities for 4-H or dog training club get-togethers.

Sit Around the World

This game is not only fun, but it also practices that all-important "coming when called" behavior and reinforces polite greetings.

- **Step 1:** Arrange all available human players in a large circle in a safely enclosed area. Begin with Fido sitting in front of one person.
- **Step 2:** Have the next person in the circle call the dog with a cheerful, enthusiastic, "Fido, come!" You can use toys and squeakers initially, if necessary, to get Fido excited about playing the game. When Fido comes, he must sit before he gets his treat reward. Lure the sit, rather than giving the "Sit" cue, so he learns to sit in greeting without being asked.
- **Step 3:** Have the next person in the circle call the dog.
- **Step 4:** When Fido is really good about coming around the circle, you can start calling him randomly *across* the circle.
- **Step 5:** To play this game as a competition, be sure the humans are equally spaced, and then use a stopwatch to keep track of the time it takes for Fido to come and sit for each person. The holder of the fastest time, or fastest average times, is the winner.

Practical applications: Coming when called and polite greetings—how much more practical can you get? If you have a multi-dog household, try this with two or more dogs at a time, after each dog has learned the game individually.

Caution: If Fido is large and tends to jump up, small children may not be able to play this game until the dog understands the rules.

Musical Sits

For a group of dog people, this is far more fun than the human-only version of musical chairs. It can be played on several different levels, from beginner to advanced. As a another variation, each game can be played with downs instead of sits.

- **Easy version:** Have dogs and handlers walk to the music around orange cones in a large circle. When the music stops, all players ask the dogs to sit. Luring with treats is allowed; physically forcing the dogs to sit is not. First dog to sit wins! Repeat until everyone has had enough play.

Caution: Players can get pretty enthusiastic with this game. You may need to establish safety rules based on the footing of the play area, and the energy level, size, and strength of various players.

- **Intermediate version:** Space rug sample squares evenly around a large circle, with one fewer rug than there are dog/handler teams. Have dogs and handlers walk to the music, outside the circle of rugs. When the music stops, players must proceed to the next available rug square and have their dogs sit. The team that doesn't get a rug is out. Repeat until one team wins.
- **Advanced version:** Set out a double line of chairs back to back, in the center of the room, with one fewer chair than dog/handler teams. Put rug sample squares in a large circle around the chairs, one rug per team. Have dogs and handlers walk to the music outside the circle of rugs. When the music stops, players must proceed to the next available

The canine (hot dog) version of "bobbing for apples" has no real training applications; it's just fun to watch!

get the hot dogs out of the water and eat them. The dog who eats all his hot dog pieces the fastest wins.

Caution: We have never seen it happen, but you might want to watch for a dog who risks drowning himself while "diving for dogs." Stop the game if a dog starts sputtering!.

Practical applications: None we can think of, but it sure is fun and the dogs love it! Actually, if you want to teach your dog to retrieve underwater, this can get him started.

My Dog Can Do That

This is a commercially produced board game that you play with your dog. The game consists of three decks of cards—beginner, intermediate, and advanced. Any dog with basic good-manners training can play.

rug, put their dogs on a sit-stay, and run for a chair. The player who doesn't get a chair is out. *However*, if a dog breaks his sit-stay, the player must return to the dog, re-establish the sit-stay, and then return to her chair. Meanwhile, of course, another player can sit in the chair.

Practical applications: Great opportunity to practice leash-walking in groups, fast sits, downs, and reliable stays with *lots* of distractions.

Diving for Dogs

- **Step 1:** Slice several hot dogs into an equal number of discs. Keep each hot dog separate from the others.
- **Step 2:** Put 2 to 12 inches of water in a pan or tub. Small dogs will require a shallower "pool."
- **Step 3:** Drop one hot dog's worth of discs into the pan. Let the dog watch you do this. Be sure he knows they are hot dogs.
- **Step 4:** With your stopwatch in hand, say, "Ready, set, go!" and start the stopwatch. On "Go," the handler releases the dog and encourages him to

Resolve to play games with your dog at least three times a week—and then stick to your resolution!

Set aside one night a week as Family/Dog Game Night and get the whole family together to play.

Call all your dog friends and arrange for a regular monthly game day when you all get together and play.

Organize a dog games fund-raiser for your favorite animal charity. You can charge entry fees and invite the public, to introduce even more people to the fun of playing games with their dogs.

Do Not Pass "Go": Games You Should Not Play with Your Dog

A few canine games have high potential for reinforcing undesirable behaviors. While some dogs manage to play these games without apparent ill effect, the risks are great enough that we strongly suggest you avoid them, and thus avoid the risks altogether. After-the-fact behavior modification may be time-intensive and ineffective. Here are a few games we suggest you and your dog pass on:

- **Rough physical games.** *Some owners like their dogs to get very physical in play, encouraging behavior such as mutual body slamming and jumping up on humans. The problem is, it's very difficult for a dog to distinguish between ready-and-able play partners and frail and frightened ones.*

  It's best to redirect high-contact physical activities to acceptable games such as tug-of-war (with rules). If you must teach your dog to jump up on you, or into your arms (we'll admit this trick is cute), be sure to teach her that she can do it only when you give her some obscure verbal cue or hand signal that your grandmother or toddler is never likely to exhibit accidentally.

- **Chasing laser lights.** *It is entertaining to watch a dog chase a laser light beam with frenetic intensity, but BEWARE! The dog who most delights in chasing a laser light is the very dog who is most likely to turn the game into an obsessive-compulsive behavior known as shadow chasing.*

Shadow-chasers become fixated on any movement of light, and compulsively chase any light, reflections, or shadows that happen to cross their vision.

Obsessive-compulsive behaviors are frightening in their intensity, and difficult to resolve once they occur. Be smart and avoid this game—and any others that elicit intense, compulsive responses.

- **High-energy indoor games.** *In general, indoor games should consist of activities that require the dog to use his brain, not his brawn. Games that involve mad dashes around furniture, bouncing soccer balls off noses, and burrowing for hidden treasures are best suited for the great outdoors—not just because they can cause damage to family heirlooms, but also because, in general, encouraging your dog to be calm and self-controlled inside the house is a better idea.*

  If you live in an apartment with no yard and the only way to exercise your high-energy dog is with indoor play, keep the games very structured. For example, roll a ball down stairs or a hallway, don't throw it; require your dog to "Wait!" before you release her to pursue the prey; and have her sit and politely drop the ball into your hand when she brings it back. Ask for another "Wait!" before you roll it again. Practice some "moving downs" while she is on her way to the ball, and on her way back.

Each card has a behavior described on it that you have to try to get your dog to do—from simple "Sit on a verbal cue" from the beginner deck, to "Pick up a toy and drop it in a basket" in the advanced deck. The value is listed on the card (3 spaces, 5 spaces, 12 spaces, and so on); generally the more difficult the behavior, the higher the value.

You have 30 seconds to get your dog to perform the task on the card you've drawn. If you and your dog succeed, you can move your marker that many spaces on the board (or earn that many points, if you just keep score).

If you don't succeed, the next player in line—if she thinks *her* dog can perform the behavior—says "My Dog Can Do That!" (It is perfectly acceptable to use a superior tone of voice when saying "My Dog Can Do That!") If she and her dog succeed, she moves *double* the number of spaces or earns *double* the number of points.

Caution: Official rules say to play off leash. Depending on level of players and security of your playing field, you may want to modify this to allow leashes some or all of the time.

The team that reaches "Finish" on the board first, or that has the highest number of points at the previously agreed-upon ending time of the game, wins.

My Dog Can Do That is available from many pet supply sources, including DogWise (dogwise.com or 800-776-2665).

Practical applications: Lots of opportunities to practice a wide variety of good manners behaviors. Great motivator for teaching your dog tricks, including "Roll over," "Say your prayers," and "Balance a treat on your nose."

Personal preferences

Different types of games appeal to different human and canine personalities. There are many more games to be played than the ones we have described for you here, although we hope you found some that you like. Talk to your dog friends and see what ideas they have. Look up "dog training games" on the Internet and see if you can find more. Pick out the ones you and your dog are most likely to enjoy, gather the equipment you need to set them up—and then go play in the yard!

Sit, Stay, Cha, Cha, Cha: Musical Freestyle

Participants in musical freestyle (aka "dancing with dogs") say the sport is great for training, exercise, bonding, and just plain fun.

Dance fever is sweeping through the canine community. Dogs are spinning and twirling to country western, rock 'n' roll, movie theme songs, and more. What's driving these dogs (and their handlers!) to move to the beat? It's none other than the tail-wagging sport of canine musical freestyle.

Musical freestyle is a choreographed routine performed by handlers and their dogs. A relatively new addition to the dog sport world, freestyle came onto the scene less than 20 years ago. According to a few sources, freestyle seemed to pop up simultaneously in several countries, the way dog sports often do.

Today, freestyle is an established sport, but it continues to evolve and grow. The sport's early beginnings may have been rooted in formal heeling. But musical freestyle has moved beyond heeling routines into a true crowd-pleasing performance sport that incorporates a variety of trick-like movements such as spinning,

Laurel Rabschutz of Willington, Connecticut, and her five-year-old Newfoundland, Rollo. All three of Rabschutz's Newfs hold freestyle titles and frequently perform for dog-related fundraising and public service events. Here they perform to "Drunken Sailor" during the "Celebrating the Sea Dog" exhibit at the Mystic (CT) Seaport. (Photo courtesy of Laurel Rabschutz)

backing up, weaving through legs, and jumping over arms.

It's about the relationship!

We've all seen a couple on the dance floor that rivets an audience. When partners dance—really dance!—it isn't just the footwork or the fancy moves that fascinate; it's their connection, chemistry, and relationship. In musical freestyle, in which the dance partners are dog and handler, the relationship and the chemistry are also key.

Unlike other dog sports, in which the course or expected performance is essentially the same for each team, the focus of freestyle is the individuality of routines. Each team determines the music, moves, and interactions that will highlight the physical ability and personality of each team member. This aspect of freestyle readily lends itself to building on both the dog's and the handler's strengths—and thus on strengthening their relationship.

While the relationship-building aspect of freestyle is part of what makes it so attractive, the obvious joy—and just plain fun—of dancing with your dog cannot be overlooked.

Moving to the music

The first step in developing a musical freestyle routine is picking the music. The primary consideration is how well it fits the natural movement of the dog and handler; its rhythm needs to complement the dog's and the handler's rhythm, too. The music should also

Having Fun with Your Dog

highlight the personality of the team. Music can create a mood that reflects the seriousness, power, or playfulness of the team. Or it can conjure an atmosphere of romance or joy.

Uncommon moves

Once you have a music choice, the moves in a routine are designed to complement the music. The moves used in freestyle can be quite varied, depending on whether the routine is being developed for competition, demonstration, or just for fun.

Focus and attention are required in part because they are considered a demonstration of the bond between the handler and dog, but also because they are necessary for the dog to see the handler's cues within the routine.

Various movements are commonly incorporated into freestyle routines. Traditional heelwork, for example, is often at the foundation of a dance. Heelwork includes right- and left-side heeling, turns with the dog in the heel position, and right- and left-side finishes.

Backing up is another common movement in freestyle routines. Backing can be done with the dog in the

right- or left-side heel position, with the dog in front of the handler, or with the dog backing away from the handler.

Sidestepping or lateral moves are often incorporated. Lateral movements can be done in conjunction with the handler's movements, in a right- or left-side heel position. Sidestepping can also be done with the dog moving away from the handler, or with the dog moving in front of the handler.

Seventy-year-old Oklahoma freestyler Janet Chadwick says her two-year-old Lab-mix, Maggie, is the first dog she's really trained, despite having had dogs all of her life. Freestyle makes it fun and rewarding. (Photo courtesy Janet Chadwick)

Circles can be incorporated in which the dog circles the handler or another object. Spins, in which the dog turns in a 360-degree circle independent of the handler, are also popular in freestyle routines.

Other more advanced moves include a dog weaving between the handler's legs. This can be done as a figure 8, as a moving weave through the legs, or when a dog simply goes through the handler's legs. Teams can also incorporate tricks such as rolling over, crawling, or jumping. Distance work (when a dog does any of these movements away from the handler) is also considered to be advanced.

Taking the show on the road

It is important to note that in a freestyle competition, certain movements may be required at each level, depending on the organization. For example, in Canine Freestyle Federation (CFF), a beginning routine is done on leash, and should include specific elements of heeling, working in front, turns or pivots, and spins or circles.

There are four levels of competition in CFF, and in the most advanced level, the routine is done off leash and includes distance work, lateral movements, and backing up. All levels can also incorporate movements like weaving through legs, crawling, rolling over, and jumping over arms or legs. Even in competition, however, the required elements allow for a great deal of flexibility and creativity.

Plus, there are quite a few different organizations that promote freestyle, and each has its own unique philosophy. By investigating the different avenues for competition, a team is sure to find a match that will work for them. And for demonstration, exhibition, or "just for fun" freestyle routines, of course, anything goes.

Acknowledgments

I'd like to acknowledge and express my gratitude to a number of people who have helped shape and create *Whole Dog Journal* over the past decade. Horse trainer and instructor Diana Thompson's vision of a magazine full of holistic healthcare instruction for *horse* owners inspired Belvoir Media Group publisher Tim Cole to create *Whole Dog Journal*, and put me at the helm. Dog trainer and writer Pat Miller, an early adopter and promoter of positive dog training techniques, gently but assertively guided my development of an "all-positive" ethos for WDJ's training articles, and continues to generate warm and helpful positive instruction for WDJ readers. In the process of contributing health-related articles, noteworthy for their breadth and depth, holistic veterinarian Randy Kidd, PhD, DVM, typically proposes further inquiry into a dozen additional article topics. (He may be retired from veterinary practice, but his professional and intellectual curiosity are eternal!) Longtime WDJ contributor and book author CJ Puotinen continues to explore the wonders of holistic medicine and offer enthusiastic and practical advice about the most effective and accessible alternative and complementary healthcare methods available to dog owners. Sandi Thompson, who has taught positive puppy training classes in Berkeley, California for more than 20 years, offered early on to model with some of her canine friends for our instructional photographs . . . and a decade later, she still cheerfully answers the phone and agrees to demonstrate for our training articles. Amazing!

In addition to these stalwarts, I'm also in debt to dozens of other writers and experts who have contributed important articles and article ideas to *Whole Dog Journal* over the years – as well as to my friends and neighbors, who have generously shared their dogs, yards, living rooms, and children for photo shoots! Thanks, too, to my family, all animal lovers, who have sustained a heroic level of enthusiasm for (or at worst, tolerance of) my work and never-ending deadlines for a very long time. I'm especially grateful for the early and unconditional support of my mom, now on the far side of "the rainbow bridge," who was a reliable co-conspirator in secret plots to bring an endless number and variety of animals home when Dad was away, and who taught me to observe and treat all animals with kindness, humor, and patience. Thanks, everyone.

Index

A

Academy of Veterinary Homeopathy (AVH), 235
activities. *See also* games; training programs
  agility sport, 350–54
  camping, 362–66
  flyball racing, 355–56
  games, 367–73
  hiking, 357–61
  musical freestyle, 374–76
  "targeting," 121
  trick training, 345–49
acupuncture. *See also* holistic care, 272, 276, 279–81
  and cancer treatment, 327
adaptogens. *See* herbs
Addison's disease, 274
adoption, 34–37
aggressive behavior. *See also* behaviors, 111, 148
  and alpha roll, 50
  biting, 151, 153–54
  idiopathic aggression, 156–59
  and predatory behavior, 138
  and stress, 32, 36, 44, 148, 151
  types of, 158
agility sport, 350–54
Airedale Terriers, 261
Akitas, 261
All You Ever Wanted to Know about Herbs for Pets (Wulff-Tilford & Tilford), 330
aloe (*Aloe vera*), 272, 301–2

alpha roll, 50
American Animal Hospital Association (AAHA), 250
American Holistic Veterinary Medical Association (AHVMA), 235, 296
American Institute of Baking (AIB), 170
American Veterinary Chiropractic Association (AVCA), 235, 283
American Veterinary Medical Association (AVMA)
  on cost of cancer, 323
  on vaccinations, 246, 247, 250
angiogenesis. *See also* cancer, 322–23
Angiogenesis Foundation, 322
Animal Cancer Foundation, 323
animal shelters
  and microchips, 216, 217, 218
  "no-kill," 245
  puppies in, 244
animal-source protein. *See also* food, 194–96
  factory farmed, 194–95
  pasture fed, 196
antibiotics, 268–72
antioxidants, 271, 329, 340
  Protocel, 342
anxiety. *See* separation anxiety (SA); stress
Armstrong, Russell, 175–76, 176–77

arnica (*Arnica montana*), 302
aromatherapy. *See also* holistic care, 285–91, 327, 343
hydrosols, 290–91
Aronson, Linda, 133
artemisinin, 332–33, 342
arthritis
  chiropractic for, 283
  herbs/supplements for, 302
ashwagandha (*Withania somnifera*), 301
Association of American Feed Control Officials (AAFCO), 186
astragalus (*Astragalus membranaceous*), 271, 301, 331, 343
Atkins, Tracy, 20
attention deficit hyperactivity disorder (ADHD). *See also* hyperactivity, 131, 134
Australian Shepherds, 131

B

babies. *See* children, and dogs
Bach, Dr. Edward, 292–93
bacteria. *See* antibiotics
Ballner, Maryjean, 309, 310
barking, 41–42, 78–79, 142–47
basil (*Ocimum basilicum*), 271
Basset Hound, 261
Beagles, 317, 318
bedding
  cleaning, 205
  and flea control, 201–2
  and housetraining, 69, 72

behaviors. *See also* training
programs
after adoption, 34
aggressive, 50, 156–59
barking, 78–79, 142–47
basic for living with humans,
29–33
basic for vet exams, 239
bite inhibition, 15–18
biting, 151–55
canine compulsive disorder,
122–25
changing unwanted or difficult,
39–42, 109–13
and classical conditioning,
43–45
destructive, 114–16
establishing in puppies, 3–4, 14,
19, 21
growling, 148–50
hyperactivity, 131–37
jumping up/greeting, 52, 64,
76–79
with other dogs, 33, 222–29
physical causes for, 112
predatory, 138–41, 225
rage syndrome or idiopathic
aggression, 156–59
recall (coming when called),
84–88
and rewards or punishments,
5–6, 51–56
roaming, 211–15
separation anxiety, 31, 126–30
shaping, 83, 91
sitting, 80–83, 100–101, 103
sniffing, 94
and stress, 32, 36, 44, 148, 151
and submissive or excitement
urination, 11–12, 13, 69

unsocialized dogs, 117–21
walking on leash, 33, 89
Bell, Kristen Leigh, 285, 288
Bernese Mountain Dogs, 156,
314, 316
beta glucan, 330
Bielakiewicz, Gerilyn, 23
Billinghurst, Ian, 182, 184
bioresonance therapy. *See also*
holistic care, 337
bite inhibition, 15–18, 222
and large dogs, 66
and stress, 32
biting behavior. *See also* behaviors,
151–55
classification of bites, 154
and growling, 148
black salves. *See* escharotic salves
bladder cancer. *See also*
cancer, 314
Blake, Audrey, 331–32
Blake, Stephen, 343, 344
bloat, 235, 259–63
Bloodhounds, 261
boarding kennel, 2
bones, raw. *See also* food,
183–85, 187
Border Collies, 131, 355
boredom. *See also* behaviors
barking, 143
chewing, 116
and daycare, 219, 221
Borzoi, 261
Boston Terriers, 317
Boswellia (*Boswellia spp.*), 302
bowls, water or food, 202–3, 359
Boxers, 261, 314, 315, 316, 317
breeds. *See also* dogs
and agility sport, 351
and barking, 142

bloat in, 259, 260, 261
breed rescue groups, 244
canine compulsive disorder
in, 123
and chemotherapy, 321
and flyball racing, 355
food allergies and metabolic
disorders in, 165
genetic behaviors in, 140
hyperactivity in, 131, 132
idiopathic aggression in, 156
suited to environment, 277
susceptibility to cancer, 314–18,
324, 338
training and size, 58–63
Brown, L. Phillips, 176
Brown, Steve, 339
Budwig, Johanna, 329
burdock root (*Arctium
lappa*), 301
Bussey, Melissa, 21

C
calendula (*Calendula officinalis*),
271, 272, 296–99
camping, 362–66
Cancell, 336–37
cancer, 281, 313–44
anticancer diet, 334–35
conventional treatments for,
320–21
cost of, 323–25
holistic care for, 326–37
new treatments for, 321–23
preventing, 338–44
survival rates of, 319–20
symptoms of, 313–14
types of, 314–18
Canine Aggression Workbook, The
(O'Heare), 112

canine compulsive disorder
(CCD). *See also* behaviors,
122–25
Canine Freestyle Federation
(CFF), 376
Canine Neuropsychology
(O'Heare), 112
Cappel, Beverly, 184
carbohydrates, and cancer. *See also*
diet, 165, 335
carpets, cleaning, 204
car restraints, 2
carrot seed *(Daucus carota)*, 288
cartilage supplements, 330
cats
    chasing, 39
    and essential oils, 202
    nutritional deficiencies in, 179
Catty, Suzanne, 291
Cautious Canine, The
    (McConnell), 27
cayenne pepper, 271, 300
cedarwood, atlas *(Cedrus atlan-
    tica)*, 288
Chadwick, Janet, 375
Chambreau, Christina, 304
chamomile, 288, 299, 300, 301
chemicals
    and cancer, 340–41
    household, 199–201, 207
    pesticides, 208
chewing. *See also* behaviors,
    32, 208
    destructive, 41, 114, 116
children, and dogs, 58, 96–104, 132
    and bites, 95, 140, 151
    children as trainers, 99–104
    and growling, 148–49
    preparing for baby, 97–98
    with puppies, 18, 25

treats and conditioning, 44, 96
chiropractic care. *See also* holistic
    care, 272, 282–84
    and cancer treatment, 327
clary sage *(Salvia sclarea)*, 288
cleaners, household, 2, 6, 199–201,
    202, 203, 204
clicker training. *See also* training
    programs, 2, 36, 58, 346
    for calm dog, 46–50
    and children, 99–104
    for crates, 73–75
    for hyperactive dog, 134–35,
    136–37
    and sitting, 80–83
    and walking on leash, 91–94
clinics. *See also* veterinarians,
    231–32
    specialized, 234–35
    staff in, 233–34
Cocker Spaniels, 156, 165, 318
coconut oil, 329, 340
collars, 2, 64, 208, 216, 217
    shock, 52, 53, 214
Collies, 261
conditioning. *See* training
    programs
Conway, Kellyann, 221
Cook, Frank, 175, 177, 178
corn, in diet. *See also* food, 192–93
corticosteroids, 273–76
cortisol. *See* glucocorticoids
counter-conditioning and desensi-
    tization (CC&D). *See* training
    programs
crates, 1, 3, 71–75
    and housetraining, 6–7, 8, 9, 10,
    69, 72
    problems with, 72–73
    size of, 7

training for, 73–75, 115, 240
cryosurgery, 334–35
curcumin, 331, 343
Curran, Nancy, 262

D
Dachshunds, 317
Dalmatians, 165, 317
dancing, with dogs. *See*
    musical freestyle
dandelion, 301, 331
Davis, Kathy Diamond, 309
daycare centers, 128, 219–21
de Bairacli Levy, Juliette, 182,
    183, 343
DeNapoli, Jean, 133
desensitization. *See also* training
    programs, 120
destructive behavior. *See also*
    behaviors, 114–16
devil's claw root *(Harpagophytum
    procumbens)*, 302
diet. *See also* food, 163
    and behavioral problems, 112
    and bloat, 261
    and cancer treatment/preven-
    tion, 327, 328–29, 330, 334,
    335, 339–40
    and disease, 164–65
    and energy requirements,
    165–66
    home-prepared, 188–97
    quality of, 203, 204, 295
    raw food, 182–86, 278
    variety in, 168, 179–81
    weight-control program, 242–43
diethylcarbamazine. *See* heart-
    worm disease
dill, 298
disasters, preparedness for, 209

diseases. *See also* health
bloat, 259–63
cancer, 313–44
and diet, 164–65
and glucocorticoids, 273, 274
heartworm, 251–54
and homeopathy, 304
treated by acupuncture, 281
and vaccinations, 249, 250
Doberman Pinschers, 156, 315, 316
Dodds, Jean, 133
Dodman, Nicholas, 133
Dog Massage: A Whiskers to Tail Guide to Your Dog's Ultimate Petting Experience (Ballner), 309
dog parks, 222, 228
dogs. *See also* behaviors; training programs; health; puppies
adopting, 34–37
body language in play, 226–27
bully behavior, 224
calming down, 46–50
and children, 95, 96–98, 102–3
crossover dogs, 57–58
daycare for, 128, 219–21
emergency health conditions of, 235
energy requirements of, 165–66
feeding cycle for, 183
hiking gear for, 358–59
marking territory, 69
microchipping, 216–18
pack behavior, 35, 225
size of and training, 58–67
socialization of, 117–21
spay/neutering, 9, 241–45
touching and handling, 237–38, 308–10
use of teeth, 32

Dogs Are From Neptune (Donaldson), 27
dominant aggression. *See also* aggressive behavior, 158
Donaldson, Jean, 27, 43–44, 225
Don't Shoot the Dog (Pryor), 58
Dr. Pitcairn's Complete Guide to Natural Health for Dogs & Cats (Pitcairn), 342
drugs. *See also* diseases; health
antibiotics, 268–72
for bloat, 262–63
for cancer, 320–21, 322, 336–37
and canine compulsive disorder, 124–25
corticosteroids, 273–76
costs of, 264–67
for heartworm, 251–54
herbs as alternative to, 295, 296
and homeopathy, 303
for idiopathic aggression, 159
for separation anxiety, 116, 128
and urination, 9, 68
Dubos, Rene J., 268
Dunbar, Ian, 23, 154

E
echinacea *(Echinacea spp.)*, 271, 272
Edgerton, Dani, 20
English Bulldogs, 317, 318
English Bull Terriers, 317
English Setters, 314
English Springer Spaniels, 165
enzyme therapy, 336
escharotic salves, 333
essential oils, 285–89
for cleaning, 202, 203
Etogesic. *See also* drugs, 266
eucalyptus, 203, 288, 291
exercise, 209–10, 242, 243

and boredom barking, 143
and calm dog, 46
and cancer prevention, 343–44
at daycare, 221
and stress, 17, 112, 116, 126, 128
underwater treadmills, 311–12
and urination, 9

F
Faggella, Alicia, 260, 261, 262
Falck, Carol, 326, 327, 343
Fallon, Sally, 190, 192, 195
fears. *See also* behaviors, 69
and classical conditioning, 44–45
puppies "fear periods," 26
triggers for, 120
feces, picking up, 207–8
Feed Your Pups with Bones (Billinghurst), 182
Feisty Fido (McConnell), 162
fences, 212, 213, 214–15
electric, 214
fennel, 298
feverfew *(Tanacetum partenium)*, 301, 302
Fife, Bruce, 329, 340
first-aid kit, 208–9
fish, wild-caught. *See also* food, 197
Fisher, Gail, 21, 23
Flat-Coated Retrievers, 314
fleas, controlling, 201–2, 253, 342
Fleming, Alexander, 268
floors
cleaning, 204
non-slip, 205
flower essences. *See also* holistic care, 287, 292–94
and cancer treatment, 327
flyball racing, 355–56

Folkman, Judah, 322
food, 163, 164
    animal-source protein, 194–97
    and bloat, 261
    and cancer treatment/prevention, 328–29, 330, 334, 335, 339–40
    canned food, 171–73
    children and dogs, 102
    commercial frozen, 187
    and counter surfing, 40, 65
    dry food, 168–70
    food allergies, 180
    grains, 190–93
    guarding, 30–31, 65–66
    identifying tainted, 174–76, 177–78
    pre-mixes, 186–87
    quality of, 203, 204
    raw, 182–86, 278
    as reward, 51
    storage of, 176–77
    variety in, 179–81
    vegetables, 188–90
Foods Pets Die For (Martin), 179
fo-ti *(Polygonum multiflorum)*, 301
Fox, Michael W., 195
Fox Terriers, 317
furniture, keeping off, 42

G
games, 367–73
    attention games, 85, 116
    and canine compulsive disorder, 124
    fetch, 17
    flyball racing, 355–56
    group games, 369–73
    not to play, 372
    for puppies, 3

    and stress, 113
    for terriers, 140
garlic *(Allium sativum)*, 272, 331, 343
gastric dilatation and volvulus (GDV). *See* bloat
Gaulin, Gigi, 337
geranium *(Pelargonium graveolens)*, 288
German Shepherd Dogs, 156, 314, 315, 316
ginger *(Zingiber officinale)*, 288, 300
ginkgo *(Ginkgo biloba)*, 299, 300
ginseng *(Panax ginseng or P. quinquefolius)*, 301
Give Your Dog a Bone (Billinghurst), 182
Gleason, Michael, 282, 283
Glickman, Lawrence, 260, 261, 262
glucocorticoids. *See also* corticosteroids, 273, 274–75
Golden Retrievers, 131, 314, 315, 316, 324
goldenseal *(Hydrastis canadensis)*, 272
Goldstein, Marty, 335
Gordon Setter, 261
gotu kola *(Centella asiatica)*, 299, 300
grains, in diet. *See also* food, 190–93
    carcinogens in, 339
Great Danes, 261, 316
Great Pyrenees, 316
greeting behavior. *See also* behaviors, 64, 76–79, 97–98
Greyhounds, 140
groomers, 2
grooming, 343–44
    tools for, 2, 287
    when camping, 366

growling behavior. *See also* behaviors, 148–50
guarding breeds. *See also* breeds, 142

H
Haber, Marion, 322
Hahnemann, Samuel, 303, 304
Hallett, Darrell, 321
Hallett, Nina, 321
Hamilton, Don, 304–5, 306
Hansen, Sharon, 259, 262
harness, 2
head halters, 64, 66, 110, 111
health. *See also* diet; diseases; holistic care
    assessing, 163–64
    and chemicals, 199–201, 208, 340–41
    and corticosteroids, 273–76
    and diet, 164–65, 179–81, 203, 205
    emergency conditions, 235
    and exercise, 209–10
    and flea control, 201–2
    fresh water for, 205
    and house plants, 207
    and housetraining problems, 68
    and hyperactivity, 131–33, 134–35
    and light, 344
    and spay/neutering, 241–45
    tooth care, 255–59
    and vaccinations, 246–50
    washing bowls, 202–3
health care, terms in. *See also* holistic care; veterinarians, 232, 233
heartworm disease, 251–54
    and temperatures, 253–54
    testing for, 254

helichrysum (*Helichrysum italicum*), 288

Help Your Dog Fight Cancer: An Overview of Home Care Options (Kaplan), 324

hemangiosarcoma. *See also* cancer, 314, 319

herbs, 295–302
  and cancer treatment, 327, 329, 330–33, 343
  dosages of, 301
  herbal antioxidants, 271–72, 296–99
  herbal steroids, 275–76
  for joints, 302
  for learning, 299–300
  and moxibustion, 280–81
  performance-enhancing, 299
  for skin and coat, 301–2
  for stress, 300–301

herding breeds. *See also* breeds, 131, 142

Hershman, Stacey, 334, 338, 339, 342

hiking, 357–61

histiocytosis. *See also* cancer, 314–15

Holistic Aromatherapy for Animals (Bell), 285

holistic care, 232, 233, 277–78
  acupuncture, 279–81
  and antibiotics, 271–72
  aromatherapy, 285–91
  for bloat, 262–63
  for cancer, 326–37, 342
  chiropractic, 282–84
  flower essences, 287, 292–94
  and glucocorticoids, 275–76
  for heartworm, 251
  homeopathy, 272, 276, 303–7, 327, 333–34

qualifications for, 235
  touch and massage, 308–10
  underwater treadmills, 311–12
  using herbs, 295–302

Homeopathic Care for Cats and Dogs: Small Doses for Small Animals (Hamilton), 305

homeopathy. *See also* holistic care, 233, 272, 276, 303–7, 333–34
  and cancer treatment, 327

Home-Prepared Dog & Cat Diets: The Healthful Alternative (Strombeck), 164, 166

hookworms, 252

hops (*Humulus lupulus*), 300

households
  air quality in, 206–7
  chemicals and carcinogens in, 199–201, 341–42
  chew-proofing, 208
  cleaning agents for, 2, 6, 199, 202, 203, 204
  confining dog in yard, 211–15
  emergency numbers/emergency plan, 208, 209
  first-aid kit in, 208–9
  flea control in, 201–2
  holistic lifestyle, 277–78
  lawn care, 206, 208
  non-slip floors in, 205
  plants in, 207
  secondhand smoke in, 205–6
  washing water & food bowls, 202–3

housetraining, 3, 5–14, 31
  adult dogs, 68–70
  problems with, 13, 40–41
  small dogs, 59–60
  and submissive urination, 11–12
  tips and reminders, 9

humans. *See* households; owners

hydrosols. *See also* aromatherapy, 285, 290–91

Hydrosols: The Next Aromatherapy (Catty), 291

hydrotherapy. *See* treadmills, underwater

hyperactivity behavior. *See also* behaviors, 131–37

hypericum (*Hypericum perforatum*), 296, 297, 298–99

I

iatrogenic illnesses, 233

identification tags, 2, 208, 209, 216, 217, 358

idiopathic aggression. *See also* aggressive behavior, 156–59

illnesses. *See* iatrogenic illnesses; diseases

insecticides, 208

International Organization for Standardization (ISO), 170

International Veterinary Acupuncture Society (IVAS), 235

International Veterinary Acupuncturist Directory, 281

Irish Setters, 261

Irish Wolfhounds, 261, 316

ivermectin. *See* heartworm disease

J

Jack Russell Terriers, 140, 355

jumping behavior. *See also* greeting behavior, 64

K

Kaplan, Laurie, 324

Katz, Ed, 334–35

Keller, Ted, 330

Kindred Spirit: How the Remarkable Bond Between Human and

Animals Can Change the Way We Live (Schoen), 310

King, Dan, 342

King, Trish, 161

Kong toys. *See also* toys, 2, 128

L

Labrador Retrievers, 131, 165, 316, 317

Lai, Henry, 332, 342

lameness, and cancer, 314

lavender, 272

    oil, 203, 286–87, 288, 289

lawns, 206, 341

lead poisoning, 133

leashes, 2, 358, 366

    and greeting behavior, 78

    and large dogs, 64

    and "off" exercise, 107–8

    and predatory behavior, 138

    retractable, 92

    walking on, 33, 89–94

Leon, Sandy, 21

leptospirosis, 250

leukemia. *See also* cancer, 315, 319

Lewis, Jamie, 221

Lhasa Apsos, 156, 165

licorice root (*Glycyrrhiza glabra*), 272, 295

light, and health, 344

long line. *See* leashes

Lonsdale, Tom, 339–40

Luescher, A. U., 125

lung cancer. *See also* cancer, 315

lymphosarcoma (lymphoma). *See also* cancer, 315, 320, 321–22, 323

M

malillumination, 344

mammary cancer. *See also* cancer, 315–16, 323

mandarin, green (*Citrus reticulata*), 288

Mandelbaum, Ann, 184

Maniet, Monique, 261, 262

maritime pine bark extract, 331

marjoram, sweet (*Origanum marjorana*), 288

Martin, Ann, 179

massage. *See also* holistic care, 240, 309, 310

    and cancer treatment, 327

McConnell, Patricia, 27, 162, 222

McDowell, Robert, 331

McKay, Pat, 185

McMillan, Franklin D., 309

meadowsweet, 275–76

meat. *See* animal-source protein

medications. *See* drugs

melatonin, 330

microchips, 208, 216–18

milbemycin oxime. *See* heartworm disease

milk. *See also* food, 197

mineralocorticoids. *See* corticosteroids

Miniature Schnauzers, 165

Morris Animal Foundation, 313, 319

Moss, Ralph, 333, 336

moxibustion. *See also* acupuncture, 280–81

mugwort (*Artemisia vulgaris*), 280

musical freestyle, 374–76

muzzles, 138–39, 239–40

myrrh (*Commiphora myrrha*), 288

N

nail trimming, program for, 154–55

neutering, 241–45, 338

Newfoundlands, 261, 316

North American Flyball Association (NAFA), 355, 356

nutrition. *See also* diet; food

    and cancer treatment/prevention, 327, 328–29, 330, 334, 335, 339–40

    and disease, 164–65

    home-prepared food, 188–97

    and hyperactivity, 133

    raw food diet, 182–86, 187

    and supplements, 271–72

    and variety of food, 179–81

O

oatstraw (*Avena sativa*), 300

"Off" exercises, 105–8

O'Heare, James, 111, 112

oils. *See* essential oils

Old English Sheepdogs, 261

On Talking Terms With Dogs: Calming Signals (Rugaas), 120

orange, sweet (*Citrus sinensis*), 288

oregano (*Origanum vulgare*), 271, 272

oseosarcoma (bone cancer). *See also* cancer, 313

osteosarcoma. *See also* cancer, 316, 319–20, 323

Other End of the Leash, The (McConnell), 222

Ott, John, 344

owners. *See also* households; training programs

    adjusting dog to children, 96–108

    and basic behaviors for dogs, 29–33

    behavior of and dog's behavior, 12, 13

    establishing routines for

puppies, 3–4

handling dog-with-dog interactions, 223–24, 225, 227

and puppies' socialization, 24–28

quality time with dog, 209, 210

touching and handling dogs, 237–38, 308

walking dogs, 89

P

passionflower (*Passiflora incarnata*), 300

Pasteur, Louis, 268

pens. *See also* crates, 1

peppermint (*Mentha piperita*), 203, 272, 288

pesticides, 208, 326, 341, 342

pet sitters, 2, 97

pharmaceuticals. *See* drugs

Phazyme, 262

Phillips, Kenneth, 151

Pitcairn, Richard, 303, 306, 307, 342

plants, poisonous, 207

play. *See also* activities; games

and barking, 143

body language during, 226–27

with children, 103

with other dogs, 33, 219, 222–29

rough, 14

Pointers, 315

Post, Gerald, 319–20, 323

predatory behavior. *See also* behaviors, 138–41, 225

probiotics. *See also* antibiotics, 263, 271

prostate cancer. *See also* cancer, 316, 323

protein. *See* animal-source protein

Protocel, 336–37, 342

Pryor, Karen, 58

Pugs, 317

punishments. *See also* training programs, 51–56

and bite inhibition, 16

and biting, 152

and conditioning, 43

and crates, 71

and housetraining, 6

negative punishment, 143

shock collars, 214

and submissive responses, 11–12

puppies. *See also* dogs; training programs, 1–28, 367

and alpha roll, 50

and bite inhibition, 15–18, 66–67, 222

and canine compulsive disorder, 124

establishing house rules for, 3–4, 29–33

housetraining, 5–13

hyperactive, 132

immune system of, 19, 22

roaming, 212–13

schools for, 20–21

socialization of, 14, 19, 23–28, 95–96, 117–18

supplies and equipment for, 1–2

vaccinations for, 249

R

rabies vaccinations. *See also* vaccinations, 247

Rabschutz, Laurel, 374

rage syndrome. *See* idiopathic aggression

ravensare aromatica (*Cinnamonum camphora*), 288, 291

recall (come when called) behavior. *See also* training programs, 84–88

red clover (*Trifolium pratense*), 301, 330–31

Reigning Cats and Dogs (McKay), 185

Rescue Remedy. *See also* flower essences, 262, 287, 294

resource guarding, 156, 157, 158

rewards. *See also* training programs, 51–56

in housetraining, 5–6

markers, 119

reward markers, 80

for walking on leash, 91

Rhodesian Ridgebacks, 317

Rioux-Forker, Mary, 21

roaming behavior. *See also* behaviors, 211–15

Roberson, Gayle, 330

rosemary (*Rosmarinus officinalis*), 203, 298, 299, 300

rose (*rosa damascena*), 288

Rottweilers, 261, 314, 316

roundworms, 252

Rowley, Kathy, 332–33

Rugaas, Turid, 120, 226

S

sage (*Salvia officinalis*), 272, 298

Saint Bernards, 156, 261, 316

Saint John's wort. *See* hypericum

salves. *See* escharotic salves

Samoyeds, 318

schizandra (*Schizandra chenensin*), 301

Schnaubelt, Kurt, 288

Schnauzers, 317

Schoen, Allen M., 233, 309–10

Schultz, Ronald D., 249, 250

Scottish Terriers, 314, 315

See Spot Live Longer (Taylor & Brown), 339

separation anxiety (SA). *See also*
 behaviors, 31, 115–16,
 126–30, 369
 and barking, 146–47
 and crates, 73, 74
serotonin, and behavior, 112
Sharp, E. V., 236, 237, 238, 240
shelters. *See* animal shelters
Sherman, John, 312
shock collars, 52, 53, 214
Singh, Narendra P., 332
sitting behavior. *See also* training
 programs, 80–83, 100
skin cancer. *See also* cancer,
 316–17, 323
Skinner, B. F., 51, 53
skullcap (*Scutellaria lateriflora*), 300
Small Animal Clinical
 Nutrition, 164
sniffing behavior. *See also*
 behaviors, 94
socialization programs. *See also*
 training programs, 117–21,
 210, 221, 222
 for being in the wild, 364
 for puppies, 14, 19–28, 44, 95–96
 and size, 64
spaying, 241–45, 338
Spontaneous Healing (Weil), 333
sporting breeds, and hyperactivity. *See also* breeds, 131
sports. *See* activities
Springer Spaniels, 156
Staffordshire Terriers, 317
Standard Poodles, 261
Stauffer, Craig, 329
stinging nettle (*Urtica dioica*), 301
Straus, Mary, 339
stress. *See also* behaviors, 32,
 109–10, 112, 113
 after adoption, 34, 36, 37

and biting, 151–52, 155
and classical conditioning, 44
and destructive behavior,
 114–16
and glucocorticoids, 276
and growling, 148–49
meeting other dogs, 226
Strombeck, Donald R., 164–65
Strouss, Nancy, 184, 324, 328, 335
submissive aggression. *See also*
 aggressive behavior, 158
Sullivan, Edmund, 321–22
supplements, nutritional, 112,
 271–72
 and cancer treatment/preven-
 tion, 327, 329–30, 334, 340
supplies
 for camping, 365–66
 for hikes, 358–59
 natural cleaning, 202, 203
 for puppies, 1–2

T
tags. *See* identification tags
Taylor, Beth, 339
Taylor, Jenny, 257–58
teeth, care of, 238, 255–59
Tellington-Jones, Linda, 240
terrier breeds, 142
 and bladder cancer, 314
 susceptibility to cancer, 314,
 315, 317
testicular cancer. *See also* cancer,
 317–18
tethers, 1–2
 and greeting behavior, 76–77
 and separation anxiety, 129
Thompson, Sandi, 59, 80, 81
thuja (*Thuja occidentalis*), 271
thyme (*Thymus vulgaris*), 271, 272,
 288, 298

thyroid dysfunction, 112
 and hyperactivity, 133
ticks, 359, 366
 repellent for, 289
Tilford, Gregory, 330
toy breeds. *See also* breeds, 142
toys, 2
 chew objects, 32, 41
 size appropriate, 61, 63
 for terriers, 140
 at vets office, 240
trainers. *See also* training programs, 2
 for puppies, 14
 website for, 162
training programs
 after adoption, 36–37
 barking, 143–47
 bite inhibition, 15–18
 biting, 152–55
 calm dog, 46–50
 and canine compulsive disorder,
 123–25
 children as trainers, 99–104
 classes for difficult dogs, 160–62
 classical conditioning, 43–45
 crate training, 71–75
 crossover dogs, 57–58
 desensitization and counter-
 conditioning, 28, 96, 120, 127
 destructive behavior, 114–16
 and dogs' size, 58–67
 greeting behavior, 76–79
 growling behavior, 149–50
 handling problems, 39–42
 and high-energy dogs, 133,
 136–37
 housetraining, 5–14
 and idiopathic aggression, 156,
 157, 159
 off limits exercise, 105–8

positive interrupt, 144

predatory behavior, 139–41

for puppies, 3–4, 19–28, 95–96

recall (coming when called), 32–33, 55, 84–88

rewards and punishments in, 51–56

roaming behavior, 211–15

and separation anxiety, 127–30

sitting behavior, 80–83, 100–101, 103

socializing adult dog, 118–21

tricks, 345–49

for vet visits, 236–41

walking on leash, 89–94

treadmills, underwater, 311–12

treats. *See also* clicker training; training programs, 25, 80

and bite inhibition, 18

children and dogs, 96, 102

and classical conditioning, 43–45

and clickers, 2

for small dogs, 60, 61

at vets office, 240

tricks, 345–49

crawl, 348

roll over, 347–48

say your prayers, 348

shake paw, 346–47

spin and twirl, 347

take a bow, 348–49

trytophan, 112

turmeric, 331

U

United States Department of Agriculture

Animal and Plant Health Inspection Service (APHIS), 170

National Organic Program (NOP), 170

V

vaccinations, 14, 22, 246–50

and cancer, 338–39

core vaccines, 249

titer tests, 248

valerian (*Valeriana officinalis*), 288, 299–300

vegetables, in diet. *See also* food, 188–89

anticancer diet, 334

lactic acid fermentation of, 189–90, 192, 340

veterinarians. *See also* holistic care, 2

and acupuncture, 279, 281

adjusting dogs to, 236–41

and canine compulsive disorder, 123

chiropractic, 282, 283–84

choosing one, 231–35

and flower essences, 293, 294

holistic, 232, 235, 296

homeopathic, 303–4, 305, 306

and housetraining problems, 9, 13, 68, 69

and pharmaceutical sales, 264–66

and physical causes of misbehavior, 112, 133

and puppies' socialization, 19, 22–23, 26

and teeth cleaning, 256–58

test for hyperactivity, 134

understanding of nutrition, 164

and vaccinations, 246–50

Vithoulkas, George, 304

W

Wagner, Herbert, 356

walking behavior. *See also* training programs, 89–94

water, fresh, 205

Weil, Andrew, 333

Weimaraners, 261, 316

Weissleader, Patricia, 33

Wen, Jiu Jia, 331

Westfall, Theresa, 321

West Highland White Terriers, 315

Whippets, 317

white willow bark (*Salix alba*), 302

Work Wonders: Feed Your Dog Raw Meaty Bones (Lonsdale), 339

wormwood (*Artemisia absinthium*), 301

Wulff-Tilford, Mary, 330

Y

yard

confining dog in, 211–15

picking up feces, 207–8

yellow dock root (*Rumex crispus*), 301

yucca (*Yucca spp.*), 302

Z

Zacharias, Marina, 343